973
Uni

99591

U. S. Adjutant-General's
     Office.
Federal aid in domestic dis-
     turbances.

Date Due

MASS VIOLENCE IN AMERICA

Advisory editors:

ROBERT M. FOGELSON   RICHARD E. RUBENSTEIN

MASS VIOLENCE IN AMERICA

FEDERAL AID
IN DOMESTIC DISTURBANCES
1787–1903

Frederick T. Wilson

ARNO PRESS & THE NEW YORK TIMES

New York · 1969

Editorial Note

NATIONS, LIKE MEN, ARE SOMETIMES INTERESTED IN BURYING THE PAST.

In early 1968, after more than five years marked by political assassinations, racial uprisings, campus disorders, mass demonstrations and the violent suppression of protest, *The New York Times Magazine* asked a group of distinguished scholars to reply to the question, "Is America by nature a violent society?" In answer, University of Chicago anthropologist Clifford Geertz wrote:

> "We do not know very well what kind of society we live in, what kind of history we have had, what kind of people we are. We are just now beginning to find out, the hard way . . ."

The proposition was astonishing but correct: what was least understood about domestic political violence was its role in American history. It was common knowledge that the United States had had a Revolution, a Civil War, some trouble with the Indians and a period of labor-management conflict. But one could search the shelves of the nation's great libraries without discovering more than a handful of works on the subject of violence in American history, and these hopelessly out of date.

Historians had generally ignored or soft-pedaled the history of farmer uprisings, native vigilantism, labor-management struggles, ethnic conflicts and race riots; comparative work in the history of social conflict was particularly weak. Sociologists and political scientists in the grip of "consensus" theory tended to treat episodes of mass violence in America as insignificant or aberrational—temporary exceptions to the norm of peaceful progress. Psychologists and behavioral scientists discussed "mob violence" in terms which suggested that riots, revolts, insurrections and official violence were the products of individual or group pathology. All such interpretations had the effect not only of minimizing group violence in America, but of depriving it of political content—hence, of relevance to the present.

As a result, as late as 1968, the rich, multifarious and often terrifying history of domestic political violence was still largely *terra incognita*. So long as most Americans wished to keep certain skeletons locked away in their closets, few scholars would attempt to open doors. Conversely, once the American people, frightened yet emboldened by the sudden reappearance of intense social conflict, began to ask new questions about the past, so did the scholars.

Our purpose in helping Arno Press and *The New York Times* select and publish significant documents in the history of political violence has not been to compound past errors by overemphasizing the role of conflict in American history. On the contrary, our aim has been to provide materials which will aid in the search for an accurate perspective on the present. MASS VIOLENCE IN AMERICA includes eyewitness reports, government documents and other descriptive and analytic material relating to mass political violence in the United States. These documents not only provide information—they give the "feel" or "flavor" of past eras of civil disorder by evoking the emotional and political context in which revolts took place. Most of them have long been out of print and are obtainable, if at all, only in the nation's largest libraries.

The scope of this series is wide, ranging from accounts of Indian warfare to descriptions of labor-management violence, from narratives of colonial insurrections to reports on modern racial uprisings. It is not, however, limitless, nor were the constituent volumes carelessly selected. The principle of coherence which guided the selections is implicit in the phrase "mass political violence." "Mass" denotes activity engaged in by large groups rather than individuals acting alone; "political" suggests a relationship between such activity and competition among domestic groups for power, property and prestige; and "violence" is narrowly construed as resulting in physical damage to persons or property. In short, the materials reproduced herein are intended to illuminate the resort to violence by American groups seeking to change or to preserve the status quo. Although historical, they are of interest to any who wishes to understand the causes, nature and direction of domestic political violence, whether they be social scientists, historians or just interested Americans.

Of course, we are particularly hopeful that these volumes will prove useful to those now engaged in curriculum-revision and the teaching of high school and college courses in the area of American studies. What Christopher Jencks and David Reisman term "the Academic Revolution" has made difficult demands on all educators, not the least of which is the demand for courses which are both relevant to the condition of modern America and of the highest academic quality. These volumes are meant to provide raw material for such courses—primary source matter which will help both instructors and students to deepen and enrich their views of the American experience.

Most important, the editors and publisher recognize that these volumes appear during a national crisis which is also a crisis of the spirit, a time in which the public response to various manifestations of civil disorder is increasingly governed by anger, fear and hysteria. In such an atmosphere it is important to recognize that one is not alone in time—that such events have taken place before in America and, unless fundamental changes in our social and political life take place, will probably recur in the future. Our fondest hope is that this work, and others like it, will help to keep alive, in a time of growing unreason, the spirit of reasoned inquiry.

RICHARD E. RUBENSTEIN
The Adlai Stevenson Institute
Chicago, Illinois

ROBERT M. FOGELSON
Harvard-MIT Joint Center
for Urban Studies
Cambridge, Massachusetts

FEDERAL AID

IN DOMESTIC DISTURBANCES

1787–1903

57TH CONGRESS, }   SENATE.   { DOCUMENT
2d Session. }   { No. 209.

FEDERAL AID

IN

DOMESTIC DISTURBANCES.

1787-1903.

The Congress shall have power * * * to raise and support armies; * * * to provide for the calling forth the militia to execute the laws of the Union, suppress insurrections and repel invasions. (Art. I, sec. 8, Constitution of the United States.)

The United States shall guarantee to every State in this Union a republican form of government, and shall protect each of them against invasion; and on application of the legislature, or of the executive (when the legislature cannot be convened), against domestic violence. (Art. IV, sec. 4, Constitution.)

PREPARED UNDER THE DIRECTION OF

MAJOR-GENERAL HENRY C. CORBIN,

Adjutant-General, U. S. Army,

BY

FREDERICK T. WILSON,

Chief of Division, Adjutant-General's Office.

MARCH 2, 1903.—Ordered to be printed.

WASHINGTON:

GOVERNMENT PRINTING OFFICE.

1903.

CONTENTS.

EMPLOYMENT OF TROOPS

IN THE

ENFORCEMENT OF THE LAWS.

[The small letters in the body of the text refer to notes at the bottom of each page, the small figures to documents in Part XIII.]

Whenever, in the judgment of the President, it becomes necessary to use the military forces under this title, the President shall forthwith, by proclamation, command the insurgents to disperse and retire peaceably to their respective abodes, within a limited time. (Sec. 5300, Rev. Stat.)

It is unlawful to employ any part of the Army of the United States, as a posse comitatus or otherwise, for the purpose of executing the laws, except in such cases and under such circumstances as such employment of said force may be expressly authorized by the Constitution or by act of Congress; and any person wilfully violating this provision will be deemed guilty of a misdemeanor, and, on conviction thereof, will be punishable by a fine not exceeding $10,000 or imprisonment not exceeding two years, or by both such fine and imprisonment.[a] (563, Army Regulations, 1901.)

The provisions of the Constitution and of acts of Congress understood as intended to be excepted from the operation of the act of June 18, 1878 (20 Stat. L., 145), authorizing the employment of the military forces for the purpose of executing the laws, are as follows (564, Army Regulations, 1901):

ARTICLE IV OF THE CONSTITUTION.

§ 4. The United States shall guarantee to every State in this Union a republican form of government, and shall protect each of them against invasion; and on application of the legislature, or of the executive (when the legislature can not be convened), against domestic violence.

REVISED STATUTES OF THE UNITED STATES.

CIVIL RIGHTS.

SEC. 1984. The commissioners authorized to be appointed by the preceding section [sec. 1983] are empowered, within their respective counties, to appoint, in writing, under their hands, one or more suitable persons, from time to time, who shall

---

[a] Sec. 15, act June 18, 1878.

execute all such warrants or other process as the commissioners may issue in the lawful performance of their duties, and the persons so appointed shall have authority to summon and call to their aid the bystanders or posse comitatus of the proper county, or such portion of the land and naval forces of the United States, or of the militia, as may be necessary to the performance of the duty with which they are charged; and such warrants shall run and be executed anywhere in the State or Territory within which they are issued.

SEC. 1989. It shall be lawful for the President of the United States, or such person as he may empower for that purpose, to employ such part of the land or naval forces of the United States, or of the militia, as may be necessary to aid in the execution of judicial process issued under any of the preceding provisions, or as shall be necessary to prevent the violation and enforce the due execution of the provisions of this title.

SEC. 1991. Every person in the military or civil service in the Territory of New Mexico shall aid in the enforcement of the preceding section [abolishing peonage].

INDIANS.

SEC. 2118. Every person who makes a settlement on any lands belonging, secured, or granted by treaty with the United States to any Indian tribe, or surveys or attempts to survey such lands, or to designate any of the boundaries by marking trees, or otherwise, is liable to a penalty of one thousand dollars. The President may, moreover, take such measures and employ such military force as he may judge necessary to remove any such person from the lands.

SEC. 2147. The Superintendent of Indian Affairs, and the Indian agents and subagents, shall have authority to remove from the Indian country all persons found therein contrary to law; and the President is authorized to direct the military force to be employed in such removal.

SEC. 2150. The military forces of the United States may be employed in such manner and under such regulations as the President may direct—

First. In the apprehension of every person who may be in the Indian country in violation of law; and in conveying him immediately from the Indian country, by the nearest convenient and safe route, to the civil authority of the Territory or judicial district in which such person shall be found, to be proceeded against in due course of law;

Second. In the examination and seizure of stores, packages, and boats, authorized by law;

Third. In preventing the introduction of persons and property into the Indian country contrary to law; which persons and property shall be proceeded against according to law;

Fourth. And also in destroying and breaking up any distillery for manufacturing ardent spirits set up or continued within the Indian country.

SEC. 2151. No person apprehended by military force under the preceding section shall be detained longer than five days after arrest and before removal. All officers and soldiers who may have any such person in custody shall treat him with all the humanity which the circumstances will permit.

SEC. 2152. The superintendents, agents, and subagents shall endeavor to procure the arrest and trial of all Indians accused of committing any crime, offense, or misdemeanor, and of all other persons who may have committed crimes or offenses within any State or Territory, and have fled into the Indian country, either by demanding the same of the chiefs of the proper tribe, or by such other means as the President may authorize. The President may direct the military force of the United States to be employed in the apprehension of such Indians, and also in preventing or terminating hostilities between any of the Indian tribes.

THE PUBLIC LANDS.

SEC. 2460. The President is authorized to employ so much of the land and naval forces of the United States as may be necessary effectually to prevent the felling, cutting down, or other destruction of the timber of the United States in Florida, and to prevent the transportation or carrying away any such timber as may be already felled or cut down; and to take such other and further measures as may be deemed advisable for the preservation of the timber of the United States in Florida.

Be it enacted by the Senate and House of Representatives of the United States of America in Congress assembled, That if any person or persons shall, after the passing of this act, take possession of, or make a settlement on any lands ceded or secured to the United States, by any treaty made with a foreign nation, or by a cession from any State to the United States, which lands shall not have been previously sold, ceded, or leased by the United States, or the claim to which lands, by such person or persons, shall not have been previously recognized and confirmed by the United States; or if any person or persons shall cause such lands to be thus occupied, taken possession of, or settled; or shall survey, or attempt to survey, or cause to be surveyed, any such lands; or designate any boundaries thereon, by marking trees, or otherwise, until thereto duly authorized by law, such offender or offenders shall forfeit all his or their right, title, and claim, if any he hath, or they have, of whatsoever nature or kind the same shall or may be, to the lands aforesaid, which he or they shall have taken possession of, or settled, or cause to be occupied, taken possession of, or settled, or which he or they shall have surveyed, or attempt to survey, or cause to be surveyed, or the boundaries thereof he or they shall have designated, or cause to be designated, by marking trees or otherwise. And it shall moreover be lawful for the President of the United States to direct the marshal, or officer acting as marshal, in the manner hereinafter directed, and also to take such other measures, and to employ such military force as he may judge necessary and proper, to remove from lands ceded or secured to the United States by treaty or cession as aforesaid any person or persons who shall hereafter take possession of the same, or make, or attempt to make, a settlement thereon, until thereunto authorized by law. And every right, title, or claim forfeited under this act shall be taken and deemed to be vested in the United States, without any other or further proceedings: *Provided,* That nothing herein contained shall be construed to affect the right, title, or claim of any person to lands in the Territories of Orleans or Louisiana before the boards of commissioners established by the act intituled "An act for ascertaining and adjusting the titles and claims to land within the Territory of Orleans and the District of Louisiana," shall have made their reports and the decision of Congress been had thereon.

[Section 1 of an act approved March 3rd, 1807, perpetuated by sec. 5596, Revised Statutes.]

The Secretary of War, upon the request of the Secretary of the Interior, is hereafter authorized and directed to make the necessary detail of troops to prevent trespassers or intruders from entering the Sequoia National Park, the Yosemite National Park, and the General Grant National Park, respectively, in California, for the purpose of destroying the game or objects of curiosity therein, or for any other purpose prohibited by law or regulation for the government of said reservations, and to remove such persons from said parks if found therein. (*Act of June 6, 1900, 31 Stat. L., 618.*)

The President is hereby authorized to take such measures as shall be necessary to remove and destroy any unlawful inclosures of said (public) lands, and to employ civil or military force as may be necessary for that purpose. (*Act of February 25, 1885, 23 Stat. L., 321.*)

THE PUBLIC HEALTH.

SEC. 4792. The quarantines and other restraints established by the health laws of any State respecting any vessels arriving in, or bound to, any port or district thereof, shall be duly observed by the officers of the customs revenue of the United States, by the masters and crews of the several revenue cutters, and by the military officers commanding in any fort or station upon the seacoast; and all such officers of the United States shall faithfully aid in the execution of such quarantines and health laws, according to their respective powers and within their respective precincts, and as they shall be directed, from time to time, by the Secretary of the Treasury. * * *

EXTRADITION.

SEC. 5275. Whenever any person is delivered by any foreign government to an agent of the United States for the purpose of being brought within the United States and tried for any crime of which he is duly accused, the President shall have power to take all necessary measures for the transportation and safe-keeping of such accused person, and for his security against lawless violence, until the final conclusion of his trial for the crimes or offenses specified in the warrant of extradition, and until his final discharge from custody or imprisonment for or on account of such crimes or offenses, and for a reasonable time thereafter, and may employ such portion of the land or naval forces of the United States, or of the militia thereof, as may be necessary for the safe-keeping and protection of the accused.

NEUTRALITY.

SEC. 5286. Every person who, within the territory or jurisdiction of the United States, begins or sets on foot, or provides or prepares the means for, any military expedition or enterprise, to be carried on from thence against the territory or dominions of any foreign prince or state or of any colony, district, or people with whom the United States are at peace, shall be deemed guilty of a high misdemeanor, and shall be fined not exceeding three thousand dollars and imprisoned not more than three years.

SEC. 5287. * * * In every case in which a vessel is fitted out and armed, or attempted to be fitted out and armed, or in which the force of any vessel of war, cruiser, or other armed vessel is increased or augmented, or in which any military expedition or enterprise is begun or set on foot, contrary to the provisions and prohibitions of this title; and in every case of the capture of a vessel within the jurisdiction or protection of the United States as before defined; and in every case in which any process issuing out of any court of the United States is disobeyed or resisted by any person having the custody of any vessel of war, cruiser, or other armed vessel of any foreign prince or state, or of any colony, district, or people, or of any subjects or citizens of any foreign prince or state, or of any colony, district, or people, it shall be lawful for the President, or such other person as he shall have empowered for that purpose, to employ such part of the land or naval forces of the United States or of the militia thereof for the purpose of taking possession of and detaining any such vessel, with her prizes, if any, in order to the execution of the prohibitions and penalties of this title, and to the restoring of such prizes in the cases in which restoration shall be adjudged, and also for the purpose of preventing the carrying on of any such expedition or enterprise from the territories or jurisdiction of the United States against the territories or dominions of any foreign prince or state, or of any colony, district, or people with whom the United States are at peace.

SEC. 5288. It shall be lawful for the President, or such person as he shall empower for that purpose, to employ such part of the land or naval forces of the United States, or of the militia thereof, as shall be necessary to compel any foreign vessel to depart the United States in all cases in which, by the laws of nations or the treaties of the United States, she ought not to remain within the United States.

INSURRECTION.

SEC. 5297. In case of an insurrection in any State against the government thereof it shall be lawful for the President, on application of the legislature of such State, or of the executive when the legislature can not be convened, to call forth such number of the militia of any other State or States which may be applied for as he deems sufficient to suppress such insurrection, or, on like application, to employ for the same purposes such part of the land or naval forces of the United States as he deems necessary.

SEC. 5298. Whenever, by reason of unlawful obstructions, combinations, or assemblages of persons, or rebellion against the authority of the Government of the United States, it shall become impracticable, in the judgment of the President, to enforce by the ordinary course of judicial proceedings the laws of the United States within any State or Territory, it shall be lawful for the President to call forth the militia of any or all the States and to employ such parts of the land and naval forces of the United States as he may deem necessary to enforce the faithful execution of the laws of the United States or to suppress such rebellion in whatever State or Territory thereof the laws of the United States may be forcibly opposed or the execution thereof forcibly obstructed.

SEC. 5299. Whenever insurrection, domestic violence, unlawful combinations, or conspiracies in any State so obstructs or hinders the execution of the laws thereof and of the United States as to deprive any portion or class of the people of such State of any of the rights, privileges, or immunities or protection named in the Constitution and secured by the laws for the protection of such rights, privileges, or immunities, and the constituted authorities of such State are unable to protect or from any cause fail in or refuse protection of the people in such rights, such facts shall be deemed a denial by such State of the equal protection of the laws to which they are entitled under the Constitution of the United States, and in all such cases, or whenever any such insurrection, violence, unlawful combination, or conspiracy opposes or obstructs the laws of the United States or the due execution thereof, or impedes or obstructs the due course of justice under the same, it shall be lawful for the President, and it shall be his duty, to take such measures, by the employment of the militia or the land and naval forces of the United States, or of either, or by other means, as he may deem necessary for the suppression of such insurrection, domestic violence, or combinations.

Among the laws to be enforced under sections 5298 and 5299 are the following:

(1) Section 3995, Revised Statutes, which prohibits the obstructing or retarding the passage of the mail, and all other laws relating to the carrying of the mails.

(2) The following sections of an act approved July 2, 1890, entitled:

AN ACT to protect trade and commerce against unlawful restraints and monopolies.

SEC. 1. Every contract, combination in the form of trust or otherwise, or conspiracy in restraint of trade or commerce among the several States, or with foreign nations, is hereby declared to be illegal.

Every person who shall make any such contract or engage in any such combination or conspiracy shall be deemed guilty of a misdemeanor, and, on conviction thereof, shall be punished by fine not exceeding five thousand dollars or by imprisonment not exceeding one year, or by both said punishments, in the discretion of the court.

SEC. 3. Every contract, combination in form of trust or otherwise, or conspiracy in restraint of trade or commerce in any Territory of the United States or of the District of Columbia, or in restraint of trade or commerce between any such Territory and another, or between any such Territory or Territories and any State or States or the District of Columbia, or with foreign nations, or between the District of Columbia and any State or States or foreign nations, is hereby declared illegal.

Every person who shall make any such contract or engage in any such combination or conspiracy shall be deemed guilty of a misdemeanor, and, on conviction thereof, shall be punished by fine not exceeding five thousand dollars or by imprisonment not exceeding one year, or by both said punishments, in the discretion of the court.

(3) The following section of an act approved July 2, 1864, entitled:

AN ACT granting lands to aid in the construction of a railroad and telegraph line from Lake Superior to Puget Sound, on the Pacific coast, by the northern route.

SEC. 11. *And be it further enacted*, That said Northern Pacific Railroad, or any part thereof, shall be a post route and a military road, subject to the use of the United States for postal, military, naval, and all other Government service, and also subject to such regulations as Congress may impose restricting the charges for such Government transportation.

(4) The following section of an act approved July 1, 1862, entitled:

AN ACT to aid in the construction of a railroad and telegraph line from the Missouri River to the Pacific Ocean, and to secure to the Government the use of the same for postal, military, and other purposes.

(The Union and Central Pacific Railway companies.)

SEC. 6. *And be it further enacted*, That the grants aforesaid are made upon condition that said company shall pay said bonds at maturity and shall keep said railroad and telegraph line in repair and use, and shall at all times transmit dispatches over said telegraph line, and transport mails, troops, and munitions of war, supplies, and public stores upon said railroad for the Government whenever required to do so by any department thereof, and that the Government shall at all times have the preference in the use of the same for all the purposes aforesaid. * * *

(5) The following sections of an act approved July 27, 1866, entitled:

AN ACT granting lands to aid in the construction of a railroad and telegraph line from the States of Missouri and Arkansas to the Pacific coast.

SEC. 11. *And be it further enacted*, That said Atlantic and Pacific Railroad, or any part thereof, shall be a post route and military road, subject to the use of the United States for postal, military, naval, and all other Government service, and also subject to such regulations as Congress may impose restricting the charges for such Government transportation.

SEC. 18. *And be it further enacted*, That the Southern Pacific Railroad, a company incorporated under the laws of the State of California, is hereby authorized to connect with the said Atlantic and Pacific Railroad, formed under this act, at such point near the boundary line of the State of California as they shall deem most suitable for a railroad line to San Francisco, and shall have a uniform gauge and rate of freight or fare with said road; and in consideration thereof, to aid in its construction, shall have similar grants of land, subject to all the conditions and limitations herein provided, and shall be required to construct its road on the like regulations, as to time and manner, with the Atlantic and Pacific Railroad herein provided for.

SEC. 5316. It shall be unlawful to take any vessel or cargo detained under the preceding section [sec. 5315] from the custody of the proper officers of the customs, unless by process of some court of the United States; and in case of any attempt otherwise to take such vessel or cargo by any force, or combination, or assemblage of persons too great to be overcome by the officers of the customs the President, or such person as he shall have empowered for that purpose, may employ such part of the Army or Navy or militia of the United States, or such force of citizen volunteers, as may be necessary to prevent the removal of such vessel or cargo and to protect the officers of the customs in retaining the custody thereof.

GUANO ISLANDS.

SEC. 5577. The President is authorized, at his discretion, to employ the land and naval forces of the United States to protect the rights of the discoverer [of a guano island] or of his widow, heir, executor, administrator, or assigns.

Officers of the Army will not permit troops under their command to be used to aid the civil authorities as a posse comitatus, or in execution of the laws, except as provided in the foregoing paragraph. (565, Army Regulations, 1901.)

If time will admit, applications for the use of troops for such purposes must be forwarded, with statements of all material facts, for the consideration and action of the President; but in case of sudden and unexpected invasion, insurrection, or riot, endangering the public property of the United States, or in case of attempted or threatened robbery or interruption of the United States mails, or other equivalent emergency so imminent as to render it dangerous to await instructions requested through the speediest means of communication, an officer of the Army may take such action before the receipt of instructions as the circumstances of the case and the law under which he is acting may justify, and will promptly report his action and the circumstances requiring it to the Adjutant-General of the Army by telegraph, if possible, for the information of the President. (566, Army Regulations, 1901.)

In the enforcement of the laws, troops are employed as a part of the military power of the United States and act under the orders of the President as Commander in Chief. They can not be directed to act under the orders of any civil officer. The commanding officers of troops so employed are directly responsible to their military superiors. Any unlawful or unauthorized act on their part would not be excusable on the ground of an order or request received by them from a marshal or any other civil officer. (567, Army Regulations, 1901.)

Troops called into action against a mob forcibly resisting or obstructing the execution of the laws of the United States or attempting to destroy property belonging to or under the protection of the United States are governed by the general regulations of the Army and apply military tactics in respect to the manner in which they shall act to accomplish the desired end. It is purely a tactical question in what manner they shall use the weapons with which they are armed—whether by fire of musketry and artillery or by the use of the bayonet and saber, or by both, and at what stage of the operations each or either mode of attack shall be employed. This tactical question will be

decided by the immediate commander of the troops, according to his
judgment of the situation.   The fire of troops should be withheld until
timely warning has been given to the innocent who may be mingled
with the mob.   Troops must never fire into a crowd unless ordered by
their commanding officer, except that single selected sharpshooters
may shoot down individual rioters who have fired upon or thrown
missiles at the troops.   As a general rule the bayonet alone should be
used against mixed crowds in the first stages of a revolt.   But as soon
as sufficient warning has been given to enable the innocent to separate
themselves from the guilty, the action of the troops should be governed solely by the tactical considerations involved in the duty they
are ordered to perform.   They should make their blows so effective
as to promptly suppress all resistance to lawful authority, and should
stop the destruction of life the moment lawless resistance has ceased.
Punishment belongs, not to the troops, but to the courts of justice.
(568, Army Regulations, 1901.)

FEDERAL AID IN DOMESTIC DISTURBANCES.

I. THE CONSTITUTIONAL GUARANTY: ITS HISTORY.

SHAYS'S REBELLION—THE FEDERAL CONVENTION—THE VIRGINIA CONVENTION—THE
PENNSYLVANIA CONVENTION.

The convention to frame a Constitution for the Government of the
United States, which met at Philadelphia on the 14th of May, 1787,
was confronted by a multitude of conditions such as had never before
been experienced by a similar body in the history of popular government. For their proposed undertaking there was no precedent and
scarcely an analogy. The Revolution had settled as a fundamental
principle that all sovereignty resides originally in the people, and
that consequently no powers nor privileges must be permitted to
exist in any portion, class, or section of the people that does not exist
in the whole. The spectacle was presented of thirteen State governments, each independent of the other, but each so dependable upon
the other that it were madness to hope to stand alone. None of them
possessed any standing military forces; their militia was unorganized
and uncertain; none could call upon its neighbor for assistance in
repelling an invasion or suppressing an insurrection, for the neighbor
had nothing but its militia to offer, and the militia would not have
obeyed the summons had it been issued; nor could any of them call
upon the Federal Government for aid in such emergency with any
certainty of success. The chances were against it. That the States
were in danger had been conspicuously demonstrated in Massachusetts
but a few months before the assembling of the convention.

The legislature of that State had imposed customs and revenue
duties for the purpose of raising a revenue sufficient to meet the
interest on the State debt. To a people just emerging from a long
and distressing war, already exhausted with public and private debts,
this additional burden served to exasperate to the
verge of resistance. The courts, unable to enforce
their judgments, appealed to the governor, and the
latter, after unsuccessful efforts to pacify the malcontents, called out
the militia. The Congress (October, 1786), fearing the seizure of the

Shays's rebellion,
1786-1787.

13

Government armory at Springfield, voted the enlistment of 1,300 men, but before these troops could be raised the insurrection had broken out. On the 5th of December a body of something over a thousand men, under the command of one Daniel Shays, who had been a captain in the Continental Army, took possession of Worcester, and twenty days later of Springfield. Other thousands hurried to their support, and by the 1st of January, 1787, the insurrection had reached so formidable a state that the governor was compelled to increase his militia force to nearly 5,000. Of this number the orders for embodiment called for 700 from Suffolk County, 500 from Essex, 800 from Middlesex, 1,200 from Hampshire, and 1,200 from Worcester; two companies of artillery to be raised in Suffolk and two in Middlesex; the troops from the three eastern counties to rendezvous at Boston on the 19th of January; those from Hampshire at Springfield on the 18th; those from Worcester to join the troops from the eastern counties at Worcester; the whole to be raised for thirty days unless sooner discharged. The command of the entire force was given to Maj. Gen. Benjamin Lincoln, an officer of distinction and high reputation during the war of the Revolution, to whom was given the following orders:

BOSTON, *January 19, 1787.*

SIR: You will take the command of the militia, detached in obedience to my orders of the 4th instant. The great objects to be effected are to protect the judicial courts, particularly those next to be holden in the county of Worcester, if the justices of the said courts should request your aid; to assist the civil magistrates in executing the laws, and in repelling or apprehending all and every such person and persons as shall in a hostile manner attempt or enterprise the destruction, detriment, or annoyance of this Commonwealth, and also to aid them in apprehending the disturbers of the public peace, as well as all such persons as may be named in the State warrants that have been or shall be committed to any civil officer or officers, or to any other person, to execute.

If to these important ends the militia already ordered out should, in your opinion, be incompetent you will call on the major-generals for further and effectual aid, and if you can rely on their attachment to Government you will, in the first instance, call on the militia in the neighborhood of your camp.

I can not minutely point out to you the particular line you shall pursue in executing these orders, but would observe, in general, that if, to answer the aforesaid valuable purposes, you should judge it necessary to march a respectable force through the western counties you will in that case do it. This would give confidence to the well affected, would aid and protect the civil officers in executing their duty, and would convince the misguided of the abilities of Government and its determination to pursue every legal and constitutional measure for restoring peace and order to the Commonwealth.

You are to consider yourself in all your military offensive operations constantly as under the direction of the civil officer, saving where any armed force shall appear and oppose your marching to execute these orders.

That I may be fully acquainted with all the proceedings of the armed force under your command and with all matters that respect the great objects to be effected, you will please to give me regular information by every post, and for immediate and necessary intelligence you will order the quartermaster-general to provide the necessary expresses.

On these attempts to restore system and order I wish the smiles of Heaven, and that you may have an agreeable command, the most perfect success, and a speedy and safe return; and am, with much esteem,

Sir, your most obedient servant,

JAMES BOWDOIN.

Hon. Major-General LINCOLN.

On the 25th of January Shays appeared before the arsenal at Springfield and demanded its surrender. This being refused, he proceeded to assault it, but his men, frightened at the sight of the cannon with which the commandant confronted them, and which he twice discharged over their heads, broke and fled in confusion. Two days later General Lincoln arrived at Springfield with a strong body of troops, and the insurgents dispersed. Some of the leaders were captured, tried, and sentenced to death, but none were executed, inasmuch as the great mass of the people sympathized with them or their cause.[a]

A year or two earlier Congress itself had been threatened by a body of some eighty discharged Pennsylvania soldiers of the Continental Army who had marched to Philadelphia, demanding a settlement of their accounts, and, "drawn up in line in the street before the statehouse, had uttered offensive words and wantonly pointed their muskets to the windows of the Hall of Congress."[b] It had been proposed to call upon the executive of Pennsylvania for aid in suppressing this mutiny, but that gentleman had expressed his doubt as to the willingness of the militia of Philadelphia to take arms in the matter and thought it might hazard the authority of government to make the attempt. The Secretary of War was absent in Virginia, and General St. Clair, who interviewed the mutinous troops, gave no encouragement. In this emergency the presiding officer adjourned the Congress to meet at Trenton, thus virtually fleeing from danger, when the mutineers submitted and accepted the promise of Congress to take furloughs and await its pleasure. Again, while Congress was listening to the news from the Massachusetts insurrection, intelligence came that the Indian tribes on the frontier were becoming hostile and that the settlements were threatened. On the 30th of October, 1786, a resolve had been adopted calling upon New Hampshire, Massachusetts, Rhode Island, and Connecticut for a force of 1,340 additional troops to serve for three years, but so slowly and grudgingly was this requisition

The Constitutional Convention, 1787. being honored that Congress recalled it on the 19th of February, 1787, despite the assurances of the Massachusetts members that the men would be furnished. In fact, so indisposed were certain classes of the people to recognize the Federal Congress as empowered to interfere in case of a rebellion

---

[a] Minot's History of the Insurrection in Massachusetts, Boston, 1810.
[b] Journals of Congress, June 19–21, 1783.

in any State that their numbers in New England alone were estimated at from 12,000 to 15,000 able-bodied men.[a]

It was under these circumstances and with an appreciation of these conditions that the convention assembled on the 14th of May, 1787. "The framers of the Constitution assembled for their work," says Mr. George Ticknor Curtis, in his admirable History of the Constitution, "amidst difficulties and embarrassments of an extraordinary nature. No general concert of opinion had taken place as to what was best, or even as to what was possible to be done. Whether it were wise to hold a convention; whether it were even legal to hold it, and whether, if held, it would be likely to result in anything useful to the country, were points upon which the most opposite opinions prevailed in every State of the Union." Among the many complex and embarrassing subjects the convention was called upon to consider, there was none more serious or more important than that of providing for the common defense. There must be no standing army—on that head there was no disagreement—but the right of the Federal legislature to maintain a standing army, even in time of peace, was one that should never be abandoned. The militia had fought and won the conflict; in a well-regulated militia lay the best guaranty of liberty, but the militia system presented the only defense and protection which the States could have for the security of their rights against encroachments of a general government, and it should never be placed under the power of the Federal legislature. On this the debate was long and sometimes bitter, but the conclusion was emphatic. The power to raise armies, to organize and call out and govern the militia, when in the service of the United States, was deliberately and decisively given to Congress. This is perhaps to anticipate, but is essential to our purpose.

It having been agreed that Virginia, which had originated the convention, should propose the method of its proceeding, Mr. Randolph, of that State, on the 29th of May presented a series of fifteen resolutions looking to the "common defense, security of liberty, and general welfare" of the people of the United States. Among these resolutions, and numbered eleven in his schedule, was one which looked to the necessity for a guaranty to the States of a form of government that should rest on the foundation of popular sovereignty. It read thus:

11. *Resolved*, That a republican government, and the territory of each State, except in the instance of a voluntary junction of government and territory, ought to be guaranteed by the United States to each State.

In the debate upon these resolutions section 11 came up in regular order on the 5th of June, when it was agreed to postpone consideration to a future date. That date was reached on the 11th of that month,

---

[a] Curtis's History of the Constitution, vol. 1, p. 273.

"when it was moved and seconded to amend the eleventh resolution submitted by Mr. Randolph by adding the words 'voluntary junction or partition.' Passed in the affirmative." On this question Massachusetts, New York, Pennsylvania, Virginia, North Carolina, South Carolina, and Georgia voted in the affirmative; Connecticut, New Jersey, Delaware, and Maryland in the negative. A subsequent motion to add the words "national government" was carried by a similar vote. Some desultory debate followed when, upon the motion of Mr. Madison, the eleventh resolution was amended to read as follows, and, on the question to agree to the same, it passed unanimously:

Resolved, That a republican constitution, and its existing laws, ought to be guaranteed to each State by the United States.

On the 19th of June the committee of the whole house reported the state of the Randolph resolutions as altered, amended, and agreed to, and in this report the eleventh resolution became the sixteenth. When the resolution was reached on the 18th of July, the following debate ensued:

Mr. Gouverneur Morris thought the resolution very objectionable. He should be very unwilling that such laws as exist in Rhode Island should be guaranteed.

Mr. WILSON. The object is merely to secure the States against dangerous commotions, insurrections, and rebellions.

Colonel MASON. If the General Government should have no right to suppress rebellions against particular States, it will be in a bad situation indeed. As rebellions against itself originate in and against individual States, it must remain a passive spectator of its own subversion.

Mr. RANDOLPH. The resolution has two objects: First, to secure a republican government; secondly, to suppress domestic commotions. He urged the necessity of both these provisions.

Mr. Madison moved to substitute "that the constitutional authority of the States shall be guaranteed to them, respectively, against domestic as well as foreign violence."

Dr. M'Clurg seconded the motion.

Mr. Houston was afraid of perpetuating the existing constitutions of the States. That of Georgia was a very bad one, and he hoped would be revised and amended. It may also be difficult for the General Government to decide between contending parties, each of which claim the sanction of the Constitution.

Mr. L. Martin was for leaving the States to suppress rebellions themselves.

Mr. Gorham thought it strange that a rebellion should be known to exist in the empire and the General Government should be restrained from interposing to subdue it. At this rate an enterprising citizen might erect the standard of monarchy in a particular State; might gather together partisans from all quarters; might extend his views from State to State, and threaten to establish a tyranny over the whole, and the General Government be compelled to remain an inactive witness of its own destruction. With regard to different parties in a State, as long as they confine their disputes to words they will be harmless to the General Government and to each other. If they appeal to the sword, it will then be necessary for the General Government, however difficult it may be to decide on the merits of their contest, to interpose and put an end to it.

Mr. CARROLL. Some such provision is essential. Every State ought to wish for it. It has been doubted whether it is a *casus fœderis* at present; and no room ought to be left for such a doubt hereafter.

Mr. Randolph moved to add, as an amendment to the motion, "and that no State be at liberty to form any other than a republican government."

Mr. Madison seconded the motion.

Mr. Rutledge thought it unnecessary to insert any guaranty. No doubt could be entertained but that Congress had the authority, if they had the means, to cooperate with any State in subduing a rebellion. It was and would be involved in the nature of the thing.

Mr. Wilson moved, as a better expression of the idea, "that a republican form of government shall be guarantied to each State; and that each State shall be protected against foreign and domestic violence."

This seeming to be well received, Mr. Madison and Mr. Randolph withdrew their propositions, and, on the question for agreeing to Mr. Wilson's motion, it passed, *nem. con.*

Adjourned.

On the 26th of July all the proceedings of the convention were referred to a committee of detail, consisting of Messrs. Rutledge, Randolph, Gorham, Ellsworth, and Wilson, for the purpose of reporting a constitution, and the convention adjourned until the 6th of August that the committee might have time to prepare and report. On the latter date Mr. Rutledge, from the committee, delivered its report, and in their report our resolution appears as Article XVIII in the following language:

ART. XVIII. The United States shall guarantee to each State a republican form of government; and shall protect each State against foreign invasions, and, on the application of its legislature, against domestic violence.

On the regular order, Article XVIII came up on the 30th of August. By this time the question of an army and the organization and disciplining of the militia had been disposed of. In his famous letter of January 27, 1788, Mr. Luther Martin, attorney-general of Maryland and one of its delegates to the convention, remarking upon this feature of its proceedings, has said:

I took the sense of the convention on a proposition by which the Congress should not have power, in time of peace, to keep embodied more than a certain number of regular troops, that number to be ascertained by what should be considered a respectable peace establishment. This proposition was rejected by a majority, it being their determination that the power of Congress to keep up a standing army, even in peace, should only be restrained by their will and pleasure. This section proceeds, further, to give a power to the Congress to provide for the calling forth *the militia* to execute the laws of the Union, suppress insurrections, and repel invasions. As to giving such a power there was no objection; but it was thought by some that this power ought to be given with certain restrictions. It was thought that not more than a certain part of the militia of any one State ought to be obliged to march out of the same, or be employed out of the same, at any one time, without the consent of the legislature of such State. This amendment I endeavored to obtain; but it met with the same fate which attended almost every attempt to limit the powers given to the General Government and constitutionally to guard against their abuse. It was not adopted. As it now stands, the Congress will have the power, if they please, to march the whole militia of Maryland to the remotest part of the Union, and keep them in service as long as they think proper, without being in any respect dependent upon the government of Maryland for this unlimited exercise of power over its citizens—all of whom, from the lowest to the greatest, may, during such service, be subjected to military law, and tied up and whipped at the halbert, like the meanest of slaves.

This explains the debate of the 30th of August on this section. There was an evident disinclination to limit the powers of the General Government, whatever opinions might exist as to the expediency of exercising them. The Massachusetts insurrection was yet fresh in mind, and the refusal of Rhode Island to enter the convention was still unpardoned.

Article XVIII being taken up, the word "foreign" was stricken out, *nem. con.*, as superfluous, being implied in the term "invasion."

Mr. Dickinson moved to strike out "on the application of its legislature, against." He thought it of essential importance to the tranquillity of the United States that they should in all cases suppress domestic violence, which may proceed from the State legislature itself, or from disputes between the two branches, where such exist.

Mr. Dayton mentioned the conduct of Rhode Island, as showing the necessity of giving latitude to the power of the United States on this subject.

On the question—New Jersey, Pennsylvania, Delaware, aye, 3; New Hampshire, Massachusetts, Connecticut, Maryland, Virginia, North Carolina, South Carolina, Georgia, no, 8.

On a question for striking out "domestic violence" and inserting "insurrection," it passed in the negative.

New Jersey, Virginia, North Carolina, South Carolina, Georgia, aye, 5; New Hampshire, Massachusetts, Connecticut, Pennsylvania, Delaware, Maryland, no, 6.

Mr. Dickinson moved to insert the words "or executive" after the words "application of its legislature." The occasion itself, he remarked, might hinder the legislature from meeting.

On this question—New Hampshire, Connecticut, New Jersey, Pennsylvania, Delaware, North Carolina, South Carolina, Georgia, aye, 8; Massachusetts, Virginia, no, 2; Maryland divided.

Mr. L. Martin moved to subjoin to the last amendment the words "in the recess of the legislature." On which question Maryland only, aye.

On the question on the last clause as amended—New Hampshire, Massachusetts, Connecticut, New Jersey, Pennsylvania, Virginia, North Carolina, South Carolina, Georgia, aye, 9; Delaware, Maryland, no, 2.

The revised draft was reported from the committee on style on the 12th of September, and in this revision Article XVIII became Article IV, section 4, and it now read:

SECTION 4. The United States shall guaranty to every State in this Union a republican form of government, and shall protect each of them against invasion; and, on application of the legislature or executive, against domestic violence.

Again, on the 15th of September, the section having been reached in the final consideration of the whole, Mr. Geary moved to insert after the word "executive" the words "when the legislature can not be convened," and in this form it was engrossed:

SECTION 4. The United States shall guarantee to every State in this Union a republican form of government, and shall protect each of them against invasion; and on application of the legislature, or of the executive (when the legislature can not be convened) against domestic violence. [a]

The Constitution had now been framed and signed by the members of the convention. It had yet to run the gauntlet of the States, three-fourths of whom were required to approve it. There were serious fears that this number was not to be gained. Rhode Island had not participated in the convention at all, and could not be expected to ratify it; New York had not been represented for some weeks, and a majority of her delegates were known to be hostile to it; it was boldly asserted that Maryland and at least two other States would reject it. There was a large body of the people throughout the country who exhibited violent opposition to it, and in their opposition the shadow of a standing army formed no inconsiderable part. Many believed with Patrick Henry, of Virginia, that to give Congress the power to enforce the laws by military coercion whenever the civil power fails would be to permit Congress to disregard the civil power altogether if it saw fit, or to declare that the civil authorities were powerless as an excuse for bringing in the troops; or, with Mr. George Mason, that the meeting of three or four persons might be called an insurrection and the militia called out to disperse them. But these fears were fortunately

---

[a] Madison Papers: (vol. 5 of Elliot's Debates) pp. 130, 132, 332, 378, 379, 437, 467, 497, 535, 561.

unfounded. Within four months Connecticut, New Jersey, Pennsylvania, Delaware, and Georgia had ratified the Constitution without the slightest objection; Massachusetts, Maryland, and South Carolina followed, and when on the 21st of June New Hampshire added her voice all opposition ceased and Virginia and New York hastened to record their assent.

Of all the States whose ratification was essential to the adoption of the Constitution, Virginia alone, by the preservation of her debates, has enabled us to learn the character of the objections that had most weight among the opposition. Inferentially, the letter of Luther Martin and those of "Publius" wherein Hamilton, Madison, and Jay successfully combated the popular prejudices, point out the nature of the arguments that were advanced with more of less reason against it [the *Federalist*]; but it is to the Virginia convention that we are limited for their expression. Here the opposition, led by Patrick Henry, Richard Henry Lee, Benjamin Harrison, John Tyler, and George Mason, with others of lesser note, was confronted by Madison, Chief Justice Marshall, with what Mr. Curtis calls "the almost overshadowing influence of Washington" opposed to the uncertain position of Jefferson. It is, therefore, to the Virginia convention that we must look for the best, if the only, expression of the grounds for objection to the proposed method of suppressing insurrection in the new Republic.

The Virginia convention, 1788.

Mr. Clay wished to be informed why the Congress were to have power to provide for calling forth the militia to put the laws of the Union into execution.

Mr. Madison supposed the reasons of this power to be so obvious that they would occur to most gentlemen. If resistance should be made to the execution of the laws, he said, it ought to be overcome. This could be done only in two ways—either by regular forces or by the people. By one or the other it must unquestionably be done. If insurrections should arise or invasions should take place the people ought unquestionably to be employed to suppress and repel them, rather than a standing army. The best way to do these things was to put the militia on a good and sure footing and enable the Government to make use of their services when necessary.

Mr. GEORGE MASON. Mr. Chairman, unless there be some restrictions on the power of calling forth the militia to execute the laws of the Union, suppress insurrections, and repel invasions, we may very easily see that it will produce dreadful oppressions. It is extremely unsafe without some alterations. It would be to use the militia to a very bad purpose, if any disturbance happened in New Hampshire to call them from Georgia. This would harass the people so much that they would agree to abolish the use of the militia and establish a standing army. I conceive the General Government ought to have power over the militia, but it ought to have some bounds. If gentlemen say that the militia of a neighboring State is not sufficient the Government ought to have power to call forth those of other States, the most convenient and contiguous. But in this case the consent of the State legislature ought to be had. On *real* emergencies this consent will never be denied, each State being concerned in the safety of the rest. This power may be restricted without any danger. I wish such an amendment as this—that the militia of any State should not be marched beyond the limits of the adjoining State; and if it be necessary to draw them from one end of the continent to the other I wish such a check—as the consent of the State legislature—to be provided.

There are various ways of destroying the militia. A standing army may be perpetually established in their stead. I abominate and detest the idea of a government where there is a standing army. The militia may be here destroyed by that method which has been practiced in other parts of the world before; that is, by rendering them useless— by disarming them. Under various pretenses Congress may neglect to provide for arming and disciplining the militia; and the State governments can not do it, for Congress has an exclusive right to arm them, etc. Should the National Government wish to render the militia useless they may neglect them, and let them perish in order to have a pretense of establishing a standing army.

Mr. MADISON. Mr. Chairman, I most cordially agree with the honorable member last up that a standing army is one of the greatest mischiefs that can possibly happen. It is a great recommendation for this system, that it provides against this evil more than any other system known to us, and particularly more than the old system of confederation. The most effectual way to guard against a standing army is to render it unnecessary. The most effectual way to render it unnecessary is to give the General Government full power to call forth the militia and exert the whole natural strength of the Union when necessary. Thus you will furnish the people with sure and certain protection without recurring to this evil, and the certainty of this protection from the whole will be a strong inducement to individual exertion. Does the organization of the Government warrant a belief that this power will be abused? Can we believe that a government of a federal nature, consisting of many coequal sovereignties, and particularly having one branch chosen from the people, would drag the militia unnecessarily to an immense distance? This, sir, would be unworthy the most arbitrary despot. They have no temptation whatever to abuse this power; such abuse could only answer the purpose of exciting the universal indignation of the people and drawing on themselves the general hatred and detestation of their country.

I can not help thinking that the honorable gentleman has not considered in all its consequences the amendment he has proposed. Would this be an equal protection, sir, or would it not be a most partial provision? Some States have three or four States in contact. Were this State invaded, as it is bounded by several States, the militia of three or four States would, by this proposition, be obliged to come to our aid; and those from some of the States would come a far greater distance than those of others. There are other States which, if invaded, could be assisted by the militia of one State only, there being several States which border but on one State. Georgia and New Hampshire would be infinitely less safe than the other States. Were we to adopt this amendment, we should set up those States as butts for invasions, invite foreign enemies to attack them, and expose them to peculiar hardships and dangers. Were the militia confined to any limited distance from their respective places of abode, it would produce equal—nay, more—inconveniences. The principles of equality and reciprocal aid would be destroyed in either case.

There is something so preposterous and so full of mischief in the idea of dragging the militia unnecessarily from one end of the conti nent to the other that I think there can be no ground of apprehension. If you limit their power over the militia, you give them a pretext for substituting a standing army. If you put it in the power of the State governments to refuse the militia, by requiring their consent, you destroy the General Government and sacrifice particular States. The same principles and motives which produce disobedience to requisitions will produce refusal in this case.

Mr. Clay apprehended that by this power our militia might be sent to the Mississippi. He observed that the sheriff might raise the posse comitatus to execute the laws. He feared it would lead to the establishment of a military government, as the militia were to be called forth to put the laws into execution. He asked why this mode was preferred to the old established custom of executing the laws.

Mr. Madison answered that the power existed in all countries; that the militia might be called forth for that purpose under the laws of this State and every other State in the Union; that public force must be used when resistance to the laws required it; otherwise society itself must be destroyed; that the mode referred to by the gentleman might not be sufficient on every occasion, as the sheriff must be necessarily restricted to the posse of his own county. If the posse of one county were insufficient to overcome the resistance to the execution of the laws, this power must be resorted to. He did not, by any means, admit that the old mode was superseded by the introduction of the new one. And it was obvious to him that when the civil power was sufficient, this mode would never be put in practice.

Mr. HENRY. As my worthy friend said, there is a positive partition of power between the two governments. To Congress is given the

power of "arming, organizing, and disciplining the militia, and gov-
erning such part of them as may be employed in the service of the
United States." To the State legislature is given the power of
"appointing the officers and training the militia according to the
discipline prescribed by Congress." I observed before that if the
power be concurrent as to arming them, it is concurrent in other
respects. If the States have the right of arming them, etc., concur-
rently, Congress has a concurrent power of appointing the officers
and training the militia. If Congress have that power, it is absurd.
To admit this mutual concurrence of powers will carry you into end-
less absurdity—that Congress has nothing exclusive on the one hand,
nor the States on the other. The rational explanation is that Congress shall have exclusive power of arming them, etc., and that the
State governments shall have exclusive power of appointing the
officers, etc. Let me put it in another light.

May we not discipline and arm them, as well as Congress, if the
power be concurrent? so that our militia shall have two sets of arms,
double sets of regimentals, etc.; and thus, at a very great cost, we
shall be doubly armed. The great object is that every man be armed.
But can the people afford to pay for double sets of arms, etc. Every
one who is able may have a gun. But we have learned by experience
that, necessary as it is to have arms, and though our assembly has,
by a succession of laws for many years, endeavored to have the militia
completely armed, it is still far from being the case. When this
power is given up to Congress without limitation or bounds, how will
your militia be armed? You trust to chance; for sure I am that that
nation which shall trust its liberties in other hands can not long exist.
If gentlemen are serious when they suppose a concurrent power, where
can be the impolicy to amend it? Or, in other words, to say that
Congress shall not arm or discipline them till the States shall have
refused or neglected to do it? This is my object. I only wish to
bring it to what they themselves say is implied. Implication is to be
the foundation of our civil liberties, and when you speak of arming
the militia by a concurrence of power you use implication. But implication will not save you when a strong army of veterans comes upon
you. You would be laughed at by the whole world for trusting your
safety implicitly to implication.

The argument of my honorable friend was that rulers might tyran-
nize. The answer he received was that they will not. In saying that
they would not he admitted they might. In this great, this essential,
part of the Constitution, if you are safe it is not from the Constitution,
but from the virtues of the men in government. If gentlemen are
willing to trust themselves and posterity to so slender and improbable
a chance, they have greater strength of nerves than I have.

The honorable gentleman, in endeavoring to answer the question why the militia were to be called forth to execute the laws, said that the civil power would probably do it. He is driven to say that the civil power may do it instead of the militia. Sir, the military power ought not to interpose till the civil power refuse. If this be the spirit of your new Constitution, that the laws are to be enforced by military coercion, we may easily divine the happy consequences which will result from it. The civil power is not to be employed at all. If it be, show me it. I read it attentively, and could see nothing to warrant a belief that the civil power can be called for. I should be glad to see the power that authorizes Congress to do so. The sheriff will be aided by military force. The most wanton excesses may be committed under color of this; for every man in office, in the States, is to take an oath to support it in all its operations. The honorable gentleman said, in answer to the objection that the militia might be marched from New Hampshire to Georgia, that the members of the Government would not attempt to excite the indignation of the people. Here again we have the general unsatisfactory answer, that they will be virtuous and that there is no danger. * * *

Mr. NICHOLAS. Mr. Chairman, the great object of government in every country is security and public defense. I suppose, therefore, that what we ought to attend to here is, What is the best mode of enabling the General Government to protect us? One of three ways must be pursued for this purpose: We must either empower them to employ and rely altogether on a standing army, or depend altogether on militia, or else we must enable them to use the one or the other of these two ways as may be found most expedient. The least reflection will satisfy us that the convention has adopted the only proper method. If a standing army were alone to be employed, such an army must be kept up in time of peace as would be sufficient in war. The dangers of such an army are so striking that every man would oppose the adoption of this Government had it been proposed by it as the only mode of defense. Would it be safe to depend on militia alone without the agency of regular forces even in time of war? Were we to be invaded by a powerful, disciplined army, should we be safe with militia? Could men unacquainted with the hardships and unskilled in the discipline of war—men only inured to the peaceable occupations of domestic life—encounter with success the most skilful veterans, inured to the fatigues and toils of campaigns? Although some people are pleased with the theory of reliance on militia as the sole defense of a nation, yet I think it will be found in practice to be by no means adequate. Its inadequacy is proved by the experience of other nations. But were it fully adequate it would be unequal. If war be supported by militia, it is by personal service. The poor man does as much as the rich. Is this just? What is the consequence when war is carried on by regular troops? They are paid by taxes raised from the people, according to their property, and then the rich man pays an adequate share.

But if you confine yourselves to militia alone, the poor man is oppressed. The rich man exempts himself by furnishing a substitute. And although it be oppressive to the poor, it is not advantageous to the rich, for what he gives would pay regular troops. It is therefore neither safe nor just to depend entirely on militia. As these two ways are ineligible, let us consider the third method. Does this Constitution put this on a proper footing? It enables Congress to raise an army when necessary or to call forth the militia when necessary. What will be the consequence of their having these two powers? Till there be a necessity for an army to be raised, the militia will still be employed, which will render a less numerous army sufficient. By these means there will be a sufficient defense for the country without having a standing army altogether or oppressing the people. The worthy member has said that it ought to be a part of the Constitution that the militia ought not to go out of the State without the consent of the State legislature. What would be the consequence of this? The general defense is trusted to the General Government. How is it to protect the Union? It must apply to the State governments before it can do it. Is this right? Is it not subjecting the general will to the particular will and exposing the general defense to the particular caprice of the members of the State governments? This would entirely defeat the power given to Congress to provide for the general defense, and unless the militia were to aid in the execution of the laws when resisted, the other powers of Congress would be nugatory.

*   *   *   *   *   *   *

Governor RANDOLPH. Mr. Chairman, our attention is summoned to this clause respecting the militia, and alarms are thrown out to persuade us that it involves a mutiplicity of danger. It is supposed by the honorable gentleman lately up, and another gentleman, that the clause for calling forth the militia to suppress insurrections, repel invasions, and execute the laws of the Union implies that, instead of using civil force in the first instance, the militia are to be called forth to arrest petty offenders against the laws. Ought not common sense to be the rule of interpreting this Constitution? Is there an exclusion of the civil power? Does it provide that the laws are to be enforced by military coercion in all cases? No, sir. All that we are to infer is that when the civil power is not sufficient, the militia must be drawn out. Who are they? He says (and I cheerfully acquiesce in the rectitude of the assertion) that they are the bulwarks of our liberties. Shall we be afraid that the people, this bulwark of freedom, will turn instruments of slavery? The officers are to be appointed by the States.   Will you admit that they will act so criminally as to turn against their country?   The officers of the General Government are attached to it, because they derive their appointment from it.   Admitting the militia officers to be corrupt, what is to make them be in favor of the General Government?   Will not the same reason attach them to the State governments?   But it is feared that the militia are to be subjected to martial law when not in service.   They are only to be called out in three cases, and only to be governed by the authority of Congress when in the actual service of the United States, so that their articles of war can no longer operate upon them than when in the actual service of the Union.

Can it be presumed that you can vest the supreme power of the United States with the power of defense, and yet take away this natural defense from them?   You risk the general defense by withholding this power.

*　　　*　　　*　　　*　　　*　　　*　　　*

Mr. Henry thought it necessary and proper that they should take a collective view of this whole section, and revert again to the first clause. He adverted to the clause which gives Congress the power of raising armies, and proceeded as follows: To me this appears a very alarming power when unlimited.   They are not only to raise but to support armies; and this support is to go to the utmost abilities of the United States.   If Congress shall say that the general welfare requires it, they may keep armies continually on foot.   There is no control on Congress in raising or stationing them.   They may billet them on the people at pleasure.   This unlimited authority is a most dangerous power; its principles are despotic.   If it be unbounded, it must lead to despotism; for the power of a people in a free government is supposed to be paramount to the existing power.

*　　　*　　　*　　　*　　　*　　　*　　　*

The honorable gentleman said that the militia should be called forth to quell riots.   Have we not seen this business go on very well to-day without military force?   It is a long-established principle of the common law of England that civil force is sufficient to quell riots.   To what length may it not be carried?   A law may be made that if twelve men assemble, if they do not disperse they may be fired upon. I think it is so in England.   Does not this part of the paper bear a strong aspect?   The honorable gentleman, from this knowledge, was called upon to show the instances, and he told us the militia may be called out to quell riots.   They may make the militia travel and act under a colonel, or perhaps under a constable.   Who are to determine whether it be a riot or not?   Those who are to execute the laws of the Union?   If they have power to execute their laws in this manner, in what situation are we placed?

*　　　*　　　*　　　*　　　*　　　*　　　*

Mr. Henry wished to know what authority the State governments had over the militia.

Mr. Madison answered that the State governments might do what they thought proper with the militia when they were not in the actual service of the United States. They might make use of them to suppress insurrections, quell riots, etc., and call on the General Government for the militia of any other State to aid them if necessary.

Mr. Henry replied that, as the clause expressly vested the General Government with power to call them out to suppress insurrections, etc., it appeared to him, most decidedly, that the power of suppressing insurrections was *exclusively* given to Congress. If it remained in the States it was by implication.

Mr. Corbin, after a short address to the chair, in which he expressed extreme reluctance to get up, said that all contentions on this subject might be ended by adverting to the fourth section of the fourth article, which provides " that the United States shall guaranty to every State in the Union a republican form of government, and shall protect each of them against invasion; and, on application of the legislature, or of the executive (when the legislature can not be convened), against domestic violence." He thought this section gave the States power to use their own militia and call on Congress for the militia of other States. He observed that our representatives were to return every second year to mingle with their fellow-citizens. He asked, then, how in the name of God they would make laws to destroy themselves.

* * * * * * *

Mr. Grayson, in reply to Mr. Corbin, said he was mistaken when he produced the fourth section of the fourth article to prove that the State governments had a right to intermeddle with the militia. He was of opinion that a previous application must be made to the Federal head by the legislature when in session, or otherwise - by the executive of any State, before they could interfere with the militia. In his opinion no instance could be adduced where the States could employ the militia; for in all the cases wherein they could be employed Congress had the exclusive direction and control of them.

* * * * * * *

Mr. Madison. With respect to suppressing insurrections, I say that those clauses which were mentioned by the honorable gentleman are compatible with a concurrence of the power. By the first, Congress is to call them forth to suppress insurrections and repel invasions of foreign powers. A concurrence in the former case is necessary, because a whole State may be in insurrection against the Union. What has passed may perhaps justify this apprehension. The safety of the Union, and particular States, requires that the General Government should have power to repel foreign invasions. The fourth section of the fourth article is perfectly consistent with the exercise of the power by the States. The words are, "The United States shall guaranty to every State in this Union a republican form of government, and shall protect each of them against invasion; and, on application of the legislature or of the executive (when the legislature can not be convened), against domestic violence." The word "invasion" here, after power had been given in the former clause to repel invasions, may be thought tautologous, but it has a different meaning from the other. This clause speaks of a particular State. It means that it shall be protected from invasion by other States. A republican government is to be guarantied to each State, and they are to be protected from invasion from other States as well as from foreign powers; and, on application by the legislature or executive, as the case may be, the militia of the other States are to be called to suppress domestic insurrections. Does this bar the States from calling forth their own militia? No; but it gives them a supplementary security to suppress insurrections and domestic violence. [a]

* * * * * * *

It would be interesting to following this debate to its end. There is no better rule for the interpretation of doubtful passages of law than to ascertain the intent of the lawmaking power, and this is to be found in the doubts and confidences of its members. The presumption of law that a man intends to do precisely what he does do is not to be applied to deliberative bodies. In the Pennsylvania convention Mr. James Wilson, the only member who had been a member of the Constitutional Convention, and who was afterwards a justice of the Supreme Court of the United States, discoursed at considerable length upon the use of standing armies, which seems to have been one of the foremost objections in Pennsylvania, as elsewhere, to the new Constitution. Mr. Wilson said:

I proceed to another objection that is taken against the power given to Congress of raising and keeping up standing armies. I confess I have been surprised that this objection was ever made, but I am more so that it is still repeated and insisted upon. I have taken some pains to inform myself how the other governments of the world stand with regard to this power, and the result of my inquiry is, that there is not one which has not the power of raising and keeping up standing armies. A government without the power of defense! It is a solecism.

I well recollect the principle insisted upon by the patriotic body in Great Britain; it is, that in time of peace a standing army ought not to be kept up without the consent of Parliament. Their only apprehension appears to be that it might be dangerous were the army kept up without the concurrence of the representatives of the people. Sir,

---

[a] Elliot's Debates in the Virginia Convention, p. 378 et seq.

we are not in the millennium. Wars may happen, and when they do happen who is to have the power of collecting and appointing the force then become immediately and indispensably necessary?

It is not declared in this Constitution that the Congress shall raise and support armies. No, sir; if they are not driven to it by necessity, why should we suppose they would do it by choice any more than the representatives of the same citizens in the State legislature? For we must not lose sight of the great principle upon which this work is founded. The authority here given to the General Government flows from the same source as that placed in the legislatures of the several States.

It may be frequently necessary to keep up standing armies in time of peace. The present Congress have experienced the necessity, and 700 troops are just as much a standing army as 70,000. The principle which sustains them is precisely the same. They may go farther and raise an army without communicating to the public the purpose for which it is raised. On a particular occasion they did this. When the commotions existed in Massachusetts, they gave orders for enlisting an additional body of 2,000 men. I believe it is not generally known on what a perilous tenure we held our freedom and independence at that period. The flames of internal insurrection were ready to burst out in every quarter; they were formed by the correspondents of State officers (to whom an allusion was made on a former day), and from one end to the other of the continent we walked on ashes, concealing fire beneath our feet; and ought Congress to be deprived of power to prepare for the defense and safety of our country? Ought they to be restricted from arming until they divulge the motive which induced them to arm? I believe the power of raising and keeping up an army in time of peace is essential to every government. No government can secure its citizens against dangers, internal and external, without possessing it and sometimes carrying it into execution. I confess it is a power in the exercise of which all wise and moderate governments will be as prudent and forbearing as possible. When we consider the situation of the United States, we must be satisfied that it will be necessary to keep up some troops for the protection of the western frontiers and to secure our interest in the internal navigation of that country. It will be not only necessary, but it will be economical on the great scale. Our enemies, finding us invulnerable, will not attack us, and we shall thus prevent the occasion for larger standing armies.[a]

In commenting upon this section (sec. 4, art. IV) Mr. Curtis remarks that it was necessary to complete the republican character of the system intended to be upheld; that the Constitution assumes that the gov-

---

[a] Elliot's Debates in the Pennsylvania Convention, page 521.

ernments of the States are rightfully in the exercise of their authority and will so continue until changed, but that no change shall be made by force, by public commotion, or by setting aside the authority of the existing government. It recognizes the right of that government to be protected against domestic violence—that is to say, against every species of force that may be directed against it, excepting the will of the people through constitutional forms.[a] Similarly, Mr. Justice Story: "At first view," says this eminent commentator, "it might seem not to square with the republican theory to suppose either that a majority have not the right or that a minority will have the force to subvert a government, and consequently that the Federal interposition can never be required but when it would be improper. But theoretic reasoning in this, as in most other cases, must be qualified by the lessons of practice. Why may not illicit combinations for purposes of violence be formed as well by a majority of a State, especially a small State, as by a majority of a county or a district of the same State? And if the authority of the State ought in the latter case to protect the local magistracy, ought not the Federal authority in the former to support the State authority? Besides, there are certain parts of the State constitutions which are so interwoven with the Federal Constitution that a violent blow can not be given to the one without communicating the wound to the other. Insurrections in a State will rarely induce a Federal interposition, unless the number concerned in them bear some proportion to the friends of government. It will be much better that the violence in such cases should be repressed by the superintending power than that the majority should be left to maintain their cause by a bloody and obstinate contest. The existence of a right to interpose will generally prevent the necessity of exerting it."[b]

---

[a] Curtis's History of the Constitution, vol. 2, page 472.
[b] Story on the Constitution, sec. 1820.

II. FROM THE ADOPTION OF THE CONSTITUTION TO THE SECOND WAR WITH GREAT BRITAIN.

THE WHISKY INSURRECTION, 1794—FRIES'S INSURRECTION, 1799—BURR'S CONSPIRACY, 1805—THE EMBARGO TROUBLES, 1808.

The Congress lost no time in providing the means for carrying into effect the more important features of the Constitution. Its first session was opened on the 4th day of March, 1789, and almost immediately a bill was introduced, which became a law September 29, 1789, to recognize the military establishment of October 3, 1787, and to authorize the President to call into the service from time to time such part of the militia as he may judge necessary for the purpose of protecting the frontier from Indian incursions.[a] At the third session authority was given to raise another regiment of infantry and further empowering the President in his judgment to employ "levies" in addition to the militia.[b] The Second Congress was disposed to still greater liberality. The two regiments of infantry and the battalion of artillery were increased to full strength and three additional regiments of infantry authorized for three years, while the President was empowered to call into the service, for the protection of the frontier, such number of cavalry as in his judgment might be necessary.[c] At the same time a bill was introduced, which became a law May 2, 1792, under the title of "An act to provide for calling forth the militia to execute the laws of the Union, suppress insurrections, and repel invasions;" in other words, to provide for carrying into execution the fourth section of the fourth article of the Constitution.[d] The first three sections of this act, which is the basis of all subsequent legislation in this direction, read thus:

Congress raises an army, 1789.

SECTION 1. *Be it enacted by the Senate and House of Representatives of the United States of America in Congress assembled,* That whenever the United States shall be invaded, or be in imminent danger of invasion from any foreign nation or Indian tribe, it shall be lawful for the President of the United States to call forth such number of the militia of the State or States most convenient to the place of danger or scene of action as he may judge necessary to repel such invasion, and to issue his orders for that purpose to such officer or officers of the militia as he shall think proper; and in

---

[a] 1 Stat. L., 95.   [b] 1 Stat. L., 222.   [c] 1 Stat. L., 242.   [d] 1 Stat. L., 264.

32

case of an insurrection in any State against the government thereof, it shall be lawful for the President of the United States, on application of the legislature of such State, or of the executive (when the legislature can not be convened) to call forth such number of the militia of any other State or States as may be applied for, or as he may judge sufficient to suppress such insurrection.

SEC. 2. *And be it further enacted*, That whenever the laws of the United States shall be opposed, or the execution thereof obstructed, in any State by combinations too powerful to be suppressed by the ordinary course of judicial proceedings or by the powers vested in the marshals by this act, the same being notified to the President of the United States by an associate justice or the district judge, it shall be lawful for the President of the United States to call forth the militia of such State to suppress such combinations, and to cause the laws to be duly executed. And if the militia of a State where such combinations may happen shall refuse or be insufficient to suppress the same, it shall be lawful for the President, if the legislature of the United States be not in session, to call forth and employ such numbers of the militia of any other State or States most convenient thereto as may be necessary, and the use of militia so to be called forth may be continued, if necessary, until the expiration of thirty days after the commencement of the ensuing session.

SEC. 3. *Provided always, and be it further enacted*, That whenever it may be necessary, in the judgment of the President, to use the military force hereby directed to be called forth, the President shall forthwith, and previous thereto, by proclamation, command such insurgents to disperse and retire peaceably to their respective abodes within a limited time.

Six days later a uniform system for the government of the militia was established under the title of "An act more effectually to provide for the national defense by establishing an uniform militia throughout the United States," [a] and this act, with very few changes and those of little importance, is substantially the law under which the militia exists to the present day. It carried out as nearly as possible the views of the makers of the Constitution and embodied all the features already so clearly expressed by Mr. Madison. It fixed the organization, the armament, and the rules of discipline, but left the arrangement of each State into brigades and regiments and companies, and the appointment of their officers, to the several legislatures. The organization, if primitive and in many respects for many years obsolete, was sufficient for the purpose and has met the demands of a century with reasonable satisfaction. It fought two wars, provided the nucleus for the organization of the vast armies that fought out the great rebellion, and only disappeared with the incoming of the "volunteer."

Scarcely had these laws been enacted and the people brought to a comprehension of the existence of a Federal Government when an event occurred that brought them suddenly and unexpectedly into action. In the four counties of Pennsylvania west of the Allegheny Mountains a lawless spirit had prevailed for the half

The whisky insurrection, 1794. century preceding the Revolution. These counties had been settled by people of Scottish descent, mainly farmers, men of great energy and decision, and always restive under

---

[a] 1 Stat. L., 271.

the restraints of law and order. To these the close of the war had
added many desperate characters, mere squatters, ready to engage in
lawless enterprises at the instigation of popular leaders. The farmers,
having no near market for their produce, had always been used to
converting much of their grain into whisky, which had a ready sale at
from fifty cents to a dollar a gallon, so that the still was the necessary
appendage of every farm. Excise laws are always unpopular. Among
these people, whose hatred to such laws was hereditary, their enforcement in colonial days had been always difficult; frequently impossible.

Such was the state of the public mind when in March, 1791, Congress passed an excise law, and for the following two years every
attempt to collect these taxes was stoutly resisted, until the number
and brutality of assaults on the collectors, frequently accompanied by
riots, participated in by whole communities, amounted to a practical
insurrection. In the vicinity of Pittsburg buildings were burned,
the mails intercepted and robbed, Federal officers tarred and feathered.
In many of these outrages the local militia participated, and their officers were among the most obstinate in their resistance to the laws.
The summer of 1794 witnessed an alarming increase of this lawlessness, which at last compelled the courts to confess their inability to
induce the slightest respect to their mandates or to enforce a single
one of their judgments. The office of collector for western Pennsylvania had been accepted by Gen. John Neville, a gentleman known far
and wide for his benevolence, and who in years of scarcity had thrown
open his granaries to his poor neighbors, and in other respects had
endeared himself to the people. On the 16th of July a mob of 500
or more attacked Neville's house, wounded its defenders, and burned
it to the ground. On the 1st of August 7,000 of the malcontents
assembled on Braddock's field, armed and provisioned, and marched
into Pittsburg, intending to capture Fort Pitt, but became frightened
and dispersed. The rebellion rapidly gathered force, until all law was
disregarded and all order at an end. Governor Mifflin refusing to call
out the militia of the State in response to the calls of the courts, the
latter had no recourse but an appeal to the Federal Government.
This took the form of a letter from the United States judge for the
district, an associate justice of the Supreme Court, intended to so
make a case under the Constitution as to authorize the Executive to
call out the military force.

PHILADELPHIA, *August 4, 1794.*

SIR: From the evidence which has been laid before me, I hereby notify to you
that in the counties of Washington and Allegheny, in Pennsylvania, laws of the
United States are opposed, and the execution thereof obstructed by combinations too
powerful to be suppressed by the ordinary course of judicial proceedings or by the
powers vested in the marshal of that district.

I have the honor to be, with the highest consideration and respect,

Your most obedient and humble servant,

JAMES WILSON.

The PRESIDENT OF THE UNITED STATES.

Even with this certificate before him the President was for a time uncertain how to act. It is related that Governor Mifflin's position was sustained by the Secretary of State, but that it was opposed by Hamilton, Bradford, the Attorney-General, and the Secretary of War. Be that as it may, a proclamation of the President appeared three days later, in which the insurgents were called upon to cease their resistance to the laws and to retire peaceably to their respective abodes on or before the 1st day of September, 1794. Failing this he avowed his determination to call forth the militia to suppress all unlawful combinations and to cause the laws to be duly executed. The following is the text of the proclamation:

PROCLAMATION.

Whereas, combinations to defeat the execution of the laws levying duties upon spirits distilled in the United States and upon the stills have, from the time of the commencement of those laws, existed in some of the western parts of Pennsylvania. And whereas, the said combinations, proceeding in a manner subversive equally of the just authority of government and of the rights of individuals, have hitherto effected their dangerous and criminal purpose by the influence of certain irregular meetings, whose proceedings have tended to encourage and uphold the spirit of opposition; by misrepresentations of the laws calculated to render them obnoxious; by endeavors to deter those who might be so disposed from accepting offices under them, through fear of public resentment and injury to person and property, and to compel those who had accepted such offices, by actual violence, to surrender or forbear the execution of them; by circulating vindictive menaces against all those who should otherwise directly or indirectly aid in the execution of the said laws; or who, yielding to the dictates of conscience and to a sense of obligation, should themselves comply therewith, by actually injuring and destroying the property of persons who were understood to have so complied; by inflicting cruel and humiliating punishment upon private citizens for no other cause than that of appearing to be the friends of the laws; by intercepting the public officers on the highways, abusing, assaulting, or otherwise illtreating them; by going to their houses in the night, gaining admittance by force, taking away their papers, and committing other outrages; employing for their unwarrantable purposes the agency of armed banditti, disguised in such a manner as for the most part to escape discovery. And whereas, the endeavors of the legislature to obviate objections to the said laws, by lowering the duties and by other alterations conducive to the convenience of those whom they immediately affect (though they have given satisfaction in other quarters), and the endeavors of the executive officers to conciliate a compliance with the laws, by explanations, by forbearance, and even by particular accommodations founded on the suggestion of local considerations, have been disappointed of their effect by the machinations of persons whose industry to excite resistance has increased with every appearance of a disposition among the people to relax in their opposition and to acquiesce in the laws; insomuch that many persons in the said western parts of Pennsylvania have at length been hardy enough to perpetrate acts which I am advised amount to treason, being overt acts of levying war against the United States; the said persons having, on the 16th and 17th of July last, proceeded in arms (on the second day amounting to several hundreds) to the house of John Neville, inspector of the revenue for the fourth survey of the district of Pennsylvania, having repeatedly attacked the said house, with the persons therein, wounding some of them; having seized David Lennox, marshal of the district of Pennsylvania, who previous thereto had been fired upon, while in the execution of his duty, by a party of armed men, detaining him for some time prisoner, till, for the preservation of his life and the obtaining of his liberty, he found it necessary to enter into stipulations to forbear the execution of certain official duties, touching processes issuing out of a court of the United States, and having finally obliged the said inspector of the revenue and the said marshal, from considerations of personal safety, to fly from that part of the country in order, by a circuitous route, to proceed to the seat of government; avowing as the motive of these outrageous proceedings an intention to prevent, by force of arms, the execution of the said laws, to oblige the said inspector of the revenue to renounce his said office, to withstand by open violence the lawful authority of the Government of the United States, and to compel thereby an alteration of the measures of the legislature and a repeal of the laws aforesaid.

And whereas, by a law of the United States entitled "An act to provide for calling forth the militia to execute the laws of the Union, suppress insurrections, and repel invasions," it is enacted that whenever the laws of the United States shall be opposed or the execution thereof obstructed in any State by combinations too powerful to be suppressed by the ordinary course of judicial proceedings or by the powers vested in the marshals by that act, the same being notified by an associate justice or the district judge, it shall be lawful for the President of the United States to call forth the militia of such State to suppress such combinations and to cause the laws to be duly executed.

And if the militia of a State where such combinations may happen shall refuse or be insufficient to suppress the same, it shall be lawful for the President, if the legislature of the United States be not in session, to call forth and employ such numbers of the militia of any State or States most convenient thereto as may be necessary; and the use of the militia so to be called forth may be continued, if necessary, until the expiration of thirty days after the commencement of the ensuing session: *Provided always*, That whenever it may be necessary, in the judgment of the President, to use the military force hereby directed to be called forth, the President shall forthwith and previous thereto, by proclamation, command such insurgents "to disperse and retire peaceably to their respective abodes within a limited time."

And whereas, James Wilson, an associate justice, on the 4th instant, by writing under his hand, did, from evidence which had been laid before him, notify to me "that in the counties of Washington and Allegheny in Pennsylvania, laws of the United States are opposed and the execution thereof obstructed by combinations too powerful to be suppressed by the ordinary course of judicial proceedings, or by the powers vested in the marshal of that district."

And whereas, it is in my judgment necessary, under the circumstances of the case, to take measures for calling forth the militia in order to suppress the combinations aforesaid and to cause the laws to be duly executed, and I have accordingly determined to do so, feeling the deepest regret for the occasion, but withal the most solemn conviction that the essential interests of the Union demand it; that the very existence of government and the fundamental principles of social order are materially involved in the issue; and that the patriotism and firmness of all good citizens are seriously called upon, as occasion may require, to aid in the effectual suppression of so fatal a spirit.

Wherefore, and in pursuance of the proviso above recited, I, George Washington, President of the United States, do hereby command all persons being insurgents as aforesaid, and all others whom it may concern, on or before the 1st day of September next, to disperse and retire peaceably to their respective abodes. And I do moreover warn all persons whomsoever against aiding, abetting, or comforting the perpetrators of the aforesaid treasonable acts. And I do require all officers and other citizens, according to their respective duties and the laws of the land, to exert their utmost endeavors to prevent and suppress such dangerous proceedings.

In testimony whereof, I have caused the seal of the United States of America to be affixed to these presents, and signed the same with my hand.

Done at the city of Philadelphia, the 7th day of August, seventeen hundred and ninety-four, and of the Independence of the United States of America the nineteenth.

GEORGE WASHINGTON. [L. S.]

By the President:
EDM. RANDOLPH.

It is averred by some writers that the insurgents looked upon the proclamation with contempt, regarding it as a piece of bravado unworthy their notice; others assert that a confidence in their own numbers and bravery, no less than the justice of their cause, impelled them to disregard it. Suffice to say it was received with derision and that the outrages continued without abatement. In the meantime the President had made requisition upon the governors of Pennsylvania, Maryland, New Jersey, and Virginia for 15,000 men, to be immediately organized and prepared to move at a moment's warning.

The requisitions upon New Jersey, Maryland, and Virginia were promptly filled. That from Pennsylvania was furnished from the eastern counties with little delay, so that by the 25th of September the President felt himself in a position to proceed to harsher measures. The troops from Pennsylvania and New Jersey were ordered to rendezvous at Carlisle, and those from Maryland and Virginia at Cumberland, the whole to move on command upon Bedford, the center of the disaffection, where they were to concentrate under the command of Governor Lee, of Virginia. On that date the President issued his second proclamation:

BY THE PRESIDENT OF THE UNITED STATES OF AMERICA.

A PROCLAMATION.

Whereas, from a hope that the combinations against the Constitution and laws of the United States in certain of the western counties of Pennsylvania would yield to time and reflection, I thought it sufficient in the first instance rather to take measures for the calling forth of the militia than immediately to embody them; but the moment has now come when the overtures of forgiveness with no other condition than a submission to law have been only partially accepted; when every form of conciliation not inconsistent with the being of government has been adopted without effect; when the well-disposed in those counties are unable by their influence and example to reclaim the wicked from their fury and are compelled to associate in their own defense; when the proper lenity has been misinterpreted into an apprehension that the citizens will march with reluctance; when the opportunity of examining the serious consequences of a treasonable opposition has been employed in propagating principles of anarchy, endeavoring through emissaries to alienate the friends of order from its support and inviting its enemies to perpetrate similar acts of insurrection; when it is manifest that violence would continue to be exercised upon every attempt to enforce the laws; when, therefore, government is set at defiance, the contest being whether a small portion of the United States shall dictate to the whole Union and, at the expense of those who desire peace, indulge a desperate ambition. Now, therefore, I, George Washington, President of the United States, in obedience to that high and irresistible duty consigned to me by the Constitution "to take care that the laws be faithfully executed," deploring that the American name should be sullied by the outrages of citizens on their own Government; commiserating such as remain obstinate from delusion, but resolved, in perfect reliance on that gracious Providence which so signally displays its goodness toward this country, to reduce the refractory to a due subordination to the law, do hereby declare and make known that with a satisfaction which can be equaled only by the merits of the militia, summoned into service from the States of New Jersey, Pennsylvania, Maryland, and Virginia, I have received intelligence of their patriotic alacrity in obeying the call of the present, though painful, yet commanding necessity; that a force which, according to every reasonable expectation, is adequate to the exigency, is already in motion to the scene of disaffection; that those who have confided or shall'confide in the protection of government shall meet full succor under the standard and arms of the United States; that those who, having offended against the law, have since entitled themselves to indemnity will be treated with the most liberal good faith if they shall not have forfeited their claim by any subsequent conduct, and that instructions are given accordingly. And I do, moreover, expect all individuals and bodies of men to contemplate with abhorrence the measures leading directly or indirectly to those crimes which produce this military coercion; to check in their respective spheres the effort of misguided or designing men to substitute their misrepresentations in the place of truth and their discontents in the place of stable government, and so call to mind that as the people of the United States have been permitted under the Divine favor, in perfect freedom, after solemn deliberation, and in an enlightened age, to elect their own government, so will their gratitude for this inestimable blessing be best distinguished by firm exertions to maintain the Constitution and laws. And lastly, I again warn all persons whomsoever and wheresoever not to abet, aid, or comfort the insurgents aforesaid, as they will answer the country at their peril; and I do also require all officers and other citizens according to their several duties, as far as may be in their power, to bring under the cognizance of law all offenders in the premises. In witness whereof, I have caused the seal of the United States of America to be affixed to these presents, and signed the same with my hand.

Done at the city of Philadelphia, the 25th day of September, seventeen hundred and ninety-four, and of the Independence of the United States of America the nine-.teenth.

GEO. WASHINGTON. [L. S.]

By the President:
    EDM. RANDOLPH.
True copy.
    GEORGE TAYLOR.

The New Jersey militia reported on the 10th day of October, under the command of Governor Howell; the Pennsylvania men were commanded by Generals Irvin and Chambers, those from Maryland by General Smith, those from Virginia under General Morgan. The seat of government being then at Philadelphia, the President journeyed to Bedford, by way of Carlisle, where he at once established subordination among the undisciplined troops, organized them into smaller bodies for effective handling, and prepared them for immediate movement on the insurgents, then believed to number some 16,000. His instructions to Governor Lee are dated at Bedford, October 20, 1794, and are as follows:

BEDFORD, *October 20, 1794.*

SIR: I have it in special instruction from the President of the United States, now at this place, to convey to you, on his behalf, the following instructions for the general direction of your conduct in command of the militia army with which you are charged:

'The objects for which the militia have been called forth are:

1. To suppress the combinations which exist in some of the western counties of Pennsylvania in opposition to the laws laying duties upon spirits distilled within the United States and upon stills.

2. To cause the laws to be executed.

These objects are to be effected in two ways:

1. By military force.

2. By judiciary process and other civil proceedings.

The objects of the military force are twofold:

1. To overcome any armed opposition which may exist.

2. To countenance and support the civil officers in the means of executing the laws.

With a view to the first of these two objects, you may proceed as speedily as may be, with the army under your command, into the insurgent counties to attack and, as far as shall be in your power, subdue all persons whom you may find in arms in opposition to the laws above mentioned. You will march your army in two columns from the places where they are now assembled, by the most convenient routes, having regard to the nature of the roads, the convenience of supply, and the facility of cooperation and union, and bearing in mind that you ought to act, until the contrary shall be fully developed, on the general principle of having to contend with the whole force of the counties of Fayette, Westmoreland, Washington, and Allegheny, and of that part of Bedford which lies westward of the town of Bedford, and that you are to put as little as possible to hazard. The approximation, therefore, of your columns is to be sought, and the subdivision of them so as to place the parts out of mutual supporting distance to be avoided, as far as local circumstances will permit. Parkinsons Ferry appears to be a proper point toward which to direct the march of the columns for the purpose of ulterior measures.

When arrived within the insurgent country, if an armed opposition appear, it may be proper to publish a proclamation inviting all good citizens, friends to the Constitution and laws, to join the United States. If no armed opposition exist, it may still be proper to publish a proclamation, exhorting to a peaceful and dutiful demeanor and giving assurances of performing, with good faith and liberality, whatsoever may have been promised by the commissioners to those who have complied with the conditions prescribed by them and who have not forfeited their title by subsequent misdemeanor.

Of these persons in arms, if any, whom you may make prisoners: Leaders, including all persons in command, are to be delivered to the civil magistrates; the rest to be disarmed, admonished, and sent home (except such as may have been particularly violent and also influential), causing their own recognizances for their good behavior to be taken in the cases which it may be deemed expedient.

With a view to the second point, namely, the countenance and support of the civil officers in the means of executing their laws, you will make such dispensations as shall appear proper to countenance and protect, and, if necessary and required by them, to support and aid the civil officers in the execution of their respective duties; for bringing offenders and delinquents to justice; for seizing the stills of delinquent distillers, as far as the same shall be deemed eligible by the supervisor of the revenue or chief officer of inspection; and also for conveying to places of safe custody such persons as may be apprehended and not admitted to bail.

The objects of judiciary process and other civil proceedings shall be:
1. To bring offenders to justice.
2. To enforce penalties on delinquent distillers by suit.
3. To enforce the penalties of forfeiture on the same persons by the seizure of their stills and spirits.

The better to effect these purposes, the judge of the district, Richard Peters, esq., and the attorney of the district, William Rawl, esq., accompany the army.

You are aware that the judge can not be controlled in his functions, but I count on his disposition to cooperate in such a general plan as shall appear to you consistent with the policy of the case; but your method of giving direction to proceedings, according to your general plan, will be by instructions to the district attorney.

He ought particularly to be instructed (with due regard to time and circumstances): First, to procure to be arrested all influential actors in riots and unlawful assemblies relating to the insurrection and combination to resist the laws or having for object to abet that insurrection and these combinations, and who shall not have complied with the terms offered by the commissioners or manifested their repentance in some other way which you may deem satisfactory; second, to cause process to issue for enforcing penalties on delinquent distillers; third, to cause offenders who may be arrested to be conveyed to jails where there will be no danger of rescue—those for misdemeanors to the jails of York and Lancaster, those for capital offenses to the jail of Philadelphia, as more secure than the others; fourth, prosecute indictable offenses in the court of the United States—those for penalties or delinquents, under the laws before mentioned, in the courts of Pennsylvania.

As a guide in the case, the district attorney has with him a list of the persons who have availed themselves of the offers of the commissioners on the day appointed.

The seizure of stills is of the province of the supervisor and other officers of inspection. It is difficult to chalk out a precise line concerning it. There are opposite considerations which will require to be nicely balanced, and which must be judged of by those officers on the spot. It may be useful to confine the seizure of stills to the most leading and refractory distillers. It may be advisable to extend them far into the most refractory county.

When the insurrection is subdued and the requisite means have been put in execution to secure obedience to the laws, so as to render it proper for the army to retire (an event which you will accelerate as much as shall be consistent with the object), you will endeavor to make an arrangement for attaching such a force as you may deem adequate, to be stationed within the disaffected counties in such a manner as best to afford protection to well-disposed citizens and the officers of the revenue and to suppress by their presence the spirit of riot and opposition to the laws.

But before you withdraw the army you shall promise on behalf of the President a general pardon to all such as shall not have been arrested, with such exceptions as you shall deem proper. The promise must be so guarded as not to affect pecuniary claims under the revenue law. In this measure it is advisable there should be a cooperation with the governor of Pennsylvania.

On the return of the army you will adopt some convenient and certain arrangements for restoring to the public magazines the arms, accouterments, military stores, tents and other articles of camp equipage, and entrenching tools which have been furnished, and shall not have been consumed or lost.

You are to exert yourself by all possible means to preserve discipline amongst the troops, particularly a scrupulous regard to the rights of persons and property, and a respect for the authority of the civil magistrates, taking especial care to inculcate and cause to be observed this principle, that the duties of the army are confined to attacking and subduing of armed opponents of the laws and to the supporting and aiding of the civil officers in the execution of their functions.

It has been settled that the governor of Pennsylvania will be second, the governor of New Jersey third in command, and that the troops of the several States in line, on the march, and upon detachment are to be posted according to the rule which prevailed in the army during the late war, namely, in moving toward the seaboard, the most southern troops will take the right; in moving toward the north, the most northern troops will take the right.

These general instructions, however, are to be considered as liable to such alterations and deviations in the detail as from local and other causes may be found necessary the better to effect the main object upon the general principles which have been indicated.

With great respect, I have the honor to be, sir,
     Your obedient servant,

ALEXANDER HAMILTON.

Truly copied from the original.

B. DANDRIDGE,
Secretary to President of the United States.

The alacrity with which the President's call for militia was responded to, their prompt concentration, the determined attitude of the Government, no less than the presence of Gen. Harry Lee and General Washington, who were recognized by even the more desperate element among the insurgents to be men of courage and determination, combined to settle the matter at once so far as continued resistance was concerned. The troops met everywhere the most complete submission. The insurgents held a crowded meeting at Parkinsons Ferry on the 24th of October, and passed resolutions of submission to authority, promising that the excise officers might safely proceed to their business and that all excise taxes and duties would be promptly paid. (History of the Insurrection in the Four Western Counties of Pennsylvania, by Wm. Findlay, M. C., Philadelphia, 1796; History of the Western Insurrection, by H. M. Brackenridge, Pittsburgh, 1859.)

Although the insurrection was apparently at an end, a condition of affairs whereby a disaffected section of the country or a timid governor could jeopardize the existence of the entire Republic seemed to possess elements of danger that called for serious consideration. Several bills were introduced into Congress looking to a more efficient organization of the militia; to the creation of a regular army; to increasing the powers of the President. To meet the existing emergency an act was passed (November 29, 1794) authorizing the President, in his judgment, to call out and station in the four western counties of Pennsylvania a force of militia not exceeding 2,500 officers and men for a period not to exceed three months, for the purpose of suppressing unlawful combinations and to cause the laws to be duly executed (1 Stat. L., 403). In his annual message for the year 1794 the President devoted much space to a recital of the recent events in western Pennsylvania and to a vigorous defense of his conduct.

While there is cause to lament that occurrences of this nature should have disgraced the name or interrupted the tranquillity of any part of our community, or should have diverted to a new application any portion of the public resources, there are not wanting real and substantial consolations for the misfortune. It has demonstrated that our prosperity rests on solid foundations, by furnishing an additional proof that my fellow-citizens understand the true principles of government and liberty; that they feel their inseparable union; that notwithstanding all the devices which have been used to sway them from their interest and duty, they are now as ready to maintain the authority of the laws against licentious invasions as they were to defend their rights against usurpation. It has been a spectacle displaying to the highest advantage the value of republican government to behold the most and the least wealthy of our citizens standing in the same ranks as private soldiers, preeminently distinguished by being the army of the Constitution—undeterred by a march of 300 miles over rugged mountains, by the approach of an inclement season, or by any other discouragement. Nor ought I to omit to acknowledge the efficacious and patriotic cooperation which I have experienced from the chief magistrates of the States to which my requisitions have been addressed.

In the arrangements to which the possibility of a similar contingency will naturally draw your attention it ought not to be forgotten that the militia laws have exhibited such striking defects as could not have been supplied but by the zeal of our citizens. Besides the extraordinary expense and waste, which are not the least of the defects, every appeal to those laws is attended with a doubt on its success.

The devising and establishing of a well-regulated militia would be a genuine source of legislative honor and a perfect title to public gratitude. I therefore entertain a hope that the present session will not pass without carrying to its full energy the power of organizing, arming, and disciplining the militia, and thus providing, in the language of the Constitution, for calling them forth to execute the laws of the Union, suppress insurrections, and repel invasions.

As already stated, the subject was frequently debated in both Houses during the second session of the Third Congress. It was, among other projects, proposed to enroll a "select corps of militia," to be at the special control of the President in cases of invasion or insurrection (H. R. Journal, Third Congress, p. 101); to authorize the President to call on the executives of the States "to organize, arm and equip, and hold in readiness to march at a moment's warning" 80,000 effective militia (ibid., 108); to enable the President to march the militia to suppress insurrections in the States (ibid., 114). This discussion culminated in the act of February 28, 1795 (1 Stat. L., 424), repealing the prior act of May 2, 1792, and laying down the principle that the President alone is to be the judge of the exigency. In the case of an insurrection in any State against the government of that State *it shall be lawful* for the President to call forth the militia of that or any other State to suppress it, but not imperative that he shall do so. And in the event of an opposition to the execution of any Federal law it shall be lawful for the President, without further advice of Congress or of any supreme justice, as in the prior statute, to call forth the militia of that or of any other State for the purpose of causing the law to be duly executed. This is, perhaps, to repeat what has already been stated in the first pages of this chapter, but it is necessary in connection with events that followed closely after.

Another insurrection broke out in Pennsylvania in the spring of 1799. The Congress had passed an act providing for the raising of a revenue by direct taxation, and as a means of arriving at the valuation of lands, dwelling houses, and stores commissioners were authorized to value and enumerate the same and to make written lists, which, so far as regarded dwelling houses, were to specify "their situation, their dimensions and area, their number of stories, the number and dimensions of their windows, the materials whereof they are built (whether wood, brick, or stone), the number, description, and dimensions of the outhouses appurtenant to them, etc." (Approved July 9, 1798; 1 Stat. L., 580.) Many people in all sections of the country resented this intrusion upon their personal and domestic rights, made necessary by an examination of their dwelling houses, while the provision which contemplated the measuring of every window was especially offensive. In southeastern Pennsylvania, through a section embracing the counties of Lehigh, Berks, Northampton, and a part of Bucks and Montgomery, settled largely by Germans, this process of domiciliary intrusion for the purpose of measurement met the most violent opposition. In some instances the "measurers" were deluged with scalding water by the women from upper windows; in others, were violently ejected by the men. The officials invoked the law, and warrants were issued for the arrest of some of those who had been uncommonly active in resistance. In the village of Bethlehem, in Northampton County, a marshal's posse having some thirty prisoners was attacked on the 7th day of March, 1799, by a body of mounted men numbering one hundred or more, under the command of one John Fries, and the prisoners rescued.

Fries's insurrection, 1799.

This was so plainly a case of opposition to the execution of the Federal laws that the President lost no time in calling upon the governor of the State for sufficient militia to put down the insurrection. To this Governor Mifflin responded by calling out 1,000 men from Philadelphia, Bucks, Chester, Montgomery, and Lancaster, under the command of Gen. William McPherson, and moving them at once to the scene of disturbance. The President's proclamation is dated March 12, 1799, and is as follows:

BY THE PRESIDENT OF THE UNITED STATES OF AMERICA.

A PROCLAMATION.

Whereas, combinations to defeat the execution of the laws for the valuation of lands and dwelling houses within the United States have existed in the counties of Northampton, Montgomery, and Bucks, in the State of Pennsylvania, and have proceeded in a manner subversive of the just authority of the Government, by misrepresentations, to render the laws odious; by deterring the public officers of the United States, to forbear the execution of their functions; and by openly threatening their lives; and

Whereas, the endeavors of the well-affected citizens, as well as of the executive officers, to conciliate a compliance with those laws have failed of success, and certain persons in the county of Northampton aforesaid have been hardy enough to perpetrate certain acts which, I am advised, amount to treason, being overt acts of levying war against the United States, the said persons, exceeding one hundred in number and armed and arrayed in a warlike manner, having, on the 7th day of this present month of March, proceeded to the house of Abraham Lovering, in the town of Bethlehem, and there compelled William Nichols, marshal of the United States in and for the district of Pennsylvania, to desist from the execution of certain legal process in his hands to be executed, and having compelled him to discharge and set at liberty certain persons whom he had arrested by virtue of criminal process duly issued for offenses against the United States, and having impeded and prevented the commissioner and the assessors, appointed in conformity with the laws aforesaid, in the county of Northampton aforesaid, by threats and personal injury, from executing the said laws, avowing as the motives of these illegal and treasonable proceedings an intention to prevent by force of arms the execution of the said laws and to withstand by open violence the lawful authority of the Government of the United States; and

Whereas, by the Constitution and laws of the United States I am authorized, whenever the laws of the United States shall be opposed or the execution thereof obstructed in any State by combinations too powerful to be suppressed by the ordinary course of judicial proceedings or by the powers vested in the marshals, to call forth military force to suppress such combinations and to cause the laws to be duly executed; and

Whereas, it is in my judgment necessary to call forth military force in order to suppress the combinations aforesaid and to cause the laws aforesaid to be duly executed, and I have accordingly determined so to do, under the solemn conviction that the essential interests of the United States demand it:

Wherefore, I, John Adams, President of the United States, do hereby command all persons being insurgents as aforesaid, and all others whom it may concern, on or before Monday next, being the 18th day of this present month, to disperse and retire peaceably to their respective abodes; and I do moreover warn all persons whomsoever against aiding, abetting, or comforting the perpetrators of the aforesaid treasonable acts. And I do require all officers and others, good and faithful citizens, according to their respective duties and the laws of the land, to exert their utmost endeavors to prevent and suppress such dangerous and unlawful proceedings.

In testimony whereof, I have caused the seal of the United States of America to be affixed to these presents, and signed the same with my hand.

Done at the city of Philadelphia, the 12th day of March, in the year of our Lord seventeen hundred and ninety-nine, and of the Independence of the said United States of America the twenty-third.

[SEAL.]   JOHN ADAMS.

By the President:
    TIMOTHY PICKERING,
        Secretary of State.

The appearance of the troops was the signal for the cessation of all disturbance. Not the slightest opposition was manifested to them; Fries and about thirty others most prominent in the affair were arrested and taken to Philadelphia, where they were tried for resisting the laws, and most of them convicted. Fries was indicted for treason, tried, found guilty, and sentenced to punishment. The President subsequently pardoned the entire party through a proclamation.

PROCLAMATION BY JOHN ADAMS, PRESIDENT OF THE UNITED STATES OF AMERICA.

Whereas, the late wicked and treasonable insurrection against the just authority of the United States of sundry persons in the counties of Northampton, Montgomery, and Bucks, in the State of Pennsylvania, in the year 1799, having been speedily suppressed without any of the calamities usually attending rebellion; whereupon peace, order, and submission to the laws of the United States were restored in the aforesaid counties, and the ignorant, misguided, and misinformed in the counties have returned to a proper sense of their duty, whereby it is become unnecessary for the public good that any future prosecutions should be commenced or carried on against any person or persons by reason of their being concerned in the said insurrection:

Wherefore, be it known that I, John Adams, President of the United States of America, have granted, and by these presents do grant, a full, free, and absolute pardon to all and every person or persons concerned in the said insurrection, excepting as hereinafter excepted, of all treasons, misprisions of treason, felonies, misdemeanors, and other crimes by them respectively, done or committed against the United States in either of the said counties before the 12th day of March, in the year 1799, excepting and excluding therefrom every person who now standeth indicted or convicted of any treason, misprision of treason, or other offense against the United States, whereby remedying and releasing unto all persons, except as before excepted, all pains and penalties incurred, or supposed to be incurred, for or on account of the premises.

Given under my hand and the seal of the United States of America, at the city of Philadelphia, this 21st day of May, in the year of our Lord eighteen hundred, and of the Independence of the said States the twenty-fourth.

[SEAL.]   JOHN ADAMS.

For some years following the adoption of the Constitution and the inauguration of the new Republic there were constant apprehensions of trouble with the foreign powers that still maintained colonies to the south and west. On January 18, 1798, a sweeping decree against American commerce was promulgated by the French Directory, and was followed by the capture of many American vessels, whose crews were treated with indignity and cruelty. This created a strong anti-French party. The French Republic having repeatedly violated the treaties made in 1778, Congress, by act of July 6, 1798, declared them void, and by a later act of February 9, 1799, all commercial intercourse between the United States and France and her dependencies was suspended. There was great excitement throughout the country; the militia was embodied and was in constant expectation of being called upon for active service; measures were projected for the increase of the Army, the better defense of the Atlantic coast, the creation of a navy. But a better feeling on the part of the French Government prevailed about the close of the century, occasioned by the accession of Napoleon to supreme power, and this excellent disposition rapidly developed until it culminated in the transfer of the Louisiana Territory, whereby, for a sum approximating $27,000,000, we disposed of a troublesome neighbor and added nearly a thousand million acres to our public domain.

Our south-western frontier, 1800-1807.

The attitude of Spain was less friendly; and now that Louisiana had enlarged our frontier, her possessions extended for 3,000 miles along our southwest boundary. Repeated plans had been formed by the Americans who resided within Spanish territory and formed the entire population of hundreds of settlements, to shake off the Spanish yoke and annex themselves to their countrymen on the east of the

Mississippi, so that the Government was under constant embarrassment in its endeavor to maintain the laws of international neutrality. The Spanish residents along the boundary increased this difficulty by their studied insolence and repeated aggression. The boundary line was indefinite and unsurveyed, and it had been agreed, pending such a survey, that each government should retain its military posts, but establish no others, nor attempt to occupy any part of the territory in dispute. In June, 1806, after a series of petty encroachments along the frontier, the Spanish commander advanced a force of 1,200 men across the Sabine to within 20 miles of Nachitoches, the westernmost settlement in the Orleans Territory. Our nearest military posts were at New Orleans and St. Louis. These were hurriedly put in a state for defense; the militia of Orleans and Missouri were ordered under arms, and General Wilkinson, then governor of Louisiana Territory, assembled the regular troops, something less than 600 officers and men, and marched to the frontier. "On the 4th of July, 1806," says Parton, "there were not a thousand persons in the United States who did not think war with Spain inevitable, impending, begun. The country desired it. A blow from Wilkinson, a word from Jefferson, would have let loose the dogs of war, given us Texas, and changed the history of the two continents." [a]

At this juncture appears one of the most remarkable figures in American history, as the head of a mysterious undertaking the secrets of which nearly a hundred years of research and conjecture have failed to unravel. Precisely what it was that Aaron Burr contemplated, when he first set on foot the enterprise that terminated in his arrest and trial for treason, has never been discovered. Close investigation of the man and his character before and after the event impel the conclusion that he himself could not have told. Without essaying to retrace the ground that has been followed by every American historian and holding closely to facts rather than conjecture, it will suffice to say that while confronting the Spanish camp in the Sabine country, about the 8th of October, 1806, General Wilkinson was waited upon by a gentleman bearing letters from Aaron Burr, who on the 4th of March, 1805, had finished a term as Vice-President of the United States, having failed by a single vote of reaching the Presidency, and who was, even in his retirement, one of the most conspicuous men of the country. In these letters was apparently concealed a plot which contemplated the seizure of Baton Rouge or New Orleans; the revolutionizing of the Western country; the fitting out from thence of an expedition for the capture of Mexico, and the ultimate erection of the whole into an empire of which Burr should be the head, Wilkinson second in command, with high positions for prominent officers of the Army and Navy. The whole plan was

Burr's conspiracy, 1805–1807.

---

[a] Life and Times of Aaron Burr (N. Y., 1861), p. 407.

nebulous, mysterious, vague, conjectural, and it still remains so. Wilkinson, who has been charged with complicity in the plot and whose conduct in the matter is in many respects inexplicable, sent the papers by a special messenger to Washington, and they were placed in the hands of the President on the 25th of November. On the 27th he issued a proclamation in the following words, in which the name of Burr is carefully avoided. In Wilkinson's dispatches he had stated that he did not know who was the prime mover of the conspiracy; but there was every reason for believing that Burr's association with it was well known to the President. In fact, it is admitted in his message to Congress of January 22, 1807.[a]

BY THE PRESIDENT OF THE UNITED STATES OF AMERICA.

A PROCLAMATION.

Whereas, information has been received that sundry persons, citizens of the United States or residents within the same, are conspiring and confederating together to begin and set on foot, provide, and prepare the means for a military expedition or enterprise against the dominions of Spain; that for this purpose they are fitting out and arming vessels in the western waters of the United States, collecting provisions, arms, military stores, and means; are deceiving and seducing honest and well-meaning citizens, under various pretenses, to engage in their criminal enterprises; are organizing, officering, and arming themselves for the same, contrary to the laws in such cases made and provided:

I have therefore thought proper to issue this my proclamation, warning and enjoining all faithful citizens who have been led without due knowledge or consideration to participate in the said unlawful enterprises to withdraw from the same without delay, and commanding all persons whatsoever engaged or concerned in the same to cease all further proceedings therein, as they will answer the contrary at their peril and incur prosecution with all the rigors of the law. And I hereby enjoin and require all officers, civil and military, of the United States, or of any of the States or Territories, and especially all governors and other executive authorities, all judges, justices, and other officers of the peace, all military officers of the Army or Navy of the United States, or officers of the militia, to be vigilant, each within his respective department and according to his functions, in searching out and bringing to condign punishment all persons engaged or concerned in such enterprise, in seizing and detaining, subject to the disposition of the law, all vessels, arms, military stores, or other means provided or providing for the same, and, in general, in preventing the carrying on such expedition or enterprise by all lawful means within their power; and I require all good and faithful citizens and others within the United States to be aiding and assisting herein, and especially in the discovery, apprehension, and bringing to justice of all such offenders, in preventing the execution of their unlawful designs, and in giving information against them to the proper authorities.

In testimony whereof, I have caused the seal of the United States to be affixed to these presents, and have signed the same with my hand.

Given at the city of Washington, on the 27th day of November, eighteen hundred and six, and in the year of the sovereignty of the United States the thirty-first.

[SEAL.]   TH: JEFFERSON.

By the President:

JAMES MADISON,
    Secretary of State.

---

[a] Messages and Papers of the Presidents (Richardson), Vol. I, p. 412.

In the message above referred to the President asserts that Burr's designs seem to differ as they are revealed by different informants. One was a severance of the Union by the Allegheny Mountains; a second an attack on Mexico; a third the settlement of a pretended purchase of a tract of country on the Washita. That finding the attachment of the Western country to the Union was not to be shaken, he determined to seize New Orleans, plunder the bank there, seize the military and naval stores, and proceed on his expedition to Mexico. It was upon this theory that the Government proceeded to act. Orders were dispatched to every point on the Ohio and Mississippi from Pittsburg to New Orleans for the employment of regular troops or militia to arrest all persons concerned and to suppress the further progress of the enterprise. The governor and legislature of Ohio were prompt to act; the militia were called out, and dispatched at once to Marietta, opposite Blennerhassett Island, in the Ohio River, where it was known that Burr was building boats and collecting stores; fifteen boats were captured, but Burr with two other boats had escaped. The island was a part of the State of Virginia, and the Ohio militia could not visit it; but under the authority of the proclamation the colonel of a militia regiment in Wood County, Va., called out his men and took possession of the island, where they destroyed considerable property and committed much vandalism, but failed to discover the fugitives. Many years afterwards Mrs. Blennerhassett petitioned Congress for indemnification for these depredations, but without avail.[a]

In the meantime Burr had reached Nashville. The governor of Kentucky had called out his militia and detachments had been stationed at various river points, but the two boats had passed them unnoticed. On the 19th of December the proclamation reached the governor of Tennessee, who immediately ordered out a body of militia with orders to seize the boats and arrest the men. Again the news reached Burr in time to enable him to drop down the river into the Mississippi Territory. He reached Bayou Pierre, 30 miles above Natchez, where he first learned of Wilkinson's course, and of a proclamation of the governor of Mississippi calling upon his militia to arrest him and crush his plot. The militia came up to the boats on the 15th of January, 1807, and Burr agreed to surrender upon proper legal process. A grand jury was at once impaneled, but instead of presenting the expected indictment they declared Burr innocent of any crime or misdemeanor against the laws of the United States or of Mississippi Territory, condemned the calling out of the militia as foolish and unnecessary, and denounced the arrests as unwarranted and unjustifiable. Burr then resolved to make his way across the country to Pensacola, then Spanish territory, where he hoped to find refuge. He

---

[a] Senate Doc. No. 394, Twenty-seventh Congress, second session.

succeeded in reaching the frontier, but before he could cross it he was arrested by a detachment of regular troops under Capt. (afterward Maj. Gen.) E. P. Gaines and taken to Fort Stoddart. Burr was brought before the United States circuit court at Richmond, Va., August 3, 1807, on an indictment for treason, and on August 31 the jury brought in a verdict of "not guilty." A second trial followed on the charge of misdemeanor, and on this he was again acquitted on the ground that the offense was not committed in Virginia, but in Ohio. The Government made no further prosecution and Burr left the country soon after for a long period of exile.[a]

Up to this time, and for some years later, the Regular Army was too few in numbers to warrant its employment for other purpose than the manning of the few fortifications on the seacoast and the protection of the frontier. The first recognition of the Army after the adoption of the Constitution was the act of September 29, 1789, which authorized a force of 700 men to be raised for three years, which, with the two companies of artillery then in service, made an aggregate of 886 officers and men. This was increased to 1,273 by the act of April 30, 1790, and to 2,232 by the act of March 3, 1791, but at no time was the number actually in service equal to that authorized.

A Regular Army created. The act of March 5, 1792, creating the "Legion of the United States," authorized a reorganization of this slender Army which gave it an increase up to 5,414, and this was substantially its strength until the 30th of May, 1796, when another act reduced it to 3,359. The panic of 1798–99, created by the fear of possible hostilities with France, induced Congress to clothe the President with power to raise an emergency army, and by the various acts of May 30, 1797; April 28, 1798; May 28, 1798; July 16, 1798, and March 3, 1799, all of which were vague, uncertain, and contradictory, an army was created, on paper, with a strength of 50,000 men and 2,000 officers; but although commissions were tendered and accepted to nearly the authorized number, few men were ever enlisted, and the opening of the new century found the Army reduced to about its former strength of 4,000 officers and men. Another attack upon this meager force (act of March 16, 1802) reduced it to 3,287, and it there remained until by the act of April 12, 1808, it was increased to 10,000, which maximum obtained until the breaking out of the second war with Great Britain. During this period of evolution it was quite impracticable to expect the Army to afford any assistance in case of domestic disturbances, it being generally understood and accepted that all duties of that nature were the special work of the militia.

---

[a] See also Lossing's Cyclopædia of American History, Vol. I; Pickett's History of Alabama, vol. 2, p. 213; message on the Burr conspiracy, and accompanying documents, January 22, 1807; House of Representatives report on the conduct of General Wilkinson, May 1, 1810, Eleventh Congress, second session.

The first contraproposition was advanced in the act of March 8, 1807 (2 Stat. L., 443):

> That in all cases of insurrection or obstruction to the laws, either of the United States or of any individual State or Territory, where it is lawful for the President of the United States to call forth the militia for the purpose of suppressing such insurrection or of causing the laws to be duly executed, it shall be lawful for him to employ, for the same purposes, such part of the land or naval force of the United States as shall be judged necessary, having first observed all the prerequisites of the law in that respect.

The occasion for the exercise of this judgment was already developing. The embargo act of Congress of December 22, 1807, supplemented by that of March 12, 1808, prohibiting the departure of any vessel from any port of the United States, and ordering all American vessels abroad to return home forthwith, which aroused the most violent and incessant opposition throughout the country, was nowhere received with greater dismay and consternation than by the people of northern Vermont along the shores of Lake Champlain. Depending entirely upon Canada as a market for the cattle, timber, and other products, which constituted the chief articles of export, and upon the articles of wear and sustenance received in exchange, the effect of this law was to simply take from them their sole means of support and to goad them to resistance. Immediately upon receipt of the official copy of the law the collector of the Vermont district, Mr. Penniman, advised Mr. Gallatin, the Secretary of the Treasury, that it would be impossible to execute it without a military force. This report having been sent to the President, he called the members of the Vermont delegation in Congress into consultation and, upon their advice, decided that it was most important to crush at once every example of forcible opposition to the law. The collector was accordingly instructed to arm, equip, and man as many vessels as he might think necessary—with volunteers, if possible; otherwise by force of arms. At the same time the United States marshal was authorized, if the opposition be too powerful for the collector, to raise his posse and aid in suppressing the insurrection. Should these measures prove ineffective, the Secretary of War was instructed to request the governor to publish the usual proclamation and to call out the militia. (Jefferson's Complete Works, vol. 5, p. 271.)

The embargo troubles, 1808.

On the 5th of May (1808), by order of the governor, Gen. Levi House, commanding the First Brigade of Vermont Militia, ordered out a small detachment from the First Regiment in Franklin County, and these men were stationed at Windmill Point. The proclamation appeared five days later, and was greeted with derision by the more desperate and with amazement by all. Town meetings were called at various points, in which resolutions were framed, unanimously passed, and forwarded to Washington, protesting against the implication that insurrection and rebellion existed or that there was any other cause for the charge than the acts of a few individuals whose families were on the verge of starvation and ruin because of the embargo restrictions. The proclamation is as follows:

By the President of the United States of America.

A PROCLAMATION.

Whereas, information has been received that sundry persons are combined or combining and confederating together on Lake Champlain and the country thereto adjacent for the purposes of forming insurrections against the authority of the laws of the United States, for opposing the same and obstructing their execution, and that such combinations are too powerful to be suppressed by the ordinary course of judicial proceedings or by the powers vested in the marshals by the laws of the United States:

Now, therefore, to the end that the authority of the laws may be maintained, and that those concerned, directly or indirectly, in any insurrection or combination against the same may be duly warned, I have issued this my proclamation, hereby commanding such insurgents and all concerned in such combination instantly and without delay to disperse and retire peaceably to their respective abodes. And I do hereby further require and command all officers having authority, civil or military, and all other persons, civil or military, who shall be found within the vicinity of such insurrections or combinations to be aiding and assisting by all the means in their power, by force of arms or otherwise, to quell and subdue such insurrections or combinations, to seize upon all those therein concerned who shall not instantly and without delay disperse and retire to their respective abodes, and to deliver them over to the civil authorities of the place to be proceeded against according to law.

In testimony whereof, I have caused the seal of the United States to be affixed to these presents and signed the same with my hand.

Given at the city of Washington, the 19th day of April, eighteen hundred and eight, and in the year of the sovereignty and Independence of the United States the thirty-second.

[SEAL.]   TH: JEFFERSON.

By the President:
JAMES MADISON,
     Secretary of State.

It appearing that notwithstanding the presence of the detachment at Windmill Point, several rafts owned by the smugglers passed into Canada, another detachment of 150 men from Rutland County was sent to join them. This act seems to have incited the ire of the militia from Franklin County, for on the 17th of June a meeting of all the commissioned officers of the First Brigade was held and a spirited address to the public adopted in which it was declared that the sending of the Rutland County militia into the district was "an open, direct, and most degrading insult." A few weeks later another mass meeting was held in Franklin County, in which it was declared "the inhabitants on Lake Champlain would never submit to the enforcement of the embargo law." Under these circumstances it was decided by the President that the occasion for trial of the act of March 8, 1807, had arrived; a detachment of United States artillery was sent to the point of disturbance and the governor was ordered to discharge the militia, which was done early in October. (President Jefferson to Governor Tompkins, New York, August 15, 1808; to Secretary Gallatin, August 15, 1808; to Secretary Dearborn, August 25, 1808; to Governor Wilkinson, August 30, 1808.) This was hastened, perhaps, by an unfortunate incident of the affair which occurred on the Winooski River on the 3d of August, where, in an encounter between a force of the militia and a party of smugglers, several of the former were killed and others wounded. The smugglers were arrested, tried, and convicted, one of them executed, and several others sentenced to ten years in prison.[a] President Jefferson thus refers to this disturbance in his annual message for the year 1808:

> I have not thought it necessary, in the course of the last season, to call for any general detachments of militia or of volunteers under the laws passed for that purpose. For the ensuing season, however, they will be required to be in readiness should their service be wanted. Some small and special detachments have been necessary to maintain the laws of embargo on that portion of our northern frontier which offered peculiar facilities for evasion, but these were replaced as soon as it could be done by bodies of new recruits. By the aid of these and of the armed vessels called into service in other quarters the spirit of disobedience and abuse which manifested itself early and with sensible effect while we were unprepared to meet it has been considerably repressed.

The act of January 7, 1809 (2 Stat. L., 506), which, by enlarging the scope of the embargo laws, so increased their unpopularity as to create a widespread public indignation which led to their speedy repeal, contained a clause which is of interest as showing the views of Congress at that time in the matter of the employment of the entire military power if necessary in the enforcement of the Federal laws. Sections 11 and 13 were as follows:

> SEC. 11. *And be it further enacted,* That it shall be lawful for the President of the United States, or such other person as he shall have empowered for that purpose, to employ such part of the land or naval forces or militia of the United States, or of the Territories thereof, as may be judged necessary, in conformity with the provisions of this and other acts respecting the embargo, for the purpose of preventing the illegal departure of any ship or vessel, or of detaining, taking possession of, and keeping in custody any ship or vessel, or of taking into custody and guarding any specie, or articles of domestic growth, produce, or manufacture, and also for the purpose of preventing and suppressing any armed or riotous assemblage of persons, resisting the custom-house officers in the exercise of their duties, or in any manner opposing the execution of the laws laying an embargo, or otherwise violating, or assisting and abetting violations of the same.

> SEC. 13. *And be it further enacted,* That the President of the United States be, and he hereby is, authorized to hire, arm, and employ thirty vessels, not exceeding in tonnage one hundred and thirty tons each, belonging to citizens of the United States, and so many seamen as shall be necessary to man the same, for immediate service, in enforcing the laws of the United States on the seacoast thereof and to dismiss the

---

[a] See also Records of the Governor and Council of Vermont, vol. 5, p. 472.

same from service whenever he shall deem the same expedient: *Provided, however,* That such hiring, arming, and employment shall not be for a term exceeding one year. And the said ships or vessels, when so hired and armed, shall be employed under the direction of the Secretary of the Treasury.

Immediately upon the passage of this act, and no doubt in anticipation of its reception by the country, the following letter, prepared by the President (Jefferson's Works, vol. 5, p. 418) was sent to the governor of every State:

JANUARY 17, 1809.

SIR: The pressure of the embargo, although sensibly felt by every description of our fellow-citizens, has yet been cheerfully borne by most of them, under the conviction that it was a temporary evil, and a necessary one to save us from greater and more permanent evils—the loss of property and surrender of rights. But it would have been more cheerfully borne but for the knowledge that while honest men were religiously observing it the unprincipled along our seacoast and frontiers were fraudulently evading it; and that in some parts they had even dared to break through it openly by an armed force too powerful to be opposed by the collector and his assistants. To put an end to this scandalous insubordination to the laws, the Legislature has authorized the President to empower proper persons to employ militia for preventing or suppressing armed or riotous assemblages of persons resisting the custom-house officers in the exercise of their duties, or opposing or violating the embargo laws. He sincerely hopes that during the short time which these restrictions are expected to continue no other instances will take place of a crime of so deep a dye. But it is made his duty to take the measures necessary to meet it. He therefore requests you, as commanding officer of the militia of your State, to appoint some officer of the militia, of known respect for the laws, in or near to each port of entry within your State, with orders, when applied to by the collector of the district, to assemble immediately a sufficient force of his militia, and to employ them efficaciously to maintain the authority of the laws respecting the embargo, and that you notify to each collector the officer to whom, by your appointment, he is so to apply for aid when necessary. He has referred this appointment to your excellency because your knowledge of characters, or means of obtaining it, will enable you to select one who can be most confided in to exercise so serious a power with all the discretion, the forbearance, the kindness even, which the enforcement of the law will possibly admit—ever to bear in mind that the life of a citizen is never to be endangered but as the last melancholy effort for the maintenance of order and obedience to the laws.

A few days later an occasion arose for the exercise of the powers thus vested in the Executive, the story of which is thus told in a letter from Mr. Jefferson to Col. Charles Simms, collector for Virginia, but of the results of which the official records are silent:

WASHINGTON, *January 22, 1809.*

SIR: I received last night your letter of yesterday, and this being a day in which all the offices are shut, and the case admitting no delay, I inclose you a special order, directly from myself, to apply for aid of the militia adjacent to the vessel, to enable you to do your duty as to the sloop loading with flour. But I must desire that, so far as the agency of the militia be employed, it may be with the utmost discretion, and with no act of force beyond what shall be necessary to maintain obedience to the laws, using neither deeds nor words unnecessarily offensive.

I salute you with respect.[a]

---

[a] Jefferson's Works, vol. 5, p. 418.

JANUARY, 1809.

United States of America, to wit:

Information being received that a sloop, said to be of one of the Eastern States, of about 1,500 barrels burden, is taking in flour in the Bay of Occoquan in Virginia, with intention to violate the several embargo laws, and the urgency of the case not admitting the delay of the ordinary course of proceeding through the orders of the governors of the States, I have therefore thought proper to issue these my special orders to the militia officers of the counties of Fairfax, Prince William, or of any other county of Virginia or of Maryland, adjacent to the river Potomak or any of its waters, wherein the said vessel may be found, and to such particular officer, especially to whom these my orders shall be presented by any collector of the customs, for any district on the said river or its waters, or by any person acting under their authority, forthwith on receiving notice, to call out such portion of the militia under his or their command as shall be sufficient, and to proceed with the same, in aid of the said collector, to take possession of the said sloop and her cargo wheresoever found in the said waters, and to detain the same until she shall be liberated according to law, for which this shall be his and their warrant.

Given under my hand at Washington, this 22d day of January, eighteen hundred and nine.

THOMAS JEFFERSON,
President of the United States of America.

NOTE.—President's Message (Washington) on the Embargo, March 28, 1794; Senate Journal, Third Congress, first session, p. 98; President's Message (Jefferson) on the Embargo, November 19, 1807, Executive Documents, Tenth Congress, first session; same, November 30, 1808, Executive Documents, Tenth Congress, second session; Report by (Gallatin) Secretary Treasury, December 8, 1808, Executive Documents, Tenth Congress, second session.

III. FROM THE REORGANIZATION OF THE ARMY TO THE FUGITIVE SLAVE RIOTS.

NEGRO INSURRECTIONS, 1831—THE NULLIFICATION EXCITEMENT, 1832—THE BLACK HAWK WAR, 1832—THE SABINE AFFAIR, 1836—INTRUDERS ON THE CHEROKEE LANDS, 1833—REMOVAL OF THE CHEROKEES, 1838—THE PATRIOT WAR, 1837-38—IOWA BOUNDARY LINE, 1839—THE DORR REBELLION, 1842—THE BOSTON FUGITIVE SLAVE CASES, 1851—THE ANTHONY BURNS RIOTS, 1854.

It has been said that the provision of the act of February 28, 1795, as amended by the act of March 8, 1807, which made it lawful for the President to call forth the militia or the Federal land and naval forces to suppress an insurrection in any State against the government of such State, "on application of the legislature of such State, or of the executive when the legislature can not be convened," vests in the President the widest discretion. "By this act," says the Supreme Court of the United States in the case of Luther *v*. Borden (7 Howard, 41), "the power of deciding whether the exigency has arisen upon which the Government of the United States is bound to interfere is given to the President. He is to act upon the application of the legislature or of the executive, and consequently he must determine what body of men constitute the legislature and who is the governor before he can act. The fact that two parties claim the right to the government can not alter the case, for both can not be entitled to it. If there is an armed conflict, * * * it is a case of domestic violence, and one of the parties must be in insurrection against the lawful government. And the President must, of necessity, decide which is the government, and which party is unlawfully arrayed against it, before he can perform the duty imposed upon him by the act of Congress." (See also Woodbury dissent, ibid., 49.) It was not, however, until nearly fifty years after the enactment of this law that it became necessary for the President to consider the propriety of exercising this discretion. Up to that time all disturbances requiring Federal interposition had grown out of a violation of, or opposition to, the Federal laws. So far as the provision of the law relating to invasion was concerned, some interesting questions had arisen at the beginning of the second war with Great Britian as to the power of the President or of Congress to require the militia of a State to serve outside its own borders; but in the presence of the common peril these constitutional problems had readily solved themselves or been forgotten in the hurry of events.

55

The year 1831 was one of unusual uneasiness throughout the slave-holding section of the country, consequent upon an apprehended uprising of the negroes. Early in the spring of that year strong and urgent representations were made to the War Department by the authorities of Louisiana that a revolt was threatened by the slaves, and that the presence of a military force in New Orleans was necessary to the preservation of order and to allay the apprehensions of the people. To quiet these fears two companies of infantry were sent to that city and orders were given to neighboring posts to hold the troops in readiness for any emergency. Later in the season similar reports

Negro insurrections, 1831.

of disorderly conduct upon the part of the slaves came from Delaware, Maryland, Virginia, and the Carolinas, and in order that a disposable force might be available to afford protection to such parts of the country as might require it, the garrison of Fort Monroe was augmented by five companies drawn from the northern seaboard. These apprehensions seemed well founded, when on the 24th of August intelligence was received from the mayor of Norfolk, Va., that a negro insurrection had broken out in Southampton County; that more than 50 persons had been massacred, and that the presence of the Federal troops was necessary for the preservation of order.[1] Believing the situation to be imminent and pressing, the commandant at Fort Monroe at once dispatched a force of troops to the scene of disturbance, but beyond allaying the excitement and restoring the courage of the people the active service of the troops was not required.[2] A few days later, on the application of the authorities of Newberne, in North Carolina, under the excitement which prevailed after the disturbances in Southampton, a detachment was sent from Fort Monroe to guard that city and to quiet the apprehensions of the citizens of that section.[5] At the same time arms and ammunition were issued to the citizens of Hampton, upon the requisition of the militia.[3] (Annual report of Major-General Macomb, November, 1831.) Whatever line of justification for this furnishing of troops in contravention of the statute may have been advanced at the time, does not appear of record. On the contrary, there is evidence that the presence of the troops was resented by the people of North Carolina, upon the ground that the situation was at no time beyond the control of the local authorities.[7]

A year later there was great excitement throughout the country consequent upon the determination of the President to enforce the tariff laws. The tariff bill which became a law on March 31, 1824, had been a source of much opposition in Congress, and was received with disapproval throughout the South. The section was agricultural and a heavy consumer of imported goods. Cotton sent

The nullification excitement, 1832.

abroad was usually exchanged for goods that had to be brought in through the custom-house, thus increasing the cost of living without apparent compensation. It was regarded by one portion of the community as a measure to build up a commercial and manufacturing North as a menace to the more pastoral South; by others as an attempt to discriminate against the slave-labor States; by a third, of whom Mr. Calhoun was the leader, as clearly and mischievously unconstitutional. This latter position was assumed with greatest defiance by the people of South Carolina. Immediately upon the passage of the bill the legislature passed resolutions declaring the tariff acts to be unconstitutional, and therefore null and void and not binding upon the people, and inviting other States to cooperate with South Carolina in devising measures of resistance. Although this action created considerable excitement at the time, it found its expression for some years mainly in threatening and other intemperate language in the public press, on the stump, and in Congress; but the passage of the tariff bill of 1832 caused a renewal of the manifestations of 1824 and a more determined attitude upon the part of South Carolina. At a delegate convention called to consider the situation resolutions were passed condemnatory of the law, forbidding citizens of the State from paying any taxes under it, or accepting any office as collector, or recognizing it in any manner. It was further declared that if the United States should attempt to enforce these laws by military or naval force, the Union was to be dissolved and a convention called to frame a new constitution for South Carolina. The legislature, which met soon after the adjournment of this convention, ratified its action by passing laws in conformity with its suggestions. Ten thousand stand of arms were ordered purchased, and measures ordered to be taken to put the State in a condition of thorough defense.

The President (Jackson) met this defiance by his proclamation of December 10, 1832, in which he declared the ordinances of the convention to be subversive of the Federal Constitution, and after appealing to the sense of justice, reason, and patriotism of the people of South Carolina, announced his determination to enforce the laws at whatever hazard. In anticipation of the reception of this warning, two companies of artillery were ordered to Fort Moultrie on the 7th of November, and on the 12th the troops then at the Citadel in Charleston were strengthened by two additional companies from the forts in the harbor. The "Citadel" was the property of the State and contained arms belonging to the State, and as it was anticipated that its delivery would be demanded, the commanding officer was instructed to turn it over upon presentation of a proper and peaceable legal demand, but to resist any attack with all the force at his command. On the 18th the following confidential instructions were sent to General Scott, then commanding the Army:

[Confidential.]

WASHINGTON, *November 18, 1832.*

SIR: The state of affairs in South Carolina has occasioned much solicitude to the President. He indulges the hope that the intelligence and patriotism of the citizens will prevent any infraction of the Constitution and laws of the General Government.

But, while he anxiously looks for this result, he deems it possible, from the information he has received, that in the first effervescence of feeling some rash attempt may be made by individuals to take possession of the forts of the United States in the harbor of Charleston. The possibility of such a measure furnishes a sufficient reason for guarding against it. * * * You are at liberty to take such measures either by strengthening these defenses, or by reenforcing these garrisons with troops drawn from any other posts, as you may think prudence and a just precaution require.

Your duty will be one of great importance and of great delicacy. You will consult fully and freely with the collector of the port of Charleston, and with the district attorney of South Carolina, and you will take no step, except what relates to the immediate defense and security of the posts, without their order and concurrence. The execution of the laws will be enforced through the civil authority, and by the mode pointed out by the acts of Congress. Should, unfortunately, a crisis arise, when the ordinary powers in the hands of the civil officers shall not be sufficient for this purpose, the President shall determine the course to be taken and the measures adopted. Till, therefore, you are otherwise instructed, you will act in obedience to the legal requisitions of the proper civil officers of the United States.

    *   *   *   *   *   *   *

LEWIS CASS.

To the proclamation South Carolina responded by an order from the governor calling out 12,000 volunteers to maintain the supremacy of the laws of the State. The winter of 1832–33 was one of great anxiety. The volunteers had been ordered " to hold themselves in readiness to take the field at a moment's notice," and recruiting offices were opened at Charleston and other points for the purpose of enlisting men to resist the enforcement of the Federal laws. On the 16th of January the President, in a special message to Congress, recited the situation and asked for further authority. February 1 had been fixed as the date when the open resistance was to take effect, but this date passed without disturbance. On the 28th of February a bill passed both houses of Congress extending the jurisdiction of the Federal courts in cases arising under the revenue laws, and empowering the use of any additional military force necessary to maintain the peace and supremacy of the laws. The effect of this unexpected action was instantaneous. South Carolina, finding herself unsupported by any other State, and realizing the hopelessness of continuing a contest that was certain to have but one result, finally rescinded the ordinances of the convention and disbanded the militia. [a]

---

[a] President's message, January 16, 1833, transmitting certain documents, proclamations, orders, etc., in relation to the opposition of South Carolina to the execution of the laws. (Senate Doc. No. 30, Twenty-second Congress, second session, 112 pages.) President's message, February 12, 1833, transmitting copies of orders given the military and naval commanders at Charleston, S. C. (Senate Doc. No. 71, Twenty-second Congress, second session.) Resolutions of the legislature of South Carolina, December 20, 1832, declaring the late proclamation of the President of the United States to be unconstitutional and unprecedented. (Senate Doc. No. 24, Twenty-second Congress, second session.)

The same year (1832) witnessed the culmination of the hostile aggressions of the Sac and Fox Indians upon the borders of Illinois and Michigan, that had been going on since the earliest settlements. While there was never any serious doubt as to the ability of these

The Black Hawk war. States to take care of themselves, these constant and unprovoked aggressions seemed to render a severe lesson necessary in the trust that its impression would be permanent and salutary. To this end a campaign having been determined upon, the executives of the States of Missouri, Illinois, Indiana, and of the Territory of Michigan were called upon to furnish a small quota of militia, and these, to the number of 3,000, in combination with some 1,500 regular troops, were concentrated under the command of Brigadier-General Atkinson, and in June–July moved in several columns upon the Indians. The campaign terminated in the unqualified submission of the hostile tribes, and the adoption of measures for the permanent security of the frontier. But the experiences of this campaign exposed some of the serious faults of our military system, and impelled the President to urge the adoption of some method by which the defects may be remedied. In his annual message December 4, 1832, the President (Jackson) remarked:

Neither our situation nor our institutions require or permit the maintenance of a large regular force. History offers too many lessons of the fatal result of such a measure not to warn us against its adoption here. The expense which attends it, the obvious tendency to employ it because it exists, and thus to engage in unnecessary wars, and its ultimate danger to public liberty, will lead us, I trust, to place our principal dependence for protection upon the great body of the citizens of the Republic. If, in asserting rights or in repelling wrongs, war should come upon us, our regular force should be increased to an extent proportioned to the emergency, and our present small Army is a nucleus around which such force could be formed and embodied. But for the purposes of defense under ordinary circumstances we must rely upon the electors of the country.

The specter of a regular army, and an assumed confidence in the heroism of the people, so eloquently set forth by the President, were an expression of the sentiment of the political party he represented, rather than of his own or of the people at large. At that time and for the ten years preceding it the Regular Army had been too insignifi-

Strength of the Regular Army, 1821–1846. cant in numbers to call forth other feelings than those of commiseration. The act of March 2, 1821, which had fixed the strength at 6,126, had been supplemented by those of April 15, and June 15 and 28, 1832, which by the addition of a regiment of mounted riflemen and a few minor changes in the organization, had increased it about a thousand, so that up to 1836 the aggregate of the Army had not exceeded an authorized strength of 7,129. This small force, something less than a European brigade, was posted along a coast line of 2,000 miles and a frontier of 3,500, garrisoning 42 to 50 posts and 10 arsenals, and pretending to afford the necessary protection and defense to a population of more than 13,000,000, scattered over an area of 2,000,000 square miles. By acts of May 23 and July 4, 1836, this meager force was increased by the addition of a regiment of dragoons to 7,957, and July 5 and 7, 1838, to 12,559, where it remained until the desirability of making certain military demonstrations against Mexico in 1846 necessitated a trifling increase.

The struggle for Texan independence, which deeply engrossed the interest and sympathy of our people, was the occasion of much embarrassment to the Government. Large numbers of adventurous Americans, in their desire to contribute to the cause of liberty, crossed the frontier and joined the Texan fighting forces, and this having been made a matter of complaint by the Government of Mexico, General Gaines, who commanded the Western Department, was instructed to preserve a strict neutrality and to prevent all armed bodies from entering Texas from this side of the border. But notwithstanding his efforts armed men crossed the line at a hundred unguarded points and contributed no inconsiderable strength to the Texan cause. As a method of prevention—perhaps of retaliation—it was rumored that the Mexican Government had sent envoys to the Indians residing along the borders of Louisiana, to arouse and entice them to join the war against Texas. To inquire into this rumor General Gaines, with a considerable escort, was directed to proceed to the frontier. He reached Natchitoches, a town on the Red River, about 50 miles east from the river Sabine, which formed the boundary between the two countries, about the middle of April, 1836, where, deeming that the rumors were well founded, and the frontier settlements exposed to danger, he called upon the Governor of Louisiana for a brigade of volunteers, and upon the governors of Tennessee, Kentucky, Alabama, and Mississippi, for a regiment each of mounted men; in all, 10,000 men. General Gaines's letters to the Secretary of War show that at the time he called for the militia, he had reason to believe that the Mexicans were on their way in force to the Sabine; that a battle with them and their Indian allies was imminent, and that a war between the two countries had already commenced. In that view of the situation, Congress was asked for an appropriation of $1,000,000 to carry on the war, and General Gaines was authorized to cross the Sabine into Texan territory, "if he deemed such a measure necessary, for the defense of the frontier." Acting upon this qualified permission, he moved a column of several hundred men across the Sabine on the 10th of July, and occupied the town of Nacogdoches, about 50 miles to the westward of the river within Texas territory.

As soon as it became known to the President that General Gaines had crossed into Texan territory and made requisition upon the neighboring States for volunteers, he refused to give it his sanction, and

The Sabine affair, 1836.

although the States upon which requisition had been made had taken prompt measures to fill their quota, the requisition was recalled, and such men as had been enrolled were mustered out and discharged. Orders were also sent to General Gaines to withdraw at once from Texas territory. The rumors of the Mexican advance having proved to be wholly unfounded, and General Houston having arrived at Nacogdoches with a considerable force of Texans, there was no further danger from Indian attack, and no longer an excuse for this extraordinary occupation of a foreign territory. On the 17th of December, 1836, he abandoned his camp at Nacogdoches and recrossing the Sabine, returned to United States soil. General Gaines was severely criticised for this movement into which he seems to have been drawn by carefully planned misinformation and too implicit a confidence in the Texan authorities, whose interest it was that the United States should countenance their plans.[a] The prompt response of the States to this sudden and unexpected call, however, demonstrated that reliance was still to be placed in the militia system.

In every emergency up to this date, and in fact for many years later, the paucity of the Regular Army rendered a call upon the militia an indispensability. This necessity was to be repeated in 1838, when the withdrawal of the troops from Camp Armistead, in the Cherokee country, had afforded the opportunity for a large number of unauthorized persons to enter upon the lands occupied by the Cherokees within the limits of North Carolina, Georgia, Alabama, and Tennessee.

Intruders on the Cherokee lands.

Under date of March 13, 1833, two companies of artillery were ordered to that section "to receive and execute any instructions they may receive from the governor of North Carolina in regard to the removal of the intruders on the Cherokee lands within the limits of that State," and three companies of the Fourth Infantry then at Augusta Arsenal were ordered to march to Fort Mitchell, Ala., to remove intruders within that State and Georgia. under the instructions of the district attorney of Alabama.[b] These efforts to protect the rights of the Cherokees proved in the end ineffectual, and it was determined to remove them to lands west of the Mississippi. To accomplish this the governors of these four States were called upon in the spring of 1838 to furnish a militia force to be mustered into the service of the United States for a period

---

[a] Secretary of War (Cass) to Major-General Gaines, January 23, April 25, May 4, July 12, August 20, 1836. General Gaines to Secretary of War, March 29, April 8, May 11, July 4, 11, 1836. Secretary of War to chairman Ways and Means, May 4, 1836. General Gaines to governor of Tennessee, August 28, 1836. Message of President Jackson to Congress, May 14, 1836. General Macomb to Secretary of War, New Orleans, April 25, 1836. Messages and Papers of the Presidents (Richardson), vol 3, pp. 234, 236. Niles Register, vols. 50, 51, index.

[b] Major-General Macomb to Brevet Major-General Scott, March 13, 1833.

of three months; from Georgia, two regiments, 1,480 men; from Tennessee, one regiment and one battalion, 1,140 men; from North Carolina and Florida, one regiment, 740 men each.[a] The successful accomplishment of this object, which was followed a few years later by the removal of the Seminoles from Florida, most satisfactorily solved one of the most serious problems that up to this time had confronted the Federal Government.

Removal of the Cherokees, 1838.

During the excitement attending these occurrences in the South, another cause for serious apprehension was developing on our northern frontier. A movement for the separation of Canada from Great Britain, which had been quietly proceeding for some years through the medium of secret societies, reached publicity somewhat prematurely in the summer of 1837, and almost immediately met with a sympathetic response among the American communities on this side of the border. For a time this found expression in the formation of similar secret societies in northern New York and Vermont and in the interchange of sympathetic messages and money contributions, but later these societies began to organize military companies, which were armed and drilled, at first secretly, and then, as popular sentiment seemed to favor them, openly, and in defiance of the local authorities. This sympathetic movement soon extended itself westward along the border. In Ogdensburg, Oswego, Lewiston, Niagara Falls, and Buffalo public meetings were held and men and arms pledged to the revolutionists, who had taken the name of "Patriots." From New York the excitement spread into western Pennsylvania, Ohio, and Michigan, and large numbers espoused the Patriot cause. Some 700 of these American sympathizers with arms, including 20 fieldpieces and abundant provisions, assembled during the month of November, 1837, on a small island in the Niagara River, about 2 miles above the Falls, known as Navy Island. This island, which contained about 350 acres, belonged to Canada, and during the second war with Great Britain had been strongly fortified. It was in bad dilapidation in 1837, but still capable of withstanding a siege. Aside from the fact that the majority of this force were American citizens, they were commanded by Rensselaer Van Rensselaer, of Albany, N. Y., a son of Gen. Solomon Van Rensselaer, an eminent citizen of that State and an officer of distinction during the war of 1812–1815. These circumstances had induced the Canadian authorities, through the Government of Great Britain, to offer at first courteous remonstrances to the Government of the United States, but

The Patriot war, 1837–38.

---

[a] Correspondence between the War Department and the governors of Georgia, Alabama, North Carolina, and Tennessee, and with General Scott. (Senate Doc. No. 403, Forty-third Congress, first session; Ex. Doc. 453, Twenty-fifth Congress, second session.)

upon the seizure of Navy Island these efforts ceased, and the Governor-General of Canada, with 4,000 regulars and militia, under one Colonel McNab, commenced operations against Navy Island.

On the night of the 29th of December, 1837, McNab surprised and seized a steamer called the *Caroline,* lying at Schlosser, on the American side, took it to the middle of the stream, set it on fire, and left it to drift down to the Falls. All on board were shot in the seizure or drowned. The next day McNab opened fire on the island, but without effect. When it became known that the *Caroline* did not belong to the Patriots nor was she concerned with them in any manner, public indignation along the border became nearly uncontrollable. On the 5th of January, 1838, the President (Van Buren) had issued a proclamation of warning to the citizens of the United States engaged in this violation of the laws of neutrality, admonishing them that they could expect no aid from the Government in extricating themselves from the consequences of whatever their folly might cost them; but on the 8th, in a message to Congress, he denounced the outrage to the *Caroline* in unmeasured terms; stated that the matter had been brought to the attention of the British Government, and asked for such appropriations as might be necessary to enforce the demands.[a] About the same time the governor of New York sent a similar communication to the general assembly of the State. To allay the excitement, General Scott had been sent to the frontier to assume the command, with authority to call into the service such a militia force from the States of New York and Vermont as he might deem necessary. The following extract from his instructions, which are dated January 5, indicates the policy of the Government:

It is important that the troops called into the service should be, if possible, exempt from that state of excitement which the late violation of our territory has created, and you will therefore impress upon the governors of these border States the propriety of selecting troops from a portion of the State distant from the theater of action. The Executive possesses no legal authority to employ the military force to restrain persons within our jurisdiction, and who ought to be under our control, from violating the laws, by making incursions into the territory of neighboring and friendly nations with hostile intent. I can give you, therefore, no instructions on that subject, but request that you will use your influence to prevent such excesses and to preserve the character of this Government for good faith and a proper regard for the rights of friendly powers.[b]

On his arrival at Buffalo, General Scott called upon the governor of New York for 1,500 militia, but before they could be assembled the Patriot forces on Navy Island had determined to evacuate that

---

[a] The British Government subsequently held itself responsible for the burning of the *Caroline* and remunerated the owners.

[b] Messages of the President, and accompanying documents, January 5 and 8, 1838. (Richardson, III, 399, 401.)

point as possessing no strategic advantage. Accordingly, on the 13th of January, in the presence of General Scott, Governor Marcy, and such of the militia as were drawn from Buffalo, the Patriots crossed over in boats to Grand Island where they surrendered their arms, and from thence to the mainland, where General Van Rennselaer was arrested by the United States marshal. After this the Patriots established themselves at various points along the border of lakes Erie and Ontario, and on the frontiers of Vermont and Michigan, and carried on a guerrilla warfare. Some 800 fortified themselves on Gibraltar Island in Detroit River and another considerable body gathered at Clayton. On the 5th of February, about 2,000 of them crossed to the Canada side below Malden; but, evidently dismayed at their own temerity, recrossed to the American shore and surrendered to General Brady at Fort Wayne. A few days later the State arsenals at Watertown and Batavia, N. Y., were broken open and plundered, as was the United States arsenal at Elizabethtown. By the middle of June these outrageous acts had become so annoying that the Government determined to end them. Regular troops were stationed at or near Buffalo and along the Niagara frontier; at Sacketts Harbor, Fort Covington, Champlain, and Plattsburg in New York, and at Swanton, Derby, and Troy in Vermont. The governor of New York recalled his militia—which had been mustered out after the surrender of Navy Island—and every possible avenue between the two countries was carefully guarded; and these precautions were kept up for the following six months.

The Patriot war terminated somewhat ignominiously and unexpectedly about the middle of November, when in an attack upon Prescott, where they were many times outnumbered, they were beaten and compelled to surrender unconditionally. The President now issued a second proclamation. This is dated November 21, 1838, and again warned the people against the consequences of their folly. By this time, however, the " Patriot" cause had shown itself to be no less hopeless than ill timed, and sympathy with it was fast declining. Its adherents gradually slipped away, the societies disbanded, and although as late as 1840 the Patriot refugees on this side of the line were arrested while attempting incursions into Canada, the insurrection may be said to have ended with the attack upon Prescott.[a]

In December, 1839, the militia of Iowa were ordered into the service by the governor of the Territory on a statement made to him by the United States marshal that the civil authorities of Missouri were seek-

---

[a] Senate Ex. Doc. No. 215, Twenty-fifth Congress, second session; Senate Ex. Doc. No. 64. H. R. Docs. Nos. 73, 193, 302, 440, all of Twenty-fifth Congress, second session. Niles's Register, vols. 53, 54, index. Hastings's American Politics, 132; Robert's New York, vol. 2, pp. 590–594; and Canada in 1837–38, by E. A. Theller, brigadier-general in the Canadian Republican Army, Philadelphia, 1841.

ing to extend the jurisdiction of that State over a part of the Territory of Iowa which Missouri claimed to be within her limits; that she was assembling a large military force in the immediate neighborhood of the disputed ground for the purpose of taking immediate possession and enforcing her laws; and that he was unable with any force at his control successfully to resist the effort. Upon this representation the governor of Iowa immediately issued an order for the militia to march to the scene of controversy. In response to this a regiment of militia, 42 officers and 1,133 men, assembled and were placed under the direction of the marshal, but they do not appear to have ever been called into active service. Congress subsequently recognized this service by admitting the right of this regiment to payment for one month.[a]

Iowa boundary line, 1839.

From this time until the acceptance on the part of the Republic of Texas of the terms of annexation offered by our Government excited the ill will of the Government of Mexico and thus compelled the sending of troops to the Rio Grande, there was, with one exception, comparative quiet from domestic disturbances throughout the country. This exception, however, furnished the first occasion for the President to decide whether as a matter of fact an insurrection against the government of a State actually existed, and whether it would be lawful for him to intervene between two persons, each claiming to be the executive, and two organized bodies, each claiming to be the legal one.

The State of Rhode Island, which was the last of the thirteen colonies to ratify the National Constitution, was also the last to abandon her charter government. For nearly two hundred years the people of that State possessed no fundamental law except the charter granted by Charles II in 1663, and the usage of the legislature under it. This charter, among other features, restricted the right of suffrage to owners of a freehold and to their eldest sons; framed at a time when Newport was the principal town it gave her six deputies in the lower house of the legislature, while Providence was given but four. In the meantime Providence had increased its population to nearly three times that of Newport, while in 1840 the landholders numbered scarcely one-eighth of the adult male population. These restrictions, as their inequalities increased with time, became more and more obnoxious, and finally produced open discontent. Many attempts of the minority in the legislature to secure reform having failed, the people in mass meeting at Providence in July, 1841, authorized the assembling of a convention to frame a constitution. This constitution having been submitted to the people in December, 1841, it was claimed that a vote equal to a majority of the adult male citizens of the State was given for its adoption; and it was further

The Dorr Rebellion, 1842.

---

[a] H. R. Report No. 371, Twenty-eighth Congress, first session.

asserted that this affirmative vote included as well a clear majority of the freeholders, or those entitled to vote under the charter. In the meantime, under the authority of the legislature, the "charter party," so called, had held a convention and framed a constitution which was submitted to the people in March, 1842, and rejected. The opposition, disregarding this, ordered an election for the 18th of April, 1842, and boldly announced their intention to see that the officers chosen at such election should be seated. On the 4th of April the governor made the following formal requisition upon the President of the United States:

PROVIDENCE, *April 4, 1842.*

The PRESIDENT OF THE UNITED STATES.

SIR: The State of Rhode Island is threatened with domestic violence. Apprehending that the legislature can not be convened in sufficient season to apply to the Government of the United States for effectual protection in this case, I hereby apply to you, as the executive of the State of Rhode Island, for the protection which is required by the Constitution of the United States. To communicate more fully with you on this subject I have appointed John Whipple, John Brown Francis, and Elisha R. Potter, esqs., three of our most distinguished citizens, to proceed to Washington and to make known to you in behalf of this State the circumstances which call for the interposition of the Government of the United States for our protection.

I am, sir, very respectfully, your obedient servant,

SAM. W. KING,
Governor of Rhode Island.

Messrs. Whipple, Francis, and Potter were the bearers of a letter from the governor in which the situation is given in detail.[9] In this letter the governor advances the argument that a proclamation from the President and the presence in the State of an officer of the Army would convince the opposition that a contest with the State government would involve them in a contest with the Federal Government, and hence would operate as a preventive to anticipated violence and deter them from carrying out their intentions. To this the President replied on the 11th that in his opinion the time had not arrived for Federal interference; that "there must be an actual insurrection, manifested by lawless assemblages of the people or otherwise, to whom a proclamation may be addressed and who may be required to betake themselves to their respective abodes." At the same time he assured the governor that should the time arrive "when an insurrection shall exist against the government of Rhode Island, and a requisition shall be made upon the Executive of the United States to furnish that protection which is guaranteed to each State by the Constitution and the laws, I shall not be found to shrink from the performance of a duty which, while it would be the most painful, is at the same time the most imperative."[10]

On the 18th of April the election ordered under the new constitution was held, and a full board of officers chosen, of whom one Thomas W. Dorr was the governor. The new government organized at Providence on the 3d of May; both houses of the legislature assembled and resolutions were passed requesting the governor (Dorr) to inform the President of the United States that a State government had been duly elected and organized under the constitution. On the following day the general assembly of the State, under the charter, in session at Newport, passed the following resolutions:[11]

Resolved by the general assembly, That there now exists in this State an insurrection against the laws and constituted authorities thereof, and that, in pursuance of the Constitution and laws of the United States, a requisition be, and hereby is, made by this legislature upon the President of the United States forthwith to interpose the authority and power of the United States to suppress such insurrectionary and lawless assemblages, to support the existing government and laws, and protect the State from domestic violence.

Resolved, That his excellency the governor be requested immediately to transmit a copy of these resolutions to the President of the United States.

To these resolutions the President replied on the 7th of May, in a letter to Governor King, that from information in his possession he is led to believe that the danger is overestimated; "that the lawless assemblages have already dispersed and that the danger of domestic violence is hourly diminishing, if it has not already disappeared;" he reiterated his assurance that "if resistance be made to the laws of Rhode Island by such force as the civil power shall be unable to overcome, it will be the duty of this Government to enforce the constitutional guaranty."[12] The same day Dorr issued a proclamation appealing to the people from the proposed interference of the President of the United States in the affairs of Rhode Island, in which occurred the following language:

It has become my duty to say that so soon as a soldier of the United States shall be set in motion, by whatever direction, to act against the people of this State in aid of the charter government I shall call for that aid to oppose all such force, which, I am fully authorized to say, will be immediately and most cheerfully tendered to the service of the people of Rhode Island from the city of New York and from other places. The contest will then become national and our State the battle ground of American freedom.

   *   *   *   *   *   *   *

As requested by the general assembly, I enjoin upon the militia forthwith to elect their company officers; and I call upon volunteers to organize themselves without delay. The military are directed to hold themselves in readiness for immediate service.[13]

On the 18th a body of men assembled at Providence and under the leadership of Dorr attempted to seize the State arsenal, but dispersed on the approach of Governor King with a body of militia. Dorr now left the State, but rumors soon came that he was enlisting men and collecting arms in the neighboring States for the purpose of moving with an armed force upon the existing government. Acting upon this information Governor King again addressed the President on the 25th of May.[14] After reciting the situation, and expressing his fears that "a civil war of the most destructive and vindictive character" was imminent, he adds:

In this posture of affairs I deem it my duty to call upon Your Excellency for the support guaranteed by the Constitution and laws of the United States to this government. I would submit to Your Excellency whether a movement of a sufficient body of troops to this quarter, to be stationed at Fort Adams, and to be subject to the requisitions of the executive of this State whenever in his opinion the exigency should arise to require their assistance, would not be the best measure to insure peace and respect for the laws and to deter invasions.

You will see by the statement of the secret agent of the government that the time set for this incursion is very near. The mustering of the insurgents and their movement upon the city will probably be with the greatest expedition when once commenced—in a time too short for a messenger to reach Washington and return with aid. I therefore make this application before any movement of magnitude on their part, in order that we may be prepared at the briefest notice to quell domestic insurrection and repel invasion.

The President's reply is dated May 28.[15] He informs the governor that measures are being taken to ascertain the extent of the danger, and that "should the necessity of the case require the interposition of the authority of the United States it will be rendered in the manner prescribed by the laws." At the same time he indulged a confident expectation that the resources and means of the State would be abundantly adequate to preserve the public peace. On this date the Secretary of War was instructed to direct Colonel Bankhead at Newport to send a prudent officer to the scene of disturbance[16] to procure all possible information and report to the President with all possible dispatch, and at the same time to convey similar instructions to General Wool at New York, and to General Eustis at Boston.[17] For the ensuing month the Dorr party gave little or no sign of their intentions, and it was confidently believed that they had abandoned their projects, when on the 23d of June Dorr suddenly appeared at the village of Chepachet, some 10 or 12 miles to the northeast of Providence, with a force estimated at 500 to 1,000 men, fully armed and provided with cannon, camp equipage, and stores. On the receipt of this intelligence the governor again appealed to Washington, reciting the situation and reporting that in many parts of the State the civil authority is disregarded and paralyzed.[18] He adds:

Under these circumstances I respectfully submit to Your Excellency that the crisis has arrived when the aid demanded by the legislature of the State from the Federal Government is imperatively required to furnish that protection to our citizens from domestic violence which is guaranteed by the Constitution and laws of the United States.

The President now calls the attention of the governor to a fact heretofore overlooked, viz, "that the legislature of the State is now in session, and, as under the law the State executive has no authority to summon to the aid of the State the military force of the United States, except in cases when the legislature can not be convened, such summons must come from that body." "Should the legislature of Rhode

Island," he concludes, "deem it proper to make a similar application to that addressed to me by your excellency, their communication shall receive all the attention which will be justly due to the high source from which such application shall emanate."[19]   On the 25th of June the general assembly declared martial law. On the 27th a militia force of 2,500 to 3,000 men was put in motion, and by two or more roads marched upon Chepachet, where Dorr, with about 250 men, some two-thirds of whom were armed, was stationed behind some earth-works, with six pieces of cannon. On that date Colonel Bankhead, then at Providence, reported to the Adjutant-General that the insurgents, some 2,500 in number, with 1,500 muskets and 10 or 12 cannon, were strongly intrenched at Chepachet; that the militia had assembled at Providence with 2,000 men, and that it seemed impossible to avoid a conflict without the interposition of a strong regular force.[20]   At the same time an urgent appeal for aid came from the Rhode Island delegation in Congress, in which they requested an immediate compliance with the governor's requisition, as being "the only measure that can now prevent the effusion of blood and the calamities of intestine violence, if each has not already occurred."[21]   Early on the morning of the 28th the State troops moved upon these works at Chepachet and found them deserted, Dorr and his men having dispersed during the night.

On the 29th, the President having decided that the time for action had arrived, instructed the Secretary of War to proceed to Rhode Island, and, in the event of a requisition being made upon the President in conformity with the laws, he should cause the proclamation already prepared and signed to be published; that the Federal troops from Fort Adams should be placed in such positions as would enable them to defend the city of Providence, and that, should circumstances render it necessary, he should call upon the governors of Massachusetts and Connecticut for such numbers of militia as might be sufficient to terminate the insurrection.[22]   "Happily," says President Tyler in his message of April 9, 1844, to Congress, "there was no necessity for either issuing the proclamation or the requisition or for removing the troops from Fort Adams, where they had been properly stationed. Chepachet was evacuated, and Mr. Dorr's troops dispersed without the necessity of the interposition of any military force by this Government, thus confirming me in my early impressions that nothing more had been designed from the first by those associated with Mr. Dorr than to excite fear and apprehension, and thereby to obtain concessions from the constituted authorities which might be claimed as a triumph over the existing government.

"With the dispersion of Mr. Dorr's troops ended all difficulties. A convention was shortly afterwards called, by due course of law, to amend the fundamental law, and a new constitution, based on more liberal principles than that abrogated, was proposed, and adopted by the people. Thus the great American experiment of a change in government under the influence of opinion and not of force has been again crowned with success, and the State and people of Rhode Island repose in safety under institutions of their own adoption, unterrified by any future prospect of necessary change and secure against domestic violence and invasion from abroad. I congratulate the country upon so happy a termination of a condition of things which seemed at one time seriously to threaten the public peace. It may justly be regarded as worthy of the age and of the country in which we live."

Mr. Dorr returned to the State on the 29th of October, was arrested, tried upon a charge of high treason, convicted and sentenced to imprisonment for life, but was released in 1847, under a general act of amnesty.[a]

After the termination of the political contention, and pending the trial of Dorr, the matter reached the courts through an action of trespass brought by one Martin Luther, one of the Dorr partisans, against Luther M. Borden et al., militiamen, who at the command of their captain had broken and entered plaintiff's house and searched the rooms, supposing him to be there concealed, in order to arrest him. The defendant plead that martial law had been declared by the legislature of the State, and he, being a military officer and acting under the orders of his superior, had entered as he lawfully might. The United States circuit court for Rhode Island found for the defendants, thus recognizing the established government, and on this the case went to the Supreme Court of the United States on writ of error. The latter affirmed the judgment of the circuit court, upon the ground that the government of a State, by its legislature, has the power to protect itself from destruction by armed rebellion by declaring martial law, and that the legislature is the sole judge of the existence of the necessary exigency. The language of the court, so far as it relates to the power of the President to interfere in cases of domestic violence, is interesting, as forming the earliest judicial interpretation of the subject:[b]

The fourth section of the fourth article of the Constitution of the United States provides that the United States shall guarantee to every State in the Union a republican form of government, and shall protect each of them against invasion, and on the application of the legislature or of the executive (when the legislature can not be convened) against domestic violence.

---

[a] The most complete account of this affair, though an opinionated one, is in the report of the Select Committee of the House of Representatives, submitted June 7, 1844 (H. R. Report No. 546, Twenty-eighth Congress, first session). But see, however, A Report of the Trial of Thomas Wilson Dorr, etc., Providence (B. T. Moore, printer), 1844, Rhode Island Pamphlets, vol. 1, War Department Library; Might and Right, by a Rhode Islander, Providence (A. H. Stillwell), 1844; Message of President Tyler, dated April 9, 1844, in response to a House resolution of March 23, 1844.

[b] Luther v. Borden, 7 Howard, 1.

Under this article of the Constitution, it rests with Congress to decide what government is the established one in a State; for, as the United States guarantee to each State a republican government, Congress must necessarily decide what government is established in a State before it can determine whether it is republican or not; and when the Senators and Representatives of a State are admitted into the councils of the Union the authority of the government under which they are appointed, as well as its republican character, is recognized by the proper constitutional authority, and its decision is binding on every other department of the Government and could not be questioned in a judicial tribunal. It is true that the contest in this case did not last long enough to bring the matter to this issue; and as no Senators or Representatives were elected under the authority of the government of which Mr. Dorr was the head, Congress was not called upon to decide the controversy; yet the right to decide is placed there, and not in the courts.

So, too, as relates to the clause in the above-mentioned article of the Constitution, providing for cases of domestic violence. It rested with Congress, too, to determine upon the means proper to be adopted to fulfill this guaranty. They might, if they had deemed it most advisable to do so, have placed it in the power of a court to decide when the contingency had happened which required the Federal Government to interfere. But Congress thought otherwise, and no doubt wisely; and by the act of February 28, 1795, provided that "in case of an insurrection in any State against the government thereof it shall be lawful for the President of the United States, on application of the legislature of such State, or of the executive when the legislature can not be convened, to call forth such number of the militia of any other State or States, as may be applied for, as he may judge sufficient to suppress such insurrection."

By this act the power of deciding whether the exigency had arisen upon which the Government of the United States is bound to interfere is given to the President. He is to act upon the application of the legislature, or of the executive, and consequently he must determine what body of men constitute the legislature, and who is the governor, before he can act. The fact that both parties claim the right to the government can not alter the case, for both can not be entitled to it. If there is an armed conflict, like the one of which we are speaking, it is a case of domestic violence, and one of the parties must be in insurrection against the lawful government. And the President must, of necessity, decide which is the government and which party is unlawfully arrayed against it before he can perform the duty imposed upon him by the act of Congress.

After the President has acted and called out the militia is a circuit court of the United States authorized to inquire whether his decision was right? Could the court, while the parties were actually contending in arms for the possession of the government, call witnesses before it and inquire which party represented a majority of the people? If it could, then it would become the duty of the court (provided it came to the conclusion that the President had decided incorrectly) to discharge those who were arrested or detained by the troops in the service of the United States, or the government which the President was endeavoring to maintain. If the judicial power extends so far, the guaranty contained in the Constitution of the United States is a guaranty of anarchy, and not of order. Yet, if this right does not reside in the courts when the conflict is raging, if the judicial power is, at that time, bound to follow the decision of the political, it must be equally bound when the contest is over. It can not, when peace is restored, punish as offenses and crimes the acts which it before recognized, and was bound to recognize, as lawful.

It is true that in this case the militia were not called out by the President. But upon the application of the governor under the charter government the President recognized him as the executive power of the State, and took measures to call out the militia to support his authority if it should be found necessary for the General

Government to interfere; and it is admitted in the argument that it was the knowl-edge of this decision that put an end to the armed opposition to the charter govern-ment and prevented any further efforts to establish by force the proposed constitution. The interference of the President, therefore, by announcing his determination, was as effectual as if the militia had been assembled under his orders; and it should be equally authoritative, for certainly no court of the United States, with a knowledge of this decision, would have been 'justified in recognizing the opposing party as the lawful government, or in treating as wrongdoers or insurgents the officers of the gov-ernment which the President had recognized and was prepared to support by an armed force. In the case of foreign nations the government acknowledged by the President is always recognized in the courts of justice. And this principle has been applied by the act of Congress to the sovereign States of the Union.

It is said that this power in the President is dangerous to liberty, and may be abused. All power may be abused if placed in unworthy hands. But it would be difficult, we think, to point out any other hands in which this power would be more safe and at the same time equally effectual. When citizens of the same State are in arms against each other and the constituted authorities unable to execute the laws, the interposition of the United States must be prompt or it is of little value. The ordinary course of proceedings in courts of justice would be utterly unfit for the crisis. And the elevated office of the President, chosen as he is by the people of the United States, and the high responsibility he could not fail to feel when acting in a case of so much moment, appear to furnish as strong safeguards against a wilful abuse of power as human prudence and foresight could well provide. At all events, it is conferred upon him by the Constitution and laws of the United States, and must, therefore, be respected and enforced in its judicial tribunals.

A question very similar to this arose in the case of Martin v. Mott, 12 Wheat., 29–31. The first clause of the first section of the act of February 28, 1795, of which we have been speaking, authorizes the President to call out the militia to repel inva-sion. It is the second clause in the same section which authorizes the call to suppress an insurrection against a State government. The power given to the President in each case is the same, with this difference only, that it can not be exercised by him in the latter case except upon the application of the legislature or executive of the State. The case above mentioned arose out of a call made by the President by virtue of the power conferred by the clause, and the court said that "whenever a statute gives a discretionary power to any person, to be exercised by him upon his own opinion of certain facts, it is a sound rule of construction that the statute constitutes him the sole and exclusive judge of the existence of those facts." The grounds upon which that opinion is maintained are set forth in the report, and, we think, are conclusive. The same principle applies to the case now before the court. Undoubtedly if the President, in exercising this power, shall fall into error or invade the rights of the people of the State, it would be in the power of Congress to apply the proper remedy. But the courts must administer the law as they find it.

The condition of the Army at this time (1842) was one of compara-tive inactivity, as indeed its strength amply justified. On the 1st of October the whole number of troops in service was 9,847, being then nearly 2,000 in excess of the number authorized, and these were occu-pying 72 posts, while 1,644 officers and men were still in Florida.

Condition of the Army, 1842–1846.

"The invasion of Texas by Mexico," says the Secretary of War in his annual report, "and the threatening appearances of some of the wild tribes at the south-west, renders it expedient that a strong corps of observation should be placed near our southwestern boundary line, as well to keep the Indians in that quarter at peace among themselves, as to check any disposition and prevent any attempts to engage in the conflict in which Texas was about to be involved." The apprehensions of the Administration were to be speedily realized, as indeed there was the best of reasons for expecting. The ready acceptance on the part of Texas of the terms of annexation preferred by this Government excited the ill will of the Government of Mexico, which at once set on foot extensive preparations to invade and subjugate Texas. General Taylor was accordingly sent to the Rio Grande frontier with an "army of occupation," to supply which troops were drawn from the seaboard and northern frontier. The exaggerated accounts of the strength of the Mexican forces, and the meagerness of his own, induced General Taylor to make requisition on Louisiana for militia, and the two companies of artillery from New Orleans, thus unwarrantably called out, though subsequently authorized by Congress, were the first volunteer troops to enter the Mexican war. Later, General Taylor called upon Texas and Louisiana for four regiments each, which were promptly furnished. As soon as it became known that Mexico had commenced hostilities, Congress recognized the existence of war between the United States and Mexico, and by act of May 13, 1846, authorized the President to accept 50,000 volunteers. Under this authority requisitions were made upon the States of Arkansas, Mississippi, Alabama, Georgia, Tennessee, Kentucky, Missouri, Illinois, Indiana, Ohio, and Texas, and the Regular Army was increased to 17,000. The response to these requisitions was prompt and unhesitating, and the situation was thus removed from one of invasion or domestic violence to that of actual war. The official date for the beginning of this war is April 24, 1846; for its termination, May 30, 1848.

Notwithstanding the enlargement of the national domain growing out of the acquisition of the vast territory gained from Mexico and the consequent expansion of frontier, the Regular Army was not increased; on the contrary, it was reduced nearly 2,000 below the The Regular Army, authorized strength of 1838. By the act of July 7, 1848-1855. 1838, it was fixed at 12,539, and by acts of May 13, 15, and 19, June 18 and 26, 1846, February 11 and March 3, 1847, it had been gradually enlarged, until the termination of hostilities found an authorized force of 30,865. But this, by the acts of August 14, 1848, was cut down to 10,317, and with that inconsiderable number it continued to garrison its 60 to 75 posts and guard the coast and frontier until 1855, when, by the act of March 3 of that year, it was increased to 12,698, and thus remained until the breaking out of the civil war.

During all this period (1842–1855) the country was singularly free from domestic disturbances. The exception was in the territories recently gained from Mexico. "The peculiar condition of the territories of California and New Mexico," says the Secretary of War in his annual report for 1849, "in respect to their internal governments and the absence of any clearly defined authority by Congress for this object, has imposed delicate and difficult duties on the Army. One of its assigned duties is to aid civil functionaries, when required, in the preservation of public tranquillity. But it is believed that the civil authority, so far as it had its origin in political power, in a great measure disappeared by the transfer of the sovereignty and jurisdiction from Mexico to the United States. The military regulations established for their government during the war were superseded by the return of peace. A large concourse of foreign emigrants, not familiar with our institutions and habits, has been assembled in one of the territories and engaged in a pursuit eminently calculated to produce collisions and bloodshed. Amidst all these difficulties the Army, aided by the confirmed habit of self-government in which the American citizen is reared, has protected these territories from general or unusual disorders."

As time progressed, these seeming difficulties adjusted themselves. The governors of California and Oregon deemed the small regular force wholly inadequate to protect their territories from the disorders incident to the incoming of the vast hordes of adventurers called thither by the unexpected discovery of gold, and from the predatory bands of bad Indians. Under these circumstances they requested permission to organize companies of rangers to be called out at such times and for such periods as emergencies might demand. But this the President deemed incompatible with the Constitution and laws, and declined to authorize. Two additional regiments were sent to the Pacific coast, and with this force the new territories were speedily quieted.

The next serious disturbance was to come from New England, a section heretofore remarkable for its domestic quiet and order. "The passage of the fugitive slave act," says Mr. Wilson in his history of the slave power, " was the signal for a general commotion throughout the land. * * * Its uplifted hand was directed first against the fugitives, of whom it was estimated that there were more than 20,000 in the free States * * * for beside them there were large numbers of free persons with whom these fugitives had intermarried, and to whom they were joined in the various relations of social and religious life."[a] The specially offensive features of this law (act of September 18, 1850), which was a revival of the law of 1793, were those which made it the duty of United States marshals to arrest and return all fugitives brought to their attention, authorizing them to summon for that purpose as large a posse as might be necessary, and making the Government responsible for their delivery to their former masters. Immediately upon the passage of this bill public meetings were held all over the North; Massachusetts and New York were especially

---

[a] Rise and Fall of the Slave Power in America. Henry Wilson (Boston, 1874), Vol. II, p. 304 et seq.

active in denunciation of the measure.   The execution of the law was everywhere opposed; in many cases successfully.   At Harrisburg, Pa., Syracuse, N. Y., Philadelphia, and other places, slaves who had been arrested were rescued and their captors severely handled.

The two cases which attracted the most attention at the time, and served perhaps to accelerate the zeal of the officers, were those of Simms and Shadrach.   On February 15, 1851, Shadrach, a waiter in a coffee-house in Boston, was arrested under a warant issued by a United States commissioner, and brought before the latter for examination.   The hearing had been postponed and the prisoner remanded to the custody of the deputy marshal. While the counsel were conferring, the door was forcibly broken open, the prisoner seized, carried away, and sent to Canada, where he arrived safely.   The excitement was intense.   On the 18th of February the President issued a proclamation in which, after reciting the incident at Boston, he called upon all well-disposed citizens to rally to the support of the laws of their country; required and commanded all officers and persons, civil and military, to aid and assist by all means in their power in quelling this and all similar combinations and assisting the marshal to recapture the prisoner, and further commanding the officers of the courts to cause all persons concerned in the rescue to be immediately arrested and proceeded with according to law.[a]   At the same time the following instructions were sent to the commanding officer of the United States troops in Boston Harbor:

The Shadrach case, February 15, 1851.

WAR DEPARTMENT,

Washington, February 17, 1851.

SIR: Information has just been communicated to the President that a number of persons, principally people of color, in the city of Boston did a few days since combine to resist the execution of the law providing for the arrest of fugitive slaves, and did forcibly rescue a slave who had been arrested from the custody of the officers of justice.   It is possible that the civil authorities may find it necessary to call in the military force to aid in the execution of the law.   If such should be the case, and the marshal or any of his deputies shall exhibit to you the certificate of the circuit or district judge of the United States in the State of Massachusetts, stating that in his opinion the aid of a military force is necessary to insure the due execution of the laws, and shall require your aid and that of the troops under your command as a part of the posse comitatus, you will place under the control of the marshal yourself and such portion of your command as may be deemed adequate to the purpose.   If neither the circuit or district judge shall be in the city of Boston when the exigency above referred to shall occur, the written certificate of the marshal alone will be deemed sufficient authority for you to afford the requisite aid.

Very respectfully, etc.,

C. M. CONRAD,

Secretary of War.[b]

---

[a] Messages and Papers of the Presidents.   Richardson's compilation, vol. 5, p. 109.

[b] See also Attorney-General Cushing: "A marshal of the United States, when opposed in the execution of his duty by unlawful combinations, has authority to summon the entire able-bodied force of his precinct as a posse comitatus.   This authority comprehends, not only bystanders and other citizens generally, but any and all organized armed force, whether militia of the State or officers, soldiers, sailors, and marines of the United States."   (6 Opin., 466.)

On the 3d of the following April a second case occurred, which, if less fortunate for the fugitive, was more exasperating to the anti-slavery element in Boston.   Thomas M. Simms, a fugitive slave from Georgia, was on that day arrested by the Boston police on a warrant issued by United States Commissioner Curtis, on the application of the United States marshal, on the pretence of being a thief,

The Simms case, April 3, 1851.   and taken to the court-house and put under guard.

Intelligence of the arrest spread quickly throughout the city and an immense crowd hurried to the scene.   The court-house was surrounded by chains, the entire police force put on duty, and a serious riot happily averted.   A writ of habeas corpus was refused and Simms was ordered to be returned to his master.   At 5 o'clock the next morning he was taken from his cell, placed in a hollow square of 300 policemen heavily armed, and put on board a vessel under orders for Savannah.   A large body of militia occupied Faneuil Hall and other points prepared to render assistance, but the early hour prevented the anticipated outbreak.   Great popular excitement succeeded; indignation meetings attended by immense throngs were held at several points in Boston and throughout New England.   That serious riots were averted at this time seems to have been solely due to the forbearance of the people, a majority of whom were unalterably opposed to slavery.

The impending outbreak was merely delayed.   On the 23d of May, 1854, one Charles F. Suttle, of Virginia, applied to United States Commissioner Edward G. Loring, of Boston, for a warrant under the fugitive-slave law for the seizure of one Anthony Burns, then residing in that city, whom he claimed had fled from his home

The Anthony Burns riots, May 26, 1854.   some two years before.   A warrant was granted, and

Burns, who had not the slightest warning of his apprehension, was arrested on a false pretext, taken to the court-house, and turned over to the United States marshal.   On the 25th he was brought before the commissioner, who adjourned the hearing until the 27th.   This arrest and the unwonted publicity given to all its details created the most intense excitement throughout the city.   On the night of the 26th immense meetings were held at Faneuil Hall and other places for large assemblages, and it was openly avowed that Burns should not be taken from the city.   The meetings counseled a rescue of the prisoner; a night attack on the court-house was proposed and carried; 50,000 people were in the streets.   Without apparent plan or hope of success the assault was made, but easily repulsed, and the rioters, who included some of the leading anti-slavery men of Boston, were driven from the scene, to be arrested later by the police. One of the marshal's guard was killed and several of the assailants badly wounded.   At 3 a. m. on the morning of the 27th there was delivered to the commanding officer at Fort Independence the following papers:

To WATSON FREEMAN, Esq.,
    Marshal of the United States, Massachusetts District.
    From facts which have been made known to me, I am of opinion that it is necessary that an efficient posse comitatus should be called out to aid you in enforcing the laws of the United States in the case of Anthony Burns, now held by you by warrant from Edward G. Loring, esq., one of the commissioners of the circuit court of the United States in the district of Massachusetts, an alleged fugitive from labor.
    Dated at Boston the 26th day of May, A. D. 1854.
                                                        P. SPRAGUE,
                    Judge of the United States for the District of Massachusetts.

To the COMMANDER OF THE UNITED STATES TROOPS AT FORT INDEPENDENCE:
    SIR: I send you a certified copy of the judge's certificate that in his opinion an efficient posse comitatus should be called out to enforce the laws of the United States. You will please to send me all the military force at your disposal as soon as possible, to report to me at the court-house, Boston.
    Respectfully yours,   WATSON FREEMAN,
                                                        United States Marshal.
    P. S.—I refer you to the order of the Department of February 17, 1851.

In response to this demand two batteries of the Fourth Artillery, 2 officers and 42 men, with two field pieces, under the command of Brevet Maj. S. C. Ridgely, left Fort Independence at 5 a. m. of the 27th, and reported to the marshal. A similar demand on the commandant of the navy-yard at Charlestown brought a detachment of marines and sailors, while an order of the governor called out all the militia of Boston and neighboring towns. At the hearing Burns was ordered to be returned to his master; there was great excitement, occasioned by the severe denunciation against the officers of the Government made by the counsel for Burns, among them the most eminent lawyers in the State, and there were fears of a renewal of the scenes of the 26th. To provide for this the United States marshal and attorney telegraphed General Scott on the 29th that—

A larger military force is necessary to execute the laws of the United States. You are requested to forward forthwith all the troops you can spare to Fort Independence. Let these report to the United States marshal at Boston court-house.

General Scott, conceiving that he had no authority to act without the orders of the President, telegraphed to Washington for instructions, at the same time directing the troops in New York Harbor to be held in readiness to move at a moment's notice; but fortunately there was no occasion for their services. Guarded by a large armed force of police and military, Burns was taken through masses of shouting, angry, and excited people, estimated to number 200,000, to the wharf and placed on board a United States revenue cutter, which sailed for Virginia under the escort of several naval vessels. The troops were discharged by the marshal on the 2d of June and returned to their stations.[a]

---

[a] H. R. Doc. No. 30, Forty-fourth Congress, second session, pp. 89–91.

About the same time one Joshua Glover was arrested at Racine, Wis., as a fugitive slave and taken to Milwaukee. The people of Racine, enraged by the arrest, held a public meeting at which a vigilance committee was appointed; 100 men fully armed went to Milwaukee, where they were joined by many hundreds of the citizens of that town; assaulted the jail and rescued the prisoner, who was taken back to Racine and sent to Canada. The affair created great excitement, and the commanding officer of the troops at Fort Brady was called on for aid, but the excitement subsided before he could obtain instructions from Washington.

Racine, Wis., 1854.

IV. FROM THE KANSAS TROUBLES TO THE END OF THE WAR OF THE REBELLION.

DISTURBANCES IN KANSAS, 1854–1858—THE SAN FRANCISCO, CAL., VIGILANCE COMMIT-
TEE, 1856—THE MORMON REBELLION, 1851–1858—THE UTAH EXPEDITION, 1857—DIS-
TURBANCES AT PROVO, UTAH, 1859—THE AFFAIR AT HARPERS FERRY, VA., 1859—THE
WAR OF THE REBELLION, 1861–1865.

The act of May 31, 1854, providing for the erection in the mid continent of two immense Territories under the names of Nebraska and Kansas, and permitting the inhabitants of those Territories to decide for themselves whether slavery should or should not exist within their limits (10 Stat. L., 277), was the occasion for a political struggle that forms one of the most important chapters in the history of the United States. Almost immediately after the passage of the act emigration commenced to flow into those Territories from the free-labor States, largely from New England, accelerated by the investment of large sums of money by industrial capitalists; and these settlers not unreasonably brought with them the political principles, the prejudices, and habits of their section. They settled along the streams of the eastern section of both Territories and founded in Kansas the towns of Lawrence, Topeka, Pawnee, Grasshopper Falls, and a few others. At the same time another stream of settlers came in from the slaveholding States, very considerably from Missouri, which formed the eastern border of Kansas, and settled at points which they called Atchison, Kickapoo, Donaphan, Lecompton. It is not too much to assume with equal impartiality that the settled convictions of generations of sires were not left behind by the sons who left the slaveholding States to take up homes in Kansas. "As a result of this state of things," says Mr. Douglas in his report of March 12, 1856, to the Senate (Senate Report, Committee 34, Thirty-fourth Congress, first session), "the great mass of emigrants from the Northwest and from other States who went there on their own account, with no other object and influenced by no other motives than to improve their condition and secure good homes for their families, were compelled to array themselves under the banner of one of these hostile parties in order to insure protection to themselves and their claims against the aggressions and violence of the other."

Disturbances
in Kansas,
1856-1858.

In October, 1854, A. H. Reeder, who had been appointed governor of the Territory of Kansas, arrived at Fort Leavenworth and took

79

the necessary measures for the election of a Territorial legislature, as required by the act of May 31. This election was held in March, 1855, and resulted in a large pro-slavery majority. The legislature met at a small settlement near the Missouri line, known as "Shawnee Mission," where they proceeded to enact laws; the most of which were vetoed by Governor Reeder, and instantly passed over his veto. This condition of affairs culminated in an attempt of the governor to remove the seat of government to an equally obscure settlement on the military reservation of Fort Riley, known as "Pawnee City," when he was removed from office (August, 1855) and Wilson Shannon, of Ohio, appointed to the vacancy. In October the anti-slavery citizens assembled in convention at Topeka and framed another constitution, which made Kansas a free-labor State, and on this demanded admission to the Union. From this date a reign of terror was inaugurated in Kansas; all classes of men went about armed, and little or no regard was had to either law or order. On the 28th of November Governor Shannon reported to the President that he was satisfied that a secret military organization existed in the Territory, in numbers estimated at 1,000 to 2,000, having for its object a forcible resistance to the laws; that prisoners had been rescued from the hands of the officers; cattle were being killed, crops and other personal property destroyed, and women and children driven out of the Territory; that a sheriff had called on him for 3,000 men to aid him in executing warrants in his hands, and that in order to avoid civil war he had directed that all the militia at his disposal be sent to the aid of the sheriff. Three days later he dispatched the following telegram to the President:[a]

WESTPORT, Mo., *December 1, 1855.*

His Excellency FRANKLIN PIERCE:

I desire authority to call on the United States forces at Leavenworth to preserve the peace of this Territory; to protect the sheriff of Douglas County, and enable him to execute the legal process in his hands. If the laws are not executed civil war is inevitable. An armed force of 1,000 men, with all the implements of war, it is said, are at Lawrence. They have rescued a prisoner from the sheriff, burnt houses, and threatened the lives of citizens. Immediate assistance is desired. This is the only means to save bloodshed.

Particulars by mail.

WILSON SHANNON.

This was received at Washington at 10 o'clock on the morning of the 3d, and immediately responded to as follows:[a]

WASHINGTON, *December 3, 1855.*

WILSON SHANNON,
    Governor of the Territory of Kansas:

Your dispatch is received. All the power vested in the Executive will be exerted to preserve order and enforce the laws. On the receipt of your letter the preliminary measures necessary to be taken before calling out troops will be promptly executed, and you will then be fully advised.

FRANKLIN PIERCE.

---

[a] Senate Ex. Doc. No. 23, Thirty-fourth Congress, first session, p. 26.

On the 11th Governor Shannon reported that he had received the President's dispatch of the 3d, and transmitted a copy at once to Colonel Sumner, the commandant at Fort Leavenworth, but that the latter declined to march until he had himself received orders from his superior commanders; that in the meantime he (Governor Shannon) had proceeded to Lawrence and had succeeded in persuading the rival forces to disband, but that this peace was but temporary, and hostilities might break out at any moment. He concludes his report with the remark that—

I am satisfied that the only forces that can be used in this Territory in enforcing the laws or preserving the peace are those of the United States, and with this view I would suggest that the executive of this Territory be authorized to call on the forces of the United States when in his judgment the public peace and tranquillity or the execution of the laws may require their assistance. Should there be an outbreak it will most probably be sudden, and before orders can be obtained from Washington the crisis will have passed.[a]

Before the end of January, 1856, the forebodings of the governor were fully realized. The President was credibly advised that a force of armed men, with several pieces of artillery, were about to enter Kansas from Missouri with the avowed intention of burning the towns occupied by the free-labor party, and that the latter were arming and assembling in considerable numbers to resist them.[27] Realizing that the time had arrived when Federal interference was not only justified but imperative for peace and order, he issued the following proclamation:[b]

A PROCLAMATION.

Whereas, indications exist that public tranquillity and the supremacy of law in the Territory of Kansas are endangered by the reprehensible acts or purposes of persons both within and without the same, who propose to direct and control its political organization by force; it appearing that combinations have been formed therein to resist the execution of the Territorial laws, and thus, in effect, subvert by violence all present constitutional and legal authority; it also appearing that persons residing without the Territory, but near its borders, contemplate armed intervention in the affairs thereof; it also appearing that other persons, inhabitants of remote States, are collecting money, engaging men, and providing arms for the same purpose; and it further appearing that combinations within the Territory are endeavoring, by the agency of emissaries and otherwise, to induce individual States of the Union to intervene in the affairs thereof, in violation of the Constitution of the United States;

And whereas, all such plans for the determination of the future institutions of the Territory, if carried into action from within the same will constitute the fact of insurrection, and if from without, that of invasive aggression, and will in either case justify and require the forcible interposition of the whole power of the General Government, as well to maintain the laws of the Territory as those of the Union;

Now, therefore, I, Franklin Pierce, President of the United States, do issue this my proclamation to command all persons engaged in unlawful combinations against the constituted authority of the Territory of Kansas or of the United States to disperse and retire peaceably to their respective abodes, and to warn all such persons

---

[a] Ibid., p. 30.　　　　　　　　[b] 11 Stat. L., 791.

that any attempted insurrection in said Territory, or aggressive intrusion into the same, will be resisted not only by the employment of the local militia, but also by that of any available forces of the United States, to the end of assuring immunity from violence and full protection to the persons, property, and civil rights of all peaceful and law-abiding inhabitants of the Territory.

If, in any part of the Union, the fury of faction or fanaticism, inflamed into disregard of the great principles of popular sovereignty, which, under the Constitution, are fundamental in the whole structure of our institutions, is to bring on the country the dire calamity of an arbitrament of arms in that Territory, it shall be between lawless violence on the one side and conservative force on the other, wielded by legal authority of the General Government.

I call on the citizens, both of adjoining and of distant States, to abstain from unauthorized intermeddling in the local concerns of the Territory, admonishing them that its organic law is to be executed with impartial justice; that all individual acts of illegal interference will incur condign punishment; and that any endeavor to intervene by organized force will be firmly withstood.

I invoke all good citizens to promote order by rendering obedience to the law; to seek remedy for temporary evils by peaceful means; to discountenance and repulse the counsels and the instigations of agitators and of disorganizers, and to testify their attachment to their country, their pride in its greatness, their appreciation of the blessings they enjoy, and their determination that republican institutions shall not fail in their hands, by cooperating to uphold the majesty of the laws and to vindicate the sanctity of the Constitution.

In testimony whereof, I have hereunto set my hand and caused the seal of the United States to be affixed to these presents.

Done at the city of Washington, the 11th day of February, in the year of our Lord eighteen hundred and fifty-six, and of the Independence of the United States the eightieth.

[SEAL.]   FRANKLIN PIERCE.

By the President:

W. L. MARCY,
    Secretary of State.

At the same time instructions were sent by the Secretary of War to Colonel Sumner, commanding at Fort Leavenworth, and Colonel Cooke, at Fort Riley, to the effect that should the governor make requisition upon them for a military force to aid him in the suppression of insurrectionary combinations or armed resistance to the execution of the law such aid should be promptly furnished. "In executing this delicate function of the military power of the United States," says the Secretary, "you will exercise much caution to avoid, if possible, collision with even insurgent citizens, and will endeavor to suppress resistance to the laws and constituted authorities by that moral force which, happily, in our country, is ordinarily sufficient to secure respect to the laws of the land and the regularly constituted authorities of the Government. You will use a sound discretion, as to the moment at which the further employment of the military force may be discontinued, and avail yourself of the first opportunity to return with your command to the more grateful and prouder service of the soldier, that of the common defense." [30]

Early in April several hundred men came into the Territory from Missouri and other Southern States, and were at once enrolled as a posse of the United States marshal and supplied with arms by the governor. These men assembled in camps at various points in the Territory, but their principal objective point was the town of Lawrence, the scene of the disturbances of 1855, the citizens of which had been organized and armed since the anticipated attack of that winter. During the month of May the marshal's posse gradually assembled in the country around Lawrence, and threats were freely exchanged. On the 21st the marshal entered the town with several hundred armed men, blew up and burned several houses and plundered a large number of others. A few days later a collision between the two parties occurred at the village of Osawatomie where five men were killed; another at Black Jack on the 2d of June. On the 14th of August the anti-slavery party in turn attacked and captured a military work near Lecompton occupied by pro-slavery men and made prisoners of the commandant and his garrison. Convinced by this time of the inability of Governor Shannon to preserve order, the President now removed him and appointed John W. Geary, of Pennsylvania. Governor Shannon threw up his office at the first rumor of his removal, and Daniel Woodson, the secretary of the Territory, as acting governor, declaring the Territory in a state of "insurrection," put himself at the head of the armed body that had plundered Lawrence, and attacked Osawatomie, which was defended by a small force under John Brown. The latter was defeated; some ten men were killed in the affray and twenty or more wounded, and the town of some thirty buildings was burned to the ground.[a]

Governor Geary arrived at Fort Leavenworth on the 9th of September, bearing the following instructions from the President:

DEPARTMENT OF STATE,
Washington, September 2, 1856.

SIR: Reliable information having reached the President that armed and organized bodies of men, avowedly in rebellion against the Territorial government, have concentrated in such numbers as to require additional military forces for their dispersion, you will have the militia of the Territory completely enrolled and organized, to the end that they may, on short notice, be brought into the service of the United States. Upon requisition of the commander of the military department in which Kansas is embraced, you will furnish by companies, or regiments, or brigades, or divisions, such number and composition of troops as from time to time you may find in his report to you to be necessary for the suppression of all combinations to resist the laws of the United States too powerful to be suppressed by the civil authority and for the maintenance of public order and civil government.

I am, sir, your obedient servant,

W. L. MARCY.

His Excellency JOHN W. GEARY,
Governor of the Territory of Kansas, Lecompton.

---

[a] House Ex. Doc. No. 1, Thirty-fourth Congress, third session, p. 87.

He at once issued proclamations disbanding the volunteer militia, ordering all armed bodies to quit the Territory, and directing the immediate enrollment of a militia.[34]   Disregarding this, the Missouri men who had burned Lawrence and Osawatomie, in numbers estimated at 2,000, formed into companies and regiments and marched to another attack upon the town of Lawrence.   As soon as this intelligence had reached him, Governor Geary made requisition upon the commandant of the United States troops at Fort Riley,[37] and a force of 300 mounted men and a battery of four pieces of artillery, under the command of Col. P. St. George Cooke, accompanied by the governor, proceeded by forced march to Lawrence, which they reached on the morning of September 14, finding a force of so-called Territorial militia under the command of several "generals," all from Missouri, and numbering some 2,700 men.   After considerable parleying, the Missourians decided to disband, and on the 15th they departed, promising to return to their homes, and the United States troops returned to Lecompton.   (Governor Geary to Secretary Marcy, September 16, 1856.)

During the following two or three months frequent calls were made by the governor upon the commandants at Fort Leavenworth and Fort Riley for troops, and these, having been authorized by the Secretary of War, were promptly furnished.   (See also Mr. Marcy to Governor Geary, September 9, 1856.)   Confidence, however, was being rapidly restored; the settlers who had been driven from the Territory gradually returned; business resumed its ordinary channels, so that by the 30th of September the governor announced his intention of shortly issuing a proclamation that tranquillity prevailed.[42]   But it was not until the 11th of November that he found himself able to dispense with the United States troops, and two troops of cavalry, with a company of infantry, were retained at Lecompton through the winter.

Quiet had for the time been restored throughout the Territory.   But when early in 1857 the bill for the admission of Kansas under the Topeka constitution came up in Congress it created a political agitation that extended to a greater or less degree throughout the country, and naturally reacted upon the exceedingly tense situation in Kansas. Upon the change of administration Governor Geary had been succeeded by Robert J. Walker, of Michigan, and almost immediately upon his arrival the disturbances of the past two years were revived. Lawrence, always the center of restlessness, became the headquarters for a new movement looking to the overturning of the Territorial government.   On the 14th of July, believing that a dangerous rebellion existed at Lawrence, Governor Walker called upon the commanding officer of the United States troops serving in Kansas (General Harney) for a regiment of dragoons to proceed at once to the vicinity "to act as a posse comitatus in aid of the civil authorities."[46]   In response to this requisition, Lieutenant-Colonel Cooke, with seven companies of the First Dragoons, proceeded to Lawrence on the 15th and went into camp near the city, where they remained for some months, or until after the elections in October, which, contrary to expectations, passed off quietly. From this time until the admission of Kansas as a State (January 29, 1861), there was more or less disorder, but the presence within the Territory of a considerable force of Federal troops, and the knowledge that under the policy adopted by the Administration these troops were prepared at any moment to act as a posse to the civil authorities,[a] acted as a deterrent to further open violence and insurrection.

The discovery of gold in the newly acquired territory of California, followed by the flocking to that section of the adventurous of every land, not unreasonably resulted in the gathering of large numbers of resolute, high-spirited men, among whom the lawless element, as usual in such spontaneous movements, formed no inconsiderable part. Society, not merely at the mines, but in San Francisco, was for a time in a state of utter disorganization. As early as July, 1849, when the population scarcely numbered 5,000, so outrageous had become the conduct of this lawless element that the better class of people in San Francisco formed themselves into a volunteer police force and proceeded to measure their strength against the rioters, with a result that the town was purged for a while of the more violent ruffians that infested it. Two years later, when the astonishing emigration had added 30,000 people, mostly male adults, to the population of San Francisco and a quarter of a million to the State, a second uprising of indignant citizens had performed a similar service to peace and good order, if not to the letter of the law. The first "vigilance committee" was organized in June, 1851, and numbered some 300 of the wealthiest, most influential, orderly, and respectable citizens of

---

[a] The correspondence in this case is particularly interesting in showing the views of the Buchanan Administration as to the relation of the military forces of the United States to the posse comitatus. See in detail Senate Ex. Doc. No. 8, Thirty-fifth Congress, first session, notably pages 50, 77, 82, and 111; also Documents Nos. 25 to 48; report of Senator Douglas, from the Committee on Territories, March 12, 1856; Senate Report No. 34, Thirty-fourth Congress, first session; papers accompanying President's Annual Message, 1856, House Ex. Doc. No. 1, Thirty-fourth Congress, third session; President's Message, February 18, 1856, in response to Senate resolution of February 4, 1856, Senate Ex. Doc. No. 23, Thirty-fourth Congress, first session; President's Message, May 22, 1856, upon employment of military forces in Kansas, House Ex. Doc. No. 106, Thirty-fourth Congress, first session; papers accompanying Annual Report of the Secretary of War, 1856, House Ex. Doc. No. 1, Thirty-fourth Congress, third session; House of Representatives investigation into affairs in Kansas, July 2, 1856, H. R. Report No. 245, Thirty-fourth Congress, first session; Secretary of War, report on the furnishing of troops, Senate Ex. Doc. No. 97, Thirty-fourth Congress, first session; President's Message, December 23, 1857, transmitting correspondence upon the employment of troops for the preservation of order in Kansas, Senate Ex. Doc. No. 8, Thirty-fifth Congress, first session.

San Francisco. Their constitution set forth that the members united themselves into an association "for the maintenance of the peace and good order of society and the preservation of the lives and property of the citizens of San Francisco;" that they bound themselves "to do and perform every lawful act for the maintenance of law and order, and to sustain the laws when faithfully and properly administered; but we are determined that no thief, burglar, incendiary, or assassin shall escape punishment, either by the quibbles of the law, the insecurity of prisons, the carelessness or corruption of the police, or a laxity of those who pretend to administer justice." The operations of this committee, which arrested, tried, sentenced, and executed criminals and malefactors concerning whose guilt there was no manner of doubt, and whom the police had been unable to apprehend or hold when arrested, were so sudden, resolute, and determined, that within two months nearly every lawless character, including hundreds that were merely suspected, had been driven from the city. The success of the San Francisco experiment was so speedy as well as salutary that Sacramento, Stockton, San Jose, and other towns, and the more thickly populated mining districts likewise, formed their committees of vigilance and safety, and pounced upon all the rascals within their reach, with a result that for the following five years the whole of California remained comparatively free from outrages against persons or property. The vigilance committee of 1851 suspended its operations indefinitely on the 16th of September. They did not disband or disorganize, they merely rested, as they said, "to enable the law to show its ability to maintain its supremacy," but it was not seriously believed that its work would ever be resumed.[a]

The awakening was as sudden and unexpected as had been all of its earlier movements. On the 14th of May, 1856, one James King, the editor of a leading newspaper in San Francisco, whose comments on the gambling fraternity had been unusually severe, was murdered in cold blood on Montgomery street, crowded with carriages and pedestrians, at 5 o'clock in the afternoon, by one James Casey, an ex-convict, a leader of roughs, and the proprietor of a weekly newspaper that was the special apologist for the lawless element. This was the second time within a month or so that a murder had been perpetrated thus publicly and inexcusably; that offender, one Cora, an Italian gambler, was still unpunished; so that scarcely had the bolts of the police station been turned upon Casey when the machinery had already been set in motion for the resurrection of the vigilance committee. The committee was invited to meet on the morning of the 15th at 9 o'clock for reorganization. Within twenty-four hours 1,500 men had enrolled

The Vigilance Committee of San Francisco.

---

[a] Soulé, Gihon and Nisbet's Annals of San Francisco (New York, 1855), p. 562; Bancroft's Works, Vol. XXXVI.

their names; 15 military companies of 100 men each had been organized, officered, and armed; $75,000 had been paid into the treasury, and these cool, resolute men were facing the organized municipal authorities, the militia, and the police. The next day, the 16th, the committee organized its police force, which was joined by the majority of the regular city police; all but one of the militia companies abandoned their organizations and joined the committee, whose numbers by nightfall had reached 5,000. On the 17th a large building on Sacramento street, between Front and Davis, was secured as quarters, fitted up with guard rooms, armory and drill halls, and offices; later it was fortified; cannon were mounted on the roof, and the bui'ding became known, from the peculiar composition of the breastworks—gunny bags filled with sand—as Fort Gunny Bags; officially it was styled Fort Vigilance. On the 1st of July the vigilance committee consisted of 1 battalion of 4 companies of artillery, 1 squadron of 2 troops of dragoons, 4 regiments of 32 companies of infantry, in all 6,000 men under arms, well equipped and supplied with every munition of war.

It is not to be understood that the constituted authorities during these proceedings were at all idle or supine. In fact there was scarcely less activity manifested in the circles of law and order than at the headquarters of the vigilants. The police force was increased; the armories supplied and barricaded; the sheriff summoned a posse of several thousand; the militia were called out. The governor arrived from Sacramento and assumed command of the so-called forces of "law and order." Gen. William T. Sherman, who was then living in San Francisco and had accepted a commission as major-general of the militia, from which he resigned in disgust a few days later, is authority for the opinion that but for the timidity of the State authorities the vigilance committee, with all their enthusiasm, could have been snuffed out of existence in a few hours after their organization.[a] It is clear, however, that much valuable time was lost, and when the governor had decided upon some positive line of action the time had passed when it was of any consequence which side of the controversy he favored. It is in evidence that he visited the committee on the night of the 16th, and made certain promises in the way of a compromise; promises which he failed to keep. It is also in evidence—General Sherman confirms it in his Memoirs—that from the roof of his hotel the governor witnessed the capture of the jail on the afternoon of the 17th by the vigilance committee, and the taking therefrom of the men Casey and Cora, who were both tried and executed a few days later.[b] King died on Thursday, the 20th of May, and was buried on the 22d, at the same hour that Casey was hung from a window of the fort on Sacramento street.

---

[a] Memoirs of Gen. William T. Sherman, vol. 1, p. 124.
[b] H. H. Bancroft's Works, Vol. XXXVII, p. 237.

It does not appear that the acts of the vigilance committee during the two weeks or more following the execution of Casey and Cora were especially lawless. That they were active is shown by the fact that some twenty-five of the leading gamblers and dangerous characters who had been most prominent in defying the law, were deported or had fled from the city. Be that as it may, there seems to have been no conflict between the committee and the authorities until about the 1st of June, when a judge of the supreme court having issued a writ of habeas corpus for a prisoner in the hands of the committee, the latter refused to surrender him. The governor now directed General Sherman, commanding the Second Division of California Militia, to call out such numbers of the militia under his command as may be necessary "to aid the civil authorities, especially the sheriff and his deputies, in enforcing the laws and rendering obedience thereto." [a] On the 3d of June, the governor issued a proclamation declaring the county in a state of insurrection, calling out the militia of the whole State, and commanding the disbandment of all unlawful associations, particularly the one known as the Vigilance Committee of San Francisco.[49] The response to this call does not appear to have been enthusiastic, either in numbers or ardor, while it was greeted with derision by the committee and their adherents. On the 7th of June the governor called upon General Wool, then commanding the Pacific Division, for arms and ammunition with which to equip his anticipated forces; "3,000 stand of arms, 50 rounds of ammunition, 2 mortars, 300 shells, and 2 guns of large caliber as you have, with their ammunition and appliances." His letter concludes as follows:

I would further represent that it is now manifest that the power of the military of this State is urgently and absolutely demanded for the suppression of such disregard of the constitution and laws, and for that object a large military force is now in course of organization, under my sanction and authority. It is a large force we will necessarily have to encounter; and for the due protection and maintenance of the authority of the State, I now request of you a sufficient supply of arms, accouterments and munitions of war, for the use of the State forces; and I guarantee, as the executive of the State, that the same shall be returned or paid for.

Very respectfully, your obedient servant,

J. NEELY JOHNSON,
Governor of California.

Maj. Gen. JOHN E. WOOL,
Commanding Pacific Division, U. S. A., Benicia.

General Wool's official reply to this request was to the effect that the authority to furnish arms in such cases rested solely with the President of the United States. Verbally he informed the governor that when the jail had surrendered without resistance, the golden opportunity of putting down the vigilance committee had been lost;

[a] Governor Johnson to Major-General Sherman, June 2, 1856.

that if it were true, as he (the governor) had stated, that a large majority of the citizens—not only of San Francisco but of the State—were in favor of the vigilance committee, he would advise against too great precipitation.[a] It was two weeks later before the governor made another move. On the 19th of June he addressed the President a long communication, which he sent by the hand of the postmaster of San Francisco and the United States land commissioner. Omitting the recital of events which have constrained him to call upon the General Government, the following is his letter, and the reply of the Secretary of State, Mr. Marcy:

EXECUTIVE DEPARTMENT,
Sacramento City, California, June 19, 1856.

SIR: In view of the existing condition of affairs in the city and county of San Francisco in this State, I am constrained to call upon the General Government, through the intervention of Your Excellency, for aid and assistance in the enforcement of the laws of this State; and that you may the better understand the propriety of readily granting such request, I would beg leave to present a brief recital of events which have recently transpired and rendered necessary such application.

* * * * * * *

The power and authority of the State is set at naught. These unlawful proceedings can not be arrested simply because we are destitute of arms and ammunition whereby to equip a force capable of coping with them, which, it is now said, numbers 6,000 or 7,000, with their sympathizers in large numbers outside. At most we have not muskets and rifles enough to arm 600 men; ordnance and ammunition we have none. I would, therefore, most urgently ask that you transmit orders to the officer who is or may be commanding the Pacific Division to issue to the State authorities, on the requisition of the executive, such arms and ammunition as may be needed for the purpose of suppressing the existing insurrection, at least the number and quantity specified in the requisition I made on General Wool, as appears in the postscript of the inclosed copy of communication to him of June 7. I would also urge the importance of transmitting such orders to the officer commanding this department to render such assistance in arms and ammunition at any future period as may be required by the executive for the purpose of enforcing obedience to the constitution and laws, as it is feared the example afforded by the present organization may extend its influence to other localities, in all probability to renew the present one, even after disbanding their forces. In conclusion, I would add, without the aid which is now sought at the hands of the General Government the State authorities can no longer afford protection to its citizens or punish the lawless acts this body of men have been guilty of; and with impunity they may and doubtless will proceed with their acts of aggression and disobedience toward the government as will ultimately result in its entire destruction.

* * * * * * *

Your earliest possible attention to this matter is extremely desirable.

 Very respectfully, your obedient servant,

J. NEELY JOHNSON,
Governor of California.

His Excellency FRANKLIN PIERCE,
 President of the United States, Washington, D. C.

---

[a] General Wool to Governor Johnson, September 17, 1856.

DEPARTMENT OF STATE,
Washington, July 19, 1856.

SIR: The President has received your communication of June 19, representing that an illegal association in the city of San Francisco had overpowered by force public authority there, and requesting the aid of the United States to enable you to maintain the government and enforce the laws of the State.

The President has given to the subject the most careful consideration. He is deeply impressed by the anomalous condition and dangerous tendency of affairs in San Francisco, as set forth in your letter, and is prepared, whenever exigency arises demanding and justifying his interposition, to render assistance to suppress insurrection against the government of a State, and maintain the supremacy of the laws in the mode and to the extent of the authority vested in him by the Constitution and acts of Congress of the United States.

In the present case, serious doubts of his lawful power to proceed in the manner indicated by you having occurred to the mind of the President, he referred the question to the Attorney-General for advisement, and the conclusions submitted by that officer have, on full reflection, been decided by the President to constitute insuperable obstacles to the action now desired of the General Government. The report of the Attorney-General is inclosed for your information. The President will not allow himself to believe that the prevalence of rash counsels and lawless violence still continues in San Francisco. He confidently trusts that the citizens of California who have suffered themselves to be betrayed, by whatever inducements, into violations of the public peace of so dangerous a character, will already have resumed their obedience to the laws, and that hereafter, instead of assuming to act independently of the constituted authority, they will, as good citizens, cooperate with it in the earnest endeavor to secure a prompt, impartial, and vigorous administration of justice, in the only way in which the life, property, and rights of the people can be protected effectually; that is, by faithful conformity with the constitution and laws of the State.

I am, sir, very respectfully, your obedient servant,

W. L. MARCY.

His Excellency J. NEELY JOHNSON,
Governor of California.

The substance of the opinion of Attorney-General Cushing, which forms so important a document in the history of this incident and is given in full elsewhere in this volume,[51] is that there is no evidence that in the occurrences at San Francisco "there has been committed or threatened, any act of resistance or obstruction to the Constitution, laws, or official authority of the United States;" that there were no conditions of "superlative exigency;" there is obstruction of law, but no actual shock of arms. "Besides," he remarks, "the whole constitutional power of the State in the case has not yet been exerted; for, in the space of time which the illegal incidents had already occupied, of one whole month, it does not appear that the governor took any steps to convene the legislature of the State, although that remedy might have been adopted and have had its effectual application to the evil long before any such remedy could be derived from the President of the United States."[a]

---

[a] 8 Opin. Attorney-General, 8.

An incidental affair which occurred on the 21st of June again induced the governor to apply for Federal assistance. It had been ascertained that there was due the State some three hundred stand of arms under the annual appropriation, and these were turned over to an officer representing the governor, from the arsenal at Benicia. This officer, one Maloney, put them on a sailing vessel to convey them to San Francisco, but was intercepted by the vigilants and the arms taken to their headquarters. Maloney was then released, but it was subsequently determined to rearrest him, and in the attempt one of the arresting party was severely wounded by David S. Terry, a judge of the supreme court of California, who happened to be present. As a consequence of this successful resistance to the committee's police, the vigilance army was called out, Terry was arrested, and one after another of the militia armories visited and plundered until every musket known to be in the city had been seized and taken to Fort Vigilance. On the 27th the governor, who had been refused the aid of the army, called upon the commanding officer of the war sloop *John Adams*, then lying in the harbor, to protect Judge Terry from the lawless violence of the committee:

From the state of affairs now existing in San Francisco, and I may say in other portions of the State, I have no hesitation in saying that his life is in imminent danger and peril from the lawless violence of said vigilance committee, and it is wholly beyond the civil or military power of this State to protect him from such threatened violence, without the resort to means which would, in all probability, involve the State in civil war—a calamity greatly to be deprecated under all circumstances, and which I am most earnestly desirous shall be averted.

Wherefore, in the name and by authority of the power vested in me as the governor of the State of California, I ask at your hands, and with the power and means under your command, the protection and security of the said D. S. Terry from all violence or punishment by said committee or any other power, except such punishment as may be inflicted on him in due course of law.

In testimony whereof, I have hereunto subscribed my name and caused to be affixed the great seal of the State of California on the 27th day of June, A. D. 1856.

[SEAL.]   J. NEELY JOHNSON.

Commander E. B. BOUTWELL,
    Commanding Sloop-of-war John Adams.

To this Commander Boutwell replied on the 29th, regretting that he could not see his way to complying with the governor's wishes. "I am sorry to be compelled to inform you," he writes, "that the unanimity with which the people of the city of San Francisco deprecate any interference on the part of the Federal Government with their affairs, would, I think, were I to interfere, do much injury, endanger the life of Judge Terry, and delay the settlement of the unhappy controversy now existing between the State government and a very large proportion of the citizens of the city of San Francisco."

At the same time Commander Boutwell sent a communication to the vigilance committee, requesting that Judge Terry be dealt with as a prisoner of war and placed on board his ship, or that he be surrendered to the lawful authority of the State. Not receiving an immediate reply, he wrote a more peremptory letter on the 30th. The committee responded by placing the whole correspondence in the hands of Commodore Farragut, the senior naval commander at San Francisco. The latter at once informed Commander Boutwell that he had no right to interfere in the matter, and that he must wait instructions from Washington. He says:

The Constitution requires, before any interference on the part of the General Government, that the legislature shall be convened, if possible, and (if it can not be convened) then upon the application of the executive. Now, I have seen no reason why the legislature could not have been convened long since, yet it has not been done, nor has the governor taken any steps that I know of to call them together.

In all cases within my knowledge the Government of the United States has been very careful not to interfere with the domestic troubles of the States, when they were strictly domestic and no collision was made with the laws of the United States, and they have always been studious in avoiding as much as possible collision with State right principles. The commentators Kent and Story agree that the fact of the reference to the President of the United States by the legislature and executive of the State is the great guarantee of State rights.

I feel no disposition to interfere with your command, but so long as you are within the waters of my command it becomes my duty to restrain you from doing anything to augment the very great excitement in this distracted community until we receive instructions from the Government. All the facts of the case have been fully set before the Government by both parties, and we must patiently await the result.

Very respectfully, your obedient servant,   D. G. FARRAGUT,

Commandant Mare Island.

Commander E. B. BOUTWELL,

Commanding United States Ship John Adams, California.

P. S.—We must not act except in case of an overt act against the United States.

Yours,

D. G. F.

The vigilance committee continued its sessions until the 18th of August, during which a large number of the unruly element were severely handled and many driven from the city; two were executed. On the last-mentioned date a grand review and military parade was held, in which over 6,000 men participated, after which the fort was dismantled. The cannon and other State arms were delivered up to the State and the membership disintegrated. That it was permitted to carry on its operations so long in defiance of law and order is quite inconceivable. The responsibility for this, already so forcibly expressed by General Sherman and General Wool, is further confirmed by the language of Commodore Farragut in a letter to the Secretary of the Navy dated July 2, 1856: [a]

---

[a] Message of the President (Pierce), August 6, 1856, in compliance with Senate resolution of July 28, in relation to the self-styled Vigilance Committee in California. (Senate Ex. Doc. No. 101, Thirty-fourth Congress, first session.)

That the governor has acted unwisely from the beginning there is scarcely a doubt; that he could have done anything but call the legislature together, or appeal to the Executive of the United States is equally clear to me; and it seems to me that was what he should have done, as he had neither arms, ammunition, or supporters. After having surrendered the prisoners, Casey and Cora, in the beginning of the outbreak (or virtually sanctioning it), and thus giving satisfactory evidence of his weakness, his proclamation should have been conciliatory and not, as it was, belligerent; and, as it was, should not have allowed his forces to be concentrated in the enemy's camp.

These are my humble views of the conduct of the governor and his general of militia, all of which is respectfully submitted for your consideration, with the hope that my course in the affair will meet with your approbation.

In the midst of the difficulties which attended the conduct of affairs in Kansas during the three or four years following the creation of that Territory, the Government had found itself confronted with another social problem of no less complication. A Territorial government had been established for Utah by the act of September 9, 1850, and Brigham Young, the supreme head of the Mormon Church, whose members made up almost the entire population of the Territory, had been appointed the first governor. Young's administration had from the beginning been antagonistic to that of the General Government.

In the fall of 1851 his tyrannous conduct toward the anti-Mormon population, and his defiant attitude toward the United States officials whose duties required their residence at Salt Lake City, had become so offensive that the latter were compelled to resign and the former to remove from the Territory.[a] The people of Utah, believing with the spirit of fanatics that Young's appointment of governor was an exercise of Divine selection, and obeying his commands as if they were the revelations from Heaven that he represented them to be, resisted all laws not emanating from him and defied their execution. This situation was laid before Congress by the President in December, 1851,[b] and at other opportunities, but no action was had at that time. Without entering upon a recital of the occurrences of the following years, it will suffice to say that by the 1st of June, 1857, every officer of the United States, judicial and executive, with the exception of two Indian agents, had found it necessary for their own personal safety to withdraw from the Territory, so that there was no government in Utah but the despotism of Brigham Young. Under these circumstances, the situation offering no other solution, the President summarily removed Young from the position of governor, appointed Alfred Cumming as his successor, and other gentlemen to fill the places of those Federal officers who had been driven from the Territory, and sent them with a military force to aid as a posse comitatus.

[a] H. R. Ex. Doc. No. 25, Thirty-second Congress, second session.

[b] Annual message of President (Buchanan) December 8, 1857 (Richardson's edition, Vol. V, p. 455).

This military force which left Fort Leavenworth on the 18th of July, 1857, was made up of the Second Regiment of Dragoons, the Fifth and Tenth regiments of infantry and Phelps's Battery of light artillery (B, Fourth)—about 2,500 officers and men, and was known as the "Utah expedition." It was first proposed that the command of this force should be given to Gen. W. S. Harney, but as it was especially desirable that the supervision of the very delicate affairs in Kansas, then in the hands of that officer, should not be disturbed, Col. Albert Sidney Johnston, Second Dragoons, was assigned to the Utah column. The instructions to the commanding officer of the troops, after premising that "the community, and in part the civil government of Utah, are in a state of substantial rebellion against the laws and authority of the United States," go on to say:

> If the governor of the Territory, finding the ordinary course of judicial proceedings of the power vested in the United States marshals and other proper officers inadequate for the preservation of the public peace and the due execution of the laws, should make requisition upon you for a military force to aid him as a posse comitatus in the performance of that official duty, you are hereby directed to employ for that purpose the whole or such part of your command as may be required; or should the governor, the judges, or marshals of the Territory find it necessary directly to summon a part of your troops to aid either in the performance of his duties, you will take care that the summons be promptly obeyed. And in no case will you, your officers or men, attack any body of citizens whatever, except on such requisition or summons or in sheer self-defense.
>
> In executing this delicate function of the military power of the United States the civil responsibility will be upon the governor, the judges, and marshals of the Territory. While you are not to be, and can not be, subjected to the orders, strictly speaking, of the governor, you will be responsible for a jealous, harmonious, and thorough cooperation with him, or frequent and full consultation, and will conform your action to his requests and views in all cases where your military judgment and prudence do not forbid nor compel you to modify in execution the movements he may suggest. No doubt is entertained that your conduct will fully meet the moral and professional responsibilities of your trust and justify the high confidence already reposed in you by the Government.

The head of the column left Fort Leavenworth July 18, and was followed closely by the other battalions, arriving at Camp Winfield, about 30 miles north of Salt Lake City, on the 28th of September, where it was met by a letter from Governor Young, inclosing a copy of a proclamation, in which he declares martial law in the Territory, forbids all armed forces from entering it under any pretense whatever, and directing all the Territorial forces to hold themselves in readiness to march at a moment's notice to repel any and all such invasion.[53] In his letter he directed Colonel Johnston to retire forthwith from the Territory by the same route he entered, or that he could remain in his present camp until spring upon depositing his arms and ammunition with the quartermaster-general of the Territory. To this rodomontade Colonel Alexander, the officer in command of the advance, replied that the troops were there "by the orders of the President of the United States, and their future movements and operations will depend entirely upon orders issued by competent military authority." Governor Young responded by intercepting the supply trains destined for the United States troops, burning their contents—some 150,000 rations—and stampeding the animals; by setting fire to the prairie grass along the line of march; by blocking the road with fallen trees and destroying the fords.[a] When the troops reached Fort Bridger, they found it had been burned to the ground by the Mormons, as well as Fort Supply, 12 miles distant. It was estimated that the number of Mormon militia under the command of Wells was between 5,000 and 7,000. This number is perhaps excessive, but there is reason for believing that his forces largely outnumbered those of Colonel Johnston on their arrival at Fort Bridger.[b] In another letter, dated October 14, Governor Young warns Colonel Johnston of the consequences of his folly in entering the Territory, and concludes:

It, therefore, becomes a matter for your serious consideration, whether it would not be more in accordance with the spirit and institutions of our country to return with your present force, rather than force an issue so unpleasant to all, and which must result in much misery and, perhaps, bloodshed, and, if persisted in, the total destruction of your army. And, furthermore, does it not become a question whether it is more patriotic for officers of the United States army to ward off, by all honorable means, a collision with American citizens, or to further the precipitate move of an indiscreet and rash administration, in plunging a whole Territory into a horrible fratricidal and sanguinary war.

And in a third dated October 16, in which he seeks to defend his position and that of his people, he again counsels them to leave the Territory:

By virtue of my office as governor of the Territory of Utah, I command you to marshal your troops and leave this Territory, for it can be of no possible benefit to you to wickedly waste treasures and blood in prosecuting your course upon the side of a rebellion against the General Government by its administrators. You have had and still have plenty of time to retire within reach of supplies at the east, or to go to Fort Hall. Should you conclude to comply with so just a command and need any assistance to go east, such assistance will be promptly and cheerfully extended. We do not wish to destroy the life of any human being, but, on the contrary, we ardently desire to preserve the lives and liberty of all, so far as it may be in our power. Neither do we wish for the property of the United States, notwithstanding they justly owe us millions.

Governor Cumming arrived at the camp near Fort Bridger on the 19th of November and at once took measures to organize a Territorial government. He issued a proclamation to the people on the 21st, in which, as commander in chief of the militia of Utah, he commanded all armed bodies of individuals by whomsoever organized, to disband and return to their respective homes. "The penalty of disobedience to this command," he concludes "will subject the offenders to the

---

[a] Instructions of Major-General Wells, commanding Nauvoo Legion, to Major Taylor, October 4, 1857.

[b] History of Utah, H. H. Bancroft, pp. 481–542.

punishment due to traitors." [54]   It was received by the Mormons with much contempt, and without adequate means of enforcing it it was made by them to appear somewhat ridiculous.   The troops, who were short of clothing, rations, and short forage, with timber many miles distant, and with the snow from three to five feet deep, were compelled to winter at Fort Scott, while the Mormon militia returned to the more comfortable valleys, closed all the passes, and waited for spring.[a]   In the meantime supplies were being hurried forward and additional troops being assembled to reenforce the army of Utah—the First Regiment of cavalry, the Sixth and Seventh Regiments of infantry, and two light batteries of artillery.   Captain Marcy, who had been dispatched to New Mexico for horses and forage, rejoined, after consummating one of the most remarkable marches on record.   On the 6th of April, 1858, the President issued a proclamation promising a free and full pardon to all who submit themselves to the just authority of the Federal Government, and warning those " who shall persist in the present rebellion against the United States that they must expect no further lenity, but look to be vigorously dealt with according to their deserts," and declaring that "the military forces now in Utah and hereafter to be sent there will not be withdrawn until the inhabitants of that Territory shall manifest a proper sense of the duty which they owe to this government." [b]   This proclamation was sent to Utah by the hands of two commissioners, vested with authority to restore peace.   They reached Salt Lake City on the 7th of June, and were followed by the advance troops of the reenforcing column, who reached Camp Scott on the 8th, and entered the valley a few days later, accompanied by Governor Cumming and the new Territorial officers.   The surrender of the Mormons was complete and unconditional.   Their first determination was to leave the Territory and move southward, burning all their property behind them; and in fact many thousand had commenced the exodus, but were persuaded to return.   On the 14th of June Colonel Johnston [55] and Governor Cumming [56] issued proclamations declaring that peace was restored to the Territory and civil law resumed.   The troops entered Salt Lake City on the 28th and found it abandoned, but most of the inhabitants returned within a few days, and by the 1st of August the business and social affairs of the Territory had resumed their ordinary channels.   The number of troops that were employed to bring about this situation, which was fortunately accomplished without bloodshed, was, in the aggregate, 251 officers and 5,335 men; the total cost a trifle less than $15,000,000.[c]

---

[a] H. R. Ex. Doc. No. 71, Thirty-fifth Congress, first session.

[b] 11 Stat. L., 796.

[c] Documents accompanying report of Secretary of War, December 6, 1858, Senate Ex. Doc. No. 1, Thirty-fifth Congress, second session; Message of the President, June 10, 1858, relative to the termination of the difficulties in Utah, Senate Ex. Doc. No. 67, Thirty-fifth Congress, first session.

An incident growing out of the instructions of June 29, 1857, to Colonel Johnston, which occurred in the spring of 1859, is illustrative of the necessity of restricting the use of the Army as a posse comitatus to cases where the services of a civil posse are either inadequate or unobtainable. Under date of March 6, 1859, Judge Cradlebaugh, of the second judicial district of Utah, advised the department commander that he had issued a warrant for the apprehension of a large band of organized thieves and murderers, who would be tried at the city of Provo; that there was no jail within the district, and the prisoners would therefore need to be held under military guard; and that without such aid he would be unable to secure their trial and conviction. In accordance therewith, a company of infantry was sent to Provo under the command of Captain Heth, of the Tenth Infantry, with instructions to guard the prisoners and witnesses. On arriving at Provo Captain Heth found himself obliged to encamp within the city limits, there being no available ground beyond them. This act certain of the citizens, including the mayor and council, were pleased to regard as "a military occupation," and a direct interference with the municipal regulations, while others, perhaps a small minority of the residents, insisted that the presence of the troops was an absolute necessity. When the arrests came to be made it was discovered that among them was the mayor of Provo and other leading Mormons, who were charged with having been engaged in one or more atrocious murders. The arrest created intense excitement, and thousands of people crowded into the town from the surrounding country. A rescue was feared, and the city marshal summoned 200 additional policemen. The department commander, without withdrawing Captain Heth, sent a considerable additional force, under Major Paul of the Seventh Infantry, with instructions to camp outside the city and act only in an emergency. The governor now visited Provo, decided that the civil authorities were able to maintain the peace, and requested that the troops be withdrawn. This request was refused by General Johnston, who declined to make any change in the disposition of Captain Heth's company or to withdraw the reinforcements. To Governor Cumming he writes, under date of March 22, 1859:

Disturbances at Provo, Utah, March–April, 1859.

To prevent any misunderstanding hereafter, I desire to say to your excellency that I am under no obligation whatever to conform to your suggestions with regard to the military disposition of the troops of this department, except only when it may be expedient to employ them in their civil capacity as a posse, in which case, should the emergency arise, your requisition for any portion of the troops under my command will be complied with, and they will be instructed to discharge the duty pointed out.

Two days later General Johnston was advised by the United States marshal for the Territory that the whole community about Provo were engaged in aiding offenders to evade arrest; that he finds it impossible with the means at his command to execute the processes of the court, and therefore he needs at least 200 troops. This number Major Paul was directed to furnish under these instructions:

The General wishes you to direct the officer in command in all matters relative to the civil duties required of him, to be governed by the marshal or other United States officer under whose direction he acts; and if, in the ar. est of any person or in the execution of any duty, resistance is offered, he will require of the civil officer how that resistance is to be overcome, whether by the bayonet or firing, etc., and give distinct notice to his men how it is to be done, and that it is to be done by order of the United States marshal or other persons; for example: "The United States marshal orders that this crowd be dispersed, to arrest so and so, and that you charge bayonets upon it, or fire upon it," as the case may be; "charge bayonets, forward, march, etc.; or ready, aim, fire," etc.

The punishing of these men, and the consequent trial and conviction of a large number of lawless men who had long enjoyed immunity from punishment, created great indignation among the Mormon element and deep complaints to the authorities at Washington. This resulted in the following instructions to General Johnston, which, while they satisfied one part of the community, gave great offense to the other, and, as was soon made manifest, caused much discontent and seriously retarded the administration of the courts:

WAR DEPARTMENT, *Washington, May 6, 1859.*

SIR: The change which seems to have taken place in the condition of things in Utah Territory, since the date of your former instructions, renders some modifications of those instructions necessary.

Peace being now restored to the Territory, the judicial administration of the laws will require no help from the army under your command. If the service of the United States troops should be needed under any circumstances, it could only be to assist the executive authority in executing the sentence of law or the judicial decrees of the court; and that necessity could only arise when the services of a civil posse were found to be insufficient. You will therefore only order the troops under your command to assist as a posse comitatus in the execution of the laws, upon the written application of the governor of the Territory, and not otherwise.

The fidelity with which you have obeyed the instructions of this Department heretofore given you is the fullest guarantee that you will with the same zeal and efficiency conform to these.

I am, General, very respectfully, your obedient servant,

JOHN B. FLOYD, *Secretary of War.*

Brevet Brig. Gen. A. S. JOHNSTON,
Commanding Department of Utah, Camp Floyd, Utah Territory.

Immediately on receipt of these instructions General Johnston called upon Judge Cradlebaugh to make arrangements to take over the prisoners and witnesses then under charge of the troops, and later, no response being made to his first communication, advised the marshal that he "will deeply regret to turn loose upon this community men charged with committing the most atrocious crimes, and holding in terror a portion of its members, but unless they are soon taken from the custody of the army he will have no other alternative."

The United States marshal, having no jail or other place of confinement for his prisoners, was forced to see them released, save one or two men who, having been convicted of murder under particularly atrocious circumstances, were held until he had raised a strong posse to conduct them to Salt Lake City.[a]

Whether the occurrences at Harpers Ferry, Va., on the 16th, 17th, and 18th days of October, 1859, are to be characterized as an "insurrection" within the meaning of the law is believed to depend largely upon the point of view. On the 14th of December, 1859, the Senate of the United States appointed a select committee "to inquire into the facts attending the late invasion and seizure of the armory and arsenal of the United States at Harpers Ferry, in Virginia, by a band of armed men, and report," among other things, "whether the same was attended by armed resistance to the authorities and public force of the United States, and by the murder of any of the citizens of Virginia, or of any troops sent there to protect the public property, and whether such invasion and seizure was made under cover of any organization intended to subvert the government of any of the States of the Union." The majority of this committee, composed of Senators J. M. Mason, Jefferson Davis, and G. N. Fitch, reported that in their opinion the *invasion* was in no sense of that character implied by the language of the fourth section of the fourth article of the Constitution, but was "simply the act of lawless ruffians, under the sanction of no public or political authority—distinguishable only from ordinary felonies by the ulterior ends in contemplation by them, and by the fact that the money to maintain the expedition, and the large armament they brought with them, had been contributed and furnished by the citizens of other States of the Union, under circumstances that must continue to jeopard the safety and peace of the Southern States, and against which Congress has no power to legislate."

The minority, composed of Senators Jacob Collamer and J. R. Doolittle, while agreeing that the affair was a senseless and deplorable outrage, found no evidence that any other citizens of the Union than those with Brown were accessory to the outbreak, had any complicity with the conspiracy, or any suspicion of its existence or design before its explosion. Briefly, the facts as disclosed by the Congressional inquiry, are these:

On Sunday night, the 16th of October, 1859, between 11 and 12 o'clock, a party of 18 armed men, led by one John Brown, who had been active in the disturbances in Kansas in 1855–1857, crossed the bridge connecting the States of Maryland and Virginia at Harpers Ferry, and, entering that village, proceeded quietly to take possession of the buildings of the United States armory and arsenal, which were

---

[a] Annual Report of the Secretary of War for the year 1859, pp. 124–244, "Affairs in the Department of Utah."

guarded by a single watchman.   Establishing themselves in a strong
brick building near the gate, used as an engine house,
they stationed sentinels at the bridge, the street corners, and at the main buildings of the armory, sent
out and arrested several gentlemen living in the country near the
Ferry, and by morning had them and some ten others confined in the
engine house.   When the workmen and others left their houses in
the morning they were seized and taken to the watchhouse adjoining
the engine house until, with those already there, they numbered some
thirty to forty.   The first alarm came through the stopping of a train
of the Baltimore and Ohio Railroad at about half past 1 in the morning
by a sentinel at the bridge and its unnecessary detention for some
hours.   The passengers when released carried the intelligence to
Charlestown, some 10 miles to the west, and to Martinsburg, about
10 miles farther, when the citizens assembled, armed themselves, and
lost no time in proceeding to Harpers Ferry.

The affair at
Harpers Ferry, Va.,
October 16–18, 1859.

By noon of Monday, the 17th, the citizens of Harpers Ferry, aided
by those from the neighboring towns, assembled in front of the gate
of the armory, which they carried by assault, and succeeded in liber-
ating all of the prisoners in the watchhouse, but were unable to dislodge
the party in the engine house.   During the day an irregular fire was
kept up on both sides, resulting in the killing of three and the wounding of many others, but there was no organized attack until late in the
afternoon.   By that time volunteer companies from Charlestown,
Sheppardstown, and Martinsburg had arrived, followed by a company
from Winchester and three from Frederick, Md., and later in the
evening by four companies from Baltimore, but it was then too late
for aggressive operations.

Immediately upon the receipt of the intelligence at the War Department,[57] the most available troops—a detachment of marines from the
Washington Navy-Yard—were sent to Harpers Ferry, and by a later
train Lieut. Col. Robert E. Lee, Second Cavalry, proceeded to the
scene of disturbance, under special instructions of the Secretary of
War to take command of the troops and of all operations at that
point.   In the belief that this was merely the outbreak of a serious
insurrection, orders were sent to Fort Monroe for troops to proceed
at once to Baltimore, and a detachment of 11 officers and 142 men
left by the night boat of the 17th.   Another party was dispatched
from New York Harbor, and the troops at Fort McHenry were
directed to hold themselves in readiness to move at an hour's notice.
The President issued the usual proclamation, which was intrusted in
manuscript to Colonel Lee, to be published at Harpers Ferry on his
arrival.   Colonel Lee arrived at Harpers Ferry about midnight of the
17th, by which time the excitement had reached a panic, and at once
marched the marines to the armory grounds and surrounded the building within which the insurgents were concealed.   At daylight he sum-

moned them to surrender, and upon their refusal lost no time in storming the building. The contest was over in ten minutes, by which time of Brown's party of 19, 12 were killed, 2 had managed to escape, and 5, including Brown, were prisoners. During the various assaults 5 citizens of Harpers Ferry and 1 marine had been killed, and 8 citizens and 1 marine wounded. In the conviction that with the suppression of this party nothing was left of the conspiracy, and that the insurrection was at an end, Colonel Lee decided that the publication of the President's proclamation was unnecessary, and returned it with his report to the Secretary of War. The prisoners were turned over to the civil authorities, and the troops returned to their proper stations.[a]

It will scarcely be contended that these circumstances establish anything beyond an insane demonstration on the part of a handful of reckless men, without definite purpose, plan, or hope of success. There was nothing elicited during the long trial of Brown, or the careful investigation by the Senate, to show that the negroes in the vicinity of Harpers Ferry or elsewhere had any knowledge of Brown's intentions, much less of any sympathy or purpose to join him. The negro insurrection at Southampton, already referred to, in which over fifty persons were murdered, was of infinitely more consequence in the light of a menace to the State government. Whatever measure of success is associated with the affair grows out of the fact that the Government property at Harpers Ferry was for the moment unguarded. Had there been a garrison of even the smallest detachment usually located at arsenals and armories, it is probable that these marauders would have never passed through the outer gates.[57b] Viewed in the light of an invasion or a serious insurrection against government, the incident possesses little or no value.

It is not within the plan of this work to enter upon a discussion of the circumstances which led up to the condition of public affairs that existed on the 4th day of March, 1861, at the installation of President Lincoln. It will suffice for the purposes of continuity of narrative to say that on the 20th of December, 1860, the people of South Carolina in convention declared themselves absolved from any allegiance to the United States, and that this was followed by successively similar action on the part of Georgia, Alabama, Mississippi, Louisiana, and Florida. The forts, arsenals, and other military depots in those States, with few exceptions, as well as in North Carolina, Arkansas, and Texas, had been surrendered by their commanders or seized by the authorities of those States, and to all intents and purposes the functions of the Federal Government were suspended. As remarked by the President in his message

---

[a] Senate Report Committee 278, Thirty-sixth Congress, first session; Report of Secretary of War, 1859, p. 17. Original papers on file in A. G. O. 386, W. 1859, and papers filed therewith.

of July 4, 1861, to Congress: "A disproportionate share of the Federal muskets and rifles had somehow found their way into these States and had been seized to be used against the Government. Accumulations of the public revenue lying within them had been seized for the same object. The Navy was scattered in distant seas, leaving but a very small part of it within the immediate reach of the Government. Officers of the Federal Army and Navy had resigned in great numbers; and of those resigning a large proportion had taken up arms against the Government. Simultaneously, and in connection with all this, the purpose to sever the Federal Union was openly avowed. In accordance with this purpose an ordinance had been adopted in each of these States, declaring the States, respectively, to be separated from the National Union. A formula for instituting a combined government of these States had been promulgated, and this illegal organization, in the character of Confederate States, was already invoking recognition, aid, and intervention from foreign powers." "Under these circumstances," he adds, "no choice was left but to call out the war powers of the Government, and so to resist force, employed for its destruction, by force for its preservation." Accordingly on the 15th of April, 1861, he issued a proclamation calling upon the militia of the several States to the number of 75,000 to aid in suppressing certain combinations in the States above mentioned "too powerful to be suppressed by the ordinary course of judicial proceedings, or by the powers vested in the marshals by law." "I deem it proper to say," he goes on, "that the first service assigned to the forces hereby called forth will probably be to repossess the forts, places, and property which have been seized from the Union; and in every event the utmost care will be observed, consistently with the objects aforesaid, to avoid any devastation, any destruction of or interference with property, or any disturbance of peaceful citizens in any part of the country; and I hereby command the persons composing the combinations aforesaid to disperse and retire peaceably to their respective abodes within twenty days from this date."[a] And again, on the 3d of May, he called for an additional force to the number of nearly 83,000, one-half of whom he designated "volunteers" to serve three years unless sooner discharged; the remainder to be used for increasing the Regular Army and Navy—22,714 to the former, 18,000 to the latter.[b]

The response to these calls was so instantaneous and measureless that the Government found itself seriously embarrassed in the endeavor to properly receive and equip them. By the 1st of July the Government had at its command a total force of 310,000 men. Congress met on the 4th of July and at once passed laws enlarging the war powers of the President and placing at his command all the resources of the

The war of the rebellion, 1861–1865.

---

a 12 Stat. L., 329.   b 12 Stat. L., 331.

Government. The fifth section of the act of July 13, 1861, modified the act of February 28, 1795, which up to that time had governed all proceedings for the suppression of insurrection, as follows:[a]

SEC. 5. *And be it further enacted,* That whenever the President, in pursuance of the provisions of the second section of the act entitled "An act to provide for calling forth the militia to execute the laws of the Union, suppress insurrections, and repel invasions, and to repeal the act now in force for that purpose," approved February twenty-eight, seventeen hundred and ninety-five, shall have called forth the militia to suppress combinations against the laws of the United States and to cause the laws to be duly executed, and the insurgents shall have failed to disperse by the time directed by the President, and when said insurgents claim to act under the authority of any State or States and such claim is not disclaimed or repudiated by the persons exercising the functions of government in such State or States, or in the part or parts thereof in which said combination exists, nor said insurrection suppressed by said State or States, then and in such case it may and shall be lawful for the President, by proclamation, to declare that the inhabitants of such State, or any section or part thereof, where such insurrection exists, are in a state of insurrection against the United States; and thereupon all commercial intercourse by and between the same and the citizens thereof and the citizens of the rest of the United States shall cease and be unlawful so long as such condition of hostility shall continue; and all goods and chattels, wares and merchandise, coming from said State or section into the other parts of the United States, and all proceeding to such State or section, by land or water, shall, together with the vessel or vehicle conveying the same, or conveying persons to or from such State or section, be forfeited to the United States.

In accordance with this authority, and the former given him in the act of July 22, 1861, to call into the service 500,000 volunteers, the President on the 16th of August issued a third proclamation, in which, after reciting the fact that in defiance of his proclamation of 15th of April calling upon the insurgents in certain States to disperse within twenty days, "and whereas such insurrection has since broken out and yet exists within the States of Virginia, North Carolina, Tennessee, and Arkansas, and whereas the insurgents in all the said States claim to act under the authority thereof, and such claim is not disclaimed or repudiated by the persons exercising the functions of government in such States," he said:

Now, therefore, I, Abraham Lincoln, President of the United States, in pursuance of an act of Congress approved July 13, 1861, do hereby declare that the inhabitants of the said States of Georgia, South Carolina, Virginia, North Carolina, Tennessee, Alabama, Louisiana, Texas, Arkansas, Mississippi, and Florida (except the inhabitants of that part of the State of Virginia lying west of the Allegheny Mountains and of such other parts of that State and the other States hereinbefore named as may maintain a loyal adhesion to the Union and the Constitution, or may be, from time to time, occupied and controlled by forces of the United States engaged in the dispersion of said insurgents) are in a state of insurrection against the United States. [b]

From this date (July 13, 1861) until the 20th day of August, 1866, when President Johnson declared all insurrection at an end, [c] the civil

---

[a] Act approved July 13, 1861; 12 Stat. L., 255.

[b] 12 Stat. L., 333.

[c] Proclamations April 2, 1866, and August 20, 1866; 14 Stat. L., 811–814.

war was territorial; that is to say, "it was conducted between the contending parties with all the rights of war recognized by the law of nations." "When the course of justice is interrupted by revolt, rebellion, or insurrection, so that the courts of justice can not be kept open, civil war exists, and hostilities may be prosecuted on the same footing as if those opposing the Government were foreign enemies invading the land."[a] (2 Black, 667, 668.) "The act of Congress of July 13, 1861," said the Supreme Court in the Prize cases, "we think, recognized a state of civil war between the Government and the Confederate States and made it territorial." Hence, like the second war with Great Britain and the war with Mexico, unlike an insurrection within a State, its conduct was within the control of Congress and not of the President. "By the Constitution Congress alone has the power to declare a national or foreign war. It can not declare war against a State or any number of States. The Constitution confers on the President the whole executive power. He is Commander in Chief of the Army and Navy and of the militia of the several States when called into the actual service of the United States. He has no power to initiate or declare war against a foreign or a domestic State. By the act of Congress of February 28, 1795, and March 3, 1807, he is authorized to call out the militia and use the military and naval force of the United States in case of invasion by a foreign nation and to suppress insurrection against the government of a State or of the United States."[b] It was still an insurrection, but an insurrection that had culminated in organized rebellion.

Congress having now assumed its war powers, lost no time in bringing them to bear upon the situation. By an act approved July 22, 1861,[c] it legalized the calls already made and authorized the President to accept the services of not to exceed 500,000 more. These men are designated in the act as "volunteers." Heretofore when calls had been made upon the States for military aid in the suppression of insurrection or the repelling of invasion, requisition had been made upon the *militia*, following the act of February 28, 1795, and as a rule upon the militia of the State or States nearest to the scene of disturbance. Thus, in the Florida war the force employed was from Georgia, Alabama, Mississippi, and South Carolina; in the war with Mexico the States first called upon were Louisiana and Texas, followed by Arkansas, Mississippi, and States bordering the Gulf of Mexico. Nor was this rule by any means abandoned by the introduction of the "volunteer" as a separate military factor. For by the proclamation of June 15, 1863, based upon the fact that "armed insurrectionary combinations now existing in several of the States are threatening to make inroads into the States of Maryland,

The "volunteer" as a new military factor.

---

[a] The Prize cases, 4 Miller, 878.   [b] Supra, 880.   [c] 12 Stat. L., 268.

West Virginia, Pennsylvania, and Ohio, requiring immediately an additional military force for the service of the United States," the President called into the service 100,000 *militia*—from Maryland, 10,000; from Pennsylvania, 50,000; from Ohio, 30,000; from West Virginia, 10,000.[a] But with this, and a few minor exceptions, the militia practically disappeared during the war of the rebellion and was succeeded by the volunteer.

It is to be remarked that the volunteer was an evolution or a development of the situation rather than a predetermined quantity. Under the proclamation of April 15, 1861, the 75,000 called for were apportioned from those States not then in insurrection, and the governors of these States were requested to "detach from the militia" under their command a certain specified number, to serve for three months unless sooner discharged. Of the States thus called upon, Virginia, North Carolina, Tennessee, Arkansas, Kentucky, and Missouri peremptorily refused; Maryland was prevented from furnishing its quota owing to the outbreak in Baltimore; Virginia and Missouri, notwithstanding the refusal of their governors, subsequently organized and tendered far more than their quota. Under the call of May 4, 1861, "for [60,000] volunteers to serve during the war," the response was so overwhelming that, unwilling to discriminate and equally indisposed to decline, the Government had accepted 208 regiments, or nearly 200,000 men, before the meeting of Congress on the 4th of July. In his special report of July 1, 1861, Mr. Secretary Cameron thus remarks concerning the volunteer system, which had so unexpectedly superseded the militia:

I can not forbear to speak favorably of the volunteer system as a substitute for a cumbrous and dangerous standing army. It has heretofore by many been deemed unreliable and inefficient in a sudden emergency, but actual facts have proved the contrary. If it be urged that the enemies of order have gained some slight advantages at remote points by reason of the absence of a sufficient regular force, the unexampled rapidity of concentration of volunteers already witnessed is an ample refutation of the argument. A government whose every citizen stands ready to march to its defense can never be overthrown, for none is so strong as that whose foundations rest immovably in the hearts of the people.

The spectacle of more than a quarter of a million of citizens rushing to the field in defense of the Constitution must ever take rank among the most extraordinary facts of history. Its interest is vastly heightened by the lavish outpouring from States and individuals of voluntary contributions of money, reaching an aggregate thus far of more than ten millions of dollars. But a few weeks since the men composing this great army were pursuing the avocations of peace. They gathered from the farm, from the workshop, from the factory, from the mine. The minister came from his

---

[a] It is further noted that the call of March 14, 1864, is for "200,000 men for the military service;" that of July 18, 1864, for "500,000 volunteers," and December 19, 1864, for "300,000 volunteers." The terms are employed interchangeably. The rule was to apportion the number of men desired among the States and to permit them to fill the requisition in their own way. (Report Provost-Marshal-General, 1865.)

pulpit, the merchant from his countingroom, the professor and student from the college, the teacher and pupil from the common schools. Young men of fortunes left luxurious homes for the tent and the camp. Native and foreign born alike came forward with a kindred enthusiasm. That a well-disciplined, homogeneous, and efficient force should be formed out of such a seemingly heterogeneous mass appears almost incredible. But what is the actual fact? Experienced men who have had ample opportunity to familiarize themselves with the condition of European armies concede that in point of *personnel* this patriot army is fully equal to the finest regular troops of the Old World. A more intelligent body of men or one actuated by purer motives was never before marshaled in the field.

The calling forth of this large and admirable force in vindication of the Constitution and the laws is in strict accordance with a wise prudence and economy, and at the same time in perfect harmony with the uniform practice of the Government. But three years ago, when the authority of the nation was contemptuously defied by the Mormons in Utah, the only safe policy consistent with the dignity of the Government was the prompt employment of such an overwhelming force for the suppression of the rebellion as removed all possibility of failure.

Congress followed up its legislation of July 22, 1861, which called half a million men into the field by an act which was approved July 17, 1862, authorizing an additional 100,000 for nine months, and as many as would be necessary to fill up the regiments then in the field. By the terms of this act, which directed the militia when called into the service of the United States to be organized in the mode prescribed by law for volunteers, it was provided that—

If by reason of defects in existing laws or in the execution of them in the several States or any of them it shall be found necessary to provide for enrolling the militia and otherwise putting this act into execution, the President is authorized in such cases to make all necessary rules and regulations; and the enrollment of the militia shall in all cases include all able-bodied male citizens between the ages of eighteen and forty-five, and shall be apportioned among the States according to representative population.[a]

This was followed, on the 27th of February, 1864, by an act which authorized the President, "whenever he shall deem it necessary during the present war, to call for such number of men for the military service of the United States as the public exigencies may require," thus vesting in the President a practically unlimited power to create armies and navies for the suppression of the rebellion then nearing its end.[b] Under this and the various preceding authorizations there were mustered into the service of the United States during the period covered by the war a total of nearly three million men (2,772,408), while the insurgent States opposed to them a force that amounted to very little less than one million more.

Contrary to all prior experiences of history the period covered by the war of the rebellion was singularly free from domestic disturbances. In one or more localities there was forcible opposition to the draft, but this was promptly suppressed by the State authorities without the intervention of any armed force of the General Government.

---

[a] 12 Stat. L., 597.	[b] 13 Stat. L., 6.

V. THE RECONSTRUCTION PERIOD.

BRIGANDAGE IN MISSOURI, 1866—RIOTS AT NORFOLK, VA., 1866—THE MEMPHIS, TENN., RIOTS, 1866—FENIAN INVASION OF CANADA, 1866—RIOTS AT MOBILE, ALA., 1867—RIOT AT FRANKLIN, TENN., 1867—THE NASHVILLE, TENN., ELECTION, 1867—THE KU-KLUX-KLAN, 1866-1872—DISORDERS IN GULF STATES, 1868—LAWLESSNESS IN ARKANSAS, 1868—RIOTS AT CAMILLA, GA., 1868—LAWLESSNESS IN TEXAS, 1868-1870—RIOT AT MILLICAN, TEX., 1868—RIOT AT MOBILE, ALA., 1869—RIOT AT UNIONVILLE, S. C., 1871.

The first step toward the restoration of the seceding States was a proclamation by President Lincoln of December 8, 1863,[a] in which, was promised full pardon with restoration of rights of property (excepting slaves) to such as should take and maintain an oath of allegiance, etc., and providing that when there shall be in any such State a number equal to 10 per cent of the Presidential vote of 1860 who shall have taken such oath, these people shall be authorized to reestablish a republican form of government, which shall be recognized as the true and legal government of the State. Under this authorization Louisiana and Arkansas had organized governments in 1864 and Tennessee in 1865, which had been recognized, while provisional governors had been appointed by the President for all the other States, with instructions to call conventions to formulate new constitutions and take other formal measures for restoring these States to their constitutional relations to the General Government. Congress, however, did not approve this method of reconstruction, and, after long debate throughout the year 1866 and up to the close of the Thirty-ninth Congress, developed another plan which found expression in the act of March 2, 1867,[b] and the supplementary acts of March 23 and July 19, each of which was opposed by the President and passed over his veto. These acts declared that no legal governments existed in the States of Virginia, North Carolina, South Carolina, Georgia, Alabama, Mississippi, Louisiana, Florida, Arkansas, and Texas, and divided them into five military districts, each under the command of a general officer of the Army, with sufficient military force to enforce his authority. It was made the duty of these commanders to make a registration of legal voters, these to elect delegates to a convention which should frame a new constitution, which constitutions should be approved by Congress; after which, the State, having ratified the fourteenth amendment to the Constitution, should

The reconstruction period, 1866-1870.

---

[a] 13 Stat. L., 737.   [b] 14 Stat. L., 428.

be restored to its former relations, and its Senators and Representatives entitled to admission to Congress. The conditions of these acts were complied with in 1868 by North and South Carolina, Florida, Alabama, Louisiana, and Arkansas; by Virginia, Mississippi, and Texas in 1869, and by Georgia in 1870, and thus reconstruction was fully accomplished.

The period of time during which this scheme of rehabilitation was in progress was not unnaturally one of great disorder throughout the section lately engaged in insurrection, requiring the constant presence of troops and the frequent necessity of employing them for the preservation of order. There were many reasons for this, not altogether political. The return to the pursuits of ordinary life of several hundred thousand men from the armies, many of them turbulent in disposition, disinclined to labor, and impatient of control, introduced an element of discord not easily suppressed. In several of the border States these restless men banded together for purposes of mischief and plunder, roamed the country, riding at breakneck speed through the streets, swaggering about the hotels and public places with revolvers in their belts, overawing the police, and setting the laws at defiance. These men robbed travelers, burned the huts of colored people, and were in fact brigands. To such an extent was this carried on in Missouri that the governor, finding the civil authorities powerless to maintain the peace, ordered out the entire militia of the State—34 companies—and hunted these marauders from one hiding place to another until they were finally forced to leave the State. But a more prolific source of disturbance was the intense feeling toward the colored people, many of whom perhaps allowed their freedom to take unnecessary prominence in the presence of their former owners.

Brigandage in Missouri, 1866.

Of this character were the riots at Norfolk, Va., in the spring of 1866. The close of the war had left some 700 or 800 colored soldiers at Norfolk, and many of these had availed themselves of the privilege granted by the Government to honorably discharged soldiers of purchasing the arms they had carried during the war.[a] It was not shown during the subsequent investigation that these men had any organization, or that there was any mutual understanding as to their rights to self-protection, beyond the natural bonds of race sympathy. On the other hand, it was shown that the surviving members of companies that had served in the Confederate armies had maintained their organization, although there was no evidence that these organizations proposed to resist any laws of the United States or that they entertained any insurrectionary plans. Norfolk possessed at the time a floating population of disorderly and abandoned characters, and between these and the colored

Riots at Norfolk, Va., April 16–18, 1866.

[a] General Orders, No. 101, War Department, 1865.

population there was some considerable enmity, though there was abundant proof that the relations between the colored people and their old employers and owners were eminently satisfactory. On the 16th of April the colored population of Norfolk and Portsmouth celebrated the passage of the civil rights bill by a procession and public speaking at grounds near town. The commanding officer of the United States troops at Norfolk, Captain Stanhope, Twelfth Infantry, witnessed the procession, which passed off peaceably, and had returned to his quarters when firing commenced at the grounds where the speaking was going on. He then ordered out a company, and proceeding to the grounds, where he found a white man had been killed, disarmed every negro, dispersed the meeting, and escorted the Portsmouth delegation home. He then saw the mayor of the city, who informed him that his police force was worthless, that he could not control the disturbance, and asked for Federal aid. This was about noon. During the afternoon there were rumors that the white people were organizing, and that they would attack the negroes as soon as darkness would permit. Captain Stanhope disposed his troops to best advantage and awaited the progress of events. There was desultory but constant firing during the night, and a number of negroes were killed and wounded; bodies of men were marching the streets, numbering in the aggregate several hundred, but on the appearance of the troops they dispersed. The following day there was great excitement. Large bodies of men collected about the city, and threats were openly made of a night attack that would crush the soldiers and exterminate the negroes. The troops, who had been on duty almost constantly for thirty-six hours, were reenforced about dark by about 200 men from Fort Monroe, and but for their timely arrival there is reason for believing that a desperate riot would have occurred on the night of the 17th, as both blacks and whites had matured plans that were to culminate at that time. It was afterwards discovered that every colored man who had shown himself on the streets on the night of the 16th had been fired upon.[a]

The conditions that brought about the disturbances at Norfolk and New Orleans were no different from those that existed elsewhere throughout the South during the years immediately following the close of the war. The affair at Memphis, which immediately followed that at Norfolk, was a conspicuous illustration of the intensely bitter feeling throughout the former slaveholding States toward the blacks, and particularly toward such of them as had served in the Federal armies and had thus contributed toward the suppression of the rebellion. The Third Regiment of United States Colored Artillery had

---

[a] Finding of the board of officers to inquire into the causes of the riots at Norfolk, Va., on the 16th of April, 1866. (154 V., A. G. O., 1866.) Letter of Secretary of War, January 21, 1867, in answer to H. R. resolution of December 10, 1866, calling for information relative to riots at Norfolk. (H. R. Ex. Doc. No. 72, Thirty-ninth Congress, second session.)

been organized at Memphis in 1863 under the title of the First Tennessee Heavy Artillery, and had been made up of the negroes of that vicinity who had sought the protection of the Federal Government. It had been stationed at Memphis from the time of its organization and had been employed in the various police and other semi-military duties that brought its members into frequent contact with the lawless white element.   Many negro soldiers had from time to time been arrested by the white police, and many whites, including policemen, had been arrested by the negro soldiers, and in both cases those arrested had not infrequently been treated with unnecessary harshness.   On the 30th of April, 1866, this regiment was officially mustered out of the United States service, and the men discharged.   Many of them had what they called families living at South Memphis, and having been paid off, strolled about the city on the evening of the 30th and during the 1st of May in bodies of from ten to seventy-five, gradually reached a state of intoxication, became noisy and subjects for police attention.   On the night of the 1st a body of six policemen arrested two boisterous negroes and were conducting them to the station house, when they were attacked by a crowd of negroes.   The police turned and fired into the crowd, wounding one; the prisoners escaped.   The negroes returned the fire, wounding one of the policemen.   The latter being reenforced and supported by a large crowd of citizens, proceeded to shoot, beat, and arrest every negro in sight, and this was kept up at intervals until midnight, when it was quelled by the appearance of a small detachment of United States troops.[a]

> *The Memphis riots, May 1–3, 1866.*

On the morning of the 2d the rioting was renewed, but the scene had been transferred to South Memphis, where the negroes were most congregated.   The regular troops at Memphis, after the muster out of the colored regiment, numbered less than 150, and as there was much public property to guard, but few men could be spared to aid in preserving the peace, and these devoted their efforts to keeping the discharged soldiers inside the fort and the infuriated white people out of it.   On the night of the 2d a party of mounted whites rode about the suburbs, setting fire to the negro schoolhouses, churches, and dwellings, shooting, beating, and maltreating all who resisted.   The civil authorities, as was fully proven in the subsequent investigation, were not only indisposed to quell the rioting, but many of them actually and actively participated in it.   This continued throughout the night of the 2d and during much of the 3d, with a total result of 46 colored and 2 white persons killed; 75 wounded; 100 robberies, more or less aggravated; 91 houses and cabins, 12 schoolhouses, and 4 churches burned; individual property destroyed to the value of $100,000.[b]

---

[a] Telegram: General Stoneman to General Grant, May 12, 1866.

[b] Testimony taken at Memphis May 22–June 6, 1866, before a select committee of Congress.   (H. R. Report No. 101, Thirty-ninth Congress, first session; ibid, p. 36.)

On the afternoon of the 3d General Stoneman decided to assume military control of the situation and to suspend the civil power. He remarked in his testimony before the Congressional committee that he first endeavored to communicate with the mayor of the city, but was informed that he was not in a condition to be communicated with. He accordingly issued the following open letter, which was published in the evening papers and circulated by handbills:

HEADQUARTERS DEPARTMENT OF TENNESSEE,
MEMPHIS, TENN., *May 3, 1866.*
To the mayor, city council, and all civil authorities of the county of Shelby, and city of Memphis:
GENTLEMEN: Circumstances compel the undersigned to interfere with civil affairs in the city of Memphis. It is forbidden for any person, without the authority from these headquarters, to assemble together any posse, armed or unarmed, white or colored. This does not include the police force of the city, and will not so long as they can be relied upon as preservers of the peace.
I am, gentlemen, very respectfully, your obedient servant,
GEO. STONEMAN,
Major-General, Commanding.

The effect of this action was instantaneous. All the available United States troops were stationed at various points throughout the city, which was thoroughly patrolled and the smallest assemblages dispersed wherever encountered. Every officer and man was on constant duty, day and night, for more than forty-eight hours. The next morning a considerable body of troops arrived from Nashville, but their active services were not called into requisition. On the 5th General Stoneman called upon the civil authorities for information as regarded their future intentions and ability to preserve the peace, and concluded his letter as follows:

In conclusion, I have to assure you, and, through you, the people of Memphis, that if they can not govern themselves as a law-abiding and Christian community, they will be governed, and that hereafter it will be my duty and privilege to see that there are no more riotous proceedings or conduct, either on the part of whites or blacks, or city authorities.
I am, sir, very respectfully, your obedient servant,
GEO. STONEMAN,
Major-General, Commanding.
His honor, JOHN PARK,
Mayor of the City of Memphis.

Order having been restored, and the excitement consequent upon the riot having abated, military control was withdrawn and the civil authorities resumed their functions.

An attempted invasion of Canada, not dissimilar to that attempted by the Patriots of 1837, was among the historical incidents of the year 1866. The "Fenian Brotherhood," an organization of Irish-Americans having for their object and aim the independence of Ireland, had been founded in New York in 1857, but its operations had been interrupted, if not diverted, by the breaking out of the civil war.

Several of the regiments that so promptly responded to the first call of President Lincoln, were composed of members of the "circles" of this fraternity, and officered almost entirely by Fenians. In November, 1863, there were over 15,000 members of the brotherhood in the United States, over half of whom it is claimed were in either the Federal or Confederate armies. The surrender of the latter and the disbandment of the former, not only released this membership, but furnished an excellent recruiting field for the army with which it was proposed to invade Ireland. A congress of the Fenian Brotherhood assembled at New York on the 2d of January, 1866, at which more than 400 delegates were present; this was followed on the 22d of February by a military convention, and at this time plans were adopted for an invasion of Canada. Of this the Government was early advised, and precautionary measures were taken to prevent any violation of the neutrality laws. Early in April a party of some 500 men assembled at Eastport, Me., under suspicious circumstances. It was soon learned that an attempt was to be made by the Fenians to occupy the island of Campo Bello, New Brunswick, and that a vessel had sailed from Portland laden with arms and ammunition. One company of artillery was stationed at Eastport and three more were sent there. The vessel was seized on its arrival and the arms held in military custody. The expedition being thus frustrated, its members dispersed and the troops returned to their stations.[a]

During the month of May large numbers of men quietly assembled at several points along the northern frontier—at Buffalo, Ogdensburg, Malone, and St. Albans—and all the available force of United States troops in the vicinity of New York were sent to the frontier. On the 19th of that month, 1,200 rifles and a large quantity of ammunition were seized at Rouses Point, and on the 30th another similar consignment was taken possession of at the same place. Numbers of men in small parties were observed making their way into Canada all along the line but were unmolested. In the meantime the entire militia force of Canada were in the field, and considerable bodies of these men were stationed at points opposite those occupied by our troops. On the 1st of June a party of Fenians numbering from 1,200 to 1,500, armed but ununiformed, crossed the Niagara River below Buffalo and took possession of an old earthwork on the Canada side, which, under the name of Fort Erie, had been the scene of a severe engagement during the second war with Great Britain. On the 2d, they advanced into the province along a road known as the "Ridge," where they were attacked by a force of Canadian militia; several were killed on both sides and many wounded. The invaders, however, withdrew the same night; some 700 were picked up by the United States steamer

Fenian invasion of Canada, June, 1866.

_____

[a] Major-General Meade to Adjutant-General, April 10, 1866.

Michigan on attempting to return, and the remainder surrendered the following day to General Barry, commanding at Buffalo. On the 7th, the President issued a proclamation declaring the obligation of the United States to prevent the carrying on of unlawful expeditions and enterprises from its territory; warned all persons against the consequences of such unlawful proceedings, and authorized and enforced Major-General Meade to employ the land and naval forces of the United States and the militia to arrest and prevent it.[a] From this date the invasion ceased. The Fenians continued to pour into Buffalo, but were ordered back by their leaders. Others were turned back from Ogdensburg and Malone, in New York, and from St. Albans, Vt. Large quantities of arms and munitions of war as well as supplies were captured; the men, without means and illy provided with clothing or food, were returned to their homes at the expense of the Government. Fully 10,000 men were engaged in this foolhardy enterprise, which never possessed the slightest elements of success.[b]

An active center of disturbance during the reconstruction period was the city of Mobile, Ala., due to a considerable negro population and to the aggressive attitude of the whites. Mobile had contributed an unusually large percentage of her male population to the Southern armies, and since their return there had been many occasions when the presence alone of United States troops had prevented a collision between these inharmonious elements. An attempt of the colored people to ride in the street cars had created so violent a commotion that riots were only averted by their abstaining, on the advice of the military commandant, from an exercise of their right to use the cars. On the 14th of May, 1867, a public meeting was held by the Republicans, at which the Hon. William D. Kelley, a member of Congress from Pennsylvania, was the leading speaker. During his address a disturbance occurred on the edge of the crowd, followed by indiscriminate firing, in which two men were killed and several wounded. The police made no attempt to arrest anyone, and were, as they admitted, powerless to suppress disturbances or to preserve the peace. The district commander directed the commandant of the post to assume the maintenance of public order in the city of Mobile. The city police force was suspended; a provost guard established; all outdoor assemblages prohibited; the carrying of firearms forbidden. A few days later the mayor and chief of police were removed and Union men appointed.[c]

Riots at Mobile, May, 1867.

---

[a] 14 Stat. L., 813.

[b] Reports of Major-General Meade, for the year 1866; General Hooker to General Meade; General Barry to General Meade; Major Gibson to General Meade.

[c] Major-General Swayne to Major-General Pope, May 20, 1867; General Orders, No. 37, Post of Mobile, May 19, 1867; 977 M., 1867; General Orders, No. 25, Third Military District, May 29, 1867.

A riot which occurred at Franklin, Tenn., on the 6th of July, 1867, is to be grouped in the same class as those at Memphis and Norfolk; on the one side a body of returned Confederate soldiers, banded ostensibly for the purpose of keeping alive war memories and comradeship; on the other a colored "Loyal League," made up in the majority of discharged colored soldiers. The latter, as appears from manuscript reports on file in the War Department, had been in the habit of marching about the outskirts of town with drum and fife, and having on one or more of such occasions been annoyed by other colored men, several of the members had armed themselves for self-protection. On the afternoon of July 6 political meetings had been held by both the radicals and conservatives, the "League" attending the former in a body. There was some bad feeling created by the attempt of a colored conservative to speak at the radical meeting, and some shots had been fired in the air. The "League" had withdrawn from the meeting and gone to a grove some distance from town. While they were absent the conservatives in town were busy in collecting arms and ammunition and promising the "League" a warm reception. The latter marched into town about half past 8 in the evening, and as they turned into the public square they were met by a volley from the conservative party, who to the number of some 25 to 30 were in position behind a low wall. The fire was promptly returned, and desultory firing continued for something over an hour. On the side of the conservatives 1 white man was killed, 6 whites and about 10 colored men wounded; of the League, 27, possibly 30, were wounded. There was no appearance of the police at any time during the affray; the mayor was singularly ignorant of its going on, although residing in the square. Troops were hurried to the scene from Nashville and arrived early on the morning of the 7th, but found everything quiet, the people on both sides regretful of the occurrence and anxious that the troops should remain. The circuit court met at Franklin on the 8th and the matter was turned over to the civil authorities, the troops withdrawing.[a]

Riot at Franklin, Tenn., July 6, 1867.

With the approach of the municipal elections in Memphis and Nashville there were indications of trouble, and as a precautionary measure the troops were so disposed as to be readily at hand should riot or violence occur. Differences had arisen between the governor and the mayor of Nashville as to who were qualified voters, and who the proper authorities to appoint the officers of election. The governor threatened to call upon the militia to sustain his appointees; the mayor declared that the election would be held under the municipal supervision "unless pre-

The Nashville election, September 28, 1867.

----

[a] Brevet Maj. Gen. W. P. Carlin to Commissioner R., F., and A. L., July 15, 1867, 622 Cumberland, 1867.

vented by the military power of the United States."[a] The governor followed up his proclamation by calling out the entire State militia and ordering it to proceed to Nashville. There was great excitement and both parties appealed to Washington. As a result the following instructions were issued on the 24th of September:

WASHINGTON, D. C., *September 24, 1867 –3.30 p. m.*

Maj. Gen. GEORGE H. THOMAS:

The mayor, city attorney, and common council of Nashville express great fear of collision at time of charter election on the 28th. Go to Nashville to-morrow, to remain until after election, to preserve peace. If you think more troops necessary for that purpose order them there from the most convenient posts in your command. The military can not set up to be the judge as to which set of election judges have the right to control, but must confine their action to putting down hostile mobs. It is hoped, however, by seeing the governor and city officials here referred to, your presence and advice may prevent disturbances. Please keep me advised of condition of affairs.

U. S. GRANT,
General.

General Thomas proceeded at once to Nashville, but his efforts to bring about an amicable adjustment of the difficulty were futile; both parties persisted in holding their election, and refused any compromise. He accordingly ordered to Nashville all the troops at Louisville, Bowling Green, and Franklin, two companies from Memphis, two from Paducah and Humboldt, and one from Union City, as well as Lieb's troop of cavalry. In response to his request for specific instructions, General Thomas was informed on the 26th that his first duty was to *prevent conflict:*

WASHINGTON, D. C., *September 26, 1867—5 p. m.*

Maj. Gen. GEORGE H. THOMAS:

I neither instruct to sustain the governor or mayor, but to prevent conflict. The governor is the only authority that can legally demand the aid of United States troops, and that must be by proclamation declaring invasion or insurrection exists beyond the control of other means at his hands. It is hoped your presence and good judgment and advice will prevent conflict.

U. S. GRANT,
General.

WASHINGTON, D. C., *September 26, 1867—4 p. m.*

Maj. Gen. GEORGE H. THOMAS:

You are to prevent conflict. If the executive of the State issue his proclamation declaring insurrection or invasion to exist too formidable to be put down by force at his own command, and calls upon the United States to aid him, then aid will have to be given. Your mission is to preserve peace, and not to take sides in political difference until called out in accordance with law. You are to prevent mobs from aiding either party. If called upon legally to interfere, your duty is plain.

U. S. GRANT,
General.

---

[a] Proclamation of Governor Brownlow, September 18, 1867; Proclamation Mayor W. Matt Brown, September 24, 1867; Papers accompanying Report Secretary of War, 1867, p. 83.

WASHINGTON, D. C., *September 26, 1867—9 p. m.*

Maj. Gen. GEORGE H. THOMAS:

I will send you further instructions to-morrow. Nothing is clearer, however, than that the military can not be made use of to defeat the executive of a State in enforcing the laws of the State. You are not to prevent the legal State force from the execution of its orders.

U. S. GRANT,
General.

These dispatches were shown to the mayor, but the latter persisted in his former decision, that unless prevented by the armed interference of the Federal troops he would hold the election under the city charter. On the morning of the 28th, the day of election, United States troops were posted at every polling precinct, as, under the orders of the governor, were also detachments of the State militia, but the latter almost immediately withdrew. The mayor filed a protest; the election proceeded without disturbance, and, there being no further excitement, the troops returned to their stations on the 29th.[a]

The beginning of the year 1868 was approximately the date for the first appearance of the organization of restless, reckless, and lawless spirits, which, under various names, disguises, and appellations, is best known under the generic term Ku-Klux-Klan. The Confederate general, N. B. Forrest, in his testimony before the Congressional committee,[b] fixes the earliest date for the existence of this organization as the spring of 1866, and the first scene of its operations as middle Tennessee; that it was a sort of offset to the "Loyal Leagues;" was not at first military in its character, and had no political purpose.

The
Ku-Klux-Klan,
1866–1872.

Question. You mean what is called Ku-Klux?

Answer. Yes, sir. I think that organization arose about the time the militia were called out, and Governor Brownlow issued his proclamation stating that the troops would not be injured for what they should do to rebels. Such a proclamation was issued. There was a great deal of insecurity felt by the Southern people. There were a great many Northern men coming down there, forming leagues all over the country. The negroes were holding night meetings; were going about; were becoming very insolent, and the Southern people all over the State were very much alarmed. I think many of the organizations did not have any name. Parties organized themselves so as to be ready in case they were attacked. Ladies were ravished by some of these negroes, who were tried and put in the penitentiary, but were turned out in a few days afterwards. There was a great deal of insecurity in the country, and I think this organization was got up to protect the weak, with no political intention at all.

The earliest official report of the existence of the organization as a distinct menace to the peace and good order of the community was in a report of Major-General Thomas, who commanded the Department

---

[a] Annual Report Major-General Thomas, with accompanying papers, September 30, 1867, pp. 82–94.

[b] Testimony of Gen. N. B. Forrest, vol. 13, p. 32. (Senate Report No. 41, Forty-second Congress, second session.)

of the Cumberland, dated October 1, 1868, followed a few days later
by a similar report from Major-General Reynolds, commanding the
Fifth military district at Austin, Tex., and by Maj. Gen. O. O. Howard, at the head of the Freedmen's Bureau.   General Thomas says:

With the close of the last and beginning of the new year the State of Tennessee
was disturbed by the strange operations of a mysterious organization known as the
Ku-Klux-Klan, which first made its appearance in Giles County. Within a few
weeks it had spread over a great part of the State, and created no little alarm.
Accounts of it from many sources were received at these headquarters. The newspapers recognized its existence by publishing articles on the subject, either denun-
ciatory or with an attempt to break its proceedings as harmless jokes, according to
the political opinions of their editors. The assistant commissioner of the Bureau of
Refugees, Freedmen, and Abandoned Lands for Tennessee in his reports, copies
of which were furnished me, narrated many of the proceedings of the organization,
whose acts were shown to be of a lawless and diabolical nature. Organized companies of men, mounted and armed, horses and riders being disguised, patrolled the
country, making demonstrations calculated to frighten quiet citizens, and in many
instances abused and outraged them, especially that class of colored people who by
their energy, industry, and good conduct are most prominent.

I did not think it necessary to take any action on the information furnished until
the month of March, when a member of the legislature of Tennessee sent me a written statement of the doings of this organization, saying it carried terror and dismay
throughout the country; that the civil authorities were powerless and appeared
terror struck; that his own life was threatened, and asked if something could not be
done by the General Government to protect the community; if not, there was danger
of a bloody collision.

The cases referred to by General Thomas had been duly forwarded
by him to the General in chief for instructions, with the remark that
"as Tennessee is a fully constituted State I consider that the State
authorities should deal with and suppress this organization of lawless,
desperate men, and I have not up to the present time considered myself
authorized to take active measures against them." These papers
were laid before the President, who returned them with the following
decision:

The Constitution provides that the United States shall protect each State "on
application of the legislature or the executive (when the legislature can not be convened) against domestic violence. As the legislature of Tennessee is now in session,
and as no application for Federal aid has been received from that body, or any information communicated by the governor of that State, it is not at this time deemed
within the province of the Executive to give any instructions upon the subject to
which these papers refer.

The publication of this decision seems to have given encouragement
to these midnight prowlers, for their operations which were heretofore limited to a few counties in middle Tennessee were now extended
into eastern Tennessee, North Carolina, and Georgia, and almost daily
reports were received of their outrages. On the 16th of April Governor Brownlow called for troops to be sent to Maury County, and again
in June the disturbances had reached such a degree of intolerance that
he asked for troops to be sent to eight separate points. It was declared

on the authority of General Forrest that the Ku-Klux-Klan at this time numbered 40,000 members in Tennessee alone. As every available soldier was already in pursuit of these ruffians it was found impossible to fill the governor's requisition. The latter then called a special session of the legislature and laid the matter before them. The legislature passed resolutions calling upon the Federal Government for troops to preserve order in the State and appointed a committee to visit Washington and lay the condition of affairs in Tennessee before the President. Assurances were given this committee that the power of the United States would be employed to protect the State against lawless violence. On the 16th of September Governor Brownlow issued a proclamation against the Ku-Klux-Klan, in which he announced his purpose "to put down armed marauders" whatever the consequences, and calling upon all "good, loyal, and patriotic people, white and colored, of every county in the State to proceed without delay and raise companies of loyal and able-bodied men" and report to him at Nashville. A second proclamation was issued on the 20th of January, 1869, as follows:

Whereas, there exists in middle and west Tennessee lawless bands who set at defiance civil law, and in certain localities render it impossible for civil officers to enforce the laws of the State; and whereas, those masked villians, called Ku-Klux, are taking prisoners from jails and hanging them without trial, and are abducting passengers from railroad trains and notifying conductors of Northern birth to leave the State, thus having driven four conductors from one road, the Decatur and Alabama road; and whereas, certain ambitious men have made incendiary speeches, advising the overthrow of the State government, thereby encouraging these bands; and whereas, certain rebel newspapers have encouraged these men by denying the existence of the Ku-Klux by ridiculing their acts, and failing to condemn them; and whereas, the legislature has amended the militia law and given me authority to meet such outrages: Now, therefore, I, William G. Brownlow, governor of Tennessee, do call upon all good and loyal citizens to enter the ranks of the State guards, be mustered into service, and aid in suppressing lawlessness. Those enrolling in east Tennessee will be transported to Nashville and armed and placed under the command of Gen. James A. Cooper.

Another proclamation will be duly issued designating the counties in which I shall declare martial law, the effect of which will be to set aside civil law and turn over offenders to the military to be tried and punished summarily. These outrages have been long borne, but the executive is not to be cajoled or trifled with. The citizens are warned against harboring any Ku-Klux. The governor will make the guards numerous and effective enough to make middle and west Tennessee as orderly and quiet as east Tennessee is to-day.

In testimony whereof, I have signed the foregoing and affix the great seal this the 20th day of January, 1869.

WILLIAM G. BROWNLOW.

Governor Brownlow followed this up by calling into the field the entire State militia, which he increased by active recruiting until it had reached a strength of 1,600 men. On the 20th of February he declared martial law in nine counties, and by pressing this policy with determination and imposing the expense on the counties, succeeded in restoring order. The United States troops were not further called upon in Tennessee and the Ku-Klux operations seem to have ceased as suddenly and mysteriously as they were commenced. General Forrest claims to have disbanded the organization in 1868, but his control seems to have been confined to Tennessee and perhaps Kentucky.

From Tennessee, if this be regarded as the initial point, of which there is reasonable doubt, the organization seems to have passed into Georgia. Gen. John B. Gordon, who admitted that he refused to become its head, in his testimony before the committee (p. 308) remarked:

> We were afraid to have a public organization, because we supposed it would be construed at once by the authorities at Washington as an organization antagonistic to the Government of the United States. It was therefore necessary, in order to protect our families from outrage and preserve our own lives, to have something that we could regard as a brotherhood—a combination of the best men of the country— to act purely in self-defense, to repel the attack in case we should be attacked by these people. That was the whole object of this organization. I never heard of any disguises connected with it; we had none, very certainly. This organization I think extended nearly all over the State. It was, as I say, an organization purely for self-defense. It had no more politics in it than the organization of the Masons. I never heard the idea of politics suggested in connection with it.

There was little or no difference in the operations of these marauders in Georgia, North Carolina, Mississippi, and Alabama from the methods that were followed in Tennessee. Testimony taken by the committee covered well-defined outrages in 24 counties of Georgia, 14 counties in North Carolina, 24 counties in Alabama, 18 counties in Mississippi. In 6 specified counties of Alabama the total number of proven cases of individual violence was 371, of which 33 were murders; in 4 counties of Mississippi 31 murders were committed in 1868–69.

There is abundant evidence on file in the War Department to establish these facts and thousands of similar ones. The number of proven outrages, murders, and mutilations committed by these secret organizations is appalling.

In South Carolina the operations of the Ku-Klux, which had ceased after the Presidential election of 1869, were renewed in 1870. Before the election of that year Governor Scott had organized and armed a militia composed entirely of colored men, upon the plea that it was necessary that they should protect themselves against violence. This action was most offensive to the whites, and was resented by them at every opportunity. Some of the arms belonging to this colored militia were stored at the town of Laurens, where repeated encounters

Riot at Laurens, S. C., October 20, 1870.

between individual blacks and whites had developed a state of feverish excitement. On the 20th of October, 1870, an altercation between two men of opposite opinions occurred in the public square at Laurens; several colored men rushed to the armory, evidently to procure arms; they were followed by a party of whites, armed with pistols; firing commenced on both sides, and a riot ensued. This was about noon. Within an hour or two armed white men commenced to pour into Laurens from the surrounding country, and by midnight fully 2,500 strangers were in town. The riot commenced in Laurens, extended into the county within a radius of many miles, and continued until the night of the 21st, by which time 13 men had been killed and several hundred wounded. There is nothing to connect this affair with the Ku-Klux organizations, but the testimony showed that almost immediately after the Laurens riot the Ku-Klux appeared in several places in the State, and that for the following twelve months their midnight operations were quite unrestrained. It was shown that in Spartanburg County alone 227 persons were whipped, maimed, killed, or otherwise maltreated; that hundreds of persons slept in the woods all winter under fear of these raiders.[a]

On the 31st of December, 1870, a company of negro militia left Unionville, Union County, ostensibly for drill; the real purpose of their march is not clear. On their way they met a white wagoner who had been a Confederate soldier, whom they abused, and, on his resisting, chased and killed him. The Congressional committee characterized the murder as cruel and unprovoked. This excited intense feeling in Unionville, and the citizens determined to disarm the militia company. On the 1st of January, 1871, several of the negroes who participated in the shooting were arrested and lodged in the jail.

Riot at Unionville, S. C., January 12, 1871.

Three days later a party of undisguised Ku-Klux rode into town, surrounded the jail, took out five prisoners, shot two of them; the others escaped. They were recaptured, and, with seven or eight others, again lodged in the jail, where they remained until the 12th, when another body of armed and disguised Ku-Klux, variously estimated at from 400 to 800, came into Unionville, took possession of the jail, took out eight of the prisoners and hung them. In Chester, Fairfield, and York counties the same state of affairs existed as in Union and Spartanburg. Murders, whippings, and intimidations followed each other until, in response to a call from the governor, United States troops were sent to Yorkville. On the night preceding their arrival the Ku-Klux raided the county treasury, and, being advised of the coming of the troops, tore up the railway track to obstruct their passage. The commanding officer of these troops reported a few days later:

From the best information I can get, I estimate the number of cases of whipping, beating, and personal violence of various grades, in this county, since the 1st of last November, at between 300 and 400, excluding numerous minor cases of threats,

[a] Vol. 2, pp. 1305–1319; Senate Report No. 41, Forty-second Congress, second session.

intimidation, abuse, and small personal violence, as knocking down with a pistol or gun, etc. The more serious outrages, exclusive of murders and whippings, noted hereafter.

The result of these persistent outrages, and the repeated calls of the civil authorities for aid, was the act of Congress approved April 20, 1871 (17 Stat. L., 13), entitled "An act to enforce the provisions of the fourteenth amendment to the Constitution of the United States, and for other purposes," which, after prescribing the penalty for conspiring by force to put down the Government, or to hinder the execution of any law, or for going in disguise upon the public highway, etc., goes on to say:

SEC. 3. That in all cases where insurrection, domestic violence, unlawful combinations, or conspiracies in any State shall so obstruct or hinder the execution of the laws thereof, and of the United States, as to deprive any portion or class of the people of such State of any of the rights, privileges, or immunities, or protection, named in the Constitution and secured by this act, and the constituted authorities of such State shall either be unable to protect, or shall, from any cause, fail in or refuse protection of the people in such rights, such facts shall be deemed a denial by such State of the equal protection of the laws to which they are entitled under the Constitution of the United States; and in all such cases, or whenever any such insurrection, violence, unlawful combination, or conspiracy shall oppose or obstruct the laws of the United States, or the due execution thereof, or impede or obstruct the due course of justice under the same, it shall be lawful for the President. and it shall be his duty to take such measures, by the employment of the militia or the land and naval forces of the United States, or of either, or by other means, as he may deem necessary for the suppression of such insurrection, domestic violence, or combinations; and any person who shall be arrested under the provisions of this and the preceding section shall be delivered to the marshal of the proper district, to be dealt with according to law.

SEC. 4. That whenever in any State or part of a State the unlawful combinations named in the preceding section of this act shall be organized and armed, and so numerous and powerful as to be able, by violence, to either overthrow or set at defiance the constituted authorities of such State, and of the United States within such State, or when the constituted authorities are in complicity with, or shall connive at, the unlawful purposes of such powerful and armed combinations; and whenever, by reason of either or all of the causes aforesaid, the conviction of such offenders and the preservation of the public safety shall become in such district impracticable, in every such case such combinations shall be deemed a rebellion against the Government of the United States, and during the continuance of such rebellion, and within the limits of the district which shall be so under the sway thereof, such limits to be prescribed by proclamation, it shall be lawful for the President of the United States, when in his judgment the public safety shall require it, to suspend the privileges of the writ of habeas corpus, to the end that such rebellion may be overthrown: *Provided,* That all the provisions of the second section of an act entitled "An act relating to habeas corpus, and regulating judicial proceedings in certain cases," approved March third, eighteen hundred and sixty-three, which relate to the discharge of prisoners other than prisoners of war, and to the penalty for refusing to obey the order of the court, shall be in full force so far as the same are applicable to the provisions of this section: *Provided further,* That the President shall first have made proclamation, as now provided by law, commanding such insurgents to disperse: *And provided also,* That the provisions of this section shall not be in force after the end of the next regular session of Congress.

This was followed on the 3d of May, 1871, by a proclamation by the President, in which he exhorted the people of those parts of the land which was lately the theater of insurrection and military conflict to suppress all such combinations by their own voluntary efforts, and warning them that their failure so to do will "impose upon the National Government the duty of putting forth all its energies for the protection of its citizens of every race and color, and for the restoration of peace and order throughout the entire country." This failing of its desired effect a second proclamation was issued October 12, naming the counties of Spartanburg, York, Marion, Chester, Laurens, Newberry, Fairfield, Lancaster, and Chesterfield, all in South Carolina, as places where organized and armed combinations and conspiracies exist so numerous and powerful as to be able to defy the constituted authorities, and concluding as follows:

Now, therefore, I, Ulysses S. Grant, President of the United States of America, do hereby command all persons composing the unlawful combinations and conspiracies aforesaid to disperse and to retire peaceably to their homes within five days of the date hereof, and to deliver, either to the marshal of the United States for the district of South Carolina, or to any of his deputies, or to any military officer of the United States within said counties, all arms, ammunition, uniforms, disguises, and other means and implements used, kept, possessed, or controlled by them for carrying out the unlawful purposes for which the combinations and conspiracies are organized.[a]

The five days having expired, and the insurgents engaged in these combinations having failed to disperse, the President next suspended the writ of habeas corpus in the said counties,[b] and strengthened the Federal troops by the addition of every available man from the adjoining military departments. Troops were stationed at Charleston, Columbia, Chester, Yorkville, Spartanburg, Newberry, Unionville, and Sumter, and numerous other points; all persons known or suspected to be connected with the Ku-Klux-Klan were pursued and arrested. Upward of 600 arrests were made up to January 1, 1872. A supplementary proclamation excepted Marion from the list of counties in which insurrection existed, and the county of Union was added to the number; the trials took place in the United States court at Columbia, and large numbers of the accused were convicted, heavily fined, or imprisoned.

It is not to be understood that all the disorders in the southern tier of States during this period are to be charged to the account of the Ku-Klux organization. In some of the States the brotherhood had no recognized footing, and many disturbances set down to their account were brought about by causes totally different. Of such nature were the disturbances at Augusta, Ga., in July, 1868. The

---

a 17 Stat. L., 949–950.   b 17 Stat. L., 952, 953, 954.

municipal officers had been military appointees, and on the restoration
of the State to its former political status, it was
Disorders in Gulf States, 1868. claimed by the opposition that all military authority
having ceased those officials who derived their powers
solely from the military were *functus officio*. Refusing to vacate
they were threatened with summary ejection, and an organization for
this purpose was put on foot. The mayor and his associates appealed
to the governor, and the latter called upon United States troops for
assistance. General Meade referred him to Washington, and the
President upon the ground of informality in the call declined to interfere. On the 4th of August a similar request was received from the
mayor and council of Montgomery, Ala., and the governor in transmitting the request remarked that until the State could pass a militia
law it was expected that United States troops would be permitted to
lend their moral support for the preservation of the peace. On the
12th of that month another application came from Florida, followed on
the 29th of September by a call from the governor of South Carolina,
and on the 7th of October from the governor of North Carolina.[a] To
all of these, reply was made that the several State governments must
first exhaust all their resources; that whenever their attempts to
execute the laws met with greater resistance than they could overcome
the General Government would come to their assistance, but that until
that point had been reached, the United States under existing laws was
powerless to aid them.[b]

In harmony with these instructions are those of Mr. Attorney-
General Evarts in his letter of August 20, 1868, to the United States
marshal of the northern district of Florida.[c] The marshal had
requested that instructions be given to the military commander in
Florida to aid him when necessary. To this Mr. Evarts replied in
part:

The 27th section of the judiciary act of 1789 establishes the office of marshal, and
names among his duties and powers the following: "And to execute throughout the
district all lawful precepts directed to him, and issued under the authority of the
United States, and he shall have power to command all necessary assistance in
the execution of his duty, and to appoint, as there may be occasion, one or more
deputies." (1 Stat., p. 87.)

You will observe from this that the only measure of the assistance which you have
power to command is its necessity for the execution of your duty, and upon your
discreet judgment under your official responsibility, the law reposes the determination of what force each particular necessity requires. This power of the marshal is
equivalent to that of a sheriff, and, with either, embraces, as a resort in necessity,

---

[a] See also 43 V, A. G. O., 1870; 1240, A. G. O., 1870; 1751, A. G. O., 1871; 506,
A. G. O., 1871; 60, A. G. O., 1871.

[b] 375 A, A. G. O., 1868, and accompanying papers.

[c] Also published in General Orders, No. 96, A. G. O., September 7, 1876.

the whole power of the precinct (county or district) over which the officer's authority extends. In defining this power, Attorney-General Cushing—and, as I understand the subject, correctly—says it "comprises every person in the district or county above the age of 15 years, whether civilians or not, and including the military of all denominations—militia, soldiers, marines—all of whom are alike bound to obey the commands of a sheriff or marshal."

While, however, the law gives you this "power to command all necessary assistance," and the military within your district are not exempt from obligation to obey, in common with all the citizens, your summons in case of necessity, you will be particular to observe that this high and responsible authority is given to the marshal only in aid of his duty "to execute throughout the district all lawful precepts directed to him, and issued under the authority of the United States," and only in case of *necessity* for this extraordinary aid. The military persons obeying this summons of the marshal will act in subordination and obedience to the civil officer, the marshal, in whose aid in the execution of process they are called, and only to the effect of securing its execution. [a]

This special duty and authority in the execution of process issued to you must not be confounded with the duty and authority of suppressing disorder and preserving the peace, which, under our Government, belongs to the civil authorities of the States, and not to the civil authorities of the United States   Nor are this special duty and authority of the marshal, in executing process issued to him, to be confounded with the authority and duty of the President of the United States, in the specific cases of the Constitution and under the regulations of the statutes, to protect the States against domestic violence, or with his authority and duty, under special statutes to employ military force in subduing combinations in resistance to the laws of the United States. For neither of these duties or authorities is shared by the subordinate officers of the Government, except when and as the same may be specifically communicated to them by the President.

I have, thus, called your attention to the general considerations bearing upon the subject to which your letter refers, for the purpose of securing a due observance of the limits of your duty and authority in connection therewith. Nothing can be less in accordance with the nature of our Government or the disposition of our people than a frequent or ready resort to military aid in execution of the duties confided to civil officers. Courage, vigor, and intrepidity are appropriate qualities for the civil service which the marshals of the United States are expected to perform, and a reinforcement of their power by extraordinary means is permitted by the law only in extraordinary emergencies.

If it shall be thought that any occasion, at any time, exists for instructions to the military authorities of the United States, within any of the States, in connection with the execution of process of the courts of the United States, these instructions will be in accordance with the exigency then appearing.

I am, sir, very respectfully, your obedient servant,

Wm. M. Evarts,
Attorney-General.

While the Ku-Klux movement is not known to have reached Arkansas, there were serious and disgraceful disturbances in various parts

---

[a] But see to the contrary Mr. Attorney-General Devens (16 Opin., 162), as well as the fifteenth section of the act of June 18, 1878: "From and after the passage of this act it shall not be lawful to employ any part of the Army of the United States as a posse comitatus, or otherwise, for the purpose of executing the laws, except in such cases and under such circumstances as such employment of said force may be expressly authorized by the Constitution or by act of Congress."

of the State through much of the year 1868.   Especially was this the
case in the counties of Conway, Perry, and Columbia, where the law

Lawlessness
in Arkansas,
1868.

was openly defied, court officials driven from their
seats, and enormities perpetrated that were disgraceful to the name of humanity.   These counties were in
open and defiant rebellion against the laws of the State; the courts of
justice were broken up, and the civil authorities overpowered by
bodies of armed men who rode about the country driving peaceable
citizens from their homes, burning their houses and crops, and destroying all they were unable to carry away.   In Perry County several
men were assassinated; hundreds shot at and wounded.   In this emergency the legislature authorized the enrollment of a militia, which was
set immediately on foot and rapidly proceeded with, until a force of
some 1,500 had been raised and organized.   On the 27th of August,
1868, the governor issued a proclamation reciting the facts as above
stated, and concluding as follows:

Now, therefore, I, Powell Clayton, governor of the State of Arkansas, do hereby
enjoin upon all persons within said State to keep the peace, and command all bodies
of armed men (not organized in pursuance of the laws of the State, or of the United
States) to immediately disperse and return to their homes.

I do furthermore make known that I shall at once cause to be enrolled and organized the reserve militia in pursuance of said act, and shall use, as far as may be
necessary, all the power and authority vested in me by the constitution and laws of
the State of Arkansas to preserve order, enforce the law, and protect the lives and
property of every person within the State.

Contrary to expectations, the appearance of the militia in the field
did not put an end to the disorders in the infected district; they
increased in frequency and in extent of territory, so that on the 9th of
November the governor placed the ten counties of Ashley, Bradley,
Columbia, Lafayette, Mississippi, Woodruff, Craighead, Greene,
Sevier, and Little River under martial law.   To the determination
and energy of the governor, and to his vigorous execution of this
measure, which was sustained by a formal act of the legislature and
which made repeated appropriations to pay the militia thus called into
the field, is due the ultimate suppression of these disgraceful disorders.
There was much complaint from the residents of the counties under
martial law, who suffered heavy losses both from the insurgents and
the militia, and it is believed that this fact had no insignificant bearing
upon the final termination of the troubles.   At mass meetings held in
the ten counties men of both political parties joined in condemnation of
these violations of law, engaged to keep the peace themselves, and to
cause others to keep it.   The United States troops were stationed at
various points in the State during this period—at Little Rock, Pine
Bluff, Batesville, Fort Smith, Camden, Washington, Madison, Dover,
and Fayetteville—and by their presence contributed to a suppression
of the insurrection, but were not called upon for active service.   On

March 22, 1869, the governor announced that the insurrection having been suppressed, martial law would cease throughout the State.[a]

The constant friction between men of opposite political sentiments in the years following the close of the war was the apparent reason for the formation of political clubs, armed, drilled, and sometimes uniformed, in nearly all of the Southern States. Constant apprehensions of collision between these bodies of men induced the legislature of Georgia in 1868 to empower the governor to prohibit them. This he did by a proclamation, dated September 14 of that year, in which he declared that "no authority has been granted by the executive for the formation of armed or unarmed organizations of any kind or character; that the drilling or exercising in military tactics, with arms, of any organized body of men within the State, except the Army of the United States, is unauthorized, unlawful, and against the peace and good order of the State and must be immediately suspended."[b] About the time of the appearance of this proclamation a mass meeting

Riot at Camilla, Ga., September 19, 1868.

of Republicans was called at the village of Camilla, in Mitchell County, and was attended by marching clubs of negroes from the surrounding country. A procession of some three hundred, a majority carrying guns and pistols, marched from Albany toward Camilla; they were met just outside the town by the sheriff, who told them of the proclamation and endeavored to persuade them to return or to lay aside their weapons. The negroes refused and the sheriff returned to the town and summoned a posse. On the arrival of the procession a conflict ensued in which eight or nine were killed and twenty or thirty wounded. The governor at once communicated the facts to the legislature and recommended that the Federal Government be called upon for troops to be stationed in Mitchell County. A committee of the legislature visited the section, decided that the civil authorities were fully able to preserve order, and reported that there was no necessity for military interference. General Meade, in reporting this affair, concurred with the committee, but later sent a company of infantry to Albany, and others to Columbus, Macon, Augusta, Washington, Americus, Thomasville, and others, with the following instructions to their commanding officers. As a consequence the elections passed off without serious disturbance:

They will impress on post commanders that they are to act in aid of and cooperation with, and in subordination to, the civil authorities; that they are to exercise discretion and judgment, unbiased by political or other prejudices; that their object should be exclusively to preserve the peace and uphold law and order, and they must be satisfied such is the object of the civil officer calling on them for aid; that they must in all cases, where time will permit, apply for instruction to superior

---

[a] Reports, Brevet Major-General Rousseau, Brevet Major-General Smith, Brevet Major-General Gillam, to Adjutant-General, 1868–1869.

[b] Proclamation of Governor R. B. Bulloch, September 14, 1868.

authority, but they must at all hazards preserve the peace, and not be restrained by technical points when, in their conscientious judgment under the rules above set forth, it is their duty to act. Post commanders, on being notified of the proposed holding of political meetings, may send an officer, and if necessary, a detachment, to watch the proceedings and see that the peace is preserved.[a]

It is believed that the condition of lawlessness that prevailed in Texas from the close of the war of the rebellion up to the readmission of the State in 1870, and for some years later, was due to a variety of causes not altogether political. "It is safe to say," reports Mr. Evans, the United States attorney for the western district of Texas, to the Attorney-General, under date of March 2, 1876, "that in Texas, with a population of 1,000,000, there are 3 men killed each day, amounting to 1,095 per year. One-fourth of these or more, are negroes, and killed mostly from political hatred to the race."[b] In his annual report for November 4, 1868, General Reynolds, the military commander, had remarked that:

Lawlessness
in Texas,
1868–1870.

*   *   *   *   *   *   *

Armed organizations, generally known as "Ku-Klux-Klans," exist independently or in concert with other armed bands in many parts of Texas, but are most numerous, bold, and aggressive east of Trinity River.

The precise objects of the organizations can not be readily explained, but seems in this State to be to disarm, rob, and in many cases murder Union men and negroes, and, as occasion may offer, murder United States officers and soldiers; also to intimidate everyone who knows anything of the organization, but who will not join it.

*   *   *   *   *   *   *

The murder of negroes is so common as to render it impossible to keep an accurate account of them.

Many of the members of these bands of outlaws are transient persons in the State, the absence of railroads and telegraphs and great length of time required to communicate between remote points facilitating their devilish purposes.

These organizations are evidently countenanced, or at least not discouraged, by a majority of the white people in the counties where the bands are most numerous. They could not otherwise exist.

I have given this matter close attention, and am satisfied that a remedy to be effective must be gradually applied and continued with the firm support of the army until these outlaws are punished or dispersed.

*   *   *   *   *   *   *

Free speech and a free press, as the terms are generally understood in other States, have never existed in Texas. In fact, the citizens of other States can not appreciate the state of affairs in Texas without actually experiencing it. The official reports of lawlessness and crime, so far from being exaggerated, do not tell the whole truth.

And in his report for October 24, 1869, he said that "the number of murders in the State during the nine months from January 1, 1869, to September 30, 1869, according to the official records, necessarily

---

[a]General Meade to Adjutant-General, October 8, 1868; General Orders, No. 27, Department of the South, 1868.

[b]H. R. Ex. Doc. 30, Forty-fourth Congress, second session, p. 139.

imperfect, is 384, being an average of about one and a half per day."
To similar import is a report made by a special committee of the constitutional convention on the 30th of June, 1868, which states that
about 900 murders had been committed in the State since the close of
the war; of those, 304 had been perpetrated since January 1, 1869.
The reason for this, as viewed from another standpoint, is expressed
in a report made by a special committee on " crime and lawlessness,"
appointed by a Democratic convention which met on the 6th of July,
1868:

1. The "general demoralization resulting from the war, and the absence of any
government, civil or military, for several months after the conclusion of the war, and
the sudden disbandment of a large number of Federal and Confederate soldiery who
were thus released from military restraint at a time when the checks of civil law
were also wanting;" 2. The "disorders had been increased in many localities by
taking the execution of the laws from the civil authorities without replacing them
by any other power;" 3. The "inefficiency of judicial and ministerial officers
appointed by the military authorities;" and, 4. The "changed condition of society
resulting from the emancipation of the negroes, the indolent habits and thievish disposition evinced by them, and the turbulent spirit which they have manifested,
instigated by bad and designing men, and in many instances supported by the officers of the Freedmen's Bureau."

To this explanation of the existing conditions it may be stated that
while this committee was in pursuit of its investigation a rumor was
being circulated among the negroes in the valley of the Brazos that a
colored man had been lynched by a body of white men
and his body left hanging by the wayside. An armed
band of negroes was hastily assembled near Millican
under the leadership of an itinerant minister and marched to the town,
intending "vengeance on the lynchers." On their way they encountered the sheriff with a posse. Both parties commenced firing, and
when the affray was over some 20 colored people and 4 whites
had been killed and several times as many wounded.[a] This is a fair
example of the incidents of reconstruction in Texas as reported by the
military commander from time to time. The immense territory covered by the State and the long extent of frontier necessitated the
presence of a large number of troops—three regiments of cavalry and
from five to seven regiments of infantry, with an aggregate strength
of nearly 5,000—and these were almost constantly employed. Aside
from the frontier posts, from one to three companies were stationed
at from fifteen to twenty points to aid the civil authorities. Galves-
ton, Austin, Waco, Jefferson, Bryan, Huntsville, Livingston, Greenville, Nacogdoches, Brenham, Corpus Christi, Columbus, Helena,
Lampasas, Tyler, and Indianola were among the towns thus garrisoned
by Federal troops.

*Riot
at Millican, Tex.,
July 15, 1868.*

---

[a] General Reynolds to Adjutant-General, August 1, 1868.

Soon after the readmission of the State the legislature organized the militia, together with an efficient mounted police force; a law was passed prohibiting the carrying of deadly weapons; a number of jails were built, and most determined efforts were made by the State authorities for the suppression of lawlessness. Up to the end of 1870 reports had been made showing a total of 2,790 persons charged with crime and evading arrest; of this number, 702 were charged with murder, in some cases two or more, even seven murders being charged to a single individual. In addition 972 had been arrested, 109 of them charged with murder. By the end of 1871 the courts were in good working order; offenders were promptly arrested and punished and the civil law respected, so that the troops were withdrawn and resumed their frontier stations.

Mobile was the scene of another riot on the 5th of August, 1869. There had been considerable excitement in the city for some days over the political issues that were to be determined at the August elections. Both parties had held meetings nightly, and the Republican meetings, participated in almost exclusively by colored men, had been frequently interrupted. On election day, August 3, there had been some rioting, but this the sheriff had been able to suppress. On the night of the 5th the Republicans, having won the election, held a meeting to celebrate their victory; and, it having been rumored that the meeting was to be broken up, an immense crowd was present, and many of them were armed. The police, numbering about 100 men, were all on duty at the place of meeting, and, apprehending trouble, the sheriff had called upon the commandant of the United States troops. Before they could reach the spot firing had commenced, and within a few minutes, according to a newspaper report, "the bullets were falling like hail." The whites formed themselves into squads and marched about the streets, committing all sorts of depredations. When the troops arrived it was found that six men had been killed and twelve severely wounded.[a]

---

[a] Mobile *Nationalist*, August 6, 1869; report United States Marshal Watson and of Maj. M. A. Cochran, Second Infantry, 1127, Department South, 1869.

S. Doc. 209——9

Marginal note: Riot at Mobile, Ala., August 5, 1869.

VI. POLITICAL DISTURBANCES IN LOUISIANA, 1866–1876.

RIOTS AT NEW ORLEANS, 1866—OUTRAGES IN FRANKLIN COUNTY, 1868—CONFLICT IN ST. LANDRY PARISH—RIOTS AT NEW ORLEANS, 1871–72—THE COUSHATTA TRAGEDY, 1874—RIOTS AT NEW ORLEANS, 1874—THE AFFAIR OF JANUARY 4, 1875.

It has been observed that the obligation of acting upon the application of a State legislature, or of its executive, devolves upon the President the necessity of determining what body of men constitute the legislature, or who is the governor, before he can act. The Supreme Court has remarked in the Rhode Island case (Luther *v.* Borden, 7 Howard, 1) that the fact that two parties claim the right to the government can not alter the case, for both can not be entitled to it; that if there is an armed conflict it is a case of domestic violence, and one of the parties must be in insurrection against the lawful government, and that the President must, of necessity, decide which is the government, and which party is unlawfully arrayed against it, before he can perform the duty imposed upon him by the law. But it will be remembered that in the Rhode Island case the President (Tyler) had declined to accept this doctrine. In his message of April 9, 1844, he remarked, "I also with equal strength resist the idea that it falls within the Executive competency to decide, in controversies of the nature of that which existed in Rhode Island, on which side is the majority of the people, or as to the extent of the rights of a mere numerical majority. For the Executive to assume such a power would be to assume a power of the most dangerous character." Moreover, the dispersion of Mr. Dorr's slender army rendered it unnecessary for either issuing the proclamation or for removing the troops from Fort Adams. It was reserved for President Grant, in the Louisiana and afterwards in the Arkansas case, to apply this doctrine in responding to a call for Federal aid to suppress an insurrection, from each of two contestants, by reviewing their respective claims, and recognizing one of them as the lawful governor of the State.

The Louisiana cases are, moreover, of considerable interest and importance in presenting, as they do, about all the phases that are likely to attend a political situation of that character. Extending over a period of nearly ten years, during which the titles of five executives and of six rival legislative bodies were in dispute, besides involving two Presidential and four Congressional elections, there was necessity

130

for frequent and prompt, if not arbitrary, decision upon the part of the President in the interest of peace and public order. These cases are still further of interest in demonstrating the cheerfulness and alacrity with which the insurgents in every instance surrendered their pretensions at the demand of the General Government. In the more than twenty occasions on which United States troops were required to interpose between armed bodies of disputing partisans, there was no single instance in which they were called upon to fire a shot.

A dispassionate record of the circumstances and events that make up the history of the State of Louisiana for the more than ten years following the war of the rebellion exhibits a political and social condition that is little short of anarchy. "Since the year 1866," reports Lieutenant-General Sheridan to the Secretary of War, in a dispatch dated New Orleans, January 10, 1875, "nearly 3,500 persons, the majority of whom were colored men, have been killed and wounded in this State.[a] In 1868 the official record shows that 1,884 were killed and wounded. From 1868 to the present time no official investigation has been made, and the civil authorities in all but a few cases have been unable to arrest, convict, and punish the perpetrators. Consequently there are no correct records to be consulted for information. There is ample evidence, however, to show that more than 1,200 persons have been killed and wounded during this time on account of their political sentiments. Frightful massacres have occurred in the parishes of Bossier, Caddo, Catahoula, St. Bernard, St. Landry, Grant, and Orleans. The general character of the massacres in the above-named parishes is so well known that it is unnecessary to describe them. The isolated cases can best be illustrated by the following instances, which I take from a mass of evidence now lying before me, of men killed on account of their political principles: In Natchitoches Parish the number of isolated cases reported is 33; in the parish of Bienville the number of men killed is 30; in Red River Parish the isolated cases of men killed is 34; in Winn Parish the number of isolated cases where men were killed is 15; in Jackson Parish the number killed is 20; in Catahoula Parish the number of isolated cases reported where men were killed is 50; and most of the country parishes throughout the State will show a corresponding state of affairs."

To similar effect is the language of the President (Grant) in his message of January 13, 1875, in response to a Senate resolution calling for information as to the existing political situation in Louisiana. "To say that lawlessness, turbulence, and bloodshed have characterized the political affairs of that State since its organization under the reconstruction acts is only to repeat what has become well known as a part

---

[a] That the aggregate of these murders greatly exceeded the number stated by General Sheridan, see the documentary proof published in H. R. Ex. Doc. No. 30, Forty-fourth Congress, second session, pp. 150 to 546.

of its unhappy history."[a]   Nor is it just to latter-day history to attribute, as most writers have done, this disorderly condition of an entire community to the unpopularity of the reconstruction policy of the Government.   On the contrary, upon no less an authority than Governor Wells, a native and life-long resident of Louisiana, "it is within the knowledge of all citizens resident here before the war that for years preceding the rebellion elections in the parish of Orleans were a cruel mockery of free government.   Bands of organized desperadoes, immediately preceding and during an election, committed every species of outrage upon the peaceful and unoffending citizens to intimidate them from the exercise of the inestimable privilege of freemen—the elective franchise.   A registry of 14,000 names in the days alluded to could scarcely furnish one-fourth of that number of legal votes at the polls, although 6,000 or 7,000 votes were usually returned as cast."[b]

From the distance of thirty years or more it may be safely asserted that two circumstances, perhaps three, operated to bring about the occurrences of July 30, 1866, which first specially attracted the attention of the country to the domestic affairs of Louisiana.   The first was the election in March of that year of one John T. Monroe to be mayor of the city of New Orleans, and the refusal of Major-General Canby, the military commander, to permit him to exercise the functions of that office upon the ground that he had never taken the oath of allegiance to the United States.   Although this disability was soon after removed, so that the mayor-elect assumed the office on the 15th of May, the incident occasioned much bad feeling, which increased with the action of the mayor in removing the appointees of his predecessor and supplying their places, especially on the police force, with ex-Confederate soldiers, thugs, and desperadoes.[c]   Monroe had been mayor of the city at the time of its capture and occupation by General Butler; had been always an irreconcilable; opposed to the national policy, and a recognized leader of the restless portion of the population.   General Sheridan distrusted him, and kept him and his associates under close observation. The absorbing political subject at this time was the proposed reassembling of the convention of 1864, which had framed the constitution under which the State was operating and had adjourned subject to the call of its chairman.   There was no apparent reason why this convention should reconvene; it had performed the purpose of its creation; had framed a constitution which had been adopted by the people; 52

Riots at New Orleans July 30, 1866.

---

[a] Senate Ex. Doc. No. 13, Forty-third Congress, second session.

[b] Veto message of Governor J. Madison Wells to legislature of Louisiana February 9, 1866.

[c] Testimony taken before the board of officers convened by General Baird August 1, 1866, to investigate the New Orleans riots.   (H. R. Ex. Doc. No. 68, Thirty-ninth Congress, second session, pp. 43, 151, 152, 153, 166, et seq.

of its membership of 150 had died, resigned, or removed from the State; its chairman had been appointed to a Federal judgeship.   In the midst of the excitement consequent upon an agitation of this question the chairman pro tempore of the 1864 convention, Judge Howell, issued a call reconvening that body on the 30th of July at the Mechanics' Institute in New Orleans.   The grand jury was invoked to declare this proposed assemblage an unlawful one, and found a bill of indictment against its members.   The mayor announced his intention of preventing the meeting of the body, which he denominated "an extinct convention," and of arresting its members if they attempted to assemble. This was the second and most important cause for what followed.

The third circumstance was the absence of Major-General Sheridan, the military commander of the Department of the Gulf, who had been called to Texas, another part of his military department, on pressing duty, and of Governor Wells, the chief executive of the State, who, if present in the city, was invisible for some days preceding the 30th of July.   It is in evidence that the opposition to the convention was the main topic of conversation for some weeks in and about New Orleans; that it had been proposed at first to treat it with ridicule; then to go into the convention and to control it by superior numbers; and lastly to treat it as an unlawful assemblage, and as such to break it up at all hazards.[a]   On the 25th of July the following letter was received from Mayor Monroe, and was the first intimation of the changed plans of the conspirators:

MAYORALTY OF NEW ORLEANS,
City Hall, July 25, 1866.

GENERAL: A body of men, claiming to be members of the convention of 1864, and whose avowed object is to subvert the municipal and State governments, will, I learn, assemble in this city on Monday next.

The laws and ordinances of the city, which my oath of office makes obligatory upon me to see faithfully executed, declare all assemblies calculated to disturb the public peace and tranquillity unlawful, and as such to be dispersed by the mayor, and the participants held responsible for violating the same.

It is my intention to disperse this unlawful assembly, if found within the corporate limits of the city, by arresting the members thereof and holding them accountable to existing municipal law, provided they meet without the sanction of the military authorities.

I will esteem it a favor, General, if at your earliest convenience you will inform me whether this projected meeting has your approbation, so that I may act accordingly.

I am, General, very respectfully,

JOHN T. MONROE,
Mayor.

Brevet Major-General BAIRD,
Commanding, etc.

---

[a] Report of Brevet Major-General Baird to Major-General Sheridan, August 15, 1866.

To this communication General Baird replied at some length. While remarking that the proposed assemblage had neither requested nor obtained the sanction or approbation of the military authorities for its meeting, he suggested that such an assemblage would not be contrary to the universally conceded right of all loyal citizens to meet peaceably, and discuss freely all questions concerning their civil government; that "if the assemblage has the legal right to remodel the State government it should be protected in so doing; if not, then its labors must be looked upon as a harmless pleasantry, to which no one ought to object." "If, however, the mayor is to be understood as intimating that the projected meeting is calculated to disturb the public peace and tranquillity; that the number of its opponents and the lawlessness of their character is so well established that he doubts the ability of his small force of police to control them, it will be merely necessary to call upon him (General Baird) for assistance, when not only all the troops in the city, but if necessary the entire force in his power to assemble, either upon the land or water, will be brought to his aid."[a] On the 28th General Baird was called upon by the mayor, who was accompanied by Mr. Voorhees, the lieutenant-governor of the State, who informed him that the plan of breaking up the proposed meeting by arresting its members by the city police had been abandoned, and that it was now designed to have them arrested by the sheriff upon the grand jury indictments. To this action General Baird demurred, and it was agreed that nothing should be done until he had received instructions from the Secretary of War, to whom he agreed to telegraph the situation immediately, the lieutenant-governor having already telegraphed to the President. With this the interview closed. No application was made for troops or for any military assistance, the impression left upon the mind of General Baird being that every effort would be made by the civil authorities to prevent any popular commotion; in short, so amicable was the conversation that General Baird expressed his gratification at the pleasure the interview had afforded him.[b] On their departure he dispatched the following telegram:

HEADQUARTERS DEPARTMENT OF LOUISIANA,
New Orleans, La., July 28, 1866.
Hon. E. M. STANTON,
Secretary of War, Washington, D. C.
A convention has been called, with the sanction of Governor Wells, to meet here on Monday. The lieutenant-governor and city authorities think it unlawful, and propose to break it up by arresting the delegates. I have given no orders on the subject but have warned the parties that I should not countenance or permit such an action without instructions to that effect from the President. Please instruct me by telegraph.

A. BAIRD,
Brevet Major-General, Commanding.

---

[a] Brevet Major-General Baird to Hon. John T. Monroe, mayor of New Orleans, July 26, 1866.

[b] Brevet Major-General Baird to Major-General Sheridan, August 15, 1866.

It may be observed at this juncture that to this dispatch no reply was ever received. To provide, however, for emergencies the troops at Jackson Barracks and in the upper part of the city were ordered to hold themselves in readiness on the 30th to move at a moment's notice; a steamer was directed to be ready at the barracks wharf with steam up to rush the troops up to the city, and a swift tug held as a dispatch boat. At the same time it was ordered that all soldiers be kept out of the streets; all this with the view of avoiding the excitement or attracting the attention which might be occasioned by the presence of United States troops in and about the city. The following telegraphic correspondence was passed on the 28th and 30th, and which if known to the military authorities would have had a most important bearing on their conduct, was not received at department headquarters until nearly a week later, when it was sent to General Sheridan in compliance with his request. The New Orleans papers of the 30th published the President's telegram of the 28th to Voorhees, but its vague and ambiguous language, together with the absence of any instructions for himself, warranted General Baird in doubting its authenticity:

OFFICE UNITED STATES MILITARY TELEGRAPH,
HEADQUARTERS WAR DEPARTMENT.

The following telegram received 2 p. m. July 28, 1866, from New Orleans, July 28, 1866:

President JOHNSON:

Radical mass meeting, composed mainly of large number of negroes, last night, ending in a riot. The committee of arrangements of said meeting assembling to-night. Violent and incendiary speeches made; negroes called to arm themselves; you bitterly denounced. Speakers: Field, Dostie, Hawkins, Henderson, Heirward, and others. Governor Wells arrived last night, but sides with the convention move. The whole matter before grand jury, but impossible to execute civil process without certainty of riot. Contemplated to have the members of the convention arrested under process from the criminal court of this district. Is the military to interfere to prevent process of court?

ALBERT VOORHEES,
Lieutenant-Governor of Louisiana.
ANDREW J. HERRON,
Attorney-General of Louisiana.

EXECUTIVE MANSION,
Washington, D. C., July 28, 1866—5.40 p. m.

ALBERT VOORHEES,
Lieutenant-Governor of Louisiana, New Orleans, La.:

The military will be expected to sustain and not to obstruct or interfere with the proceedings of the courts. A dispatch on the subject of the convention was sent to Governor Wells this morning.

ANDREW JOHNSON.

EXECUTIVE OFFICE,
Washington, D. C., July 28, 1866.

His Excellency Governor WELLS,
New Orleans, La.:

I have been advised that you have issued a proclamation convening the convention elected in 1864. Please inform me under and by what authority this has been done, and by what authority this convention can assume to represent the whole people of the State of Louisiana.

ANDREW JOHNSON.

OFFICE UNITED STATES MILITARY TELEGRAPH,
HEADQUARTERS WAR DEPARTMENT.

The following telegram received 8.30 p. m. July 28, 1866, from New Orleans, July 28, 1866:

President JOHNSON:

Your telegram received. I have not issued a proclamation convening the convention of 1864. This was done by the president of that body, by virtue of a resolution adjourning the convention subject to his order; and in that case also authorizing him to call on the proper officers to issue writs of election in unrepresented parishes. My proclamation is in response to that call, ordering an election on the 3d of September. As soon as vacancies can be ascertained an election will be held to fill them, when the entire State will be represented.

Your obedient servant,   J. MADISON WELLS,
                                                Governor Louisiana.

EXECUTIVE MANSION,
Washington, D. C., July 30, 1866.

ANDREW J. HERRON,
Attorney-General of Louisiana, New Orleans:

You will call on General Sheridan, or whoever may be in command, for sufficient force to sustain the civil authority in suppressing all illegal or unlawful assemblies which usurp or assume to exercise any power or authority without first having obtained the consent of the people of the State. If there is to be a convention let it be composed of delegates chosen fresh from the people of the whole State. The people must first be consulted in reference to changing the organic law of the State. Usurpation will not be tolerated. The law and the Constitution must be sustained, and thereby peace and order.

ANDREW JOHNSON.

Sunday the 29th was quiet; the city displayed less than its usual restlessness; the members of the convention appeared on the streets and moved around the hotels without attracting the slightest attention. On Monday morning, the 30th, the city papers contained the following proclamation of the mayor, which, being apparently in harmony with the agreement of the 28th, was read by General Baird with much gratification:

MAYORALTY OF NEW ORLEANS,
City Hall, July 30, 1866.

Whereas, the extinct convention of 1864 proposes meeting this day; and

Whereas, intelligence has reached me that the peace and good order of the city might be disturbed;

Now, therefore, I, John T. Monroe, mayor of the city of New Orleans, do issue this my proclamation calling upon the good people of this city to avoid with care all disturbance and collision; and I do particularly call upon the younger members of the community to act with such calmness and propriety as that the good name of the city may not be tarnished and the enemies of the reconstruction policy of President Johnson be not afforded an opportunity, so much courted by them, of creating a breach of the peace, and of falsifying facts to the great injury of the city and State. And I do further enjoin upon all good citizens to refrain from gathering in or about the place of meeting of said extinct convention, satisfied from recent dispatches from

Washington that the deliberations of the members thereof will receive no countenance from the President, and that he will sustain the agents of the present civil government and vindicate its laws and acts to the satisfaction of the good people of the city and State.

JOHN T. MONROE,

Mayor.

At 11 o'clock of the 30th the lieutenant-governor again called upon General Baird and was advised by the latter that he was still without specific instructions from Washington, but that his arrangements to preserve the peace had been well taken.   On his departure General Baird sent an officer to Jackson Barracks to bring up four companies, which, at the suggestion of the lieutenant-governor, he decided to locate near the levee on Canal street, so as to be out of the way, yet within reach if needed.   It was now about 12 o'clock, and General Baird left his office and drove to the house of Judge Howell to consult with him as to any protection he might require, but learning that he had already gone to the meeting, he returned to his office.   Here he found the following letter from Lieutenant-Governor Voorhees:

NEW ORLEANS, *July 30, 1866.*

SIR: I am informed that squads of the colored population are going about in the Third district of the city; that they have abandoned their work, and that others are coming into the city also from the upper part and from Jefferson.   How reliable this news is, or, at least, to what extent, I can not say positively.   At all events, I would suggest that an inquiry be made.   The colored population is not answerable for these things, for, goaded as they are by inflammatory appeals to their passions and prejudices, it is astonishing that they have not already fallen into excesses.

After leaving you I called upon the mayor, who was pleased to hear what cooperation he could have from the military department.   As a measure of prudence it would be well, should you, however, concur in this view, to have a military force disseminated throughout the city to act in concert with the city police, but by all means in the vicinity of Mechanics' Institute.

At this very moment my messenger comes in and brings the information that a large number of freedmen are at the Mechanics' Hall and that a great number of white people are in the vicinity.   The excitement is increasing.   The appearance of soldiers, with policemen, at this moment would be very beneficial.

I remain, very respectfully, your obedient servant,

ALBERT VOORHEES,

Lieutenant-Governor, Louisiana.

Major-General BAIRD,

    New Orleans.

Meanwhile, some 25 members of the convention had arrived at the Mechanics' Institute, which is on Dryades street, between Canal and Common, and, the hour of 12 noon having arrived, were called to order, but no quorum being present, a recess of one hour was taken.   The galleries and halls of the building were not crowded—perhaps 150 men altogether, mostly colored men; in Dryades street, in front of the institute, were a few colored men, women, and children—not more than 20—

drawn thither by curiosity.   What followed is from the dispatch of General Sheridan of August 6 to the President:

About 1 p. m. a procession of, say, from 60 to 130 colored men marched up Burgundy street and across Canal street, toward the convention, carrying an American flag.   These men had about one pistol to every 10 men, and canes and clubs in addition.   While crossing Canal street a row occurred.   There were many spectators on the street, and their manner and tone toward the procession unfriendly.   A shot was fired, by whom I am not able to state, but believe it to have been by a policeman, or some colored man in the procession.   This led to other shots, and a rush after the procession.   On arrival at the front of the institute there was some throwing of brickbats by both sides.   The police, who had been held well in hand, were vigorously marched to the scene of disorder.   The procession entered the institute with the flag, about six or eight remaining outside.   A row occurred between a policeman and one of these colored men, and a shot was again fired by one of the parties, which led to an indiscriminate fire on the building through the windows by the policemen.   This had been going on for a short time, when a white flag was displayed from the windows of the institute, whereupon the firing ceased and the police rushed into the building.

From the testimony of wounded men and others who were inside the building, the policemen opened an indiscriminate fire upon the audience until they had emptied their revolvers, when they retired, and those inside barricaded the doors. The door was broken in and the firing again commenced, when many of the colored and white people either escaped out through the door or were passed out by the policemen inside; but as they came out the policemen who formed the circle nearest the building fired upon them, and they were again fired upon by the citizens that formed the outer circle.   Many of those wounded and taken prisoners, and others who were prisoners and not wounded, were fired upon by their captors and by citizens.   The wounded were stabbed while lying on the ground, and their heads beaten with brickbats in the yard of the building, whither some of the colored men had escaped and partially secreted themselves.   They were fired upon and killed or wounded by policemen.   Some were killed and wounded several squares from the scene.   Members of the convention were wounded by the policemen while in their hands as prisoners—some of them mortally.

Less guarded in language, if more graphic in expression, is the report of the special committee of Congress that visited New Orleans in December for the purpose of making a thorough investigation of the riots.   They say (p. 10):

The committee examined 74 persons as to the facts of violence and bloodshed upon that day.   It is in evidence that men who were in the hall, terrified by the merciless attacks of the armed police, sought safety by jumping from the windows, a distance of 20 feet, to the ground, and as they jumped were shot by police or citizens.   Some, disfigured by wounds, fought their way downstairs to the street, to be shot or beaten to death on the pavement.   Colored persons, at distant points in the city, peaceably pursuing their lawful business, were attacked by the police, shot, and cruelly beaten. Men of character and position, some of whom were members and some spectators of the convention, escaped from the hall covered with wounds and blood, and were preserved almost by miracle from death.   Scores of colored citizens bear frightful scars, more numerous than many soldiers of a dozen well-fought fields can show— proofs of fearful danger and strange escape; men were shot while waving handkerchiefs in token of surrender and submission; white men and black, with arms uplifted praying for life, were answered by shot and blow from knife and club; the bodies of some were "pounded to a jelly;" a colored man was dragged from under a street crossing and killed at a blow; men concealed in outhouses and among piles of lumber were eagerly sought for and slaughtered or maimed without remorse; the dead bodies upon the street were violated by shot, kick, and stab; the face of a man "just breathing his last" was gashed by a knife or razor in the hands of a woman; "an old, gray-haired man," peaceably walking the street at a distance from the institute, was shot through the head; negroes were taken out of their houses and shot; a policeman riding in a buggy deliberately fired his revolver from the carriage into a crowd of colored men; a colored man, 2 miles away from the convention hall, was taken from his shop by the police, at about 4 o'clock on the afternoon of the riot, and shot and wounded in side, hip, and back; one man was wounded by fourteen blows, shots, and stabs; the body of another received seven pistol balls. After the slaughter had measurably ceased, carts, wagons, and drays, driven through the streets, gathered the dead, the dying, and the wounded in "promiscuous loads," a policeman, in some cases, riding in the wagon seated upon the living men beneath him.

The result of the encounter is reported by Assistant Surgeon Hartsuff, U. S. Army, from those found on the streets and in the hospitals, to have been 38 killed, 48 severely and 99 slightly wounded. Many more known to have been wounded were hid by their relatives, and a larger number known to have fled from the city.

It was nearly half past 2 when the troops arrived in the city, and the shooting had then been over for some time. They were quickly moved up Canal street to Dryades and proceeded at once to clear the street of the crowds that were pouring into it from all directions. It was then that General Baird first learned of the atrocities that had been perpetrated, and of the scarcely credible fact that the police themselves had led the riot. Conceiving it to be his first duty to take that force in hand and hold it to a strict accountability, there being great excitement and further outbreaks probable, he proclaimed martial law and took military possession of the city. As he testified later before a committee of Congress, "there was nothing else to be done." The following is the order:

GENERAL ORDERS, }   HEADQUARTERS DEPARTMENT OF LOUISIANA,
    No. 60.   }   *New Orleans, La., July 30, 1866.*

In consequence of the notorious and unlawful proceedings of to-day, martial law is proclaimed in the city of New Orleans. Brevet Maj. Gen. A. V. Kautz is appointed military governor of the city. He will make his headquarters in the city hall, and his orders will be minutely obeyed in every particular.

All civil functionaries will report at once to General Kautz and will be instructed by him with regard to such duties as they may be hereafter required to perform.

By order of Bvt. Maj. Gen. A. Baird:

NATHANIEL BURBANK,
First Lieutenant, Acting Assistant Adjutant-General.

The same evening (Monday, 30th) the sheriff came to General Baird with a warrant for the arrest of certain members of the convention, and upon this the General indorsed: "The sheriff will withhold action on this writ until further orders." This fact was at once telegraphed by Attorney-General Herron to the President, with the result that the following instructions were sent on the 1st of August:

[Telegram.]

EXECUTIVE OFFICE,
Washington, D. C., August 1, 1866.

Maj. Gen. ABSALOM BAIRD,
  Commanding, etc., New Orleans, La.:

You will not interpose any obstacle in the way of the civil authorities, but render whatever aid may be required by them for the preservation of the public peace.

The foregoing telegram is transmitted to you by order of the President. You will acknowledge its receipt.

E. D. TOWNSEND,
Assistant Adjutant-General.

On receipt of these instructions General Baird sent for the writ and wrote below his former indorsement: "The necessity for the above order having ceased to exist, no further impediment will be placed in the way of executing the writ." In consequence of this the arrests were soon after made.

General Sheridan arrived at New Orleans on the 1st of August and resumed command. Having investigated the affair of the 30th, he made the following telegraphic report to Washington, which he supplemented by another on the 2d and again on the 3d. To these are added the instructions of General Grant, dated 6 p. m. of the 3d:

OFFICE UNITED STATES MILITARY TELEGRAPH,
HEADQUARTERS, WAR DEPARTMENT.

The following telegram received in cipher, 6.15 p. m., August 1, 1866, from New Orleans, La., August 1, 1866:

U. S. GRANT, General:

You are doubtless aware of the serious riot which occurred in this city on the 30th. A political body styling themselves the convention of 1864 met on the 30th for, as it is alleged, the purpose of remodeling the present constitution of the State. The leaders were political agitators and revolutionary men, and the action of the convention was liable to produce breaches of the public peace. I had made up my mind to arrest the head men if the proceedings of the convention were calculated to disturb the tranquillity of the department, but I had no cause for action until they committed the overt act. In the meantime official duty called me to Texas, and the mayor of the city during my absence suppressed the convention by the use of the police force, and in so doing attacked the members of the convention and a party of 200 negroes with firearms, clubs, and knives in a manner so unnecessary and atrocious as to compel me to say that it was murder. About 40 whites and blacks were thus killed and about 160 wounded. Everything is now quiet, but I deem it best to maintain a military supremacy in the city for a few days until the affair is fully investigated. I believe the sentiment of the general community is great regret at this unnecessary cruelty, and that the police could have made any arrest they saw fit without sacrificing lives.

P. H. SHERIDAN,
Major-General, Commanding.

OFFICE UNITED STATES MILITARY TELEGRAPH,
HEADQUARTERS, WAR DEPARTMENT.

The following telegram received in cipher, 6 p. m., August 2, 1866, from New Orleans, La., August 2, 1866:

Gen. U. S. GRANT, *Washington, D. C.:*

The more information I obtain of the affair of the 30th in this city the more revolting it becomes. It was no riot; it was an absolute massacre by the police, which was not excelled in murderous cruelty by that of Fort Pillow. It was a murder which the mayor and police of this city perpetrated without the shadow of a necessity; furthermore, I believe it was premeditated, and every indication points to this. I recommend the removing of this bad man. I believe it would be hailed with the sincerest gratification by two-thirds of the population of the city. There has been a feeling of insecurity on the part of the people here on account of this man, which is now so much increased that the safety of life and property does not rest with the civil authorities, but with the military.

P. H. SHERIDAN,
Major-General, Commanding.

OFFICE UNITED STATES MILITARY TELEGRAPH,
HEADQUARTERS, WAR DEPARTMENT.

The following telegram received in cipher, 10 p. m., August 3, 1866, from New Orleans, La., August 3, 1866:

Gen. U. S. GRANT, *Washington, D. C.:*

I have the honor to report quiet in the city, but considerable excitement in the public mind. There is no interference on the part of the military with the civil government, which performs all its duties without hindrance.

I have permitted the retention of the military governor appointed during my absence, as it gives confidence and enables the military to know what is occurring in the city. He does not interfere with civil matters.

Unless good judgment is exercised there will be an exodus of Northern capital and Union men, which will be injurious to the city and to the country. I will remove the military governor in a day or two. I again strongly advise that some disposition be made to change the present mayor, as I believe it would do more to restore confidence than anything that could be done. If the present governor could be changed also it would not be amiss.

P. H. SHERIDAN,
Major-General, Commanding.

HEADQUARTERS ARMIES OF THE UNITED STATES,
Washington, D. C., August 3, 1866.

Major-General SHERIDAN, *New Orleans, La.:*

Continue to enforce martial law so far as may be necessary to preserve the peace, and do not allow any of the civil authorities to act if you deem such action dangerous to the public safety. Lose no time in investigating and reporting the causes that led to the riot, and the facts which occurred.

U. S. GRANT,
General.

The persons arrested by the military were subsequently released without trial; the grand jury exculpated the city government and threw the onus of responsibility for the affair upon the convention.

The lieutenant-governor, the attorney-general, and the mayor of New Orleans united in an exhaustive report to the President, in which they claimed that they had used every possible effort to prevent trouble on the 30th of July; that they had been in constant communication with the military authorities, but that their efforts could not counteract the incendiary counsels of those who for sinister purposes had in end this very result in order to reap a political harvest.[a] In December a committee appointed by the House of Representatives visited New Orleans, and having made a thorough investigation of the affair of July 30 reported on the 11th of February, 1867, that in the opinion of the majority of the committee "the condition of affairs in Louisiana requires temporary establishment of a provisional government."[b] The reconstruction bill, which had been under debate during the entire second session of the Thirty-ninth Congress, passed on the 2d of March, 1867, and under its provisions Louisiana was joined with Texas to form the fifth military district.

While domestic disturbances and disorders within the limits of Louisiana were by no means wholly suppressed during the following three years, the changed conditions were so entirely

The reconstruction period, 1867–1868.

novel in the experience of both the Federal and State governments that a different line of conduct was both necessary and expedient. The State being under military government, the military authorities were under obligations to preserve the peace at all times and under all circumstances, either with or without the concurrence of the civil officers. Among the first acts of General Sheridan, who had been assigned to the command of the Fifth Military District, was the summary removal of Attorney-General Herron, Mayor Monroe, and Judge Abell of the district court of New Orleans, all of whom he regarded as responsible for the riots of July 30, 1866. On the 3d of June he removed Governor Wells, as being an impediment to the faithful execution of the act of March 2, 1867, and appointed B. F. Flanders as his successor. Subsequently he removed the city treasurer, the chief of police, surveyor, attorney, and twenty-two members of the board of aldermen for similar reasons. As a result of this energetic policy, which was not in accord with that of the President, General Sheridan was relieved from the command of the Fifth Military District on the 17th of August and General Hancock appointed in his place. A constitutional convention in which the entire people were represented met at New Orleans on the 23d of November and continued in session until the 9th of March, 1868, and under its provisions an election took place on the 17th and 18th of April, at which the new constitution was adopted by a small majority, and Henry C. Warmoth, Republican, elected governor. In the meanwhile, General Hancock was relieved from the command and was succeeded by the senior officer in the department, Brevet Maj. Gen. R. C. Buchanan. On the 25th of June, 1868, the act of Congress for the

---

[a] H. R. Ex. Doc. No. 68, Thirty-ninth Congress, second session, p. 14.
[b] H. R. Report No. 16, Thirty-ninth Congress, second session, 596 pages.

readmission of the Southern States became a law, and Louisiana being restored to her status as it existed before the act of secession, this fact was announced to the people in orders from military headquarters, as follows:

SPECIAL ORDERS,   HEADQUARTERS FIFTH MILITARY DEPARTMENT,
No. 154.   *New Orleans, La., July 13, 1868.*

*   *   *   *   *   *   *

2. The commanding general having been officially notified of the ratification of the fourteenth article of amendment to the Constitution of the United States by the legislature of the State of Louisiana on the 9th instant, it becomes his duty, under the act of Congress which became a law June 25, 1868, and the orders of the General of the Army, to announce to the people of the State and to the troops under his command that the provisions of the reconstruction acts of Congress cease to operate in Louisiana from this date. Military authority will no longer be exercised under the reconstruction acts in said State, and all officers commanding posts or detachments are forbidden to interfere in civil affairs, unless upon a proper application by the civil authorities *to preserve the peace,* or under instructions duly received from the commanding general of the district. Military law no longer exists; the civil law is supreme.

*   *   *   *   *   *   *

The commanding general can not sever the relations heretofore existing between the State and himself without congratulating the people upon an event which fully restores Louisiana to her former position among the other States of the Union and to all her rights under the Constitution.

Peace and quiet marked the late election, showing the softening influences of mutual forbearance. Should such forbearance animate the councils of the State, the era of kind feeling will return and the highest prosperity of the people will be attained.

That this may be the result under the guidance of a merciful Providence is his devout and earnest prayer. May her restoration to the benefits of our beloved Union mark the commencement of a new era of prosperity and happiness for her people. * * *

By command of Brevet Maj. Gen. R. C. Buchanan:

THOS. H. NEILL,
Major Twentieth Infantry, Brevet Brigadier-General, U. S. A., A. A. A. G.

These pleasing anticipations, however, were not destined to be immediately realized. It was inevitable, in the disorganized condition of society which accompanied the violent transition through which these States had been passing for more than eight years, that intense partisan feelings should have developed and that the lawless elements should come to the surface. Scarcely had the felicitous congratulations of General Buchanan reached the communities to whom they were addressed, when information came from the upper parishes of outrages, assassinations, and destruction of property exceeding in horror and barbarity the worst days of the rebellion. On the 10th of July the governor received a petition from northern Louisiana for relief and protection, in which it was asserted that more than 50 murders had occurred during the past few days in Franklin County alone. These papers he at once laid before the legislature, with the result that a resolution was passed calling upon the President of the United States for the assistance

Outrages in Franklin County, July, 1868.

guaranteed by the Constitution, it being alleged that the courts were powerless to execute the laws in the disturbed districts. This was forwarded to Washington by a messenger, accompanied by a letter from the governor, in which he remarked:

From the very best information, Mr. President, I have no doubt that 150 men have been murdered in Louisiana in the last month and a half. Startling as this statement is, letters of the most reliable character fully confirm it.

*   *   *   *   *   *   *

It has now transpired that the mob which threatened the legislature some weeks since were only prevented from enacting it on the 30th of July, 1866, by the presence of United States troops.

It was a deliberate determination of this secret organization to assassinate the lieutenant-governor and the speaker of the house of representatives for having decided questions, preliminary to the organization of the general assembly, in a manner obnoxious to them. There are military organizations on foot in this city under the auspices of this secret organization. They drill openly in our streets at night, or in halls, easily to be seen.

In short, I fully believe that there is meditated a bloody revolution, certainly the fruit of which would be a long-continued if not hopeless confusion and disaster and ruin to the State. The presence of the United States troops, in my judgment, is necessary to prevent this. The organization of militia is of very questionable expediency, inasmuch as it will be, under the present excited state of mind, one political party armed to the support of the government against another. I wish to avert this, if possible, and respectfully request your Excellency to put two regiments of cavalry, a regiment of infantry, together with a battery of artillery, under the command of some competent officer, with orders to cooperate with me in repressing disorder and violence, arresting criminals, and protecting the officers of the law in trying them. The breaking up of all secret political organizations and a few examples of condign punishment of offenders will secure peace in the State as soon as the excitement attending the present campaign is over.

As a result of this appeal, General Buchanan was instructed by General Grant to maintain such a disposition of his troops that they might be ready to act without delay on the receipt of the President's order, and calling his attention to the conditions under which the military forces of the United States may be employed to suppress insurrections and domestic violence against the government of any State, as expressed in section 4, article IV of the Constitution, as well as in the acts of February 28, 1795, and March 3, 1807.[a] As a consequence of these instructions, General Buchanan, in orders of September 1, 1868, thus defined the official relations between military commanders and United States marshals and the sheriffs of parishes and counties and the conditions under which assistance was to be rendered them.[62]

The sheriff, being a State officer usually appointed for a particular county or parish, is restricted in the execution of his duties to the territorial limits of such county or parish. His right to require the assistance of the posse comitatus is supreme within such limits. He is therefore authorized, in cases of unlawful resistance to his authority clearly shown to exist, to require the assistance of any troops serving within his

---

[a] Adjutant-General Townsend to General Buchanan, August 10, 1868.

district.   In such cases the military commander will be required to render the assistance called for; provided, that in the exercise of a sound discretion he is satisfied that the necessity for such service exists.   But should he not be thoroughly satisfied of this, he will decline to act until he can make a report to and receive special instructions from these headquarters in each case.

The official relations of military commanders and United States marshals are to be defined as follows: The marshal, being a United States officer, is acting under the same authority as that which governs the military commander himself, and his district being ordinarily restricted to the limits of the State, his authority to call for the assistance of troops in cases arising out of a resistance to the laws of the United States is coextensive with the limits of such State.   He will, therefore, have a right to call upon any military commander within his district for such assistance as the nature of the case may require, but the military commander will, as before indicated, exercise a sound discretion in deciding upon the necessity for the use of his troops.

In no case is it deemed proper to consider a mere riotous demonstration as a case calling for the interposition of the military forces, which should not be displayed until it shall be absolutely necessary for them to act.[a]

During the succeeding months several cases of riotous disturbances occurred both in New Orleans and in the interior parishes, and many calls were made for military assistance.   On the night of the 12th of September all the troops within reach were brought into the city upon a requisition of Governor Warmoth to prevent an apprehended attack upon a political procession, and again on the 22d of that month another serious disturbance occurred in the streets of New Orleans, during which five persons were killed and a large building attacked and set on fire before the troops could be brought to the scene.   This occasioned the issuing of the following proclamation:

EXECUTIVE DEPARTMENT, STATE OF LOUISIANA,
New Orleans, September 25, 1868.

I call upon the good people of New Orleans to at once repair to their residence and abstain from any exciting acts or conversation.   The civil authorities are capable of suppressing any difficulties that may arise and arresting any offenders, or, if found inefficient, will be promptly assisted by the military.

I call upon all political clubs to abstain from any display whatever for the present.

H. C. WARMOTH,
Governor of Louisiana.

On the 28th occurred the climax of an affair that had been brooding for some weeks in the parish of St. Landry between the hostile bands of extreme political partisans.   Upon a rumor that the editor of the leading Republican paper had been murdered several bands of armed negroes collected in the county and marched upon the town of Opelousas.   The citizens went out to meet them, and a fight ensued in which several persons were killed on each side.   Another similar affair

Conflicts in St. Landry and St. Bernard parishes.

occurred on the 26th of October in the parish of St. Bernard, in which a family of whites were murdered and their house burned, and in the resulting affray eight or ten negroes were killed and perhaps twice as many wounded.

---

[a] Circular No. 2, Department of Louisiana, New Orleans, September 1, 1868.

Again were the State authorities compelled to admit their inability to preserve the peace or to bring the offenders to justice. On the 26th of October the governor made the following appeal to General Rousseau, who had succeeded General Buchanan in the command of the department:

Maj. Gen. L. H. ROUSSEAU,
  Commanding Department of Louisiana:
  The evidence is conclusive that the civil authorities in the parishes of Orleans, Jefferson, and St. Bernard are unable to preserve order and protect the lives and property of the people. The act of Congress prohibiting the organization of the militia in this State strips me of all power to sustain them in the discharge of their duties, and I am compelled to appeal to you to take charge of the peace of these parishes and use your forces to that end. If you respond favorably to my request, I will at once order the sheriffs and police forces to report to you for orders.
    Very respectfully, your obedient servant,
                    HENRY C. WARMOTH,
                      Governor of Louisiana.

This was forwarded at once to Washington with request for instructions, and General Rousseau was informed that he was "authorized and expected to take such action as may be necessary to preserve the peace and good order and to protect the lives and property of citizens."[a]

The following two years were marked by comparative quiet throughout the State, so that the troops were gradually withdrawn, a strong force being maintained at New Orleans and the river forts. If this quiet was occasionally interrupted by the political quarrels that were constantly arising between two factions of the dominant party, the fact that they were encouraged by the minority party, as it would see in the situation, from time to time, an apparent advantage to itself, created a situation that prevented, for a time at least, any serious outbreak. In 1871 these factions were divided between the supporters and the opponents of the governor, H. C. Warmoth, and from the opening of the legislature, in January, there was more or less bad feeling, manifested principally by occasional affrays in the interior parishes. In July the calling of a Republican convention, to be held at the custom-house in New Orleans on the 9th of August, was the occasion for the development of this feeling, which culminated in the organized assembling of large bodies of the factions at the capital for several days before the one appointed for the meeting. Early in the morning of the 9th of August from 3,000 to 5,000 excited whites and blacks, many of them armed, had collected about the custom-house, and so threatening was the situation that, in order to preserve the peace, the department commander (General Emory) ordered the troops from the barracks to march to the scene. Three companies of infantry, numbering perhaps 150 officers and men, with two Gatling guns, made their way

Riots
at New Orleans,
1871-72.

---

[a] Secretary of War Schofield to Brevet Major-General Rousseau, October 26, 1868.

through a howling crowd and occupied the custom-house. The disputants then separated, one party withdrawing to a hall in another part of the city, and order was restored.[a] With the assembling of the legislature, on the 1st of January, 1872, the war of the factions was resumed with increased bitterness. The building occupied as a State capitol was surrounded by an excited crowd exasperated to a high degree by the presence of an armed police force, which had been called into existence by the governor, and urged on by the disorderly element of the city. Within, the majority faction had proceeded to unseat its opponents, to depose their leader, the speaker of the house, and to expel the latter from the building. The ex-speaker (Carter) and his supporters, aggregating very nearly a quorum of the legislature, assembled in another hall, and were guarded by armed bodies of their adherents, who hastened to New Orleans from all sections of the State. Each of these rival bodies sent out sergeants-at-arms to coerce the attendance of their opponents in sufficient numbers to constitute a quorum. Many arrests were made on both sides, and in the resistance to arrest several people were wounded and one member·was killed. On the 20th of January Carter issued a proclamation declaring his intention to take forcible possession of the capitol building, and two days later he appeared on Canal street at the head of several thousand men, many of them armed, with the avowed purpose of carrying out his threat. The governor assembled his armed police force, and with a mob behind him of several thousand, defied him. Again did the threatening situation demand the interposition of the Federal troops for the preservation of the peace, and again did the timely interference of General Emory prevent an outbreak at a moment when bloodshed was imminent. The arrival of a committee of Congress at this juncture prompted a compromise, and the legislature continued its session until its expiration by limitation, on the 1st of March.[b]

The political excitement continued with more or less intensity throughout the year. Both factions of the Republican party held conventions; the Warmoth wing nominating William Pitt Kellogg for governor; another wing nominating P. B. S. Pinchback, a colored man of some ability and then lieutenant-governor of the State, while a third, made up of liberal Republicans and Democrats nominated John McEnery for governor and D. B. Penn for lieutenant-governor. Pinchback subsequently withdrew and assumed to turn over his strength to Kellogg. The returning board, of which Governor Warmoth was the chairman, and all the other members his appointees, declared that the ticket of which McEnery was the head had received

---

[a] General Emory to Adjutant-General, August 9, 1871.

[b] Report of select committee to investigate the condition of affairs in Louisiana, H. R. Report No. 92, Forty-second Congress, second session; H. R. Misc. Doc. No. 211, Forty-second Congress, second session.

a majority of the votes and was elected; while another board, of which John Lynch was the chairman, and whose legality had been maintained by the United States court, declared the election of Kellogg and the legislative ticket behind him. The members of the legislature whose elections were certified by the Lynch board, met at the building occupied as the State capitol—the Mechanic's Institute—on the 9th of December, with Lieutenant-Governor Pinchback in the chair; suspended Governor Warmoth from office pending his trial upon impeachment charges "for high crimes and misdemeanors," and directed Pinchback to assume the vacancy. To this proceeding Governor Warmoth paid no attention other than to maintain his official position supported by his armed police. The Pinchback legislature then passed resolutions calling upon the President for the protection accorded the States under the Constitution, which Pinchback at once telegraphed to Washington.[65] The members of the legislature whose elections had been certified by the Warmoth board met at the city hall of New Orleans, which the governor by a proclamation declared to be "the statehouse," on the 11th, and were recognized by the governor as the legal body. At the same time Warmoth telegraphed the President for a suspension of action pending the arrival of a committee then on its way to lay all the facts before him.[66] A similar dispatch was also sent by McEnery.[70] On the 12th the President, upon information sent him from reliable persons in New Orleans, recognized Pinchback as the lawful governor, and the body assembled at Mechanic's Institute as the legal legislature.[69] Pinchback had removed General Campbell from the command of the State militia, composed of white men exclusively, and appointed Gen. James Longstreet in his place; but although Longstreet was exceedingly popular with the white militia, they refused to recognize or to obey him. They were then ordered to surrender their arms, and on their refusal to do so, Pinchback's police, composed almost wholly of colored men, were ordered to disarm them. On the 13th these two bodies confronted each other; the militia numbering about 500, fully armed, and possessing four field pieces, stationed themselves at the State armory and arsenal, which building the armed police force were ordered to take. The militia announced their willingness to surrender to the United States troops, but defied the police. In this juncture General Emory telegraphed to the War Department for instructions,[72] and was directed to use all necessary force to preserve the peace and to recognize the authority of Governor Pinchback.[73] On the receipt of this, General Emory sent one of his aides to the armory asking its evacuation and the dispersion of the armed forces.[74] This was promptly complied with,[a] and thus for the third time within eighteen

---

[a] Message of the President, January 13, 1873, relative to the condition of affairs in Louisiana. H. R. Ex. Doc. No. 91, Forty-second Congress, second session.

months the passive interposition of the Federal military authority, operated to prevent an outbreak that would have unquestionably resulted in a civil, if not a race, war in Louisiana.

Meanwhile the committee of citizens had reached Washington and laid their case before the President. He declared his unwillingness to further interfere, upon the ground that Congress was in session, and was about to investigate the affairs of the State. He, however, saw no reason why the legislature, which had been recognized by Governor Warmoth, should not continue its meetings in order to preserve its status, and to that end declined to furnish troops upon the request of Governor Pinchback, to disperse that assemblage, so long as it did not attempt to obstruct the administration of the recognized government of the State.[a] In a special message to Congress, dated February 25, 1873, the President explains his position. "Different persons," he remarks, "are claiming the executive offices, two bodies are claiming to be the legislative assembly of the State, and the confusion and uncertainty produced in this way fall with paralyzing effect upon all its interests. * * * Two bodies of persons claimed to be the returning board for the State, and the circuit court in that case decided that the one to which Lynch belonged, usually designated by his name, was the lawful returning board; and this decision has been repeatedly affirmed by the district and supreme courts of the State. Having no opportunity or power to canvass the votes, and the exigencies of the case demanding an immediate decision, I conceived it to be my duty to recognize those persons as elected who received and held their credentials to office from what then appeared to me to be, and has since been decided by the supreme court of the State to be, the legal returning board.

"Conformably to the decisions of this board a full set of State officers has been installed and a legislative assembly organized, constituting, if not a *de jure* at least a *de facto* government, which, since some time in December last, has had possession of the offices and been exercising the usual powers of government; but opposed to this has been another government claiming to control the affairs of the State, and which has, to some extent, been *pro forma* organized.

"Recent investigation into said election has developed so many frauds and forgeries as to make it doubtful what candidates received a majority of the votes actually cast, and in view of these facts a variety of action has been proposed. I have no specific recommendation to make upon the subject, but if there is any practical way of removing these difficulties by legislation, then I earnestly request that such action may be taken at the present session of Congress."

The President goes on to say that while it is the province of the Congress to judge of the election and qualification of the members of

---

a Secretary Belknap to General Sherman, January 5, 1873.

its respective Houses, it seems to him that the decisions of State judicial tribunals as to State offices, filled and held under State laws, ought to be respected. "I am extremely anxious," he concludes, "to avoid any appearance of undue interference in State affairs, and if Congress differs from me as to what ought to be done, I respectfully urge its immediate decision to that effect; otherwise I shall feel obliged, as far as I can by the exercise of legitimate authority, to put an end to the unhappy controversy which disturbs the peace and prostrates the business of Louisiana, by the recognition and support of that government which is recognized and upheld by the courts of the State."[a]

The rival legislatures met at New Orleans on the 7th of January, 1873, and each organized and proceeded to business. There was a general suspension of business; the city was crowded with excited people, but the United States troops from the barracks were stationed at several points in readiness to preserve order, and no serious disturbance occurred. On the 14th, the day appointed for the inauguration of the governor, there was another excited crowd and a complete cessation of business; the Metropolitan police, fully armed and accompanied by Gatling guns, surrounded Mechanics' Institute; armed bodies of whites and blacks paraded the streets. Kellogg took the oath of office as governor at noonday at the Mechanics' Institute, and at the same hour in Lafayette Square the same oath was administered to McEnery. Again the United States troops occupied every point of vantage, and though the situation was a grave one and a conflict between the excited people momentarily expected, the day passed without any outbreak.[b] For many months the State was practically in a condition of anarchy; so much so that a mass meeting of the best citizens of New Orleans on the 1st of March passed resolutions calling on the General Government to withdraw its support of the Kellogg government, or else place the State under martial law pending a new reconstruction. On the 6th of March a body of armed police arrested the members of the McEnery legislature, placed them between files of guards, and marched them to prison. In the river parishes there was constant disorder. Predatory bands of colored men rode about burning houses and threatening murder and outrage, while other bodies of idle white men pursued them or engaged in similar amusement on their own account. A band of some 300 negroes seized the town of Colfax about the 1st of April; they were moved upon by the sheriff with a posse of some 150 white men; an engagement ensued in which about 60 were killed on both sides and the court-house and its contents entirely consumed. Outbreaks followed everywhere throughout the State. The governor called for assistance and troops were sent to Colfax, but order had been restored before their arrival. In St. Martins Parish

---

[a] Message of the President, February 25, 1873, upon the condition of affairs in Louisiana. (Senate Ex. Doc. No. 47, Forty-second Congress, third session.)
[b] Documents 75 to 80.

the inhabitants refused to pay taxes to the Kellogg government; to enforce their collection the Metropolitan police were sent to the scene armed with rifles and fieldpieces; the people fortified themselves and successfully resisted the police for several weeks, or until the arrival of United States troops on the 1st of May, when they surrendered to the latter without offering the slightest resistance, and dispersed to their homes. They stated that " while they bowed to the mandate of the United States, they were in arms to prove that throughout Louisiana no official of the Kellogg government could extort submission from the people save at the point of the bayonet in the hands of United States soldiers." Unable to suppress these increasing disorders, the governor (Kellogg) again called on the President for aid under the constitutional guaranty. The latter, as he had intimated in his message of February 25, instructed General Emory to continue to recognize Governor Kellogg, and on the 22d of May issued the usual proclamation giving all turbulent and disorderly persons twenty days in which to disperse and retire peaceably to their homes. The proclamation was as follows:

BY THE PRESIDENT OF THE UNITED STATES OF AMERICA.

A PROCLAMATION.

Whereas, under the pretense that William P. Kellogg, the present executive of Louisiana, and the officers associated with him in the State administration were not duly elected, certain turbulent and disorderly persons have combined together with force and arms to resist the laws and constituted authorities of said State; and

Whereas, it has been duly certified by the proper local authorities, and judicially determined by the inferior and supreme courts of said State, that said officers are entitled to hold their offices respectively, and execute and discharge the functions thereof; and

Whereas, Congress, at its late session, upon a due consideration of the subject, tacitly recognized the said executive and his associates then, as now, in office, by refusing to take any action with respect thereto; and

Whereas, it is provided in the Constitution of the United States that the United States shall protect every State in this Union, on application of the legislature, or of the executive when the legislature can not be convened, against domestic violence; and

Whereas, it is provided in the laws of the United States that in all cases of insurrection in any State, or of obstruction to the laws thereof, it shall be lawful for the President of the United States, on application of the legislature of such State, or of the executive when the legislature can not be convened, to call forth the militia of any other State or States, or to employ such part of the land and naval forces as shall be judged necessary for the purpose of suppressing such insurrection or causing the laws to be duly executed; and

Whereas, the legislature of said State is not now in session, and can not be convened in time to meet the present emergency; and the executive of said State, under section 4 of Article IV of the Constitution of the United States, and the laws passed in pursuance thereof, has therefore made application to me for such part of the military force of the United States as may be necessary and adequate to protect said State and the citizens thereof against domestic violence and to enforce the due execution of the laws; and

Whereas, it is required that whenever it may be necessary, in the judgment of the President, to use the military force for the purpose aforesaid, he shall forthwith, by proclamation, command such insurgents to disperse and retire peaceably to their respective homes within a limited time:

Now, therefore, I, Ulysses S. Grant, President of the United States, do hereby make proclamation and command said turbulent and disorderly persons to disperse and retire peaceably to their respective abodes within twenty days from this date, and hereafter to submit themselves to the laws and constituted authorities of said State; and I invoke the aid and cooperation of all good citizens thereof to uphold law and preserve the public peace.

In witness whereof, I have hereunto set my hand and caused the seal of the United States to be affixed.

Done at the city of Washington, this 22d day of May, in the year of our Lord eighteen hundred and seventy-three and of the Independence of the United States the ninety-seventh.

[SEAL.]   U. S. GRANT.

By the President:

    J. C. BANCROFT DAVIS,

        Acting Secretary of State.

This tended to relieve the situation of one of its most embarrassing features, inasmuch as McEnery, with whose cause the large portion of the white community were in sympathy, published an address counseling the people to abstain from futile resistance to the General Government and await the action of Congress. This advice was generally complied with in New Orleans, but the disorders in the river parishes continued with scarcely an abatement. In August, 1874, the

The Coushatta tragedy, August 28, 1874.

the village of Coushatta, in Red River Parish, became the scene of a tragedy that rivaled the deeds of 1866. Amid the conflicting accounts that were elicited by various investigating committees it is difficult to arrive at the truth; but it seems to be agreed that on the 28th of August a body of white men, armed and mounted, assembled at the town of Coushatta for the purpose of compelling the officers of that parish to resign. The sheriff assembled a posse of whites and blacks to resist them. This posse of 65 men were attacked by a largely superior force and overpowered, some eight or ten on both sides being killed in the affray, and surrendered on the condition that their lives would be spared. The following day the objectionable officials (Twitchell, tax collector and postmaster; Dewees, supervisor De Soto Parish; Holland, supervisor Red River Parish; Howell, parish attorney; Edgerton, sheriff, and Willis, justice of the peace, all white men) were bound together, two and two, and conducted by an armed guard to a plantation just over the parish line, where they were set upon, thus bound and unarmed, and deliberately murdered. Their bodies were buried where they fell.[a] The prominence given this outrage by the press was the signal for another reign of terror in Louisiana.

---

[a] Proclamation of Governor Kellogg, September 3, 1874; report of Capt. A. W. Allyn, Sixteenth Infantry, to General Emory, dated Colfax, La., September 3, 1874. (Senate Ex. Doc., No. 13, Forty-Third Congress, second session, p. 17.)

On Monday, September 14, at about 11 a. m., a mass meeting of 5,000 to 10,000 people was held at the Clay statue in Canal street, New Orleans, for the avowed purpose of overturning the existing State government, and deposing Governor Kellogg and the other State officers under him.   Resolutions to that effect were adopted and a committee was appointed to wait upon the governor to demand his immediate abdication.   This being refused, the result was reported to the Canal street meeting, which at once recognized John McEnery, who had been the unsuccessful candidate for governor in 1872, as the rightful governor, and D. B. Penn as lieutenant-governor.   McEnery being absent from the State, Penn at once assumed the position of acting governor and circulated a proclamation—which had been prepared some days earlier—calling upon the militia of the State to assemble forthwith, "for the purpose of driving the usurpers from power."   At the same time F. N. Ogden was appointed to the head of the militia, with orders to at once assume command and organize companies and battalions.

To the People of Louisiana:

For two years you have borne with patience and fortitude a great wrong.   Through fraud and violence the government of your choice has been overthrown and its power usurped.   Protest after protest, appeal after appeal to the President of the United States and to Congress have failed to give you the relief you had a right, under the Constitution, to demand.   The wrong has not been repaired.   On the contrary, through the instrumentality of partisan judges, you are debarred from all legal remedy.   Day by day taxation has been increasing, with costs and penalties amounting to the confiscation of your property, your substance squandered, your credit ruined, resulting in the failure and bankruptcy of your valued institutions.   The right of suffrage is virtually taken from you by the enactment of skilfully devised registration and election laws.   The judicial branch of your government has been stricken down by the conversion of the legal posse comitatus of the sheriff to the use of the usurper, for the purpose of defeating the decrees of the courts, his defiance of the law leading him to use the very force for the arrest of the sheriff, while engaged in the execution of a process of the court.   To these may be added a corrupt and vicious legislature, making laws in violation of the constitution for the purpose of guarding and perpetuating their usurped authority; a Metropolitan police, paid by the city, under the control of the usurper, quartered upon you to overawe and keep you in subjection.

Every public right has been denied and, as if to goad you to desperation, private arms are seized and individuals arrested.   To such extremities are you drawn that manhood revolts at any further submission.   Constrained from a sense of duty as the legally elected lieutenant-governor of the State, acting governor in the absence of Governor McEnery, I do hereby issue this, my proclamation, calling upon the militia of the State, embracing all males between the ages of 18 and 45 years, without regard to color or previous condition, to arm and assemble under their respective officers for the purpose of driving the usurpers from power.

Given under my hand and seal, this 14th day c September, 1874.

D. B. PENN,
Lieutenant-Governor.

EXECUTIVE DEPARTMENT, STATE OF LOUISIANA.

Before 3 o'clock from 2,000 to 3,000 armed men had assembled in response to Penn's order at the appointed rendezvous in Poydras street, where a strong position was taken and barricades erected. A half hour later a force of armed Metropolitan police numbering some 500 under Gen. James Longstreet, who was commander of the militia under Governor Kellogg, and General Badger, chief of police, moved down Canal street with several pieces of artillery. The opposing forces met about 4 o'clock and a severe engagement ensued, both parties opening fire without hesitation. In this affray 32 men were killed and 48 severely wounded, some of whom subsequently died. Armed men continued to come into New Orleans in response to the call until nearly 10,000 had assembled, so that by nightfall they had entire possession of the city. This *coup d'état* having been effected, Penn sent the following dispatch to Washington:

NEW ORLEANS, *September 14, 1874.*

To U. S. GRANT,
    President of the United States:

Hopeless of all other relief, the people of this State have taken up arms to maintain the legal authority of the persons elected by them to the government of the State against the usurpers, who have heaped upon them innumerable insults, burdens, and wrong. In so doing they are supported by the great body of the intelligent and honest people of the State. They declare their unswerving loyalty and respect for the United States Government and its officers. They war only against the usurpers, plunderers, and enemies of the people. They affirm their entire ability to maintain peace and protect the life, liberty, and equal rights of all classes of citizens. The property and officials of the United States it shall be our special aim to defend against all assaults and to treat with the profoundest respect and loyalty. We only ask of you to withhold any aid or protection from our enemies and the enemies of Republican rights, and of the peace and liberties of the people.

D. B. PENN,
Lieutenant-Governor and Acting Governor.

At this time, by a combination of circumstances, there were no United States troops in or near the city. The demand for troops in the Red River parishes and at Coushatta had drawn from all disposable sources, so that detachments were posted at Baton Rouge, Monroe, Pineville, Shreveport, Colfax, Greenville, and a few other minor points, leaving but a small guard of perhaps 16 men at Jackson Barracks. Meanwhile the unexpected appearance of the yellow fever along the Gulf had necessitated the precautionary measure of withdrawing such of the troops as were unacclimated to the interior, so that at the time which the conspirators had no doubt purposely fixed upon as the date for the culmination of their plans the headquarters of the department and all the troops from New Orleans and the river forts not otherwise employed were encamped at Holly Springs, Miss., some 350 miles distant, while the department commander, General Emory, had availed himself of the opportunity to visit his home in

the North.   The repulse of the State police and the increasing accessions to the Penn forces rendered it impracticable for Governor Kel-
log to continue the contest.   He accordingly called upon the President
for help:

NEW ORLEANS, *September 14, 1874.*

To PRESIDENT GRANT,
         Washington:

Under Article IV, section 4, of the Constitution of the United States, I have the honor
to inform you that the State is now subject to domestic violence of a character that
the State forces, under existing circumstances, are unable to suppress, and the legislature not being in session and not being able to be convened within the requisite
time to take action in this matter, I respectfully make requisition upon you to take
measures to put down the domestic violence and insurrection now prevailing.

WM. P. KELLOGG,
Governor of Louisiana.

A small detachment of infantry had arrived from Jackson, Miss.,
during the afternoon in response to a request from the United States
marshal, to guard the custom-house, and as soon as intelligence of the
affair had reached Holly Springs four companies had been hurried to
the scene from that point.   These arrived about 5 o'clock, by which
time General Longstreet had retired to the statehouse, where he
awaited the attack which was momentarily expected.   The coming of
the troops, however, prevented further hostilities, although the Penn
forces took possession during the night of all the State and city property, the arsenal, armory, police, and telegraph stations, and occupied
in force the streets surrounding the statehouse.   The next morning
the entire force of metropolitan police being entirely surrounded, laid
down their arms and surrendered the statehouse and all its contents to
the insurgents.   This having been communicated to the President, he
issued the following proclamation:

BY THE PRESIDENT OF THE UNITED STATES OF AMERICA.

A PROCLAMATION.

Whereas, it has been satisfactorily represented to me that turbulent and disorderly
persons have combined together with force and arms to overthrow the State government of Louisiana, and to resist the laws and constituted authorities of said State; and

Whereas, it is provided in the Constitution of the United States that the United
States shall protect every State in this Union, on application of the legislature, or
of the executive, when the legislature can not be convened, against domestic violence; and

Whereas, it is provided in the laws of the United States that, in all cases of insurrection in any State or of obstruction to the laws thereof, it shall be lawful for the
President of the United States, on application of the legislature of such State, or of
the executive when the legislature can not be convened, to call forth the militia of
any other State or States, or to employ such part of the land and naval forces as
shall be judged necessary for the purpose of suppressing such insurrection or causing
the laws to be duly executed; and

Whereas, the legislature of said State is not now in session and can not be convened
in time to meet the present emergency, and the executive of said State, under sec-

tion 4 of Article IV of the Constitution of the United States and the laws passed in pursuance thereof, has therefore made application to me for such part of the military force of the United States as may be necessary and adequate to protect said State and the citizens thereof against domestic violence and to enforce the due execution of the laws; and

Whereas, it is required that whenever it may be necessary, in the judgment of the President, to use the military force for the purpose aforesaid, he shall forthwith by proclamation command such insurgents to disperse and retire peaceably to their respective homes within a limited time:

Now, therefore, I, Ulysses S. Grant, President of the United States, do hereby make proclamation and command said turbulent and disorderly persons to disperse and retire peaceably to their respective abodes within five days from this date and hereafter to submit themselves to the laws and constituted authorities of said State; and I invoke the aid and cooperation of all good citizens thereof to uphold law and preserve the public peace.

In witness whereof, I have hereunto set my hand and caused the seal of the United States to be affixed.

Done at the city of Washington, this 15th day of September, in the year of our Lord eighteen hundred and seventy-four, and of the Independence of the United States the ninety-ninth.

[SEAL.]   U. S. GRANT.

By the President:
    HAMILTON FISH,
        Secretary of State.

To give force and effect to this proclamation a sufficient force of troops were at once assembled at New Orleans, so that by the expiration of the five days nearly two regiments of infantry and artillery were on the ground and a third was en route from Detroit and other posts on the Great Lakes. Upon his arrival at New Orleans General Emory at once demanded the surrender of all the State property and the immediate disbanding of the insurgent forces. By this time Penn had turned over his functions to Mr. McEnery, who had returned to the city, and the latter, more discreet than his subordinate, complied without other than a formal protest. General Emory then issued orders appointing Lieut. Col. John R. Brooke, Third Infantry, "to command the city of New Orleans until such time as the State and city governments can be recognised; to take possession of the arms and other State property, and to occupy the statehouse, arsenal, and other State buildings until further orders." This order resulted in the following correspondence:

WAR DEPARTMENT, ADJUTANT-GENERAL'S OFFICE,
Washington, D. C., September 18, 1874.

Gen. W. H. EMORY,
    New Orleans:

I am directed by the President to say that your acts to this date, so far as they have been reported and received here officially, are approved, except so far as they name Colonel Brooke to command the city of New Orleans. It would have been better to have named him commander of the United States forces in that city. The State government existing at the time of the beginning of the present insurrectionary movement must be recognized as the lawful State government until some other State government can be legally supplied. Upon the surrender of the insurgents you will inform Governor Kellogg of the fact and give him the necessary support to reestablish the authority of the State government. If at the end of the five days given in the proclamation of the 15th instant there still exists armed resistance to the authorities of the State, you will summon a surrender of the insurgents. If the surrender is not quietly submitted to, it must be enforced at all hazards. This being an insurrection against the State government of Louisiana, to aid in the suppression of which this Government has been called upon in the forms required by the Constitution and laws of Congress thereunder, it is not the province of the United States authorities to make terms with parties engaged in such insurrection.

E. D. Townsend,
Adjutant-General.

To this, General Emory replied that he had "placed Colonel Brooke in command of the city as well as in command of the troops. Otherwise there would have been anarchy. Governor Kellogg did not and has not yet called on me for support to reestablish the State government. His chief of police was shot down and the next in command also, and the whole force utterly dispersed and hidden away out of sight. For one of them to have attempted to stand on his beat would have been certain destruction, and even now the State authorities, represented by Governor Kellogg, have asked to defer taking charge for the present."

McEnery made a formal surrender of all the property that had been seized by Penn and his followers, at the same time delivering a written protest, the language of which is significant as admitting and conceding the right of the United States to demand his surrender. He said:

GENERAL BROOKE: As the lawful and acting governor of this State, I surrender to you, as the representative of the Government of the United States, the capitol and remainder of the property in this city belonging to the State. This surrender is in response to a formal demand of General Emory for such surrender, or to accept as an alternative the levying of war upon our government by the military forces of the United States under his command. As I have already said to General Emory, we have neither the power nor inclination to resist the Government of the United States. Sir, I transfer to you the guardianship of the rights and liberties of the people of the State, and I trust and believe that you will give protection to all classes of our citizens, ruled and ruined by a corrupt usurpation presided over by Mr. Kellogg. Our people could bear the wrongs, tyranny, annoyance, and insults of that usurpation no longer, and they arose in their might, swept it from existence, and installed in authority the rightful government, of which I am the head. All lovers of liberty throughout the Union must admit the patriotism that aroused our people to act as one man and throw off the yoke of this odious usurpation. I know as a soldier you have but to obey the orders of the Government of the United States, but I feel that you will temper your military control of affairs with moderation, and in all things exhibit that integrity of purpose characteristic of officers of the Army. I now hand over to you, sir, the capitol and the other property of the State under my charge.

JOHN McENERY.

Governor Kellogg resumed his functions on the 19th, having been assured of the necessary support of the General Government,[a] and issued orders for the resumption of their duties by all the officials who had been deposed, and calling for a reorganization of the Metropolitan police. From this time until the November elections there was constant excitement throughout the State, so that the troops were almost constantly being moved about to prevent anticipated outbreaks.[b] The results of the election were so close—fifty-four Republicans being returned to the legislature and fifty-two Conservatives, with five disputed seats—that it was evident that the approaching assembling of the legislature would be attended by the usual violence. On the 9th of December Governor Kellogg telegraphed the President as follows:

NEW ORLEANS, *December 9, 1874.*
President GRANT,
    Washington:

Information reaches me that the White League purpose making an attack upon the statehouse, especially that portion occupied by the treasurer of the State. The organization is very numerous and well armed, and the State forces now available are not sufficient to resist successfully any movement they make; with a view of preventing such an attempt, and the bloodshed which would be likely to result should an insurgent body again take possession of the Statehouse, and in dispersing them, I respectfully request that a detachment of United States troops be stationed in that portion of the Saint Louis Hotel which is not used for any of the State officers, where they will be readily available to prevent any such insurrectionary movement as that contemplated.

WM. P. KELLOGG,
Governor of Louisiana.

To this the President replied that "It is exceedingly unpalatable to use troops in anticipation of danger. Let the State authorities be right, and then proceed with their duties without apprehension of danger. If they are then molested, the question will be determined whether the United States is able to maintain law and order within its limits or not." In view, however, of the threatening situation the President decided to send Lieutenant-General Sheridan to the scene with the following confidential instructions:

WAR DEPARTMENT,
Washington, D. C., December 24, 1874.
Gen. P. H. SHERIDAN,
    Chicago, Ill.:

GENERAL: The President sent for me this morning, and desires me to say to you that he wishes you to visit the States of Louisiana and Mississippi, and especially New Orleans, La., and Vicksburg and Jackson, Miss., and ascertain for yourself and for his information the general condition of matters in those localities. You need not confine your visit to the States of Louisiana and Mississippi, and may extend

---

[a] Message of the President, January 13, 1875, in response to Senate resolution of January 8, 1875.
[b] Senate Ex. Doc. No. 17, Forty-third Congress, second session.

your trip to other States—Alabama, etc.—if you see proper; nor need you confine your visit in the States of Louisiana and Mississippi to the places named. What the President desires is the true condition of affairs, and to receive such suggestions from you as you may deem advisable and judicious. Inclosed herewith is an order authorizing you to assume command of the Military Division of the South, or any portion of that division, should you see proper to do so. It may be possible that circumstances may arise which would render this a proper course to pursue. You can, if you desire it, see General McDowell, in Louisville, and make known to him confidentially the object of your trip, but this is not required of you. Communication with him by you is left entirely to your own judgment. Of course, you can take with you such gentlemen of your staff as you wish, and it is best that the trip should appear to be one as much of pleasure as of business, for the fact of your mere presence in the localities referred to will have, it is presumed, a beneficial effect. The President thinks, and so do I, that a trip South might be agreeable to you, and that you might be able to obtain a good deal of information on the subject about which we desire to learn. You can make your return by Washington and make a verbal report, and also inform me from time to time of your views and conclusions.

 Yours, truly, etc..

W. W. Belknap,
Secretary of War.

General Sheridan arrived in New Orleans on the 1st of January. In a later report he remarks that during the few days he was in the city prior to the meeting of the legislature on the 4th, the general topic of conversation was the scenes of bloodshed that

The affair of January 4, 1875. were likely to occur on that day, and that he repeatedly heard threats of assassinating the governor and members of the legislature and regrets expressed that the governor had not been killed on the 14th of September.[a] It is in evidence that the governor was apprehensive of impending trouble, and that at his request, and in order to preserve the peace, General Emory consented to station troops around the building. It was no doubt owing to these precautions that the statehouse was not seized on the night of the 3d. On the morning of the 4th a noisy, disorderly crowd filled the streets, requiring the constant watchfulness of the police and the surveillance of the troops. The legislature assembled, however, without serious disturbance—102 legally returned members, of which 52 were Republicans and 50 opposition. Before anyone outside the conspirators was aware of what was intended, the leaders of the opposition proceeded to carry out its plans. One Wiltz jumped on the platform, seized the speaker's chair and gavel, and declared himself speaker. On motions from the floor, and without ballots, he in the same way declared other gentlemen elected secretary and sergeant-at-arms, and having directed the latter to appoint assistants, a hundred or more men scattered about the hall suddenly opened their coats, displaying badges on which was inscribed "assistant sergeant-at-arms," and the minority were in possession of the legislature. The excitement was intense; knives and

---

[a] Telegram, General Sheridan to Secretary Belknap, January 8, 1875.

pistols were drawn; several fisticuffs occurred; the shouting was so deafening that little could be heard. A committee was appointed, however, to wait upon the commanding officer of the troops and ask his assistance in clearing the lobby. This was granted at once, and at the request of General De Trobriand, the senior officer present, the crowd became quiet and peace was restored. The Republicans then withdrew from the hall and presented their protest to the governor, who at once called upon the commanding general to aid him in restoring the status as it was before the illegal proceedings. This request also was complied with. General De Trobriand returned, accompanied by the Republican members. Five gentlemen who were not legally elected, but had been seated during the absence of the Republicans, were removed from the hall. The Democrats then withdrew in a body, and the remaining members proceeded with the organization. "In all this turmoil," says General Sheridan, "in which bloodshed was imminent, the military posse behaved with great discretion. When Mr. Wiltz, the usurping speaker of the house, called for troops to prevent bloodshed, they were given him. When the governor of the State called for a posse for the same purpose and to enforce the law, it was furnished also. Had this not been done it is my firm belief that scenes of bloodshed would have ensued."[a] The following dispatch[b] from Wiltz to the President presents the affair from the standpoint of his party:

[Telegram.]

HOUSE OF REPRESENTATIVES,
New Orleans, January 4, 1875.

The PRESIDENT OF THE UNITED STATES,
Washington, D. C.:

I have the honor to inform you that the house of representatives of this State was organized to-day by the election of myself as speaker, 58 members, two more than a quorum, voting, with a full house present. More than two hours after the organization I was informed by the officer in command of the United States troops in this city that he had been requested by Governor Kellogg to remove certain members of the house from the statehouse, and that under his orders he was obliged to comply with the request. I protested against any interference of the United States with the organization or proceedings of the house, but, notwithstanding this, the officer in command marched a company of soldiers upon the floor of the house and by force removed 13 members who had been legally and constitutionally seated as such, and who, at time of such forcible removal, were participating in the proceedings of the house. In addition to this the military declared their purpose to further interfere with force in the business and organization of this assembly, upon which some fifty-two members and the speaker withdrew, declining to participate any longer in the business of the house under the dictation of the military. As speaker I respectfully appeal to you to know by what authority and under what law the United States Army interrupted and broke up a session of the house of representatives of the State of Louisiana, and to urgently request and demand that they

---

[a] Telegram, General Sheridan to Secretary Belknap, January 8, 1875.
[b] Senate Ex. Doc. No. 13, Forty-third Congress, second session, p. 29.

be ordered to restore the house to the position it occupied when they so interfered; and, further, that they be instructed that it is no part of their duty to interfere in any manner with the internal workings of the general assembly. The house is the representation of the sovereignty of the State, and I know of no law which warrants either the executive of the State or the United States Army to interfere with its organization or proceedings.

LOUIS A. WILTZ,
Speaker of the House of Representatives of the State of Louisiana.

The excitement produced by the publication of this affair was intense throughout the country. At New Orleans the presence of the troops and the determined character of General Sheridan, who at 9 p. m. assumed command of the Department of the Gulf, sufficed to suppress any outbreak, although threats were freely made that General Sheridan would be assassinated, that the United States troops would be driven from the city, and that the Kellogg government would be deposed, the statehouse burned, and all Northern men removed from Louisiana. The following dispatches from and to General Sheridan were sent on the 4th, 5th, and 6th:

[Telegram.]

HEADQUARTERS DIVISION OF THE MISSOURI,
New Orleans, January 4, 1875. (Received 4—11.45 p. m.)
W. W. BELKNAP,
Secretary of War, Washington, D. C.:

It is with deep regret that I have to announce to you the existence in this State of a spirit of defiance to all lawful authority and an insecurity of life which is hardly realized by the General Government or the country at large. The lives of citizens have become so jeopardized that unless something is done to give protection to the people all security usually afforded by law will be overridden. Defiance to the laws and the murder of individuals seems to be looked upon by the community here from a standpoint which gives impunity to all who choose to indulge in either, and the civil government appears powerless to punish or even arrest. I have to-night assumed control over the Department of the Gulf.

P. H. SHERIDAN,
Lieutenant-General, U. S. Army.

[Telegram dated New Orleans, January 5, 1875, received at northeast corner Fourteenth street and Pennsylvania avenue, 4.47 p. m.]

W. W. BELKNAP,
Secretary of War, Washington, D. C.:

Please say to the President that he need give himself no uneasiness about the condition of affairs here. I will preserve the peace, which it is not hard to do with the naval and military forces in and about the city, and if Congress will declare the White Leagues and other similar organizations, white or black, banditti, I will relieve it from the necessity of any special legislation for the preservation of peace and equality of rights in the States of Louisiana, Mississippi, Arkansas, and the Executive from much of the trouble heretofore had in this section of the country.

P. H. SHERIDAN
Lieutenant-General, U. S. Army.

S. Doc. 209——11

[Telegram dated Headquarters Military Division of the Missouri, New Orleans, La., January 5, 1875
Received January 5.]

W. W. BELKNAP,
    Secretary of War, Washington, D. C.:

I think that the terrorism now existing in Louisiana, Mississippi, and Arkansas could be entirely removed and confidence and fair dealing established by the arrest and trial of the ringleaders of the armed White Leagues. If Congress would pass a bill declaring them banditti they could be tried by a military commission. The ringleaders of this banditti, who murdered men here on the 14th of last September, and also more recently at Vicksburg, Miss., should, in justice to law and order and the peace and prosperity of this southern part of the country, be punished. It is possible that if the President would issue a proclamation declaring them banditti, no further action need be taken, except that which would devolve upon me.

P. H. SHERIDAN,
    Lieutenant-General, U. S. Army.

[Telegram received in cipher January 6, 1875, from Lieut. Gen. P. H. Sheridan, dated New Orleans, La., January 5, 1875.]

W. W. BELKNAP,
    Secretary of War:

There is some excitement in the rotunda of the St. Charles Hotel to-night upon the publication by the newspapers of my dispatch to you calling the secret armed organization banditti. Give yourself no uneasiness. I see my way clear enough if you will only have confidence.

P. H. SHERIDAN,
    Lieutenant-General, U. S. Army.

[Telegram.]

WAR DEPARTMENT,
    Washington City, January 6, 1875.

Gen. P. H. SHERIDAN,
    New Orleans, La.:

Your telegrams all received. The President and all of us have full confidence and thoroughly approve your course.

WM. W. BELKNAP,
    Secretary of War.

[Telegram.]

WAR DEPARTMENT,
    Washington, January 6, 1875.

Gen. P. H. SHERIDAN,
    New Orleans, La.:

I telegraphed you hastily to-day, answering your dispatch. You seem to fear that we had been misled by biased or partial statements of your acts. Be assured that the President and Cabinet confide in your wisdom, and rest in the belief that all acts of yours have been and will be judicious. This I intended to say in my brief telegram.

WM. W. BELKNAP,
    Secretary of War.

[Telegram dated New Orleans, La., January 6, 1875. Received January 6, 1875.]

Gen. W. W. BELKNAP,
    Secretary of War, Washington, D. C.:

The city is very quiet to-day. Some of the banditti made idle threats last night that they would assassinate me because I dared to tell the truth. I am not afraid, and will not be stopped from informing the Government that there are localities in this department where the very air has been impregated with assassination for several years.

P. H. SHERIDAN,
    Lieutenant-General, Commanding.

[Telegram dated New Orleans, La., January 7, 1875. Received January 7, 1875.]

W. W. BELKNAP,
    Secretary of War, Washington, D. C.:
Several prominent people have for the last few days been passing resolutions and manufacturing sensational protests for Northern political consumption. They seem to be trying to make martyrs of themselves; it can not be done at this late day; there have been too many bleeding negroes and ostracised white citizens for their statements to be believed by fair-minded people. Bishop Wilmer protests against my telegram of the 4th instant, forgetting that on Saturday last he testified, under oath, before the Congressional committee that the condition of affairs here was substantially as bad as reported by me. I will soon send you a statement of the number of murders committed in this State during the last three or four years, the perpetrators of which are still unpunished. I think that the number will startle you; it will be up in the thousands. The city is perfectly quiet. No trouble is apprehended.

                                                              P. H. SHERIDAN,
                                                    Lieutenant-General, U. S. Army.

The President, in a message dated January 13, 1875, in response to a Senate resolution of January 8 calling for information in the matter, uses the following language:

I repeat that the task assumed by the troops is not a pleasant one to them; that the Army is not composed of lawyers capable of judging at a moment's notice of just how far they can go in the maintenance of law and order, and that it was impossible to give specific instructions providing for all possible contingencies that might arise. The troops were bound to act upon the judgment of the commanding officer upon each sudden contingency that arose or wait instructions which could only reach them after the threatened wrongs had been committed which they were called on to prevent. It should be recollected, too, that upon my recognition of the Kellogg government I reported the fact, with the grounds of recognition, to Congress, and asked that body to take action in the matter; otherwise I should regard their silence as an acquiescence in my course. No action has been taken by that body, and I have maintained the position then marked out.

If error has been committed by the Army in these matters, it has always been on the side of the preservation of good order, the maintenance of law, and the protection of life. Their bearing reflects credit upon the soldiers, and if wrong has resulted the blame is with the turbulent element surrounding them.

I now earnestly ask that such action be taken by Congress as to leave my duties perfectly clear in dealing with the affairs of Louisiana, giving assurance at the same time that whatever may be done by that body in the premises will be executed according to the spirit and letter of the law, without fear or favor.

Meanwhile committees had been sent to Louisiana by both Houses of Congress, and testimony taken from both sides, which was fully reported and debated, with the result that before its adjournment the House of Representatives recognized Kellogg as the legal governor, and on the 20th of March the Senate in extra session passed the following resolution:

Resolved, That the action of the President in protecting the government of Louisiana, of which W. P. Kellogg is the executive, and the people of that State against domestic violence, and enforcing the laws of the United States, is approved.

VII. POLITICAL DISTURBANCES IN ARKANSAS, 1874.

The political troubles that enter so largely into the history of Louisiana for the decade following the civil war, had their counterpart, to a greater or less extent, in Arkansas; though in but two instances was there a resort to arms or occasion for the interposition of the Federal troops. These instances, however, were of so determined a character, involving such extreme bitterness and pertinacity, that for the time they engrossed an unusual share of public attention and called for the most earnest consideration of the General Government. The disturbances of 1868 have already been described.

The contest between Joseph Brooks and Elisha Baxter, both Republicans, for the governorship of Arkansas, had its origin in 1872, when a faction of the Republican party in convention at Cincinnati having nominated Horace Greeley for the Presidency, a similar faction in Arkansas indorsed that movement and nominated Joseph Brooks for governor, while the regular Republicans approved the administration of President Grant and selected Elisha Baxter as their candidate for governor. The Democrats, whose national party had indorsed the nomination of Greeley, made no State ticket, but favored the candidacy of Brooks. The returns, when opened in the presence of the legislature, as required by law, showed 41,784 votes for Baxter and 38,673 for Brooks, and accordingly the former was declared elected and was at once inaugurated. Brooks, alleging fraud at the polls, petitioned the legislature for permission to contest, but his petition was denied, as was also his application to the supreme court of the State for a writ of *quo warranto*. During this time vague threats seem to have circulated about Little Rock to the effect that Brooks, if denied the writ, would attempt to seize the executive office, and upon this pretext, Governor Baxter called out the militia. The denial of the writ, and the equanimity with which the deci-

The militia called out, June, 1873. sion was received by the Brooks party, seem to have calmed the fears of the governor, so that five days later he issued an order mustering out the militia, in which order he takes occasion to explain his reasons for calling them into service.

1. The peace of the State having been threatened by a combination of reckless and bad men, having for its purpose the violent and illegal overthrow of the State government, it was deemed wise to prepare to meet such threatened revolutionary action

164

by an organized force, sufficient to maintain order, and enforce the law against all opposition thereto, and for that purpose alone the commander in chief directed the enrollment and muster in of the militia of the State.

2. By the solemn judgment of the supreme court of the State, the legality of the present State government is now fully recognized, and the effort made to overthrow it, through the forms of law, declared illegal and unauthorized.

3. This judgment of the supreme court puts the executive of the State in an attitude to appeal to the Executive power of the Nation to suppress any illegal, violent, or revolutionary action that may be attempted to overthrow the State government or any of its departments; and the executive of the State has assurances that such an appeal will meet with a prompt response from the President, should occasion to make the appeal occur, which it is believed will not be the case.

Brooks next brought suit against Baxter in the circuit court of Pulaski County, under the Civil Code, which provides that whenever a person usurps an office or franchise to which he is not entitled, an action at law may be instituted against him either by the State or by the party entitled thereto.[a] Baxter interposed a plea of nonjurisdiction, but having reason to believe that the court was about to decide against him, addressed a communication to the President, September 4, 1873, reciting the essential facts of the controversy and asking that Federal troops be sent to Little Rock, inasmuch as the course of events may compel him to resort to martial law. This the President refused on the ground that the application was not made in accordance with the provisions of the Constitution.[b]

On the 15th of April, 1874, the circuit court of Pulaski County rendered a judgment of ouster in favor of Brooks, and the latter immediately took possession of the State capitol, which he surrounded by a strong guard of his supporters, who, apprised of the forthcoming judgment, had assembled to the number of several hundred. A large quantity of arms and ammunition belonging to the State had been stored for safe-keeping in the United States arsenal at Little Rock, and for these arms both parties at once made demand. This was refused and each accordingly called upon the President:

Brooks seizes the capitol, April 15, 1874.

[Telegram.]

EXECUTIVE OFFICE,
Little Rock, April 15, 1874.

Having been duly installed as governor of Arkansas by the judgment of a court, I respectfully ask that the commanding officer at the arsenal be instructed to deliver the arms belonging to the State, now in his custody, or hold the same subject to my order.

JOS. BROOKS.

U. S. GRANT,
President, Washington.

---

[a] Sec. 525, Civil Code of Arkansas.

[b] Governor Baxter to President Grant, September 4, 1873, and Attorney-General Williams to Governor Baxter, September 15, 1873, in H. R. Ex. Doc. No. 229, Forty-third Congress, first session.

[Telegram.]

LITTLE ROCK, *April 15, 1874.*

The PRESIDENT OF THE UNITED STATES,
    Washington:

I have been advised by public rumor that in the State circuit court for this county, in a long pending case brought by Jos. Brooks for the office of governor of this State, a demurrer to the complaint was overruled, and immediately judgment of ouster against me given. This was done in the absence of counsel for me and without notice, and immediately thereafter the circuit judge adjourned his court. The claimant has taken possession of the State buildings and ejected me by force. I propose to take measures immediately to resume possession of the State property, and to maintain my authority as the rightful governor of the State. Armed men, acting under this revolutionary movement, are now in charge of the Government armory and capitol buildings. I deem it my duty to communicate this state of affairs to the President. I trust these revolutionary acts may be settled without bloodshed, and respectfully ask the support of the General Government in my efforts to maintain rightful government of the State of Arkansas, and that the commander of the United States arsenal at this post be directed to sustain me in that direction. I respectfully request a reply to this communication at an early moment.

ELISHA BAXTER,
Governor of Arkansas.

Governor Baxter at once called out the militia, those in Little Rock promptly responding, and established his headquarters at St. John's College. The mayor of Little Rock endeavored with a meager police force to stem the tide of events, but as the population of the city had ranged itself on one or the other side of the controversy, he found himself unable to keep the peace and appealed to the officer in command of the United States troops at Little Rock Barracks. A large number of messages representing both parties were sent to Washington, from the midst of which there was difficulty in learning the truth of the situation. As yet, however, there seemed nothing in the case warranting any interference upon the part of the General Government, so that beyond instructing the United States marshal to take notice of existing troubles and notify the officer commanding the United States troops to prevent bloodshed, should a collision be imminent, no action was immediately had. On the 16th, however, the following telegrams were sent to Messrs. Brooks and Baxter, as well as to the commanding officer at the barracks.

[Telegram.]

DEPARTMENT OF JUSTICE,
Washington, April 16, 1874.

Hon. ELISHA BAXTER, *Little Rock, Ark.:*

I am instructed by the President to say in answer to your dispatch to him of yesterday, asking for the support of the General Government to sustain you in efforts to maintain the rightful government in the State of Arkansas, that in the first place your call is not made in conformity with the Constitution and laws of the United States, and in the second place, as your controversy relates to your right to hold a State office, its adjudication, unless a case is made under the so-called enforcement acts for Federal jurisdiction, belongs to the State courts.

If the decision of which you complain is erroneous, there appears to be no reason why it may not be reviewed and a correct decision obtained in the supreme court of the State.

GEORGE H. WILLIAMS,
Attorney-General.

[Telegram.]

DEPARTMENT OF JUSTICE,
Washington, April 16, 1874.

Hon. JOSEPH BROOKS, *Little Rock, Ark.:*

I am instructed by the President to say in answer to your dispatch to him of yesterday, asking that the United States commanding officer at the arsenal be instructed to deliver the arms in his custody belonging to the State to you, or hold the same subject to your order, that he declines to comply with your request, as he is not advised that your right to hold the office of governor has been fully and finally determined by the courts of Arkansas.

GEORGE H. WILLIAMS,
Attorney-General.

[Telegram.]

WAR DEPARTMENT, ADJUTANT-GENERAL'S OFFICE,
Washington, April 16, 1874.

COMMANDING OFFICER, *Little Rock, Ark.:*

By direction of the President, the Secretary of War instructs that you take no part in the political controversy in the State of Arkansas, unless it should be necessary to prevent bloodshed or collision of armed bodies.

Acknowledge receipt.

E. D. TOWNSEND,
Adjutant-General.

During the greater part of the 16th, Brooks held quiet possession of the statehouse, though it was guarded by a force of some 250 determined men, fully armed and possessing two pieces of cannon, while every incoming train brought accessions to his forces, no less than to those of Baxter. It looked for a time as though the latter would offer no serious resistance, and that the decision of the court was to be quietly acquiesced in. So secure in fact did Brooks consider his position that about noon he issued a congratulatory proclamation addressed to "the people of Arkansas," in which, having defined his position and announced his future policy, he concluded with the following pacific language:

Efforts no doubt will be made by designing men to convey the impression that it is the duty of the people to rally to the standard of a man who, no doubt, will claim he is governor of Arkansas, that you all know was not elected, and who has no more right or claim to the office than any one of you have that was not a candidate, for the purpose of placing that man again in the executive office [*sic*]. I say frankly to you that all such attempts will lead to strife and bloodshed, for I shall resist and suppress the action of all mobs that may assemble together under the banner or at the call of Elisha Baxter! No man in the State can more deeply regret strife and bloodshed than myself. But feeling as I do that self-government, rather than self-aggrandizement, is in the issue, I shall employ every means to maintain its supremacy. Elisha Baxter forced me from the legislature to the courts, and thus far I have patiently borne with the law's delay, at all times feeling that justice would be done me. By the judgment of a court of competent jurisdiction I am in the executive office. When it is adjudicated that I am not there legally I will bow my head in silence to the decree of the court, be it what it may. The power that Elisha Baxter used to force me into the courts I will use to make him respect and abide its decrees. To one and all I say, keep quiet and pursue your different vocations; *your services are not needed at the capital* to preserve either peace or good order. Should the time come when they will be needed you will be notified in due time through proper channels.

JOSEPH BROOKS,
Governor of Arkansas.

Governor Baxter, however, was not idle. The cadets of St. John's College—young men averaging about 16 years of age, armed with cadet rifles—were put on guard about the college grounds, where the incoming troops and volunteers were assembled as they arrived under the command of General Newton, the head of the State militia. The day was fortunately not a propitious one for the opening of a revolution—a fine and drizzling rain prevailing throughout the day and no doubt deterring both parties from more active operations. About dark Governor Baxter, escorted by the cadets and some 300 citizens, left the college and took up his quarters at the Anthony House, which is in the second block east of the statehouse, and at once issued a proclamation declaring martial law in Pulaski County:

Whereas, an armed rebellion exists in the county of Pulaski against the State government and it becomes necessary to employ all the forces at my disposal to suppress it: therefore, by the authority vested in me by law, I hereby proclaim the existence of martial law within said county, and command all persons capable of military duty to assist in the putting down of the said rebellion. During the time that martial law shall thus prevail every infringement of the right of peaceable and well-disposed persons will be severely punished, by whomsoever it may be committed. The utmost respect shall be paid by all persons to citizens not in arms, and to their property, and to that of the Federal Government.

In testimony whereof, I, Elisha Baxter, governor of the State of Arkansas, do hereby set my hand, the private seal of said State being now not accessible to the governor of the State.

Done at Little Rock, this 15th day of April, 1874.

ELISHA BAXTER,
Governor of Arkansas and Commander in Chief.

At the same time he issued orders placing Brigadier-Generals Churchill and Dockery in command of the volunteers and announcing the latter as military governor of the city. It being difficult to procure weapons with which to arm the incoming volunteers, Governor Baxter took forcible possession of the entire stock of arms and ammunition belonging to dealers in firearms, and citizens possessing arms of any kind were appealed to to turn them over to the State authorities. Sentinels were regularly posted and the city was now in entire charge of the military, while every hour the three railroads entering the city, as well as steamboats at the levee, were disembarking recruits for one or other of the opposing camps. Many negroes had been recruited in the counties along the line of the Cairo and Fulton; from Lewisburg; several hundred white men from Lee and Phillips counties, and these were unloaded from the river boats by hundreds and marched into the camp, to which they were consigned like so many cattle; many of them without shoes; most without coats or sufficient clothing; all without arms.   By the 19th the numbers of these had increased to an alarming extent—the two camps had swelled to the proportion of armies.   The situation was fraught with danger.   Reckless men armed with revolvers—whites and blacks—roamed the streets, uttering threats and boasting of coming engagements.   Baxter, having decided to repossess himself of the capitol building, issued an address which concluded thus:

The executive of the State has but one obligation to perform, that to which he is bound alike by his duty as a citizen and his official oath.   The authority of the law will be immediately and effectually asserted, peaceably, if may be, but asserted in any event.   The government proposes to occupy the capitol.   As governor of Arkansas, I appeal to the people of the State to support the government of the State against shameless usurpation.   Under the solemn obligations of my oath of office, I renew my promise to be true to them.   I ask from them the support which they owe to their chief magistrate.

ELISHA BAXTER,
Governor of Arkansas.

On Saturday, the 18th, the situation increased in intensity.   A little after daylight a steamboat from Pine Bluff arrived with 300 negroes for Baxter, followed by detachments from Howard, Hempstead, and Saline counties to the number of over 900.   By this time the police of Little Rock were powerless, so that the mayor had the night before telegraphed to Washington for assistance.[84]   He stated that Governor Baxter had put the county under martial law; that armed men were patrolling the streets, stopping unarmed and peaceable citizens, setting the authority of the city officers at defiance, and arresting the police; that the city is sure to become a scene of bloodshed.   Under these circumstances, he adds:

I desire to ask if the Federal Government is powerless to protect the lives and property of 20,000 inhabitants who are situated as we are.   If you will instruct the officers in command of the arsenal to aid the city police in making the arrest of men who are openly violating the law and setting the same at defiance, I could preserve the peace of the city without being compelled to take sides with either of the contending factions.   This question of who is the rightful governor can only be settled by the courts, a thing that may not be done for the next twelve months, and I now implore you in the name of peace to aid me all in your power until the other question is settled.[a]

To this the Attorney-General had replied, as follows, on the 18th:[b]

[Telegram.]
DEPARTMENT OF JUSTICE,
Washington, April 18, 1874.

You must be aware that the President can not interfere in the domestic difficulties of a State except in conformity with the Constitution and laws of the United States.

---

[a] Kramer, mayor of Little Rock, to Attorney-General Williams, April 17, 1874. (H. R. Ex. Doc. No. 229, Forty-third Congress, first session.)

[b] Attorney-General Williams to Mayor of Little Rock, April 18, 1874.   (H. R. Ex. Doc. No. 229, Forty-third Congress, first session.)

He can not recognize a call made upon him for military aid by the mayor of a city. He has instructed the officer commanding the United States troops at Little Rock to prevent bloodshed. That is all he can do under existing circumstances. I will ask, in answer to your inquiry whether the United States are powerless to protect 20,000 people situated as the citizens of Little Rock are, if the people of Arkansas have not patriotism enough to allow a question as to who shall hold a State office to be settled peaceably and lawfully, and not bring upon their State the disgrace and ruin of civil war.

GEORGE H. WILLIAMS,
Attorney-General.

FREDERICK KRAMER, Esq.,
 Mayor, Little Rock, Ark.

In the meanwhile Captain Rose, the commanding officer of the United States troops at Little Rock, two companies of the Sixteenth Infantry, had moved his disposable forces into the city and located them at such points between the two camps as would enable him to watch both parties and prevent a collision. This accomplished, he addressed the following letter to Governor Baxter and sent a copy of the same to Brooks:

HEADQUARTERS LITTLE ROCK BARRACKS,
Little Rock, April 17, 1874.

SIR: I am informed by the United States marshal of this district that there is danger of a collision between the forces under your command and those of certain forces under the command of Joseph Brooks.

I therefore have the honor to enjoin upon you that you make no movement with your forces in any direction in the city of Little Rock, Ark., or its vicinity, with a view to bring about such a collision, or that may bring on such a collision, or to make any movement that may possibly bring about a collision with the United States troops under my command, or to impede any movement I may wish to make with the troops of my command to prevent the shedding of blood and the collision of armed forces.

Very respectfully, your obedient servant,

T. E. ROSE,
Captain, Sixteenth Infantry, Commanding Post.

Gen. ELISHA BAXTER,
 Commanding Forces in the State of Arkansas.

To this each responded that no hostile movement would be immediately made. Governor Baxter, having issued an order that all telegraphic messages should be inspected before transmission, orders were sent Captain Rose to take possession of the telegraph office and see that the sanctity of telegraphic correspondence was maintained.[86] To this the President added:

While the Government takes no part in the unhappy state of affairs existing in Arkansas at this time, you will see that official dispatches of the Government, whether from the military or civil departments, are transmitted without molestation by either of the contestants for the gubernatorial chair.

The wires having been thus opened to public use, both Brooks and Baxter now called upon the President for aid under the Constitutional guarantee:

[Telegram.]

LITTLE ROCK, ARK., *April 19, 1874.*

The PRESIDENT OF THE UNITED STATES,
Washington, D. C.:

A few days since, in the absence of my counsel and at a time wholly unexpected, the circuit judge of this county, a court of inferior jurisdiction, rendered judgment in favor of Brooks against me for the office of governor of the State, and without notice to me or my counsel. I was at once forcibly put out of the office, and that without any pretense of a writ being served on me. All this was done, too, after the supreme court of this State had twice decided that no court in the State had jurisdiction of the case at all and the legislature alone had the jurisdiction. At once, on being ejected from the office, I took steps to restore myself and to get possession of the office and to carry on the government. The people are coming to my aid and are ready to restore me at once. In making this organization I am obstructed by the interference of the United States troops in displacing my guards from the telegraph office; and now it is apprehended that there will be further interference. Such interference breaks me down and prevents any effort on my part to restore the State government and to protect the people in their rights. I beg of you to modify any order to the extent of such interference and leave me free to act in this way to restore law and peace as the legitimate governor of the State. Such interference does not leave me any chance to assert my claim to the office of governor. In the interests of peace and of those people who are flocking here to my support by the hundreds, I beg of you to remove the United States troops back to the arsenal and permit me to restore the legitimate government by my own forces, which I will do promptly if the United States will not interfere. There is an armed insurrection against the legal State government here, and I call upon you to aid in suppressing it; but if you will not, then leave me free to act, and order the United States troops without an hour's delay to their own ground and keep them out of my way. I have been thwarted and delayed thus long and in fact ejected from my office because of the fact that I had heretofore disbanded the militia of the State. I make this earnest demand to repress insurrection and prevent domestic violence under my sense of duty to the Constitution and laws of the United States as well as of the State of Arkansas, and I rely confidently, as I have all the time, upon the assurances contained in your letter of September 15, 1873, to prevent the overflow of my official authority by illegal and disorderly proceedings. An immediate answer is requested; otherwise bloodshed may be the result.

ELISHA BAXTER,
Governor of Arkansas.

[Telegram.]

LITTLE ROCK, ARK., *April 20, 1874.*

His Excellency U. S. GRANT,
President of the United States:

SIR: I hereby inform you that one Elisha Baxter, a private citizen, pretending to be governor of Arkansas, without warrant or authority of law assumed to declare martial law in the capital county of the State and to appoint a pretended militiary governor of the city of Little Rock, the seat of government; that he called out armed bodies of men for the avowed purpose of attacking and capturing the capitol of the State by military force, and forcibly installing himself as governor of such State; that large bodies of armed men have assembled and are continually assembling under said Baxter's proclamation of martial law, and are in close proximity to the statehouse, and have this day actually advanced on the statehouse and confronted a body of Federal troops stationed in front of the statehouse, under order from their commanding officer, acting under your command to preserve the peace, and were only prevented from making the attack by the presence of Federal troops; that these armed bodies have seized and appropriated private property, and are hourly seizing and appropriating private property, without compensation; have conscripted and are continually conscripting private citizens, and compelling them to aid and abet them in their insurrectionary purposes, and have seized and are daily seizing railroads in the State and appropriating them to the same illegal and insurrectionary purposes; that there are armed bodies at this moment assembled within a few hundred yards of the statehouse and threaten an immediate attack upon it; that the legislature adjourned *sine die* in April last, has not since been convened, is not now in session, and can not be convened in time to prevent the threatened attack; that domestic violence now actually exists in this State and at the seat of government which the civil and military authorities under my control are powerless to prevent or suppress.   Therefore I, Joseph Brooks, governor of the State of Arkansas, in pursuance of the Constitution and laws of the United States, hereby make application to Your Excellency to protect the State capital and the State of Arkansas against domestic violence and insurrection.

In testimony whereof, I have hereunto set my hand and caused the great seal of the State to be affixed at Little Rock, this the 20th day of April, A. D. 1874.

[SEAL.]   JOSEPH BROOKS,
                                                              Governor.

By the governor:
    EDWARD CURREY,
        Secretary of State ad interim.

Little Rock now presented the appearance of a military camp. Fully 10,000 men, indifferently armed, but organized into companies and battalions, were being constantly drilled and maneuvered. The excitement was extending to the country districts. On the 21st a body of Baxter men—mostly colored—while being addressed by the governor, became unduly hilarious and discharged pistols in the air. This, through a misapprehension, became the signal for some indiscriminate firing. A detachment of United States troops were hurried to the scene and the disturbance was promptly quelled, but not until several had been wounded and one aged noncombatant, who was sitting at a window of the Anthony House, killed. The following day Governor Baxter proposed a settlement by the legislature, and the following correspondence passed between him and the President:

[Telegram.]

                                                LITTLE ROCK, ARK., *April 22, 1874.*
The PRESIDENT OF THE UNITED STATES,
        Washington:

As I can not move with my troops to assert my claims to the office of governor without a collision with the United States troops, which I will not do under any circumstances, I propose to call the legislature together at an early day and leave them to settle the question, as they alone have the power. But to do this, the members of the legislature must have assurances of protection from you and a guaranty that they may meet in safety. This will be a peaceable solution of the difficulty, and I will readily abide by the decision of the legislature.

                                                ELISHA BAXTER,
                                                    Governor of Arkansas.

[Telegram.]

EXECUTIVE MANSION,
Washington, April 22, 1874.

Hon. ELISHA BAXTER, *Little Rock, Ark.:*

I heartily approve any adjustment peaceably of the pending difficulties in Arkansas by means of the legislature assembly, the courts, or otherwise.

I will give all the assistance and protection I can under the Constitution and laws of the United States to such modes of adjustment.

I hope that the military on both sides will now be disbanded.

U. S. GRANT.

In harmony with this method of settling a vexatious question, Captain Rose was instructed to retire with his command to the arsenal "as soon as danger to life is no longer threatened, and leave the question to be settled by the contestants, by the courts, or other peaceable methods."[88] That those well-meant dispositions were unproductive of any satisfactory results was perhaps owing to the excitement which prevailed throughout the State. Neither party was ready to listen to compromise. The drilling went on at Little Rock and reenforcements continued to arrive from the country, which by this time was thoroughly aroused. In the Brooks camp, which was composed of a larger majority of white men, there was greater order and determination; breastworks were thrown up around the yard, and preparations were made for an anticipated siege; 2,000 Springfield rifles were sent from St. Louis. Still large bodies of negroes had joined the Brooks forces. Some of these were sent back, but they assembled at points outside the city and threatened greater mischief than when under observation. On the 27th Governor Baxter, who had summoned the legislature for the 11th of May, again made formal application for Federal aid, which was followed by a second on the 28th:

LITTLE ROCK, *April 27, 1874.*

U. S. GRANT, *President:*

On the 19th day of this month, as governor of this State, I telegraphed you there was an armed insurrection against the legal government of this State, and made a requisition upon you for aid to suppress it and to prevent domestic violence. I have just now been advised that you never received the requisition. I now take occasion to say that an armed insurrection exists in this State against the lawfully constituted authority thereof, and, as the legislature can not meet until the 11th day of May, I call upon you for aid to protect the State against domestic violence.

ELISHA BAXTER,
Governor of Arkansas.

EXECUTIVE OFFICE, STATE OF ARKANSAS,
Little Rock, April 28, 1874.

His Excellency the PRESIDENT OF THE UNITED STATES:

I, Elisha Baxter, governor of the State of Arkansas, beg leave to inform your Excellency that divers evil-disposed persons, conspiring the overthrow of the government of the State of Arkansas, have unlawfully and by force of arms taken possession of the capitol building and archives of government; that the legislature is not now in session; that the insurrection aforesaid has grown into such magnitude as to seriously interfere with, if not prevent, the assembling of the legislature, which

I have called to convene at the seat of government on the 11th day of May next, and can not be suppressed by the State militia under my command without great bloodshed and loss of life.

Now, therefore, pursuant to the provision of the Constitution of the United States in that behalf, I respectfully call on your Excellency for the necessary military force to suppress such insurrection and to protect the State against the domestic violence aforesaid.

In testimony whereof, I have hereunto set my hand and affixed my private seal, the seal of the State being in the hands of the insurgents.

Done at the capitol on the day and year first above written.

[L. S.]   ELISHA BAXTER,
                                                        Governor of Arkansas.
By the governor:
    J. M. JOHNSON,
            Secretary of State.
    By A. H. GARLAND,
            Deputy Secretary of State.

As was to have been expected, this excitement was not unproductive of disturbances throughout the State. At Pine Bluff, where camps of Brooks and Baxter men had been formed, an engagement of doubtful magnitude occurred on the 30th, in which several men were wounded. At Benton, in Saline County, two judges of the supreme court were arrested and held by a military guard; troops were sent from Little Rock, but the gentlemen had escaped. On the 7th of May a steamboat having Baxter men on board was fired upon by a body of Brooks's men and some 20 were killed and wounded on both sides. On the 9th, 10th, and 12th there was rioting and some firing in Little Rock; the streets were barricaded and both camps under arms; several men were killed and numbers wounded. Brooks still held the State buildings and pretended to conduct the administration of State affairs, while Baxter's headquarters remained at the Anthony House, where he received all mail addressed to him. The Postmaster-General had instructed the local postmasters to deliver to each of the opponents such mail as bore his name, whether as " governor " or otherwise, and to hold until further orders all mail addressed simply " Governor of Arkansas." A constant excitement reigned throughout the city; business was almost entirely suspended; river boats declined to land freight at the levee; the situation amounted to a commercial paralysis. The supreme court had met on the 7th of May and upon a collateral case had held that the circuit court of Pulaski County had jurisdiction of the subject-matter, that its judgment was regular and valid, and as a consequence directed the State treasurer to honor Brooks's warrants. This decision was communicated to the President by Brooks, and on the 9th he again made an urgent appeal for help.

[Telegram dated Baring Cross, Fifth month, 9, 1874. Received at northeast corner Fourteenth street and Pennsylvania avenue at 4.20 p. m.]

President GRANT, *Washington, D. C.:*

I was elected to the office of governor of Arkansas by a large majority of votes. This I have established by the proof. In the courts I have been adjudged entitled to the office by the circuit court, the only court of general jurisdiction in this State. The force and effect of this judgment was submitted to the supreme court in a proceeding which called into question the jurisdiction of the circuit court and the force and effect of its judgment and my right to exercise the duties and office of governor, and now the supreme court has adjudicated me to be the lawful governor of the State, and directed the treasurer to honor my warrant on the treasury, to suppress violence and disorder, an act that can be performed only by the governor. I in actual possession, and exercising the functions of the office, a formidable insurrection and armed rebellion against the right and lawful authorities exists, actual conflict wages, and several lives have been lost. It is my duty to defend the government I have sworn to administer. I have appealed and do now appeal to Qour Excellency as Chief Magistrate of the United States for assistance to quell insurrection and domestic violence. Two days have the insurgents projected a desperate struggle to gain possession of the state-house and public property. I am able to hold the situation against all the force the insurgents can rally, but prompt recognition and interposition on your part would prevent the effusion of much blood.

JOSEPH BROOKS,
Governor of Arkansas.

Meanwhile the Congressional delegation at Washington, together with attorneys representing the two factions, were endeavoring to effect a compromise. On the 9th of May these parties had reached an agreement by which the entire question was to be left to an extra session of the legislature, to be convened on the fourth Monday in May, each contestant in the meantime to disband and send home his troops, retaining, if desirable, a small bodyguard at Little Rock not to exceed one company, but preserving absolute peace and noninterference. This proposition was accepted by Brooks[90] but rejected by Baxter,[89] so that matters remained as before. The legislature was to meet on the 11th of May, but the adherents of Brooks now decided to prevent the assembling of a quorum, and to assist in this scheme seized the trains of the Little Rock, Fort Smith and Memphis Road, so that members from the northern part of the State were unable to reach the capital. Those members of the legislature who succeeded in reaching Little Rock, twenty-nine in number, telegraphed the President for protection.[91] The latter, unwilling to believe that the opportunity for compromise had entirely passed, now proposed that the legislature meet and adjourn for a time—ten days, for example—in order to allow a quorum to respond, and to effect this plan promised the protection of the troops.[94] This was agreed to conditionally by Baxter but rejected by Brooks.[95] This seems to be regarded as the point at which the patience of all the friends of compromise at Washington was exhausted. The President was exceedingly anxious that a settlement should be reached and extremely desirous that it be accomplished without the necessity of exercising his judicial power. The forces on both sides were being augmented, collisions more frequent, appeals from business men and nonpoliticians for interposition more urgent. The case had been in the hands of the Attorney-General for some days and the latter had reached an opinion, but the President still hesitated to adopt it. On the 13th of May the legislature succeeded in reaching a quorum and at once passed the following resolutions:

Whereas, the legislature of the State of Arkansas has convened, a quorum of each house being present; and whereas, the capital of our State is occupied by armed and contending forces; and whereas, the statehouse is now in possession of armed troops: Therefore, be it

Resolved by the general assembly of the State of Arkansas, That the President of the United States be, and is hereby, requested to put the legislature in possession of the legislative halls, and that the public property in the statehouse square be placed under the supervision and the control of this body, the legal custodian thereof while in session, and that he make such order for the disposition of said armed and contending forces as will more perfectly protect the State against domestic violence, and insure this body due protection, and that a duly certified copy of this resolution be at once forwarded to the President of the United States.

On receipt of this the President issued the following proclamation recognizing Baxter as the legal governor, and directing all turbulent and disorderly persons to disperse and retire peaceably Baxter recognized, to their homes within ten days. At the same time May 15, 1874. instructions were sent to General Emory, commanding the Department of the Gulf, to instruct the commanding officers of all troops in Arkansas to recognize Baxter as the legal governor and to afford him all the protection in that position which the case may demand:

BY THE PRESIDENT OF THE UNITED STATES OF AMERICA.

A PROCLAMATION.

Whereas, certain turbulent and disorderly persons, pretending that Elisha Baxter, the present executive of Arkansas, was not elected, have combined together with force and arms to resist his authority as such executive and other authorities of said State; and

Whereas, said Elisha Baxter has been declared duly elected by the general assembly of said State as provided in the constitution thereof, and has for a long period been exercising the functions of said office, into which he was inducted according to the constitution and laws of said State, and ought by its citizens to be considered as the lawful executive thereof; and

Whereas, it is provided in the Constitution of the United States that the United States shall protect every State in the Union, on application of the legislature, or of the executive when the legislature can not be convened, against domestic violence; and

Whereas, said Elisha Baxter, under section 4 of Article IV of the Constitution of the United States and the laws passed in pursuance thereof, has heretofore made application to me to protect said State and the citizens thereof against domestic violence; and

Whereas, the general assembly of said State was convened in extra session at the capital thereof on the 11th instant, pursuant to a call made by said Elisha Baxter, and both houses thereof have passed a joint resolution also applying to me to protect the State against domestic violence; and

Whereas, it is provided in the laws of the United States that in all cases of insurrection in any State, or of obstruction to the laws thereof, it shall be lawful for the President of the United States, on application of the legislature of such State, or of the executive when the legislature can not be convened, to employ such part of the land and naval forces as shall be judged necessary for the purpose of suppressing such insurrection, or causing the laws to be duly executed; and

Whereas, it is required that whenever it may be necessary, in the judgment of the President, to use the military force for the purpose aforesaid, he shall forthwith, by proclamation, command such insurgents to disperse and retire peaceably to their respective homes within a limited time:

Now, therefore, I, Ulysses S. Grant, President of the United States, do hereby make proclamation and command all turbulent and disorderly persons to disperse and retire peaceably to their respective abodes within ten days from this date, and hereafter to submit themselves to the lawful authority of said executive and the other constituted authorities of said State; and I invoke the aid and cooperation of all good citizens thereof to uphold law and preserve public peace.

In witness whereof, I have hereunto set my hand and caused the seal of the United States to be affixed.

Done at the city of Washington, this 15th day of May, in the year of our Lord one thousand eight hundred and seventy-four, and of the Independence of the United States the ninety-eighth.

[SEAL.]

U. S. GRANT.

By the President:

HAMILTON FISH,
Secretary of State.

WAR DEPARTMENT,
ADJUTANT-GENERAL'S OFFICE,
Washington, May 16, 1874.

GENERAL: I am instructed by the Secretary of War to communicate to you the following orders of the President and to request you will direct the commanding officer at Little Rock, Capt. Thos. E. Rose, Sixteenth Infantry, by telegraph to see that they are properly carried out:

The President directs that, as his proclamation recognizing Baxter as lawful governor has been issued, he is to be protected in that position by the United States forces, if necessary.

I am, General, very respectfully, your obedient servant,

E. D. TOWNSEND,
Adjutant-General.

Gen. W. T. SHERMAN, *U. S. Army.*

[Telegram.]

HEADQUARTERS, ARMY OF THE UNITED STATES,
Washington, D. C., May 16, 1874.

Gen. W. H. EMORY,

Commanding Department of the Gulf, New Orleans, La.:

The President has recognized Governor Baxter as the legal governor of Arkansas by his proclamation of yesterday. You will accordingly instruct the commanding officer at Little Rock, and all other garrisons serving in Arkansas, to recognize Governor Baxter as the legal governor of that State and afford him all the protection in that position which the case calls for.

By command of General Sherman:

WM. D. WHIPPLE,
Assistant Adjutant-General.

The reasons for this recognition are fully set forth in the opinion of Attorney-General Williams, dated May 15, 1874,[a] and are substan-

---

[a] XIV Opin., 391.

tially those adopted by the supreme court of the State in denying the writ of *quo warranto* "that the courts of the State had no right to hear and determine the question presented, because exclusive jurisdiction in such cases had been conferred upon the general assembly by the constitution and laws of the State." In giving this opinion the Attorney-General remarked:

Section 4, Article IV of the Constitution of the United States is as follows: "The United States shall guarantee to every State in this Union a republican form of government, and shall protect each of them against invasion, and, on application of the legislature, or of the executive (when the legislature can not be convened), against domestic violence." When, in pursuance of this provision of the Constitution, the President is called upon by the executive of a State to protect it against domestic violence, it appears to be his duty to give the required aid, especially when there is no doubt about the existence of the domestic violence; but where two persons, each claiming to be governor, make calls respectively upon the President, under said clause of the Constitution, it, of course, becomes necessary for him to determine in the first place which of said persons is the constitutional governor of the State.

* * * * * * *

It is assumed in the argument for Brooks that the judgment of the Pulaski circuit court is binding as well upon the President as upon Baxter until it is reversed; but where there are conflicting decisions, as in this case, the President is to prefer that one which, in his opinion, is warranted by the constitution and laws of the State.

The general assembly has decided that Baxter was elected. The circuit court of Pulaski County has decided that Brooks was elected. Taking the provision of the constitution which declares that *contested elections* about certain State officers, including the governor, *shall be determined* by the general assembly, and that provision of the law heretofore cited which says that *all contested elections of governor shall be decided* by the legislature, and the two decisions of the supreme court affirming the exclusive jurisdiction of that body over the subject, and the conclusion irresistibly follows that said judgment of the circuit court is void. A void judgment binds nobody.

* * * * * * *

Respecting the claim that Brooks received a majority of the votes at the election it must be said that the President has no way to verify that claim. If he had, it would not, in my opinion, under the circumstances of this case, be a proper subject for his consideration. Perhaps if everything about the election was in confusion and there had been no legal count of the votes, the question of majorities might form an element of the discussion; but where, as in this case, there has been a legal count of the votes and the tribunal organized by the constitution of the State for that purpose has declared the election, the President, in my judgment, ought not to go behind that action to look into the state of the vote. Frauds may have been committed to the prejudice of Brooks; but, unhappily, there are few elections where partisan zeal runs high in which the victorious party, with more or less of truth, is not charged with acts of fraud. There must, however, be an end to controversy upon the subject. Somebody must be trusted to count votes and declare elections. Unconstitutional methods of filling offices can not be resorted to because there is some real or imagined unfairness about the election. Ambitious and selfish aspirants for office generally create the disturbance about this matter, for people are more interested in the preservation of peace than in the political fortunes of any man.

Either of the contestants with law and order is better than the other with discord and violence. I think it would be disastrous to allow the proceedings by which Brooks obtained possession of the office to be drawn into precedent. There is not a

State in the Union in which they would not produce conflict, and probably blood-shed.   They can not be upheld or justified upon any ground; and in my opinion Elisha Baxter should be recognized as the lawful executive of the State of Arkansas.

*   *   *   *   *   *   *

On the 11th instant the general assembly of the State was convened in extra session upon the call of Baxter, and both houses passed a joint resolution, pursuant to section 4 of Article IV of the Constitution of the United States, calling upon the President to protect the State against domestic violence.   This call exhausts all the means which the people of the State have under the Constitution to invoke the aid of the Executive of the United States for their protection, and there seems to be, under the circumstances of the case, an imperative necessity for immediate action.

*   *   *   *   *   *   *

Brooks now disbanded his troops and retired from the statehouse, of which Baxter at once resumed possession.   The adherents of both sides abandoned their organization, and those from the country districts gradually left for their homes.   The United States troops were not called upon for any future service, nor during the entire period of excitement were they ever required to exercise more than a passive force.   It is stated that the military expenses attending the disturbances exceeded $250,000, which the State was subsequently compelled to assume.   The tension of political feeling engendered by the incident was, however, merely relaxed.   The legislature adjourned on the 28th of May, but not before providing for another constitutional convention—the fourth which had been convened since 1861.   This convention met on the 14th of July and framed a new constitution, which was submitted to the people on the 13th of October and ratified by a large majority.   The Brooks Republicans held a convention in September, in which they declared that the so-called constitutional convention, having been called by a revolutionary legislature, was without warrant or authority of law; that all its acts were revolutionary, null, and void, and therefore declined to nominate candidates for the election of November 3.   As a consequence the Democratic candidate, A. H. Garland, was elected governor without opposition, and on the 12th of November entered upon his duties, relieving Baxter, whose term had expired.   A new contestant now appeared on the scene in the person of V. V. Smith, who had served as lieutenant-governor under Baxter, and with the Brooks wing had ignored the proceedings attending the May legislature, the constitutional convention, and the election, and who, claiming that the office of governor had been shamefully abandoned by Baxter and usurped by Garland, announced himself as entitled to the office of governor.   He issued a proclamation in which, having declared the acts of the Garland administration to be "revolution, and nothing but revolution," he concluded as follows:

Now, therefore, I, V. V. Smith, lieutenant-governor of the State of Arkansas, by virtue of the authority vested in the lieutenant-governor by the tenth section of Article VI of said constitution (Elisha Baxter having abdicated and abandoned the office of governor), do hereby command all persons claiming to derive political authority under and by virtue of the so-called constitution of October 13, 1874, to desist and refrain from the exercise of all official authority thereunder, and all persons that may have assumed to act under the authority of said pretended constitution, whether executive, legislative, or judicial, are hereby commanded to relinquish and surrender said offices to the persons entitled thereto under the constitution of 1868, and the laws passed thereunder, within five days from the date hereof, or I shall take such measures as will, in my opinion, result in the observance and enforcement of this command.

In testimony whereof, I have hereunto set my hand and caused the seal of the State to be affixed, at Little Rock, this the 13th day of November, A. D. 1874.

[SEAL.]   V. V. SMITH,
                                                     Governor of Arkansas.
EDWARD WHEELER,
    Secretary of State.

On the same date he addressed a long dispatch to the President reciting his position and announcing himself as the legal governor of Arkansas:

The abdication of the office of governor [he states] and the abandonment thereof by Elisha Baxter in law amounts to a constructive or *parol* resignation. In such case, under the provisions of section 10, article 6, of said constitution, the duties of the office of governor devolve upon me as lieutenant-governor. By and through the treachery and connivance of Elisha Baxter, I find A. H. Garland in the executive office discharging the duties thereof. Not only this, I find a body of men in the legislative halls who pretend to be the members of the general assembly of the State of Arkansas, and who are attempting to legislate for the people, who were not elected at the time nor in the manner provided by the constitution and laws of said State; in short, I find a new government, set up during my absence, that is not the legitimate offspring of that of 1868, and that the officers of the pretended government have in some instances by violence and force displaced officers holding similar positions under the constitution alluded to by reason of this state of affairs and other causes, all contributing to the same end. Domestic violence exists in this State which is too powerful to be suppressed by ordinary process of the law or the militia at my command:

Now, therefore, I, V. V. Smith, lieutenant-governor of the State of Arkansas— Elisha Baxter, the recognized governor of said State, having abdicated and abandoned said office—do hereby and by these presents make application to the President of the United States, and the laws passed in pursuance thereof, to guarantee to said State of Arkansas a republican form of government and protect the same against domestic violence. The legislature of said State is not now in session and can not be convened at this time without great detriment to the public interests. Any attempt to do so would result in augmenting confusion and anarchy, and would probably lead to strife and unnecessary bloodshed.

In testimony whereof, I have hereunto set my hand and caused the seal of the State to be affixed, at the city of Little Rock, this 13th day of November, 1874.

[SEAL.]   V. V. SMITH,
                                                     Governor of Arkansas.
By the governor:
    EDWARD WHEELER,
        Secretary of State.

Inasmuch as a Congressional committee, under the chairmanship of Mr. Poland, of Vermont, was at the moment inquiring into the Arkansas matter, the President declined to interfere in behalf of

Smith; but when, in February, 1875, this committee reported, the majority sustaining the proceedings under which Garland was elected and the minority declaring that Brooks had been elected in 1872 and was the lawful governor until January, 1877, the President concurred with the latter, and sent a message to Congress to that effect on the 8th of February in which he urged Congress to "take definite action to relieve the Executive from acting upon questions which should be decided by the legislative branch of the Government." This request however was not heeded, though the House ultimately adopted the Poland report.[a]

---

[a] Senate Ex. Doc. No. 25, Forty-third Congress, second session; H. R. Report No. 771, Forty-third Congress, first session; H. R. Report No. 2, Forty-third Congress, second session; House Ex. Doc. No. 229, Forty-third Congress, first session.

VIII. POLITICAL DISTURBANCES IN SOUTH CAROLINA.

THE HAMBURG RIOT, 1876—THE RIFLE CLUBS—DISORDERS AT COLUMBIA.

The participation of South Carolina in the operations of the Ku-Klux-Klan and the action of the President in locating Federal troops throughout the disturbed counties have already been recited. Although the immediate effect of these measures was to restore a degree of good order to this section, there were constant irritations and disturbances for the following five or six years. It was not until the summer of 1876, however, that these disorders attracted much attention. A company of colored militia had been organized at Hamburg, in Aiken County, during the administration of Governor Scott, in 1869-70; had been supplied with arms and had drilled frequently, but after the excitement consequent upon the operations of the Ku-Klux had subsided the company had ceased its activity, drilled but seldom, and was scarcely alive. In May, 1876, a new captain had been elected, by whose energy recruiting had been

The Hamburg riot, July 8, 1876. stimulated until the membership had increased to about eighty. On the 4th of July, 1876, the company was being drilled on one of the public streets of Hamburg when a carriage containing two of the townsmen (white) came by and tried to drive through the ranks. An altercation ensued, but the company finally opened ranks and permitted the carriage to pass through. The incident seems to have angered the white men, for they at once made complaint against the militia company for obstructing the highway, and the captain was arrested and brought before one Rivers, a trial justice, who was also a major-general of militia. The arrest seems to have caused great offense to the members of the company, and it was charged that they assembled in their armory and threatened to release the captain. It was also asserted that the company had no legal existence, but had been disbanded for years. Before the case could be heard the white men of the town seem to have determined that the militia company should be disarmed, and on the 8th of July some 200 or 300 citizens armed themselves, came into Hamburg, and, calling upon Rivers, demanded a surrender of the arms in the hands of the militia company. Rivers seems to have been willing to surrender the arms, but the captain and his men refused to turn them over. While these negotiations were going on the armed white men were sur-

182

rounding the armory, and before they were concluded firing had already commenced.

After it had commenced it was returned by the militia, and one of the attacking party was shot through the head and instantly killed. From this time up to midnight every colored man that could be found in Hamburg was pursued, shot at, and otherwise maltreated. Some twenty-five of the members of the militia company were captured. Five of these were taken out and shot to death; the rest were turned loose or broke loose and ran away, were fired upon as they ran, and several severely wounded. In the midst of this pursuit several stores and houses were broken open and robbed and a large number of cabins belonging to the colored people broken into and plundered. The matter was reported to Congress by a message from the President in answer to a Senate resolution,[a] but was lost sight of in the more pressing and exciting events of that year.

There were other outbreaks during the succeeding months, and it was alleged that white rifle clubs had been organized all over the State. There was a riot in Ellenton, not far from Hamburg, in Aiken County, which continued for several days, in which some twelve or fifteen men were killed. On the 7th of October Governor Chamberlain issued a proclamation, requiring all organizations and combinations of men, not organized militia, to disband, with the alternative of a resort to military force. At the same time he applied to the Federal Government for assistance, and in response the President issued a proclamation, dated October 17, 1876, followed by instructions to the General of the Army, as follows:

The "Rifle Clubs," 1876.

By the President of the United States of America.

A PROCLAMATION.

Whereas, it has been satisfactorily shown to me that insurrection and domestic violence exist in several counties of the State of South Carolina, and that certain combinations of men against the law exist in many counties of said State, known as "rifle clubs," who ride up and down by day and night in arms, murdering some peaceable citizens and intimidating others, which combinations, though forbidden by the laws of the State, can not be controlled or suppressed by the ordinary course of justice; and whereas, it is provided in the Constitution of the United States that the United States shall protect every State in this Union, on application of the legislature, or of the executive when the legislature can not be convened, against domestic violence; and whereas, by laws in pursuance of the above, it is provided in the laws of the United States that in all cases of insurrection in any State, or of obstruction to the laws thereof, it shall be lawful for the President of the United States, on application of the legislature of such State, or of the executive when the legislature can not be convened, to call for the militia of any other State or States, or to employ such part of the land and naval forces as shall be judged necessary for the purpose of suppressing such insurrection or causing the laws to be duly executed; and whereas, the legislature of said State is not now in session and can not be convened

---

[a] Senate Ex. Doc. No. 85, Forty-fourth Congress, first session.

in time to meet the present emergency, and the executive of said State, under section 4 of Article IV of the Constitution and the laws passed in pursuance thereof, has therefore made due application to me in the premises for such part of the military force of the United States as may be necessary and adequate to protect said State and the citizens thereof against domestic violence and to enforce the due execution of the laws; and whereas, it is required that whenever it may be necessary, in the judgment of the President, to use the military force for the purpose aforesaid he shall forthwith, by proclamation, command such insurgents to disperse and retire peaceably to their respective homes within a limited time: Now, therefore,

I, Ulysses S. Grant, President of the United States, do hereby make proclamation and command all persons engaged in said unlawful and insurrectionary proceedings to disperse and retire peaceably to their respective abodes within three days from this date, and hereafter abandon said combinations and submit themselves to the laws and constituted authorities of said State, and I invoke the aid and cooperation of all good citizens thereof to uphold the laws and preserve the public peace. In witness whereof, I have hereunto set my hand and caused the seal of the United States to be affixed.

Done at the city of Washington, this 17th of October, in the year of our Lord eighteen hundred and seventy-six and of the Independence of the United States the one hundred and first.

[SEAL.]   U. S. GRANT.

By the President:

JOHN L. CADWALLADER,
    Acting Secretary of State.

                                                        WAR DEPARTMENT,
                                                    Washington, October 17, 1876.

Gen. W. T. SHERMAN,
    Commanding United States Army.

SIR: In view of the existing condition of affairs in South Carolina, there is a possibility that the proclamation of the President of this date may be disregarded. To provide against such a contingency, you will immediately order all the available force in the military division of the Atlantic to report to General Ruger, commanding at Columbia, S. C., and instruct that officer to station his troops in such localities that they may be most speedily and effectually used in case of resistance to the authority of the United States. It is hoped that a collision may thus be avoided, but you will instruct General Ruger to let it be known that it is the fixed purpose of the Government to carry out fully the spirit of the proclamation, and to sustain it by the military force of the General Government, supplemented, if necessary, by the militia of the various States.

Very respectfully, your obedient servant,

                                                        J. D. CAMERON,
                                                            Secretary of War.

Against the assertions of this proclamation the people of the State protested, denying any intention of disturbing the peace or of resisting the General Government. They contended that the so-called "rifle clubs" were formed solely for home protection; that few of them had arms or ammunition; that others were equipped with the sanction of the governor, and frequently with his aid, and that their organization was necessitated by the reckless distribution among the colored people of arms and ammunition by the State authorities.

Their submission was immediate and unconditional, and no occasion arose for the use of the troops in disbanding these clubs.

There was much excitement in the State, as elsewhere through the country, over the delay in ascertaining the result of the Presidential election of 1876. During the disturbances growing out of the suppression of the rifle clubs and the election that followed troops were stationed, in small detachments, at 70 different points in the State, and by their presence contributed in a marked degree to the orderly manner in which the election was conducted. But as the time for the meeting of the legislature approached it was feared that there would be armed resistance to the installation of the governor, and to anticipate this the latter applied to the President for troops to preserve the peace. In response the following instructions were telegraphed on the 26th of November to the Department commander: [a]

WASHINGTON, D. C., *November 26, 1876.*

Gen. THOMAS H. RUGER, or Col. H. M. BLACK,
Columbia, S. C.:

The following has been received from the President:

EXECUTIVE MANSION, *November 26, 1876.*

Hon. J. D. CAMERON, *Secretary of War.*

SIR: D. H. Chamberlain is now governor of the State of South Carolina beyond any controversy, and remains so until the new governor shall be duly and legally inaugurated under the Constitution. The Government has been called upon to aid, with the military and naval forces of the United States, to maintain Republican government in the State against resistance too formidable to be overcome by State authorities. You are directed, therefore, to sustain Governor Chamberlain in his authority against domestic violence until otherwise directed.

U. S. GRANT.

In obeying these instructions you will advise with the governor and dispose your troops in such manner as may be deemed best in order to carry out the spirit of the above order of the President.

Acknowledge receipt.

J. D. CAMERON,
Secretary of War.

As a result of these instructions all available troops were at once assembled at Columbia. These consisted of eight companies of the Eighteenth Infantry, one battery of the First Artillery, two of the Second, and three of the Third, together with various detachments, to a total exceeding 450 officers and men. The legislature met on the 28th, when, under the instructions of the governor, only those holding certificates of election from the secretary of state were permitted to enter the hall of representatives, thus excluding certain Democrats from Edgefield and Lancaster counties. As a consequence those who were refused admission, together with those Democrats who had been admitted, organized separately, and thus the spectacle was presented for several days of two houses of representatives in session at the

---

[a] H. R. Ex. Doc. No. 30, Forty-fourth Congress, second session, pp. 16, 17.

same time in the same hall. To put an end to this anomalous state of
affairs the governor decided to eject the members who had been the
subject of contention, and to that end called upon the commanding
officer of the troops for aid. In this complication the latter (General
Ruger) determined at first to so far comply with the requisition as to
exclude those gentlemen from future admission to the hall, pending a
judicial settlement of the question, but on reflection decided that the
wisest course would be to hold closely to his general instructions—to
preserve the peace merely. To this course the governor demurred and
telegraphed the Secretary of War, asking that General Ruger be
instructed to obey his orders, to which reply was sent him on the 2d
of December and similar dispatch to General Ruger. A few days
later, fearing that the earlier instructions had been too brief or vague,
the President sent a second dispatch to General Ruger. These were
as follows: [a]

WASHINGTON, *December 2, 1876.*

Governor D. H. CHAMBERLAIN,
    Columbia, S. C.:

The President thinks that you should exercise your own resources as governor in
behalf of the legislature which you have recognized by assisting it to purge itself of
unauthorized persons.

If you are resisted in this, General Ruger has been instructed to enforce your
authority.

ALPHONSO TAFT,
Attorney-General.

EXECUTIVE MANSION,
Washington City, December 3, 1876.

Gen. T. H. RUGER,
    Columbia, S. C.:

Fearing your instructions may be conflicting and leave you in doubt as to your
duties in the present unhappy condition of affairs in South Carolina, I wish to say this:
Governor Chamberlain is the legal constituted governor of the State, and remains so
until the legislature canvasses the vote and installs his successor; and he is entitled
as such to your support and protection. It is a civil duty to organize the legislature
devolving on State authorities. All you can do is to prevent unauthorized persons
from forcibly interfering with the governor and other authorized officers in the performance of their duties. To be plain, I want to avoid anything like an unlawful
use of the military, but it will be entirely right to sustain the governor or any of his
agents or officers in the performance of any duty in connection with the legislature
if interfered with by outsiders while in the performance of that duty.

U. S. GRANT.

On the 5th of December there was increased uneasiness at Columbia.
Armed men came in from the country, openly asserting their intention
to seize the statehouse and seat the contesting governor (Wade Hampton). There were fears of violence, and under much excitement
appeals were made to the President. Under his direction the troops

---

[a] General Ruger to General Sherman, dispatches of November 30, 1876 (H. R. Ex.
Doc. No. 30, Forty-fourth Congress, second session, pp. 37–38).

were posted in and about the statehouse, with instructions to protect the legislature from outside interference.   Against this the contesting members of the legislature protested, and to their inquiries General Ruger replied as follows:

COLUMBIA, S. C., *December 8, 1876.*

The Hon. F. A. CONNER AND OTHERS.

GENTLEMEN OF THE COMMITTEE: I have the honor to say, in reply to your inquiries, based upon the resolution of which you handed me a copy on yesterday, that the United States troops in the statehouse were placed there by my order for the purpose of executing such orders as might be given; and in this connection I would say, with reference to the inquiries numbered 6 and 7, that if your body should appear at the statehouse for the purpose of entering the hall of the house of representatives, and should be refused admission by those having charge of the doors, and such persons should apply to the officers in command of the troops at the statehouse for assistance necessary to prevent your entering, the present orders to the officers would require them to render such assistance.

I am, gentlemen, your obedient servant,

THOMAS H. RUGER,
Colonel and Brevet Brigadier-General,
Department of the South.

Meanwhile the Republican senate and house had canvassed the votes and declared D. H. Chamberlain to have been elected governor, and proceeded to inaugurate him on the 7th, while the Democratic house had procured duplicate returns, which they canvassed, and from which they declared the election of Wade Hampton.   Hampton demanded the surrender of the statehouse and the public records, which Chamberlain refused, and during the entire winter of 1876–77 both these gentlemen maintained their right to the office of governor, which both pretended to exercise.   The President declined to interfere further than to preserve the peace, and although a small military force was kept up at Columbia, the city was quiet and no occasion arose for their services.   Soon after taking office President Hayes invited Messrs. Chamberlain and Hampton to a personal conference, and as a consequence on the 10th of April, 1877, the United States troops were withdrawn from the statehouse, and the State government was soon after peaceably transferred to General Hampton.[a]

There was much opposition in and out of Congress to the policy of the Administration in the matter of furnishing Federal troops to preserve the peace in this and other Southern States during the elections of 1876, and this opposition became more intense when the results of that election were apparently in doubt for some months.   The matter was warmly debated throughout the closing session of the Forty-fourth Congress, resulting in the failure of that Congress to provide the usual appropriations for the support of the Army for the ensuing year, and

---

[a] Senate Misc. Doc. No. 45, Forty-fourth Congress, second session; H. R. Misc. Doc. No. 31, ibid; H. R. Report 175, ibid.

was renewed at the first session of the Forty-fifth.[a]   Various bills were introduced looking to a limitation of the powers of the Executive in the use of the Army, and especially in forbidding its use by United States marshals as a posse comitatus.   The long debate culminated in a rider to the army appropriation bill for the fiscal year ending June 30, 1879, approved June 18, 1878, as section 29 (afterwards section 15), as follows:

SEC. 15.   From and after the passage of this act it shall not be lawful to employ any part of the Army of the United States as a posse comitatus, or otherwise, for the purpose of executing the laws, except in such cases and under such circumstances as such employment of said force may be expressly authorized by the Constitution or by act of Congress; and no money appropriated by this act shall be used to pay any of the expenses incurred in the employment of any troops in violation of this section, and any person wilfully violating the provisions of this section shall be deemed guilty of a misdemeanor, and on conviction thereof shall be punished by fine not exceeding ten thousand dollars or imprisonment not exceeding two years, or by both such fine and imprisonment.

---

[a]The debate in the House on November 8, 1877, and in the Senate June 6, 1878, is especially interesting in the way of showing the views of leading Senators and members on the question of the use of the Army as a posse comitatus.

IX. THE LABOR STRIKES OF 1877.

RIOT AT MARTINSBURG, W. VA.—RIOTS AT BALTIMORE, MD.—RIOTS AT PITTSBURG, PA.—
DISTURBANCES IN OHIO—RIOTING AT INDIANAPOLIS, IND.—RIOTING AT CHICAGO,
ILL.—RIOTING AT ST. LOUIS, MO.—DISTURBANCES IN VARIOUS STATES.

The action of the railroad companies in the summer of 1877, in suddenly precipitating a reduction of 10 per cent in the wages of their employees, was the occasion for a serious conflict between the forces of labor and capital, resulting in the most extensive domestic disturbance which the country has witnessed. In order to respond to calls for aid where violence actually existed, and to guard against danger at threatened places, it became necessary to concentrate troops in six of the States, as well as to move up others in readiness for anticipated calls, so that within six days nearly one-half the Army was in motion or under orders for immediate service. The trouble commenced on the 14th of July on the Baltimore and Ohio Railroad, where some 40 brakemen and firemen stopped work and attempted to prevent the passage of freight trains. On the 16th the crews of the freight trains at Martinsburg, W. Va., refused to work, and drove off the men sent to replace them. The police of Martinsburg were powerless to cope with the situation, and a body of the State militia sent to that point on the morning of the 17th were fired upon and driven back. By this time the strikers, whose numbers had increased to 100, had been joined by several hundred outsiders, and by night the road was effectually blocked at Martinsburg, while the strike had extended to Wheeling and Parkersburg. By the morning of the 18th the whole road was in the hands of the strikers, and the governor, perceiving the hopelessness of contending with the situation with his slender militia forces, called in the aid of the General Government. The legislature of 1875 had prohibited the enrollment of the militia, so that the only military bodies in the State were four companies of volunteers, two of whom were at Martinsburg and in sympathy with the rioters; a third was 38 miles from a railroad; the fourth, of but 40 men, was needed for home protection. The following is the call of the governor: [a]

Riot at Martinsburg, W. Va., July 14, 1877.

WHEELING, W. VA., *July 18, 1877.*

His Excellency R. B. HAYES,
      President of the United States:

Owing to unlawful combinations and domestic violence now existing at Martinsburg and at other points along the line of the Baltimore and Ohio Railroad it is

---

[a] See also Documents Nos. 99, 100, and 101.

189

impossible with any force at my command to execute the laws of the State. I therefore call upon your excellency for the assistance of the United States military to protect the law-abiding people of the State against domestic violence and to maintain the supremacy of the law. The legislature is not now in session and could not be assembled in time to take any action in the emergency. A force of from two to three hundred should be sent without delay to Martinsburg, where my aid, Colonel Delaplaine, will meet and confer with the officer in command.

HENRY M. MATHEWS,
Governor of West Virginia.

In response to this appeal the President directed Col. William H. French, Fourth Artillery, then commanding at Washington Arsenal, to proceed with every available man of his command, equipped as infantry, to Martinsburg, W. Va., there to report to and confer with Colonel Delaplaine, aid to the governor of the State.[102] At the same time similar instructions were sent to the commandant at Fort McHenry.[103] These troops left without the slightest delay and before dark on the 18th were underway. In order that the laws should be strictly complied with, the commander of these troops was instructed that a proclamation by the President was about to be promulgated, commanding the insurgents to disperse and retire peaceably to their places of abode, and that such proclamation would doubtless have been published at the scene of disturbance by the time of the arrival of the troops, but if not, he should delay action until its publication.[104] The proclamation, in accordance with section 5300 of the Revised Statutes, was issued on the night of the 18th, and was in the following words:

BY THE PRESIDENT OF THE UNITED STATES.

A PROCLAMATION.

Whereas, the governor of the State of West Virginia has represented that domestic violence exists in said State at Martinsburg and at various other points along the line of the Baltimore and Ohio Railroad in said State, which the authorities of said State are unable to suppress;

And whereas, it is provided in the Constitution of the United States that the United States shall protect every State in this Union, on application of the legislature, or of the executive when the legislature can not be convened, against domestic violence;

And whereas, by laws, in pursuance of the above, it is provided (in the laws of the United States) that in all cases of insurrection in any State (or of obstruction to the laws thereof) it shall be lawful for the President of the United States, on application of the legislature of such State, or of the executive when the legislature can not be convened, to call forth the militia of any State or States, or to employ such part of the land and naval forces as shall be judged necessary for the purpose of suppressing such insurrection or causing the laws to be duly executed.

And whereas, the legislature of said State is not now in session and can not be convened in time to meet the present emergency, and the executive of said State, under section 4 of Article IV of the Constitution of the United States and the laws passed in pursuance thereof, has made due application to me in the premises for such part of the military force of the United States as may be necessary and adequate to protect said State and the citizens thereof against domestic violence and to enforce the due execution of the laws;

And whereas, it is required that whenever it may be necessary, in the judgment of the President, to use the military force for the purpose aforesaid, he shall forthwith, by proclamation, command such insurgents to disperse and retire peaceably to their respective homes within a limited time:

Now, therefore, I, Rutherford B. Hayes, President of the United States, do hereby make proclamation, and command all persons engaged in said unlawful and insurrectionary proceedings to disperse and retire peaceably to their respective abodes on or before 12 o'clock noon of the 19th day of July, instant, and hereafter abandon said combinations and submit themselves to the laws and constituted authorities of said State;

And I invoke the aid and cooperation of all good citizens thereof to uphold the laws and preserve the public peace.

In witness whereof, I have hereunto set my hand and caused the seal of the United States to be affixed.

Done at the city of Washington, this 18th day of July, in the year of our Lord one thousand eight hundred and seventy-seven, and of the Independence of the United States the one hundred and second.

R. B. HAYES.

By the President:
    F. W. SEWARD,
        Acting Secretary of State.

Colonel French arrived at Martinsburg early on the morning of the 19th, where he found more than 100 engines and 1,500 freight cars standing idle and blocking every approach to the town. He reported his arrival as follows:

MARTINSBURG, W. VA., *July 19, 1877.*

ADJUTANT-GENERAL, *Washington:*

Proclamation printed; now being circulated. After 12 o'clock, if the insurgents have not dispersed, the troops under my command will proceed to enforce the orders of the President. At present everything seems quiet, and I doubt whether anything more than a demonstration will be required. Whatever action I may determine upon will be after consultation with and full concurrence of Colonel Delaplaine, aid to the governor.

FRENCH,
Colonel, Commanding.

Having circulated the proclamation of the President, which was supplemented by a printed notice to all concerned, warning all persons engaged in the interruption of travel on the Baltimore and Ohio road that the United States troops must not be impeded, and that whoever undertakes it does so at their peril,[105] he proceeded to carry out his instructions. In the course of the day the block at Martinsburg was untangled and several trains were sent forward under military escort. On this day, however, the strike extended over the entire length of the line, and affairs in West Virginia were no longer of consequence.

Moving eastward, the next considerable railroad point was at Cumberland, Md., some 20 miles from the West Virginia line. Here were workshops, roundhouses, car sheds, and various property of the Baltimore and Ohio Railroad Company to immense value, which it was feared the strikers, who had collected in large numbers, intended to destroy. To prevent this, the governor of Maryland ordered the Sixth Regiment of State Militia, having its headquarters in Baltimore, to proceed to Cumberland. This order was the signal for an uprising in Baltimore, and when the regiment appeared in the streets on its way to the station on the afternoon of the 20th it was stoned by the mob. The soldiers, indifferently disciplined, were unable to endure this treatment and responded by shooting into the crowd. This was done without orders or method, so that an irregular fusillade was kept up along the whole route, with a result that 9 of the rioters were killed and 30 or 40 wounded. The excitement was now intense, and the orders for the regiment to go to Cumberland were withdrawn, but not before the Baltimore and Ohio station had been set on fire and much other damage done. The Fifth Regiment, which was ordered to suppress the riot, was attacked, but no shots were exchanged. Soon after dark, the mob having increased its numbers and determination, the governor decided that the situation was beyond his control and that events justified a call upon the Government. This call and the response of the Secretary of War are subjoined:

Riot at Baltimore, July 20, 1877.

CAMDEN STATION, 20.

His Excellency R. B. HAYES.

SIR: An assemblage of rioters, [not] to be dispersed by any force at my command, has taken possession of the Baltimore and Ohio Railroad depot here, set fire the same, and have driven off the firemen who attempted to extinguish the same, and it is impossible with force at my command to disperse the rioters. Under circumstances, as governor of the State of Maryland I call upon you as President of the United States to furnish the force necessary to protect the State against domestic violence. The legislature of the State is not in session and can not be convened in time to meet the emergency.

JOHN LEE CARROLL,
Governor of Maryland.

SOLDIERS' HOME, *Washington, July 21, 1877*

Governor JOHN LEE CARROLL,
Baltimore, Md.:

The President directs me to say that he will aid you to the extent of his power. Available troops will be sent, but a call upon neighboring States will probably be necessary. Communicate with me here and I will advise you more definitely in a short time.

GEO. W. McCRARY,
Secretary of War.

Orders were immediately sent to Gen. W. F. Barry, the commandant at Fort McHenry, to respond to the call of the governor of Maryland by sending all disposable troops to his aid in suppressing the riot at Baltimore, and the President directed that if necessary the marines from Washington Navy-Yard be sent to Baltimore, as indeed they were sent within the following twenty-four hours, but fortunately were not needed.   At the same time a proclamation was issued in the following terms:

BY THE PRESIDENT OF THE UNITED STATES OF AMERICA.

A PROCLAMATION.

Whereas, it is provided in the Constitution of the United States that the United States shall protect every State in this Union on application of the legislature, or of the executive (when the legislature can not be convened), against domestic violence;

And whereas, the governor of the State of Maryland has represented that domestic violence exists in said State at Cumberland, and along the line of the Baltimore and Ohio Railroad in said State, which the authorities of said State are unable to suppress;

And whereas, the laws of the United States require that in all cases of insurrection in any State or of obstruction to the laws thereof, whenever in the judgment of the President it becomes necessary to use the military forces to suppress such insurrection or obstruction to the laws, he shall forthwith, by proclamation, command such insurgents to disperse and retire peaceably to their respective abodes within a limited time:

Now, therefore, I, Rutherford B. Hayes, President of the United States, do hereby admonish all good citizens of the United States and all persons within the territory and jurisdiction of the United States, against aiding, countenancing, abetting, or taking part in such unlawful proceedings; and I do hereby warn all persons engaged in or connected with said domestic violence and obstruction of the laws to disperse and retire peaceably to their respective abodes on or before noon of the 22d day of July, instant.

In testimony whereof, I have hereunto set my hand and caused the seal of the United States to be affixed.

Done at the city of Washington, this 21st day of July, in the year of our Lord eighteen hundred and seventy-seven and of the Independence of the United States of America the one hundred and second.

[SEAL.]   R. B. HAYES.
By the President:
    WM. M. EVARTS,
            Secretary of State.

By evening of the 21st Governor Carroll telegraphed that order had been restored at Baltimore for the present and hoped he would be able to restrain violence with the State militia and local police. He added, however, that lawlessness at Cumberland was increasing; and as it would require all the State forces to preserve order in Baltimore, he feared he might be obliged to ask the Government for aid at that point.[116]   General French was accordingly directed to send all the men he could spare from Martinsburg to Cumberland, to report to Colonel Douglass, of Governor Carroll's staff, to act under the orders of the governor.   Major-General Hancock, the commanding general of the division of the Atlantic, arrived in Baltimore early on the 22d and assumed charge of all military operations in that section. By noon some 360 Regular troops had arrived from New York and relieved the State troops at the Camden station and the Sixth Regiment Armory, so that these latter were available for duty along the

S. Doc. 209——13

line of the railroad. General French removed his headquarters to Cumberland during the day, and all disposable forces were concentrated at that point. In the meantime all available troops from posts in New England and New York State were moved toward New York Harbor, to be held in readiness for such disposition as the emergency might demand. In the same manner troops were drawn from Columbus, Ohio, to Pittsburg, and from St. Louis to Indianapolis, while others from west of the Mississippi were moved into Chicago, as all of these points had been threatened during the day. The presence of the United States troops at Cumberland seemed to be satisfactory to both sides, and before the evening of the 22d trains were running regularly and freely. In fact, the situation in this section had so far improved that General Hancock was enabled to leave Baltimore on the afternoon of the 23d for Philadelphia, where the state of affairs had become threatening.[118]

On the morning of the 19th all the crews of the freight trains of the Pennsylvania Railroad then at Pittsburg stopped work and declared a strike. All freight trains were stopped as they reached the city, and by night a mob to the number of perhaps 1,500 had collected in the yards, but beyond blocking traffic they attempted no serious disturbance. On the 20th all freight traffic on the Pennsylvania road was at a standstill, and the mob at Pittsburg was growing larger and more threatening. By this time the governor, who was hastening home from the Pacific coast with all possible speed, had

Riots
at Pittsburg, Pa., become fully impressed with the gravity of the situa-
July 19, 1877.

tion and had telegraphed orders calling out the entire national guard of the State, sending the Philadelphia regiments to Pittsburg in order to avoid any difficulty growing out of possible sympathy between the strikers and the militia. This was an unfortunate move, though inspired by the most prudent judgment. All day Saturday, the 21st, the Sixth Division of the Pennsylvania National Guard composed in the majority of the regiments from Philadelphia, was slowly making its way across the State, and each hour the mob at Pittsburg, resenting their coming, was increasing in numbers and determination. At 5 o'clock the advance of the guard reached the suburbs of the city, and was greeted by a shower of stones and other missiles, to which the troops replied by several volleys of musketry. The mob, driven to frenzy, broke open a gun shop and, having procured several pieces of ordnance, returned to the attack. In the meantime the troops had taken up their position in a roundhouse, and this was repeatedly attacked by the mob, rapid firing ensuing on both sides. Finding themselves unable to dislodge the soldiers, the mob set fire to a number of cars loaded with oil and coke, which they saturated with oil, and hurled them against the roundhouse. This continued throughout the night of the 21st, but soon after daylight the troops managed to make a successful retreat and ultimately succeeded in reaching the opposite side of the river and disbanding, but not before a large number had been killed and wounded. The mob, however, having tasted the sweets of revenge, proceeded to set fire indiscriminately to all railroad property in sight, so that by 7 o'clock the machine shops, two roundhouses, 125 locomotives, over 2,000 loaded freight cars, and all the buildings of the Pennsylvania road, to the value of between $8,000,000 and $10,000,000, were a mass of flames. To this succeeded plundering and the most indiscriminate robbery and destruction.   During the whole of Sunday the depots of the Pittsburg, Cincinnati and St. Louis, the offices, depots, and engine houses of the Panhandle line, of the Adams Express Company, and the Pullman Car Company, and many private structures were plundered and consumed. The citizens of Pittsburg viewed the destruction with apparent indifference until Monday morning, the 23d, when, the fury of the mob having spent itself, citizen companies were organized and armed for protection.

The first call from Pennsylvania for aid came on the 21st from the mayor of Philadelphia, who feared that the withdrawal of the local militia would encourage the lawless element.[119]   To this the Secretary of War replied on the 22d that troops would be immediately sent to Philadelphia to meet any emergency, and that the President would exert every constitutional power to restore order and protect property.[120]   At the same time the President directed General Hancock to go to Philadelphia as soon as he could leave Baltimore with safety, taking the battalion of marines, and halting, if necessary, any troops en route from New England.   In communicating these instructions the Secretary of War added that the state of affairs at Philadelphia was very threatening, and that, while the governor of Pennsylvania had not yet made a formal call for troops, the President wished to prepare in season for emergencies.[118]   As the news of the riots at Pittsburg was being received, every effort was made to reach Governor Hartranft, but it was not until midnight of Sunday the 22d that he could be located.   At 1 a. m. on the 23d the following dispatch was delivered to the President at the Soldiers' Home:

CRESTON, WYOMING TERRITORY,
July 22, 1877.

President HAYES, *Washington:*

I call upon you for troops to assist in quelling mobs within the borders of the State of Pennsylvania. Respectfully suggest that you order troops from adjoining States, and prepare to call for volunteers authorized by act of Congress.

J. F. HARTRANFT.

By this time General Hancock had reached Philadelphia, where he found the strikers in considerable force and demonstrative, but committing no overt acts.   He, however, ordered the troops en route from

Fort Adams, R. I., and Fort Trumbull, Conn., 194 in number, and those from Fort Warren and Independence, Mass., 102 strong, to halt in Philadelphia, so that by nightfall he had, with the marines, a force of something over 450 men and the four guns of Light Battery C, of the Third Artillery. The commanding officer of the arsenal at Pittsburg reported that all was quiet at that point, and that the troops from Columbus, Ohio, ordered to join him the night before, had arrived. During the morning the proclamation of the President was published and given the fullest circulation throughout the State. It was as follows:

BY THE PRESIDENT OF THE UNITED STATES OF AMERICA.

A PROCLAMATION.

Whereas, it is provided by the Constitution of the United States that the United States shall protect every State in this Union, on application of the legislature, or of the executive (when the legislature can not be convened), against domestic violence;

And whereas, the governor of the State of Pennsylvania has represented that domestic violence exists in said State which the authorities of said State are unable to suppress;

And whereas, the laws of the United States require that in all cases of insurrection in any State or of obstruction to the laws thereof, whenever in the judgment of the President it becomes necessary to use the military forces to suppress such insurrection or obstruction to the laws, he shall forthwith by proclamation command such insurgents to disperse, and retire peaceably to their respective abodes within a limited time:

Now, therefore, I, Rutherford B. Hayes, President of the United States, do hereby admonish all good citizens of the United States, and all persons within the territory and jurisdiction of the United States against aiding, countenancing, abetting, or taking part in such unlawful proceedings; and I do hereby warn all persons engaged in or connected with said domestic violence and obstruction of the laws to disperse and retire peaceably to their respective abodes on or before 12 o'clock noon, of the 24th day of July, instant.

In testimony whereof, I have hereunto set my hand, and caused the seal of the United States to be fixed.

Done at this city of Washington, this 23d day of July, in the year of our Lord eighteen hundred and seventy-seven, and of the Independence of the United States of America the one hundred and second.

[SEAL.]   R. B. HAYES.

By the President: ·

WM. M. EVARTS,
        Secretary of State.

The situation in Pennsylvania during the 23d, 24th, and 25th was one of comparative quiet. The blockade inaugurated at Martinsburg on the 18th and at Pittsburg on the 19th had now extended into the adjoining States, so that one after another the railroads leading into Baltimore, Philadelphia, and Pittsburg, so far as their freight business was concerned, had to come to a standstill. This situation necessitated the stopping of many roads that were otherwise innocent of participation in the strike, while a number of others whose employees were affected by sympathy suspended operations to await its outcome. Among the latter were the Erie, the New York Central, the Delaware, Lackawanna and Western, and the Canada Southern, all operating in the State of New York, but reaching across Pennsylvania into Ohio. All these roads struck on Tuesday, the 24th, so that by the morning of the 25th, when Governor Hartranft arrived at Philadelphia, there was a cessation of labor throughout the affected States that practically amounted to a paralysis. It is estimated that at that moment fully 100,000 men, ordinarily employed at good wages, were on strike, and perhaps ten times that number ready to join them on the slightest provocation.

For a time a conflict of opinion between the State and Federal authorities seemed to threaten a defeat of the very purposes of their joint action. In the cases of West Virginia and Maryland the President had been especially careful that the Federal troops should report to the governor and act under his direction, and General Hancock had been instructed to pursue a similar course in Pennsylvania; but upon reflection the President was inclined to think that when a State had exhausted all its resources and by an appeal to the General Government had confessed its defeat and admitted its inability to cope with the situation, it was for the Federal Government to assume the direction of subsequent affairs, inasmuch as by responding to the appeal of the State it had accepted the responsibility and would be held accountable for the consequences. In this view of the case and under the circumstances known to exist in Pennsylvania the President thought that General Hancock should take command of all the troops engaged in suppressing domestic violence within the State, including both the United States forces and those furnished by the State. He deferred, however, to a suggestion of General Hancock that inasmuch as the governor believed that he could maintain the supremacy of the law, and with the moral effect of the Federal cooperation was willing to undertake it, it would be time enough for the Government to insist upon its position when the governor had failed to accomplish successful results.[a] In the furtherance of this policy Major-General Schofield, who in the absence of both General Sherman and Lieutenant-General Sheridan in the far West had been ordered to Washington, was directed to stop at Philadelphia and confer with the governor and General Hancock. At this conference it was decided that an attempt should be made at once to open up the road from Philadelphia to Pittsburg by a force of State troops under the immediate command of the governor, supported by United States troops under an efficient officer to be designated by General Hancock. General Schofield arrived at Washington with the terms of this project at midnight of the 25th,

---

[a] See Documents Nos. 122 to 132.

and, the plan being approved by the President, measures were at once instituted to carry it into effect.

The combined forces, numbering over 2,000 State troops under General Beaver and 500 United States troops under the command of Maj. John Hamilton, First U. S. Artillery, left West Philadelphia at 11 o'clock on the night of the 26th, the governor having already gone forward with a strong force from Harrisburg. There was some little delay at Johnstown, where the Cambria Iron Works are located and several thousand men on strike, and a misplaced switch threw several cars from the track, but the damage was speedily repaired, and a few minutes before noon of the 28th the troops arrived at Pittsburg. The regular troops were marched directly to the United States arsenal and remained at that point for the following two weeks, but were not called upon for further service. The strikers came to terms on the 27th, and by the 30th traffic had been resumed on the trunk lines and on most of the smaller roads east of the Ohio. Disturbances had in the meantime broken out at Reading, where 13 rioters had been killed in a collision with the militia and 43 wounded, and a force of 200 men, under Major Hamilton, was sent to that point, and about the 1st of August, by which time the disturbances incident to the railroad strikes had ended, it was found necessary to send troops to the anthracite coal regions of Pennsylvania, where the miners had defied the authorities, and for a week or more detachments of the Army were stationed at Scranton, Wilkesbarre, Mauch Chunk, and Easton. But in every instance the presence of the United States troops sufficed to repress the disorders, and during the entire period of the labor troubles no serious resistance was ever made to them.

The blockade at Pittsburg commencing on the 19th and continuing through the 20th naturally resulted in the blocking of that portion of the lines crossing the State of Ohio. The train hands on the Pittsburg, Fort Wayne and Chicago road struck on the afternoon of the 19th and on the Baltimore and Ohio on the 20th. This effectually blocked everything at Steubenville and at Newark, at which points great crowds assembled, causing serious apprehensions on the part of the authorities. To quiet these fears the governor ordered out the State troops. Early in the month the governor of Ohio had made requisition upon the General Government for arms and ammunition, and although the State had but a small balance to its credit the President decided that the emergency warranted the exercise of extraordinary powers and directed the issue of as many arms as could be spared. Accordingly, 2,500 Springfield rifles, .45, were sent from the Rock Island Arsenal on the 23d to Columbus. On that date all trains were stopped on the Ohio and Mississippi road; on the Cleveland, Cincinnati and Columbus at Cleveland; on the Hocking Valley and on the Indianapolis and

Disturbances in Ohio, July 16-30, 1877.

St. Louis.   At Toledo the Lake Shore and Michigan Southern was blocked, and a similar tie up existed on the Erie at Youngstown.   At Columbus, where a dozen railroads centered, the idle railroad hands were joined by a mob of miners and tramps, who closed the rolling mills, machine shops, and factories, and at Zanesville the most of the factories and mills were closed on the plea of sympathy with the railroad strikers at Pittsburg.

Although no formal call for military aid as required by the Constitution was made by the governor of Ohio, many earnest appeals came from local authorities, but beyond the stationing of a considerable force at Newport Barracks opposite Cincinnati, a point from which they could be speedily thrown into the State, no assistance was directly rendered.   On the 2d of August, Col. E. S. Otis in command of a force of United States troops, en route to Fort Wayne, passed through Toledo, where the strikers were especially violent, and the local authorities implored him to stay and render assistance.   He submitted the question to General Hancock, who decided that unless legally summoned by the sheriff as a posse comitatus he should take no part in suppressing the rioters, inasmuch as the governor had not called for assistance.   In the end the State authorities, aided by the National Guard and citizens' committee, succeeded in quelling the disturbances at Zanesville, Columbus, Toledo, and Cleveland, but it was nearly the middle of August before order had been completely restored.

As the strike progressed westward, two points in Indiana threatened for a time to call for the most energetic measures.   These were Fort Wayne, where the headquarters of the western section of the Pennsylvania system crossed the Wabash road, and at Indianapolis, where were centered a half dozen trunk lines as well as nearly a score of shorter roads.   At both of these points there was a complete embargo as early as the 20th.   At Jeffersonville, opposite the city of Louisville, another considerable railroad point, is located the largest quartermaster's depot in the country, and at Indianapolis, an arsenal, where was stored a large quantity of small arms and ammunition.   To fully protect these points, troops had been sent, and their presence immediately prevented their attempted seizure by the immense mobs that gathered in the adjoining cities.   On the 25th United States Judge Gresham advised the President that the situation at Indianapolis was most critical and dangerous.   He stated that the State authorities were doing nothing and that the mob was for the moment the only supreme power in the State.   He thought an officer of high rank of the Army should be sent there at once.[133]   On the 26th the governor of Indiana, finding the capital surrounded by a wholly reckless mob bent on mischief, called on the commandant of the arsenal for assistance.   The latter referred him to Washington, and at 10 p. m. of that date the Presi-

Rioting at Indianapolis, Ind., July, 1877.

dent received the following telegram, to which is subjoined the reply of the Secretary of War:

INDIANAPOLIS, IND., *July 26.*

The PRESIDENT OF THE UNITED STATES,
Washington, D. C.:

In view of the threatened domestic violence growing out of the railroad strike, I request that authority be at once given to the commandant of the arsenal to render me all the aid possible in preserving the public peace.

JAMES D. WILLIAMS,
Governor of Indiana.

WAR DEPARTMENT,
Washington City, July 27, 1877.

Gov. JAMES D. WILLIAMS,
Indianapolis, Ind.:

I am directed by the President to say that in the absence of a call upon him under the Constitution and statute for military aid in suppressing domestic violence the Federal troops at Indianapolis can only be used in protecting property of the United States and enforcing process of Federal courts.

GEO. W. McCRARY,
Secretary of War.

At the same time additional troops were sent to the arsenal at Indianapolis, and on the 27th arms and ammunition were issued, at the request of the governor, to four companies of militia—360 men—who were also permitted to camp at the arsenal. The city was greatly excited from the 27th to the 30th; a committee of safety was organized by the citizens, and fears were entertained that the mob would repeat the scenes of Pittsburg. On the 28th the President, yielding to the opinions of Judge Gresham, General Harrison, and other leading citizens of the State, decided that in cases where troops should be called for by United States marshals to aid in enforcing the processes of the United States courts they might be furnished, but in such event he desired that the officers in command of troops, before resorting to extreme measures to compel obedience, should, in the name of the United States, command the insurgents to disperse and desist from resisting the process of the United States.[136] A riot occurred at Fort Wayne on the 28th, and on the same date a small force was sent to Vincennes in response to the call of the United States marshal, but on learning of their coming the rioters dispersed. This latter force was then sent to Terre Haute, where a mob of some 3,000 or 4,000 had assembled and were preventing the running of trains, but their arrival was followed by similar results as at Vincennes. The small force under Colonel Otis en route to Pittsburg was halted at Fort Wayne, but was not called upon for any service.

It was nearly a week from the inauguration of the strike at Martinsburg before its exterior circles had reached Chicago. The men stopped work on the Vandalia and the Chicago and Alton on the 23d. On the 24th General Drum, at Chicago, having telegraphed that from present indications all the trunk lines from the West into Chicago would be closed before night, the troops from Omaha (Ninth Infantry) were ordered east, the Twenty-second Infantry, from Detroit, as well as two companies from Montana being already en route to that point. Although the mayor had expressed his opinion that "the presence of troops at Chicago would only aggravate existing troubles," the mob was permitted to gather and increase in numbers and turbulence throughout the 24th and 25th, shutting up factories and committing all manner of depredations. On the 24th Governor Cullom had inquired if there were troops on the way to Chicago and had been advised of the small force from Detroit. On the 25th signs of the coming storm were so apparent that he lost no further time in calling for aid.

Rioting at Chicago, Ill., July 26–28, 1877.

SPRINGFIELD, ILL., *July 25, 1877.*

His Excellency R. B. HAYES,
    President United States, Washington, D. C.:

Lawlessness exists in this State to such an extent that I am unable with forces at my command to quell the same and protect the law-abiding citizens in their rights. I therefore call upon you for assistance by furnishing military and without delay. Can the six companies at Rock Island be forwarded to Chicago at once? Domestic violence exists in the State.

S. M. CULLOM,
Governor.

On the 26th a fierce encounter took place between the mob and the police, aided by the militia, in which 19 were killed and nearly 100 injured and wounded. It began with an attempt on the part of the police to clear the streets; the crowds resisted and again and again forced the police to retire. At last a force of some 300 policemen, properly officered and maneuvered, made a determined charge on a crowd composed of many thousands; the crowd broke but rallied, heavily reenforced. To this the police responded by another fierce charge, backed by a company of mounted militia, with results as already stated. Many similar skirmishes ensued in various parts of the city, continuing through the day and far into the night. As soon as the call of Governor Cullom was received, the following dispatch was sent to General Drum at 2.50 a. m. of the 26th:

WAR DEPARTMENT,
Washington, D. C., July 26, 1877.

Col. R. C. DRUM,
    Assistant Adjutant-General, Chicago, Ill.:

The President directs that you use the United States troops in case of emergency in suppressing riot at Chicago, under orders of governor of the State. The orders you have given for movement of troops are approved. I have ordered Major Flagler to send you the Gatlings and ammunition. Inform Governor Cullom of this in reply to his request for them. Acknowledge receipt.

E. D. TOWNSEND,
Adjutant-General.

On the receipt of this the two companies of the Twenty-second then at Chicago were reported to the mayor, and by 2 p. m. four more companies of the Twenty-second and six of the Ninth had arrived and been put on duty, but none of the regular troops were engaged in the affray with the mob.[145] On the morning of the 27th the mayor called for guards from these troops to protect the city gas and water works, and these were promptly given, as also, on the application of the Treasury officials, guards were placed at the bonded warehouses. Later in the day the following instructions were sent to General Drum:

WAR DEPARTMENT,
Washington, D. C., July 27, 1877.

Col. R. C. DRUM,
　　Chicago, Ill.:

The President directs that the troops under your command are to be used in protecting the property of the United States and in enforcing the process of the courts of the United States. Should a pressing emergency again arise for their use otherwise, you will telegraph for further orders unless circumstances make it impossible. You will make such display of your force for moral effect as you may deem expedient and will advise me as to situation.

GEO. W. McCRARY,
Secretary of War.

Although there was some rioting at Chicago for several days following, there were no serious encounters with the strikers, and when General Sheridan arrived, on the 30th, he was able to report that the city was tranquil, and he had no doubt that this was largely due to the confidence inspired by the presence of the regular troops.[147] In deference to this condition of public opinion, the troops were kept at Chicago until about the 20th of August, but at no time were they actively employed.

The strike reached St. Louis on the 23d. On the previous evening the railroad employees in that section met at East St. Louis and decided to tie up all freight trains at midnight. Information of this decision was immediately communicated to the President, who directed General Pope, then commanding the Department of the Missouri at Fort Leavenworth, to send to St. Louis all the force he could spare, and to proceed to that point himself if he deemed it necessary. In accordance with these instructions, Col. Jeff. C. Davis, with six com-

Rioting at St. Louis, Mo., July 23-26, 1877.

panies of the Twenty-third Infantry, left Fort Leavenworth at 10 p. m. of the 23d, arriving at St. Louis on the afternoon of the 24th. The commanding officer of these troops was expressly instructed that his duty was simply to protect the property of the United States; that until a call should have been made by the State upon the United States, duly responded to, he should take no part in suppressing insurrection against the State laws.[153] Later in the day General Davis was joined by two companies from Fort Riley, with two Gatling guns, and six more companies were put en route.   During the night of the 24th and throughout the 25th the mob at St. Louis was being constantly recruited, and the situation was extremely threatening.   The same practice of closing the workshops as a method of showing sympathy with the railroad strikers as was carried out in other cities was pursued at this point, so that the streets became congested with idle workmen, the shiftless unemployed and the miscellaneous rabble that is always abroad at such times, and the same spirit of riot that had exhausted itself in the East now renewed itself on the west bank of the Mississippi.   On the 25th and 26th business at St. Louis was at a standstill.   To prevent a repetition of the scenes at Pittsburg and Chicago, the citizens formed large committees, and these having called upon the General Government for 10,000 arms and sufficient ammunition, General Pope was authorized to deliver all that were required "to the State authorities upon a requisition of the governor."   On the 26th an immense crowd marched through the streets in regular column, surrounded the police headquarters and the armories of the militia, daring the latter to fight and taunting the police with cowardice.   At East St. Louis the situation was even worse.   No freight trains were permitted to leave in any direction, and the strikers were masters of the situation.   This point, however, was within the limits of the State of Illinois, and no call for troops for use at East St. Louis had been received.   In the meantime the citizens at St. Louis, to the number of more than 3,000, had been organized and armed and were doing good service.

On the 27th the judge of the United States court called for aid in enforcing the mandates of his court, and General Davis, having been directed to furnish it, immediately reported to the marshal, who, with the aid of the troops, seized and held the yards and tracks of the Ohio and Mississippi and the St. Louis and Southeastern, as well as the St. Louis bridge, and on the morning of the 28th General Davis crossed the river and took possession of East St. Louis.   This was the beginning of the end.   The governor of Illinois arrived during the day and asked for aid, but the President decided that beyond protecting United States property and enforcing the mandates of the courts the troops should not act until the States of Missouri and Illinois had exhausted all their resources in enforcing peace and order within their own borders.   The strikers by this time had opened negotiations with their employers, and within twenty-four hours freight trains were moving on the trunk lines, and by the 2d of August business had resumed its ordinary channels.   The troops remained at St. Louis until the 20th, when they were returned to their stations.

Although the more serious disturbances of the labor strikes of 1877 were confined to the States here mentioned, their reflex action affected to a greater or less degree several of the surrounding States.   In New York there were riots at Buffalo, Hornellsville, Elmira, and a half dozen other points, but in every instance the National Guard proved competent to handle the situation. On Wednesday, the 25th, every railroad man in New Jersey was on strike and traffic was entirely suspended, but there were no acts of violence, and the determined attitude of the authorities at Jersey City and Newark prevented any prolongation of the blockade. In several Western cities, other than those already mentioned, the idle and dàngerous classes attempted to intimidate the authorities, and in some cases bold and lawless mobs held towns and railway junctions and prevented the running of trains for several days. On the 24th the unsettled and threatened condition of affairs at Detroit induced the governor of Michigan to request that if necessary the troops at Fort Wayne be made subject to his orders, as it was feared an emergency might arise where their services would be absolutely necessary in maintaining peace and enforcing obedience to the laws.[154] He was advised, however, that the troops of the United States are to protect public property and by their presence promote peace and order, and that they can not take part in suppressing insurrection against State laws until call is made by the State upon the United States and responded to in the manner provided by the Constitution and the laws.[155]

A similar condition of affairs at Milwaukee on the 25th resulted in a similar request from the governor of Wisconsin,[156] and on the same day the governor of California, in the fear that the local police and State militia would prove inadequate to quell impending disturbances, desired that all the United States forces at San Francisco be placed at his disposal to be used in case of emergency.[158] In both cases the trouble had passed before the Government found it necessary to decide upon a course of action. Again, on the 27th, when the employees of the Chicago, Burlington and Quincy tied up the trains of that line at Burlington, the citizens of that city suggested that regular troops might be held within call from the governor. On that day General Pope was at St. Louis and General Ruger at Louisville, in order that they could, if necessary, advise the President as to the need of troops at those points; and all the troops in the Department of the Gulf and the Department of the South were ordered North; but happily these precautions were needless.

In his annual report to Congress for the year 1877 the President remarked as follows concerning the foregoing occurrence:

The very serious riots which occurred in several of the States in July last rendered necessary the employment of a considerable portion of the Army to preserve the peace and maintain order. In the States of West Virginia, Maryland, Pennsylvania, and Illinois these disturbances were so formidable as to delay the local and State authorities, and the National Executive was called upon, in the mode provided by the Constitution and laws, to furnish military aid. I am gratified to be able to state that the troops sent in response to these calls for aid in the suppression of domestic violence were able, by the influence of their presence in the disturbed regions, to preserve the peace and restore order without the use of force. In the discharge of this delicate and important duty both officers and men acted with great prudence and courage, and for their services deserve the thanks of the country.

Reports of President and Secretary of War.

Similarly the Secretary of War:

I am glad to be able to announce that the Army has again shown itself the staunch friend of law, the firm supporter of the lawful authorities, and in an eminent degree the conservator of peace and order. It is also a source of great pleasure to me to be able to announce that the national forces sent to quell these disturbances met with little resistance, and were able to execute all their orders without firing a gun and without bloodshed. The single instance of serious resistance, at Johnstown, Pa., it is believed may have been in ignorance of the fact that it was made against the national troops.

X. DISTURBANCES IN THE TERRITORIES, 1878–1894.

LAWLESSNESS IN NEW MEXICO, 1878—DISORDER AT HASTINGS, NEBR., 1879—APACHE OUTRAGES, 1882—DISORDERS AT SALT LAKE CITY, UTAH, 1885—CHINESE OUTRAGES, 1885–86—CHINESE AT ROCK SPRINGS, WYO.—CHINESE AT SEATTLE, WASH.—CHINESE IN NEW MEXICO—RIOTING AT CŒUR D'ALENE MINES, IDAHO, 1892—MUNICIPAL TROUBLES, DENVER, COLO., 1894.

———————

From about the middle of October, 1877, to the fall of 1878, the county of Lincoln, in the Territory of New Mexico, was in a state of anarchy. Lawlessness and murder ran riot throughout the county, and there was at no time during that period any civil or other power in the Territory with the ability or inclination to maintain order, except the regular troops, who were prohibited by law from assisting in any manner to keep the peace. Bands of armed men, comprising in the aggregate perhaps 250, roamed the country at will, robbing mail coaches, plundering stores and ranches, burning settlements, committing murder and every possible outrage. To resist them the county possessed the ordinary legal machinery, which, in that section of our frontier was somewhat rudely adjusted, and the Territory even less power and no means of exercising it in the direction of restoring order or enforcing the laws. In February the governor of the Territory had applied to the senior officer of the Army in his vicinity for assistance and had been advised that troops could only be furnished on the orders of the President, which must be based upon a proper application in the form prescribed by the statute. In March the governor forwarded a telegram from the sheriff of Lincoln County asking for aid in serving the legal processes of the courts,[162] and upon this the Secretary of War directed that the military be ordered to support the civil Territorial authorities in maintaining order and enforcing legal process.[163] The Judge-Advocate-General of the Army, however, was of the opinion that a sheriff, or other State official, had

Lawlessness
in New Mexico,
1878.

no such authority as that possessed by a United States marshal to call upon United States troops to serve as a posse; that the governor's application was not accompanied by a statement that the legislature could not be convened, and if it had been so accompanied the application would not have been within the constitutional provision, since the same applies to "States" and not to Territories.[164]

At that time there was pending before Congress a bill, which subsequently became a law, that was intended to govern the employment of

troops as a posse comitatus.   By the 15th section of this act (approved
June 18, 1878) it was provided that "it shall not be lawful to employ
any part of the Army of the United States as a posse comitatus, or
otherwise, for the purpose of executing the laws, except in such cases
and under such circumstances as such employment of said force may be
expressly authorized by the Constitution or by act of Congress."   The
effect of this act was to prohibit the military authorities of the United
States from aiding the officers of the law in making arrests and, as
expressed by the department commander (General Pope) in his annual
report, compelling them "to stand by and see houses containing
women and children attacked, and many people, and some of them
undoubtedly persons innocent of any part or lot in these quarrels,
killed or driven to seek refuge on the military reservation of Fort
Stanton."   By the middle of August the situation had become so
exasperating that upon the solicitation of all the county officers, supported by the commanding officer at Fort Stanton, the governor
addressed the following call to the President:

EXECUTIVE DEPARTMENT,
Santa Fe, N. Mex., August 20, 1878
His Excellency the PRESIDENT OF THE UNITED STATES OF AMERICA.

SIR: I have the honor as governor of New Mexico to apply to Your Excellency for
protection for this Territory from domestic violence.

The Territorial legislature is not now in session nor can it be convened at this time.
There is no Territorial militia nor has the governor authority to call for volunteers.

The southeastern portion of the Territory is overrun by bands of armed men, numbering in all about 200, who almost daily commit the most atrocious crimes, such as
murder, rape, arson, and robbery.   Some of these bands come from Texas and some
from Old Mexico.   One band when asked who they were and where they came from
replied, "We are devils just come from hell," and when ordered by the sheriff of
the county to disband and return to their homes and ordinary avocations they
replied, "We have no homes; we are at our ordinary avocations."

These men are not only living upon the good people of the Territory, but are constantly committing acts of wanton cruelty and violence.   Many men have been murdered, and several women and young girls, mere children, have been ravished, and
large quantities of property stolen and destroyed.

In corroboration of my statements I respectfully refer Your Excellency to the
inclosed petition, this day presented to me in person by the county officers of Lincoln County.

The local authorities are unable to protect the people from this domestic violence.

I, therefore, S. B. Axtell, governor of New Mexico, do hereby most respectfully
ask assistance from the United States under the Constitution and treaties thereof.

Most respectfully, Your Excellency's obedient servant,

[SEAL.]   S. B. AXTELL,
Governor, New Mexico.

By the governor:
W. G. RICH.

No immediate action was had upon this application, while affairs in
the Territory became, if possible, more disorderly than before.   A
party of renegades from Texas styling themselves the "Wrestlers"

came into Lincoln County and commenced a reign of terror such as left all former atrocities far behind. On the 28th of September they killed three men at a ranch near Fort Stanton without the slightest provocation, stealing every horse on the place, and proceeding to another ranch 15 miles below, where they killed one man and wounded another. The mail stage to the fort was robbed the same day. On the 6th of October two men were shot and killed and one hung near old Fort Sumner and three others killed at Puerta de Luna. The frequency of these outrages determined the President to lose no further time in temporizing with the situation. Accordingly, on the 7th of October he issued the following proclamation:

BY THE PRESIDENT OF THE UNITED STATES OF AMERICA.

A PROCLAMATION.

Whereas, it is provided in the laws of the United States that whenever, by reason of unlawful obstructions, combinations, or assemblages of persons, or rebellion against the authority of the Government of the United States, it shall become impracticable, in the judgment of the President, to enforce by the ordinary course of judicial proceedings the laws of the United States within any State or Territory, it shall be lawful for the President to call forth the militia of any or all the States and to employ such parts of the land and naval forces of the United States as he may deem necessary to enforce the faithful execution of the laws of the United States or to suppress such rebellion, in whatever State or Territory thereof the laws of the United States may be forcibly opposed or the execution thereof forcibly obstructed;

And whereas, it has been made to appear to me that by reason of unlawful combinations and assemblages of persons in arms it has become impracticable to enforce, by the ordinary course of judicial proceedings, the laws of the United States within the Territory of New Mexico, and especially within Lincoln County therein; and that the laws of the United States have been therein forcibly opposed and the execution thereof forcibly resisted;

And whereas, the laws of the United States require that whenever it may be necessary, in the judgment of the President, to use the military force for the purpose of enforcing the faithful execution of the laws of the United States, he shall forthwith, by proclamation, command such insurgents to disperse and retire peaceably to their respective abodes within a limited time:

Now, therefore, I, Rutherford B. Hayes, President of the United States, do hereby admonish all good citizens of the United States, and especially of the Territory of New Mexico, against aiding, countenancing, abetting, or taking part in any such unlawful proceedings; and I do hereby warn all persons engaged in or connected with said obstruction of the laws to disperse and retire peaceably to their respective abodes on or before noon of the 13th day of October instant.

In witness whereof, I have hereunto set my hand and caused the seal of the United States to be fixed.

Done at the city of Washington, this 7th day of October, in the year of our Lord eighteen hundred and seventy-eight and of the Independence of· the United States the one hundred and third.

[L. S.]   R. B. HAYES.

By the President:

F. W. SEWARD,

Acting Secretary of State.

This was followed on the 8th by a letter of instructions to the Commanding General of the Army:

WAR DEPARTMENT,
Washington City, October 8, 1878.

Gen. WM. T. SHERMAN,
Commanding Army of the United States.

GENERAL: The President has issued a proclamation that, by reason of unlawful obstructions, combinations, and assemblages of persons, the laws of the United States within the Territory of New Mexico, and especially in Lincoln County therein, can not be enforced by the ordinary course of judicial proceedings, and commanding the persons composing such combinations or assemblages to disperse and repair peaceably to their respective abodes before 12 o'clock noon on the 13th instant. This proclamation is preliminary to the employment of the troops of the United States to preserve the peace and enforce the laws in case the disturbances and unlawful combinations continue after the time named.

The President therefore directs that you instruct the proper military officer that after the time above mentioned has expired he will proceed to disperse, by military force, all such unlawful combinations or assemblages of persons within the said Territory, and that he will, by the use of such force, and so long as resistance to the laws shall continue, aid the governor and authorities of the Territory in keeping the peace and enforcing the laws.

I have the honor to remain, very respectfully, your obedient servant,

GEO. W. McCRARY,
Secretary of War.

The use of the Army in New Mexico was as effective as could have been expected. Located on the edge of a frontier, where by a few miles dash a marauding party could cross the border and find itself in Mexico, safe from pursuit, its operations were necessarily limited. Still, it succeeded almost immediately in securing the peace of Lincoln County. In fact, so thorough was its work that the Territorial authorities soon abandoned the preservation of order and the maintenance of the laws entirely to the Army, making little or no effort to enforce their own authority. So flagrant was this evasion of duty that when, in February, 1879, the governor of the Territory complained because the troops declined to assist constables in making ordinary arrests, General Pope raised the point that the troops in New Mexico under the proclamation of the President and the order of October 8, 1878, could only be used to suppress insurrections and restrain lawlessness, which were beyond the power of the usual civil machinery to control; to expect them to replace all civil posses and be used simply on demand of every small civil functionary was not only unreasonable, but unlawful. "Of course," remarked General Pope, "every constable or sheriff finds it much easier, where he wishes to arrest an offender, to call for a military guard, and no doubt the people who otherwise would be obliged to serve as a posse also find the use of the military very convenient, but such acts are not within the lawful province of the United States Army, and if persisted in would soon lead to the complete substitution of the military for the civil posse." These views were concurred in by Generals Sheridan and Sherman and approved by the Secretary of War. The following are the remarks of the Secretary of War, in his annual report for 1878, concerning this matter:

During the war numerous attacks have been made upon the mail coaches in New Mexico and Arizona for purposes of robbery and plunder, and while I have been of the opinion that the mails of the United States may be defended by the use of troops, I have been obliged to give instructions that they can not, without disregarding the act of Congress, be employed to aid the officers of the law in capturing the robbers after they have committed the crime. In doing so they would act as a posse comitatus, and this is nowhere by law "expressly authorized." In the new and sparsely populated regions of the West, to say to robbers and thieves that they shall not be taken on any writ unless the sheriff and his local posse is able to capture them without aid from the soldiers is almost to grant them immunity from arrest. In those new regions the Army is the power chiefly relied upon by the law-abiding people for protection, and chiefly feared by the lawless classes. Numerous instances might be cited, but the recent occurrences in Lincoln County, N. Mex., constitute a striking example. The inability of the officer in command of the troops in that vicinity to aid the officers of the law in making arrests was one of the principal causes which led to the most disgraceful scenes of riot and murder, amounting, in fact, to anarchy. This state of things continued until a case could be made for declaring the district in insurrection, after which a proclamation of warning was issued by the President. The troops were called into action, and at once restored quiet.

Report of Secretary of War.

The condition of affairs as thus reported by Mr. Secretary McCrary continued until February, 1880, when General Pope submitted the question that it was time to relieve the troops from all connection with civil affairs in Lincoln County, N. Mex. He added that "as matters now stand, anyone who commits crime expects to be shielded, from the vengeance of those whom his crime has incensed, in the asylum of a military post, or the civil authorities expect their prisoners to be guarded for them." The Secretary of War accordingly addressed a communication to the Secretary of State asking that the proclamation be withdrawn, which letter with its reply is subjoined:

JANUARY 19, 1880.

SIR: Referring to the proclamation of the President of October 8, 1878, declaring martial law within the Territory of New Mexico, I have the honor to state that the commanding general, Department of the Missouri, reports that the garrison of Fort Stanton is kept so reduced by the constant demands made upon it under said proclamation that it is impracticable wholly to perform its proper duties of protection against Indians; that the civil affairs in the counties covered by the proclamation are as much settled as they will ever be, and recommends that the counties referred to be relegated to their proper status as civil communities.

Withdrawal of a proclamation.

In view of said recommendation, and of the concurrence therein of the General of the Army, I have the honor to request that the proclamation of the President, above referred to, be withdrawn.

Very respectfully, your obedient servant,   ALEX. RAMSEY,
Secretary of War.

The honorable the SECRETARY OF STATE.

DEPARTMENT OF STATE,
Washington, February 3, 1880.

The Hon. ALEXANDER RAMSEY,
          Secretary of War.

SIR: I have the honor to acknowledge the receipt of your letter of the 19th ultimo, referring to the President's proclamation of the 7th of October, 1878, in relation to unlawful assemblages and combinations of persons in arms then represented to exist in Lincoln County, Territory of New Mexico, and recommending that the proclamation in question be withdrawn.

The proclamation referred to was issued, as you will perceive, in accordance with the authority vested in the President by the provisions of Title LXXIX of the Revised Statutes. It is the proclamation of preliminary warning contemplated by section 5300 of the Revised Statutes, one of the provisions of that title, and can not properly be considered a proclamation "declaring martial law;" it does not suspend or authorize the suspension of the writ of habeas corpus, and it may in the absence of any further Executive proclamation be assumed to have fulfilled the purposes for which it was made at noon on the 13th day of the same month, that being the time fixed by the President within which "all persons engaged in or connected with said obstruction of the laws" were required "to disperse and retire peaceably to their respective abodes."

In this view of the subject it is conceived the necessary orders to the commander of the military forces in New Mexico, which may properly emanate from your Department under the direction of the President, will be found sufficient to remedy the military inconveniences referred to by the commanding general of the Department of the Missouri, and at the same time to relegate the inhabitants of Lincoln County to their normal and civil condition.

I have the honor to be, sir, your obedient servant,

WM. M. EVARTS.

On the 11th of April, 1879, the commanding general of the Department of the Platte, at Omaha, Nebr. (General Crook), received a dispatch from the governor of the State requesting that a company of troops be sent at once to Hastings, the county seat of Adams County, to secure order. It appears that a man by the name of Olive and others were being tried before the court at that place for murder committed under most fiendish circumstances, and that information had been received by the governor that a party of outlaws were about to attempt their rescue. Knowing the desperate character of the Olive gang, and apprehending that if not prevented in their designs there was danger of their injuring any of the citizens who might object to their conduct, and perhaps burn the town, General Crook lost no time in sending a company of infantry to the scene, at the same time informing the governor that he must obtain the necessary authority from the President, as required by the Constitution and laws for the use of Federal troops in the suppression of domestic violence. The governor accordingly telegraphed as follows:

Disorder at Hastings, Nebr., April 11, 1879.

HASTINGS, NEBR., *April 11, 1879.*

His Excellency R. B. HAYES,
          President of the United States, Washington:

We have no well-organized system of militia in this State, and upon the demand of Sheriff Martin, of Adams County, I requested General Crook to send a company of troops here to preserve order during the trial of Olive and others for murder, which he has done. Can the sheriff use these troops as a posse comitatus if necessary?

ALBINUS NANCE,
Governor of Nebraska.

To this the Secretary of War replied on the 12th:

The President directs me to say that an act of Congress forbids the use of troops as a posse comitatus in the case you state. The troops may be so stationed as to exercise a moral influence, and in case of domestic violence they can be employed to keep the peace after a regular call for aid upon the President.

G. W. McCRARY,
Secretary of War.

General Crook's action in sending the troops without the sanction of the President was based upon his knowledge of the desperate character of the individuals referred to, and his belief that they would carry out their determination to rescue Olive at any cost; but as soon as advised that the President had declined to grant the governor's request the troops were at once withdrawn and returned to their station. (2165 A. G. O., 1879.)

The issuing of a proclamation in May, 1882, calling upon all disturbers of the peace within the Territory of Arizona to disperse and retire peaceably to their respective abodes, was occasioned by the unusual record of crime that that section had been making during the preceding few months. Under date of the 28th of April the House of Representatives had by resolution called upon the Secretary of War for information. This resolution had recited: "That whereas, a hostile outbreak has occurred in the Territory of Arizona within the Indian past few weeks, and the citizens of that Territory are outrages in Arizona, being day by day ruthlessly murdered by the Apache 1882. Indians, against whose attacks the people seem to have no adequate protection, the Secretary of War be requested to inform the House as to the number of troops in the Territory; whether they are sufficient to guarantee full protection to the people, and whether any legislation is necessary by Congress for the prompt and efficient security of the people against the destruction of life and property by hostile Indians." To this the Secretary of War replied that it would be difficult to employ in Arizona more troops than would be there after the reenforcements already ordered there had arrived, and that the only legislation necessary to a prompt and efficient security of the people of Arizona was an increase of the strength of the Army. On the same date the Secretary of the Interior received a dispatch from the mayor and other citizens of Tombstone to the effect that the Indians were on the warpath; that 80 people had been killed, and that the military were not sufficient. On the 1st of May the governor of Arizona reported that a great demand existed to have a force of militia put into the field, but having no funds at his disposal for that purpose, he was unwilling to incur the resultant debt. He proposed to arm a number of men as deputy sheriffs and send them in pursuit of Indians charged with murder, on warrants to be issued by the Territorial courts. The department commander (General Willcox) doubted the wisdom of this course, inasmuch as the citizen bodies would be likely to attack reservation Indians, in which event it would become the duty of the military commander to resist them on the demand of the Indian agent. A company of citizens was, however, at the moment being organized for the purpose indicated by the governor, and to avoid any possible conflict it was determined that an Executive proclamation as provided by the statute was expedient. Accordingly, the same appeared under date of May 3, as follows:

BY THE PRESIDENT OF THE UNITED STATES OF AMERICA.

A PROCLAMATION.

Whereas, it is provided in the laws of the United States that "whenever, by reason of unlawful obstructions, combinations, or assemblages of persons, or rebellion against the authority of the Government of the United States, it shall become impracticable, in the judgment of the President, to enforce by the ordinary course of judicial proceedings the laws of the United States within any State or Territory, it shall be lawful for the President to call forth the militia of any or all the States, and to employ such parts of the land and naval forces of the United States as he may deem necessary to enforce the faithful execution of the laws of the United States, or to suppress such rebellion, in whatever State or Territory thereof the laws of the United States may be forcibly opposed or the execution thereof forcibly obstructed;"

And whereas, it has been made to appear satisfactorily to me by information received from the governor of the Territory of Arizona and from the General of the Army of the United States, and other reliable sources, that in consequence of unlawful combinations of evil-disposed persons who are banded together to oppose and obstruct the execution of the laws, it has become impracticable to enforce by the ordinary course of judicial proceedings the laws of the United States within that Territory, and that the laws of the United States have been therein forcibly opposed and the execution thereof forcibly resisted;

And whereas, the laws of the United States require that whenever it may be necessary in the judgment of the President to use the military forces for the purpose of enforcing the faithful execution of the laws of the United States, he shall forthwith, by proclamation, command such insurgents to disperse and retire peaceably to their respective abodes within a limited time:

Now, therefore, I, Chester A. Arthur, President of the United States, do hereby admonish all good citizens of the United States, and especially of the Territory of Arizona, against aiding, countenancing, abetting, or taking part in any such unlawful proceedings, and I do hereby warn all persons engaged in or connected with said obstruction of the laws to disperse and retire peaceably to their respective abodes on or before noon of the 15th day of May.

In witness whereof, I have hereunto set my hand and caused the seal of the United States to be affixed.

Done at the city of Washington, this 3d day of May, in the year of our Lord eighteen hundred and eighty-two, and of the Independence of the United States the one hundred and sixth.

[SEAL.]   CHESTER A. ARTHUR.

By the President:

FREDK. T. FRELINGHUYSEN,
   Secretary of State.

These outrages were largely attributed to Loco's band of Warm Spring Apaches, who had broke out on the 19th and been joined a few days later by wandering lodges of Chiricahuas; but before the proclamation was issued they had been struck by Lieutenant-Colonel Forsythe with four troops of the Fourth Cavalry at Horseshoe Cañon, and later by Major Tupper with two troops of the Sixth in the Hatchet Mountains and driven into Mexico, where they were caught by Lieutenant-Colonel Garcia with a strong force of Mexican troops, and so soundly thrashed that for the succeeding few months there was comparative peace in the Territory.

The execution within the Territory of Utah of the act of Congress known as the "Edmunds law," for the suppression of polygamy, in the face of the opposition of the local, civil, and ecclesiastical authorities, was attended by scenes of great disorder.   On the 4th of July, 1885, the United States flag on the court-house, city hall, and all buildings owned or controlled by the Mormons was placed at half-mast as a sign of contempt of and toward the Federal Government, and an attempt of several ex-Union and ex-Confederate soldiers to replace it in a proper position was the occasion for serious disturbances, and an outbreak at that time was hardly avoided.   Judges and other Federal officers were assaulted, their homes assailed under cover of darkness, and other outrages perpetrated, with no effort on the part of the civil authorities to arrest or punish the offenders.

Disorders at Salt Lake City, 1885.

There was no organized militia in the Territory, and territorial laws prohibited the governor from protecting life or property.   On the 16th of July Governor Murray telegraphed the President that events likely to occur in the immediate future suggested the necessity of measures looking to the preservation of life and property. To this the President replied that no condition had so far arisen demanding the use of the troops, but that the War Department would watch events and be prepared to act when occasion required.   As arrests and convictions under the Edmunds law progressed, the situation at Salt Lake City grew so threatening that General McCook, then commanding at Fort Douglas, asked for authority to station a company of troops in the city to form a rallying point for citizens when their lives might be endangered by mob violence.   This was agreed to, and in addition a battery of light artillery was ordered to that point from Omaha early in December, and the presence of these troops contributed in the fullest measure to the subsequent execution of the laws in that Territory during the winter of 1885–86.   (3913 A. G. O., 1885.)

On the 16th of February, 1886, at the request of the governor and the United States marshal, General McCook sent a detachment of troops to Promontory, Utah, as a guard to secure the safe delivery to the United States district court at Salt Lake City of George Q. Cannon, the first president of the Mormon Church.   This action was the occasion for much controversy, in which the military authorities held that under the law and regulations a commanding officer must act upon his best judgment, leaving it to the President to decide whether or not his course was justifiable. (3913 A. G. O., 1885.)

It is difficult to arrive at the exact truth concerning the causes which combined to bring about the attack on the Chinese miners at Rock Springs, Wyo., on the 2d of September, 1885. The Union Pacific Railway Company, in a pamphlet setting forth their position in the matter (Rand, Avery & Co., Boston, 1886), have, by means of numerous citations from the local journals, very fairly presented both sides of the case; yet, with these at hand, opinions will naturally depend upon the point of view. Divested of all discrepancies and contradictions, a plain narrative of events is as follows:

Rock Springs, a small mining town of about 1,000 inhabitants, is a station on the Union Pacific Railroad, 314 miles from Cheyenne, and about midway between Rawlins and Evanston, and is one of several points along their line where the Union Pacific own and operate mines for the purpose of supplying coal for the use of the road. The company employed on the 2d of September, 1885, about 500 miners, of whom 150 were white and 330 Chinese, and there were in the town perhaps 100 idle white miners. On that date the white miners, aided by the loafers about town, all fully armed, suddenly attacked the unarmed Chinese both in and outside the mines, killing all who resisted, driving the others into the mountains, and burning and plundering their dwellings. About 25 to 30 Chinese were killed, every Chinese house in the town was burned, and of those who had fled to the hills some 50 perished from wounds, starvation, and exposure. The remainder were gathered up by the railway company and taken to Evanston. Immediately on receipt of the intelligence, the governor of Wyoming, then at Cheyenne, telegraphed the Secretary of War that the county authorities were powerless; that the Territory had no militia, and that he had applied to General Howard, at Omaha, for military aid. On the 3d he made a similar appeal to the President, adding that he believed immediate assistance imperative to preserve life and property. On receipt of this he was advised by telegraph that before action could be had in the matter he must first make personal application to the President in the manner indicated by the Constitution and statutes, but that in the meantime, in order that the public interests might not suffer, the Secretary of War had ordered two companies to Rock Springs to prevent any interruption to the United States mails or the routes over which they were carried. In response to this, Governor Warren telegraphed as follows on the morning of the 5th:

Massacre
of Chinese at
Rock Springs, Wyo.,
September 2, 1885.

EVANSTON, WYO., *September 5, 1885.*

The PRESIDENT,

    Washington, D. C.:

Unlawful combinations and conspiracies exist among coal miners and others in Uinta and Sweetwater counties, this Territory, which prevent individuals and corporations from enjoyment and protection of their property and obstruct execution of the laws; open insurrection at Rock Springs, property burned, 16 dead bodies found, probably over 50 more buried under ruins; 700 Chinamen driven from town have taken refuge at Evanston and are ordered to leave here. Sheriffs powerless to make necessary arrests and protect life and property unless supported by organized bodies of armed men. Wyoming has no Territorial militia, therefore I respectfully and earnestly request the aid of United States troops, not only to protect mail and mail routes, but that they may be instructed to support civil authorities until order is restored, criminals arrested, and the suffering relieved.

FRANCIS E. WARREN,

Governor.

ROCK SPRINGS, WYO., *September 6, 1885.*

The PRESIDENT,

Washington, D. C.:

Referring to my dispatch of yesterday, asking for United States troops in support of civil authority while subduing insurrection, I beg to add that the legislature of Wyoming is not in session and can not be convened in season to provide for emergency. Chinamen prevented from returning to their homes at Rock Springs, and are ordered to leave Evanston by unauthorized parties.

FRANCIS E. WARREN,

Governor.

In accordance with the orders of the 3d, two companies of the Seventh Infantry from Fort Fred Steele, under Lieutenant-Colonel Chipman, were sent to Rock Springs, and one company of the Fourteenth from Fort D. A. Russell, under Lieutenant-Colonel Anderson, to Evanston. It was decided by Major-General Schofield, then commanding the Division of the Missouri, within whose command the Territory of Wyoming was situated, that the Union Pacific was established under an act of Congress as a military road and mail route, and being indispensable to the military service, should be placed under the protection of United States troops; and he proposed that this protection should be extended to the property and employees of the company, including those engaged in providing the necessary fuel for the service of the road. But the exercise of this latter discretion was rendered unnecessary, inasmuch as by our treaty with China, the United States was under obligations to exert all its power to devise measures for the protection of any Chinese residing in its territory who shall meet with ill treatment at the hands of any other persons, and to secure to them all rights, privileges, immunities, and exemptions as may be enjoyed by the citizens of the most favored nation. (Article III, treaty proclaimed October 5, 1881.) During the 5th and 6th of September the excitement against the Chinese continued. All work had ceased in the mines at Rock Springs and at Almy (near Evanston), and the Chinese, still hiding in the hills, were warned by the mob not to return to either place on penalty of being fired upon. On the 7th, Governor Warren again telegraphed for aid, as follows:

EVANSTON, WYO., *September 7, 1885.*

The PRESIDENT,

  Washington, D. C.:

Referring to my several late telegrams, I respectfully submit that the unlawful organized mobs in possession of coal mines at Almy, near here, will not permit Chinamen to approach their own homes, property, or employment. From the nature of outbreak sheriff of county can not rally sufficient posse and Territorial government can not sufficiently aid him. Insurrectionists know through newspapers and dispatches that troops will not interfere under present orders, and moral effect of presence of troops is destroyed. If troops were known to have orders to assist sheriff posse in case driven back, I am quite sure civil authorities could restore order without actual use of soldiers; but unless United States Government can find way to relieve us immediately, believe worse scenes than those at Rock Springs will follow and all Chinamen driven from the Territory. I beg an early reply and information regarding the attitude of the United States Government.

          FRANCIS E. WARREN,
             Governor.

On the afternoon of the 7th General Schofield was advised that in view of the treaty stipulation and of the representation of the governor of Wyoming that the civil powers of that Territory were unable to protect lives and property and preserve the peace in certain localities, the President directed that a suitable military force be sent to the points where violence existed or was threatened; that if necessity actually existed for the employment of that force in protecting life and property and aiding the civil authorities in preserving the peace and in the arrest of those committing offenses against the laws, he was authorized to so use it, but that care should be taken that the military force was not needlessly employed.[165] On the 8th, the railroad company having decided to take the Chinese back to Rock Springs and reopen the mines, both at that point and at Almy, six companies of the Ninth Infantry, then in camp not far from Salt Lake City, Utah, were ordered to Evanston, and on the 9th four of those companies under the command of Captain Morton, of that regiment, acted as an escort to a force of some 700 Chinese laborers and miners to Rock Springs, where they arrived on the afternoon of that date without incident. The governor promptly telegraphed his thanks[167] for the prompt assistance rendered, and the following day, all fears of further disturbance being allayed, all of the troops, except two companies at Rock Springs and one at Evanston, were withdrawn and returned to their stations.

Although the prospect of any outbreak against the Chinese in the presence of troops had diminished along the line of the Union Pacific, the anti-Chinese feeling among the mining population had by no means subsided. The Chinese consuls at San Francisco and New York, under the escort of General McCook, visited the scene of the troubles in the latter part of the month and made careful investigations. On the 1st of October the miners at Carbon, Wyo., ceased work "until every

Chinaman along the Union Pacific road is discharged," and to avoid trouble those mines were closed. A day or two later a similar strike occurred at Louisville, Colo., attended by the same result. During the month of October the anti-Chinese feeling had reached Washington and Oregon and found sufficient expression for a time in the driving out of individual Chinese from the smaller towns. But about the beginning of November the immunity from punishment appears to have so far encouraged the perpetrators of these outrages as to impel them to renewed efforts. On the 2d of that month an attempt of the municipal authorities at Tacoma to protect Chinese residents led to a

Riots at Seattle, Wash., September 7, 1885.

disgraceful riot, and to a proclamation by the governor of the Territory, in which, after reciting the situation and announcing that the United States was under treaty obligations to protect these people, he trusted that the citizens of the Territory would not permit its good name to be disgraced by the necessity of interposition by Federal troops.[170] This, however, proved unavailing, and, on the appearance of signs of similar demonstrations at Seattle, the governor, on the 7th, telegraphed the situation to the President and begged for assistance. In response to this, ten companies of the Fourteenth Infantry stationed at Vancouver Barracks were ordered to Seattle, arriving on the morning of the 8th, but the announcement of their coming seems to have been sufficient to restrain the unruly disturbers of the peace from carrying out their plans. Everything was quiet in the town, and the next day four companies left for Tacoma, where they received a number of prisoners from the United States marshal and conducted them to Vancouver, where they were turned over to the court. At the same time the troops were ordered to Seattle, the following proclamation was telegraphed to all points in the disturbed territory:

BY THE PRESIDENT OF THE UNITED STATES OF AMERICA.

A PROCLAMATION.

Whereas, it is represented to me by the governor of the Territory of Washington that domestic violence exists within the said Territory, and that by reason of unlawful obstructions and combinations and the assemblage of evil-disposed persons it has become impracticable to enforce by the ordinary course of judicial proceedings the laws of the United States at Seattle, and at other points and places within said Territory, whereby life and property are there threatened and endangered;

And whereas, the legislature of said Territory can not be convened, and in the judgment of the President an emergency has arisen and a case is now presented which justifies and requires, under the Constitution and laws of the United States, the employment of military force to suppress domestic violence and enforce the faithful execution of the laws of the United States, if the command and warning of this proclamation be disobeyed and disregarded:

Now, therefore, I, Grover Cleveland, President of the United States of America, do hereby command and warn all insurgents and all persons who have assembled at any point within the said Territory of Washington for the unlawful purposes aforesaid to desist therefrom, and to disperse and retire peaceably to their respective abodes on or before 12 o'clock meridian on the 8th day of November instant.

And I do admonish all good citizens of the United States and all persons within the limits and jurisdiction thereof against aiding, abetting, countenancing, or taking any part in such unlawful acts or assemblages.

In witness whereof, I have set my hand and caused the seal of the United States to be hereunto affixed.

Done at the city of Washington, this 7th day of November, in the year of our Lord eighteen hundred and eighty-five, and of the Independence of the United States the one hundred and tenth.

[SEAL.]   GROVER CLEVELAND.

By the President:
> T. F. BAYARD,
> > *Secretary of State.*

There being no disturbances at Seattle, and all signs of the threatened trouble having disappeared, the six companies were withdrawn from that point on the 7th and returned to their station, having been absent ten days, during which no action of any kind was called for on their part.

On Sunday, the 7th of February, 1886, the disturbances on account of the Chinese suddenly broke out again at Seattle. By daylight every Chinaman in town had been called on by committees of five or six men and ordered to pack up and be ready to leave by a steamer to sail at 1 o'clock. Later in the morning wagons were sent around to collect their baggage, and when they refused to deliver it their houses were summarily entered and their belongings thrown on the wagons. The sheriff having been appealed to, directed the police to maintain the law, but they declined to interfere with the removal of the Chinese. About half past 10 the bells were rung and all the population crowded into the streets, but the city was already in the hands of the mob. The governor of the Territory chanced to be in Seattle, and, warned by his experiences of the former riots, lost no time in telegraphing to the authorities at Washington. His dispatch addressed to the Secretary of War, the Secretary of the Interior, and to General Gibbon, the military commander of the department, was as follows:

SEATTLE, *February 7, 1886.*
Immense mob forcing Chinese to leave Seattle; civil authorities arriving posse comitatus to protect them; serious conflict probable. I respectfully request that United States troops be immediately sent to Seattle. Troops at Fort Townsend can arrive soonest and probably will be sufficient. Have issued proclamation.

WATSON C. SQUIRE,
Governor.

At noon United States deputy marshals read aloud at street corners and other public places the governor's proclamation. This recited that inasmuch as the mayor of the city had reported himself unable to preserve order or keep the peace against a mob unlawfully gathered, all persons were warned to desist from breaches of the peace and

directed to return to their homes.[173] The military companies of the
city were ordered to report themselves under arms to the sheriff of
the county, and all persons disposed to assist in maintaining order to
enroll themselves immediately. The proclamation was received with
derision and the officers of the law hooted and jeered
at. Just before the hour for the vessel to sail a writ
of habeas corpus had been served upon the captain,
which prevented further proceedings until Monday. Up to midnight,
however, the mob had full control of the city. The troops at Vancouver Barracks were at once put in readiness to move, but the governor was advised that they could not move except on the order of the
President.

Riots at Seattle, Wash., February 7, 1886.

On Monday, the 8th, the disorders were renewed. The Chinese,
now thoroughly frightened, expressed a willingness to go, and about
200 of them were put on board the steamer, their passage paid to
California, and the steamer departed. The mob then attacked those
Chinamen who remained. The police and militia endeavored to protect them; a conflict ensued, shots were fired, and several wounded.
At about 1 o'clock the governor, on the advice of the chief justice,
declared martial law. Both of these officials urged the sending of
United States troops. During the day the following dispatch was
sent:

WAR DEPARTMENT,
Washington, February 8, 1886.

Hon. W. C. SQUIRE,
    Governor of Washington Territory:
    Telegram received. Troops can not be sent except upon last emergency. It would
seem that with the force you have order can and should be maintained. Is the legislature in session? Keep me advised of the situation.
    By order of the President:

W. C. ENDICOTT,
Secretary of War.

The governor claims that this dispatch never reached him. It may
have been sent to the State capital, or elsewhere; the records fail to
afford any explanation. The governor's proclamation—reproduced
elsewhere in full[174]—was followed by the most effective military measures. No citizen was permitted in the streets after dark without a
pass; orders were rigidly enforced; volunteers were called for; cadets
from the State University enrolled and sworn into the service. On
Tuesday, the 9th, more urgent dispatches were received at the War
Department, so that orders were sent to General Gibbon to "proceed
in person at once to Seattle with such troops as may be necessary to
suppress domestic violence and aid the civil authorities in overcoming
obstructions to the enforcement of the laws." At the same time the
President issued the following proclamation:

By the President of the United States of America.

A PROCLAMATION.

Whereas, it is represented to me by the governor of the Territory of Washington that domestic violence exists within the said Territory, and that by reason of unlawful obstructions and combinations and the assemblage of evil-disposed persons it has become impracticable to enforce by the ordinary course of judicial proceedings the laws of the United States at Seattle, and at other points and places within said Territory, whereby life and property are there threatened and endangered;

And whereas, in the judgment of the President, an emergency has arisen and a case is now presented which justifies and requires under the Constitution and laws of the United States the employment of military force to suppress domestic violence and enforce the faithful execution of the laws of the United States, if the command and warning of this Proclamation be disobeyed and disregarded:

Now, therefore, I, Grover Cleveland, President of the United States of America, do hereby command and warn all insurgents and all persons who have assembled at any point within the said Territory of Washington for the unlawful purposes aforesaid to desist therefrom, and to disperse and retire peaceably to their respective abodes on or before 6 o'clock in the afternoon of the 10th day of February instant.

And I do admonish all good citizens of the United States and all persons within the limits and jurisdiction thereof against aiding, abetting, countenancing, or taking any part in such unlawful acts or assemblages.

In witness whereof, I have set my hand and caused the seal of the United States to be hereunto affixed.

Done at the city of Washington, this 9th day of February, in the year of our Lord eighteen hundred and eighty-six, and of the Independence of the United States the one hundred and tenth.

[SEAL.]   GROVER CLEVELAND.

By the President:
    T. F. BAYARD,
        Secretary of State.

General Gibbon found everything quiet at Seattle on his arrival on the 10th. The city was in possession of the militia organizations with a provost marshal in charge. The governor at once transferred the military control to General Gibbon; the city was placarded with the President's proclamation; business houses and saloons were closed at an early hour every day, and patrols of regular troops, having relieved the militia organizations, were constantly on the streets. A number of the leaders and inciters of the outrages were arrested by the provost-marshal and his civilian assistants and placed under guard, and later were turned over to the United States marshal. From day to day the stringency of martial law was relaxed; stores and saloons were allowed to reopen, the guards were gradually withdrawn and business resumed, so that on the 22d, on the recommendation of General Gibbon, the governor issued a proclamation declaring martial law removed and the civil authorities resumed control of the city. On the 25th four companies returned to Vancouver Barracks; two remained until the 2d of April, and two upon the request of the governor until August 19. At no time was there any resistance to the Federal troops on the part of the disturbers of the peace, nor were they ever called upon for active service.

The ill feeling against the Chinese was not restricted to the States above mentioned, although in these alone was any action had by the Federal authorities. In Colorado, Utah, Arizona, and New Mexico there was much excitement and fears were apprehended that violence would result. In January, 1886, the governor of New Mexico, Hon.

Disturbances in New Mexico, 1886. Edmunds Ross, advised the President that at two points in that Territory, Silver City and Raton, there was a high condition of public excitement against Chinese residents; that at the latter place several hundred coal miners and others had united and there was imminent danger of an outbreak.[177] To prevent bloodshed he thought he should have authority to call on the troops if necessary, and had accordingly telegraphed for such authority. To this the Secretary of War replied by direction of the President calling attention to the Revised Statutes (5297–5300) which prescribe the circumstances and manner by which troops may be used for suppressing domestic violence, stating that the President can not order out troops except in accordance with these provisions and section 4 of Article IV of the Constitution.[178] No occasion presented itself however for the use of troops and no further call was made.

The summer of 1892 was marked by serious disturbances in several of the States, growing out of differences between employers and their workmen. These were first a disturbance caused by the strike of dissatisfied ironworkers in the rolling mills at Homestead, Pa.; second, a strike of railroad men at Buffalo, N. Y.; and third, an uprising of miners and others at Coal Creek, Tenn., against the leasing out by the State of convicts from the prisons to work the coal mines at a time when thousands of miners were idle from an inability to procure work. In each of these instances the local authorities acknowledged their inability to enforce the law, and the governors called upon the militia and National Guard to aid in securing order and preventing the destruction of property. In Pennsylvania the entire military force, aggregating about 9,000, took possession of the mills, drove out the rioters, and restored order. In New York the governor called out two brigades of National Guard, about 7,000 men, and although the effort was not unattended by stout resistance, they speedily suppressed disorder and restored quiet. In Tennessee the militia force consisted of a single company, and the majority of the people in the vicinity of the outbreak were sympathizers with the disturbers, but, presenting a determined front, they succeeded in maintaining the supremacy of the laws. A more difficult situation presented itself in the mountains of

Rioting at Cœur d'Alene mines, July 11, 1892. northern Idaho, where, on the 11th of July, an attack by members of an organization known as the Miners' Union upon nonmembers employed in certain of the mines resulted in the killing of quite a number, the destruction of much property, and the driving of the nonunion men from the vicinity of the mines. The Cœur d'Alene mining region, the scene of this disturbance, embraces the valley and country adjacent to the Cœur d'Alene River and is one of rough mountains, difficult to reach and more difficult to attack. There were but four companies of militia in the State and these were at once ordered to the scene of disturbance, but, in view of their small number and the gravity of the situation, the governor deemed it futile to move on the rioters without the aid of Federal troops. He accordingly addressed this telegram to the President:

Boise City, July 11, 1892.

The President of the United States:

This morning riot and bloodshed by the miners in the Cœur d'Alene district commenced. The mill was blown up by dynamite and many men were killed and injured. Inspector-General Curtis, I. N. G., informs me that 400 or 500 armed men constitute the mob. The legislature is not in session and can not be promptly convened. The civil authorities of the county and State are wholly inadequate to maintain peace. The immediate military force of the Idaho National Guard numbers only 196 men, which is, in my opinion, far too few to successfully cope with the mob, though I will at once order it into the field. In this emergency I deem it necessary to call for the assistance of the Federal troops. I therefore request that a sufficient force be detailed from Fort Sherman or elsewhere to act in concert with the State authorities in maintaining public order.

Norman B. Willey,
Governor.

This reached the President, then absent from Washington, on the morning of the 12th, and in response thereto he telegraphed the Secretary of War as follows:

[Telegram.]

Saratoga Depot, N. Y., July 12, 1892.

The Secretary of War,
<blockquote>Washington, D. C.:</blockquote>

The governor of the State of Idaho has called upon me under section 4 of article IV of the Constitution for assistance in suppressing a domestic disturbance which the State authorities are unable to control. You will at once send to the scene of disorder an adequate force of troops from the nearest station under an officer of rank and discretion, with orders to cooperate with the civil authorities in preserving the peace and protecting life and property.

I will reach Washington to-night.

Benj. Harrison.

Orders were accordingly sent to General Merritt at St. Paul, directing him to send three companies from Fort Missoula, [181] and to General Ruger at San Francisco, to send all available troops from Fort Sherman, [182] to Wardner, Idaho, which had been indicated as the center of the disturbance, under a discreet officer of rank, to report to the governor of the State and to support the civil authorities in preserving the peace and preventing the destruction of life and property. On the approach of the troops to Wardner the rioters dispersed, in part to the mines and others collected at the railway stations, Wardner, Wallace, and Mullan. The troops were distributed to the mines and such other points as best controlled the region of disturbance. There was at no time the slightest conflict between the United States troops and the rioters, nor did they offer any resistance to the regulations of the officers in command of the troops. On the 16th the following orders and proclamation were published as a measure of precaution:

WAR DEPARTMENT, *Washington, D. C., July 16, 1892.*

It is gratifying to know that any collision between the troops and the rioters has been avoided. As a measure of precaution, and in the hope that it may tend to allay excitement, you will cause to be published the following proclamation from the President.

S. B. ELKINS,
Secretary of War.

BY THE PRESIDENT OF THE UNITED STATES OF AMERICA.

A PROCLAMATION.

To whom it may concern:

Whereas, the governor of the State of Idaho has represented to me that within said State there exists an insurrection and condition of domestic violence and resistance to the laws, to meet and overcome which the resources at his command are unequal; and

Whereas, he has further represented that the legislature of said State is not now in session, and can not be promptly convened; and

Whereas, by reason of said conditions, the said governor, as chief executive of the State, has called upon me, as Chief Executive of the Government of the United States, for assistance in repressing said violence and restoring and maintaining the peace:

Now, therefore, I, Benjamin Harrison, President of the United States, by virtue of section 4, Article IV, of the Constitution of the United States, and of the laws of Congress enacted in pursuance thereof, do hereby command all persons engaged in said insurrection and in resistance to the laws to immediately disperse and retire peaceably to their respective abodes.

In witness whereof, I have hereunto set my hand and caused the seal of the United States to be affixed.

Done at the city of Washington, this fifteenth day of July, in the year of our Lord eighteen hundred and ninety-two, and of the Independence of the United States the one hundred and sixteenth.

[SEAL.]   BENJ. HARRISON.

By the President:

JOHN W. FOSTER,
Secretary of State.

The duty performed by the troops consisted in assistance to the civil officers in making arrests of those charged with participation in criminal acts during the riots; in guarding prisoners held in custody and preventing their rescue. In all, over 300 arrests were made. The presence of the troops extinguished open lawlessness in the whole Cœur d'Alene region, so that by the end of July, as there remained nothing for them to do except to guard the prisoners, they were withdrawn and returned to their stations. (34728 A. G. O., 1892.)

A change in the personnel of two unimportant municipal offices at Denver, Colo., in the spring of 1894, complicated by the interposition of the governor, threatened for a time to bring about a serious domestic disturbance and involve riot and bloodshed. The governor attempted to remove the offending officials, and they, refusing to surrender, obtained from the court a temporary injunction restraining the governor from interference. The governor refused to recognize the injunction and ordered out the militia with the object of removing the officials by force, while the latter, surrounding themselves in the city hall by the police and other friends to the number of several hundred, fully armed, possessed themselves of dynamite and other high explosives which they threatened to throw at the attacking force. The governor then applied to tne military commander for United States troops to preserve order in the city:

Municipal troubles at Denver, March, 1894.

DENVER, COLO., *March 15, 1894.*

General McCOOK, U. S. Army,
     Commanding the Department of the Colorado.

I have called out the militia in Denver—National Guard—to enforce the laws of the State. I find an organized opposition by the city police and detective force and the sheriff's office. I can enforce the law, but not without great bloodshed. I call upon you, as governor of the State, to assist me in preserving order and in preventing bloodshed.

DAVIS H. WAITE,
Governor of Colorado.

Believing a crisis imminent and insurrection and riot about to supervene, General McCook, under the authority given commanding officers under paragraph 585 of the Army Regulations (edition 1889), ordered the troops from Fort Logan to go at once to the city for the sole purpose of preserving the peace, at the same time reporting his action to the War Department. The following reply was also sent to Governor Waite:

HEADQUARTERS DEPARTMENT OF THE COLORADO,
Denver, Colo., March 15, 1894.

In pursuance of your demand, this moment received, I have ordered the troops from Fort Logan to come at once to the city, for the sole purpose of preserving peace. I act in the matter under paragraph 585, Army Regulations. I consider a crisis imminent, and insurrection and riot against the executive authority of the State of Colorado. The troops, upon arrival, will be directed to act with great discretion, and I will see that the laws of the land are not violated. I would recommend that an order issue that the National Guard be returned to their armory.

A. McD. McCOOK,
Brigadier-General Commanding.

DAVIS H. WAITE,
     Governor of Colorado, Denver, Colo.

S. Doc. 209——15

The following is the answer received from the governor:

STATE OF COLORADO, EXECUTIVE MANSION,
Denver, Colo., March 15, 1894.

Yours by your aide-de-camp received. I respectfully decline to order the National Guard, now endeavoring to enforce the laws of the State, to their armory, but will confer with you or Colonel Merriam, whom shall be in command when the troops arrive.

Respectfully,

DAVIS H. WAITE,
Governor.

General McCOOK.

General McCook then called upon the governor, who asked him to assist him in taking possession of the city hall. He was told that he could not be assisted. He then asked if the United States troops could be held in reserve for the National Guard to fall back upon in case they were repulsed, and was told that United States troops could not be used for such a purpose. The troops arrived at 8.30 p. m., and on their appearance the crowd dispersed, the militia returned to their armory, and peace and quiet were restored to the city. On the morning of the 16th the following dispatch was sent to General McCook:

WAR DEPARTMENT,
Washington, March 16, 1894.

Brigadier-General McCOOK,
Commanding Department of the Colorado, Denver, Colo.:

No application, as required by section 5297 of the Revised Statutes, for the employment of military forces of the United States has been received by the President from the legislature or governor of Colorado for the suppression of an insurrection against its government. Unless such an insurrection as is contemplated by the statutes exists or is threatened and the executive represents the State authorities incapable to suppress or prevent it, the use of the troops except for the protection of Government property is not authorized.

DANIEL S. LAMONT,
Secretary of War.

This having been communicated to Governor Waite, he remarked that he did not want the troops for any such purpose, and asked that they be withdrawn, and on being requested to put his wishes in writing did so, as follows:

STATE OF COLORADO, EXECUTIVE DEPARTMENT,
Denver, March 16, 1894.

Yesterday about 5 p. m., on informal notice that you had announced that you would put seven companies of United States troops in Denver at my call, I inferred that your object was to assist the State in the enforcement of the laws. As you were present in Denver and knew that the city companies of the National Guard had been called out by me as commander in chief, and were at the time on duty in the streets near the city hall, I therefore requested that you move the United States troops to the city, and I was careful to specify in my letter that the object of the call for the United States troops was that they might assist the State troops in the execution of the laws and in preventing bloodshed. In conversation with you this morning at your office I find that in your opinion you have no such right. I therefore most respectfully withdraw my request for the United States troops.

DAVIS H. WAITE,
Governor of Colorado.

A. McD. McCOOK,
Brigadier-General, U. S. Army, Department of the Colorado.

The troops were accordingly withdrawn from the scene of disturbance and quartered in a public building. There they remained until Sunday night, the 18th, when, it being apparent that there would be no further disturbance, they were returned to Fort Logan.

XI. THE RAILROAD STRIKES OF 1894.

RIOTS AT CHICAGO, ILL.—RIOTS AT HAMMOND, IND.—RIOTS IN THE WEST GENERALLY—
RIOTS IN IDAHO—RIOTS IN NEW MEXICO—RIOTS IN OKLAHOMA—RIOTS AT SACRA-
MENTO, CAL.—THE CASE OF IN RE DEBS.

The great railroad strike of 1894 originated in a movement by the employees of the Pullman Palace Car Company at Pullman, near Chicago, Ill., for higher wages, which the car company declined to grant. This was on the 9th of May, and on the 11th about 2,000 of the employees of the company quit work. A tedious period of idleness ensued and continued for several weeks with no prospect of a successful issue and the workmen were preparing to abandon the strike and go to work, when on the 26th of June the American Railway Union, an organization pretending to represent all railway employees in the West, excepting locomotive engineers, suddenly declared a "boycott" against Pullman cars. On the following day the embargo had extended to all the principal roads entering Chicago, and on the 28th it had reached nearly every road west of that point. On the 29th the boycott against the Pullman cars had resolved itself into a fight between the Railway Union and the associated managers of the railways. The former ordered a strike on the Rock Island, Chicago and Alton, Chicago and Erie, Monon, Fort Wayne, Wabash, Great Western, and Lake Shore, as well as the Union Stock Yards Transit Company, aggregating some 40,000 employees. Thus far there had been no violence, but trains through Indiana, Ohio, Illinois, and Kentucky had been stopped and Pullman cars detached and side-tracked. On the 30th trains were derailed and Pullman cars stoned in the East, and the strike had proceeded westward until it had reached the Pacific coast. By this time few trains were running in or out of Chicago, the mails were being delayed everywhere, trains were obstructed, and commerce interrupted.

On June 28th, in response to complaints regarding the interruption of the mails, the Attorney-General had instructed the United States attorney at Chicago to protect the mail trains with United States marshals. On July 1 a special attorney was appointed to enforce the laws relating to the protection of the mails, and that evening seven men were arrested on the charge of obstructing trains carrying United States mails. These arrests caused great excitement, which was increased the following day when the United States court at Chicago issued a sweeping injunction against the strikers. To provide for possible trouble the

Riots
at Chicago, Ill.,
July 3–8, 1894.

228

commanding general of the Department of the Missouri was confidentially instructed to make all necessary arrangements to move the entire garrison of Fort Sheridan—infantry, cavalry, and artillery—into Chicago at 4 o'clock, and on the 3d this order was made effective, the officers of the courts having announced their inability to enforce their mandates or to quiet the riots that had broken out all over the city. The following were the orders for the employment of the troops:

HEADQUARTERS OF THE ARMY,
Washington, D. C., July 3, 1894—4 o'clock p. m.

To MARTIN,
 Adjutant-General, Chicago, Ill.:

It having become impracticable, in the judgment of the President, to enforce by ordinary course of judicial proceedings, the laws of the United States, you will direct Colonel Crofton to move his entire command at once to the city of Chicago, leaving the necessary guard at Fort Sheridan, there to execute the orders and processes of the United States court, to prevent the obstruction of the United States mails and generally to enforce the faithful execution of the laws of the United States. He will confer with the United States marshal, the United States district attorney, and Edwin Walker, special counsel. Acknowledge receipt and report action promptly.

By order of the President:

J. M. SCHOFIELD,
Major-General.

The 4th of July was comparatively quiet in Chicago. The troops from Fort Sheridan arrived at 10.15 a. m., and were located at Blue Island, Grand Crossing, at Forty-seventh street, and at the Stock Yards. There was some rioting, but upon the whole the situation was encouraging for peace and good order. The morning of the 5th opened quietly, but about the usual time of beginning work a mob of several thousand commenced operations along the line of the Rock Island by overturning cars, burning station houses, and destroying property indiscriminately. By noon this mob numbered some 10,000 men, was 3 miles long, and moved over an area fully one-half mile wide, burning and destroying everything it could reach. Additional troops were hurried into Chicago from Fort Brady and Leavenworth and camped at Lake Front Park, while the National Guard of the State was ordered to concentrate at Chicago. During the night fires were started in a dozen different places, and a proclamation was issued by the mayor directing the police to disperse the mobs and prevent interference with the railroads. The mob wrecked many locomotives, overturned and burned several hundred cars and some 10 large buildings, while more than 20 men had been killed or injured. The 6th was a repetition of the scenes of the day before on a larger scale. During the twenty-four hours more than 1,000 cars, many of them loaded with merchandise, were burned and destroyed, and the mob held possession of Kensington, Burnside, Fordham, and Grand Crossing. Several conflicts between the mob and the National Guard and United States marshals resulted in the killing of six or eight of the rioters. The 7th was quiet as compared to the day before, but in the afternoon the police fired into the mob at several places, and at Forty-ninth street a company of the National Guard fired three volleys into a mob estimated to number 15,000. The United States troops patrolled all the railway lines, and were stationed at strategic points—the Government building, Lake Front Park, Blue Island, and the Stock Yards. By this time there were over 100,000 idle men in Chicago, and 180,000 on strike in the State of Illinois alone. Sunday was a quiet day in Chicago, although small affrays occurred at various points about the lines of railways. There was a considerable conflict at Hammond, a small town in Indiana, 20 miles from Chicago—to be mentioned hereafter—in which a company of United States troops were compelled to fire on the mob. On receipt of this intelligence the President at once issued the following proclamation:

BY THE PRESIDENT OF THE UNITED STATES OF AMERICA.

A PROCLAMATION.

Whereas, by reason of unlawful obstruction, combinations, and assemblages of persons it has become impracticable, in the judgment of the President, to enforce by the ordinary course of judicial proceedings, the laws of the United States within the State of Illinois, and especially in the city of Chicago within said State;

And whereas, for the purpose of enforcing the faithful execution of the laws of the United States and protecting its property and removing obstructions to the United States mails in the State and city aforesaid, the President has employed a part of the military forces of the United States;

Now, therefore, I, Grover Cleveland, President of the United States, do hereby admonish all good citizens and all persons who may be or may come within the city and State aforesaid, against aiding, countenancing, encouraging, or taking any part in such unlawful obstructions, combinations, and assemblages; and I hereby warn all persons engaged in or in any way connected with such unlawful obstructions, combinations, and assemblages to disperse and retire peaceably to their respective abodes on or before 12 o'clock noon on the 9th day of July instant.

Those who disregard this warning and persist in taking part with a riotous mob in forcibly resisting and obstructing the execution of the laws of the United States, or interfering with the functions of the Government or destroying or attempting to destroy the property belonging to the United States or under its protection, can not be regarded otherwise than as public enemies.

Troops employed against such a riotous mob will act with all the moderation and forbearance consistent with the accomplishment of the desired end; but the stern necessities that confront them will not with certainty permit discrimination between guilty participants and those who are mingled with them from curiosity and without criminal intent. The only safe course, therefore, for those not actually unlawfully participating is to abide at their homes, or at least not to be found in the neighborhood of riotous assemblages.

While there will be no hesitation or vacillation in the decisive treatment of the guilty, this warning is especially intended to protect and save the innocent.

In testimony whereof, I have hereunto set my hand and caused the seal of the United States to be hereto affixed.

Done at the city of Washington, this 8th day of July in the year of our Lord eighteen hundred and ninety-four, and of the Independence of the United States the one hundred and nineteenth.

[SEAL.]   GROVER CLEVELAND.

By the President:
    W. Q. GRESHAM,
        Secretary of State.

The troops in Chicago on the 9th aggregated 750 infantry, 120 cavalry, 60 artillery, in all 930 men, while 500 men were en route from Fort Riley. These were supplemented by a brigade of Illinois National Guard, numbering 2,000, and deputy United States marshals to the number of 750 to 1,000. There was no rioting on the 9th, the strikers seemingly awaiting the result of conferences. The Ninth Infantry from Madison Barracks arrived during the afternoon and were put on duty at once. On the 10th the most prominent of the leaders of the strikers were arrested charged with conspiracy to block the progress of the United States mails. By the 11th it was apparent that the worst was over. Trains were being moved on all of the twenty-two railroads centering in Chicago somewhat irregularly but without molestation; rioting had ceased, and, although there was much feverish excitement throughout the city, a better feeling existed and the troops were not called upon for anything beyond the preservation of order. On the 18th orders were issued returning the Ninth Infantry to Madison Barracks and directing all the other troops in Chicago to take station at Fort Sheridan.

The geographical position of the State of Indiana renders it an important factor in any movement involving the trunk lines between the East and West. Every railway track between the eastern seaboard and the lakes must cross its borders, and as a consequence its peace and good order are necessarily affected by any disturbance having its center in railway industries. Early in the Pullman strike the State authorities, apprehensive of impending troubles, were in correspondence with the War Department, and had taken measures to insure prompt communication should the emergency arise. From the middle of April up to the 20th of June there had been a strike among the coal miners and the entire National Guard of the State had been in the field. The State troops, about 1,000 in number, were worn out from their unaccustomed service, and at the best were too few to afford much resistance to a determined mob. In connection with the general strike the Riot at Hammond, Ind., July 7, 1894. employees of all the roads entering Indianapolis had been ordered out and trains were everywhere blocked.

On Sunday, the 7th of July, a large mob assembled at Hammond, a point on the main route from New York to Chicago, 20 miles east of that city, where five trunk lines pass through the town— the Erie, the Monon, the Michigan Central, the Nickel Plate, and the

Pennsylvania. The mob had sacked the telegraph office, cut the wires, stopped all traffic, overturned cars, and destroyed much property. The sheriff and United States marshal being powerless to restrain them, called upon the Government for aid, and the latter, in concert with the officers of the United States court, telegraphed the situation to the President and asked for the assistance of the Federal troops.[185] To this the Secretary of War replied that his request had been referred to General Miles, who had full authority to act, and at the same time General Miles was informed that he had full authority to act under his previous instructions. A company of the Fifteenth Infantry was accordingly dispatched to Hammond, and upon their arrival an effort was made to raise the blockade, and several trains under their escort were pulled through the town. This angered the mob, and volleys of stones were showered upon the Regular troops. The men stood their ground for something over three hours, by which time a mob of fully 3,000 men, who had been aroused to a frenzy by their leaders, surrounded them. Several times they rushed upon this company, numbering but 35 men, but were met each time by fixed bayonets and driven back. At last, when about to be overpowered by numbers, the order was given to fire and several volleys were poured into the mob. The result was never ascertained, as the rioters carried away their killed, if any, and all of their wounded but 12 or 15—one man only was known to be killed. An hour later three more companies arrived from Chicago, and before morning 16 companies of State militia, including a battery of artillery, had reached Hammond, and order was restored.

By the 10th of July the strike and its consequent blockade had extended westward along the line of the Northern Pacific into North Dakota, Montana, Idaho, Oregon, and Washington; the Union Pacific into Wyoming, Colorado, Utah, Nevada, and California, and the Southern Pacific into New Mexico. In Iowa there was a general suspension of traffic, with rioting at Ottumwa, Sioux City, and other points along the line of the Rock Island Road, which necessitated the calling out of the National Guard. In Missouri the tie-up was general and there was disorder at St. Louis, Moberly, Kansas City, and other points, and United States marshals were appointed in large numbers, but the governor declined to call out the militia or to ask for Federal assistance. In Nebraska the militia was called out to

Rioting in the West generally, July, 1894.

suppress lawlessness at Omaha, and there was a suspension of traffic for a week or more, but there was no occasion for Federal action. In order, however, that any possible emergency should be promptly met, all department commanders in these States and Territories west of the Mississippi were given the following instructions:

In view of the fact, as substantiated by communications received from the Department of Justice, from your official reports, and from other reliable sources, that, by reason of unlawful obstructions and combinations or assemblages of persons, it has become impracticable in the judgment of the President to enforce by the ordinary course of judicial proceeding the laws of the United States, and to prevent obstructions of the United States mails and interruptions to commerce between the States on the line of the Northern Pacific Railroad, and to secure to the United States the right guaranteed by section 11 of the act approved July 2, 1864, constituting the Northern Pacific Railroad "A post route and military road, subject to the use of the United Slates for postal, military, naval, and all other Government service," you are directed by the President to employ the military force under your command to remove obstructions to the mails, and to execute any orders of the United States court for the protection of property in the hands of receivers appointed by such court, and for preventing interruption of interstate commerce, and to give such protection to said railroad as will prevent any unlawful and forcible obstruction to the regular and orderly operation of said road "For postal, military, naval, and all other Government service."

J. M. SCHOFIELD,
Major-General, Commanding.

The situation in Idaho along the line of the Northern Pacific was complicated by a strike of the miners and their attempts to blow up mines and buildings with dynamite. On the 7th the governor requested the Senators from the State to see the President and urge the sending of troops, but it was considered that the department commander under his general instructions would take measures to provide for emergencies. A company was sent to Snake River to guard a mine and the garrison at Boise was held in readiness to move at a moment's notice. On the 9th the following dispatch was received from the governor:

Rioting in Idaho, July, 1894.

[Telegram.]

BOISE, IDAHO, *July 9.*

GROVER CLEVELAND,
President of the United States, Washington:

Domestic violence in the form of an unlawful conspiracy to destroy life and property exists in Shoshone County, Idaho. Armed men in such force that I am powerless to aid the civil authority in restoring order. Citizens residing in the county are deprived of the equal protection of the laws guaranteed by the Constitution. The legislature of the State can not be convened at this time. The presence of Regular troops is absolutely necessary. I therefore call upon you to direct that at least two companies of Regulars be stationed in said county until order is restored and the laws recognized.

W. J. McCONNELL,
Governor of Idaho.

In response to this a company was sent to Wardner, the center of the mining disturbances, and an entire regiment was scattered along the line of the Northern Pacific between Missoula, Mont., and Tacoma, Wash., to escort the trains and prevent interference with the progress of the mails. By the 17th of July all trains were moving freely and the troops were withdrawn.

The employees of the Atchison, Topeka and Santa Fe system, running from St. Louis through the southern tier of States and Territories to the Pacific, were among the first to declare their sympathy with the Pullman strikers and to quit work. This road was in the hands of receivers appointed by United States court, and the court promptly ordered the strikers to be discharged and new men employed.

New Mexico. The striking employees declared their purpose to prevent the execution of this mandate and the sheriff of one of the counties along the line of road called for aid. This the governor was unable to furnish and he telegraphed for aid. The following is his demand and its reply:

SANTA FE, N. MEX.

The employees of the Atchison, Topeka and Santa Fe Railroad Company, which is in the hands of receivers, have struck to aid in the boycott of the Pullman Palace Car Company. The court has ordered new men to be employed to take their places. There are grave fears that the old employees will prevent new employees from moving the cars. The sheriff of Colfax County wires that he can employ no deputies there upon whom he can rely and that if an outbreak occurs he would be powerless to protect property or men.

The situation is critical and demands prompt action. Owing to the failure of the last legislature to make appropriations to support Territorial militia I can not use them. Will you instruct Colonel Pearson to aid Territorial authorities in enforcing the law when called on.

W. T. THORNTON,
Governor.

[Telegram.]

WASHINGTON, D. C., July 1, 1894.

Hon. W. T. THORNTON,
Governor of New Mexico, Santa Fe, N. Mex.

Your telegram received. The United States attorney and marshal for New Mexico have been instructed to see that regular mail trains are not obstructed and that orders of Federal courts are executed by sufficient number of deputies or posse. United States troops can not in this case intervene until United States judge or attorney and marshal certify to the Attorney-General that marshal can not execute process or orders of courts.

DANIEL S. LAMONT,
Secretary of War.

At the same time, instructions were sent General McCook, the department commander, at Denver, to send at once a sufficient force from Fort Logan to Trinidad to enforce the mandates of the United States court, protect property in the hands of the receivers, and prevent obstruction to the use of said property, and the transmission of United States mails. In obedience to this, troops left Fort Logan at 5 a. m. of the 2d, arriving at Trinidad at noon of that day; other detachments were sent the same date to Raton and Pueblo, where disturbances had broken out. At Trinidad the troops were called upon that night to save railroad property from destruction by a mob numbering several thousand, and those sent to Raton were derailed at Las Vegas. A large number of the rioters were arrested, and, under escort of troops, were taken to Denver. From this point the troubles extended to the line of the Atlantic and Pacific Railroad, in Arizona. This road was also in the hands of receivers, and an appeal was made to the Attorney-General in due course. This resulted in troops being sent from Whipple Barracks, at Prescott, to Winslow, Peach Springs, and Williams, and from Fort Wingate to Los Cerrillos, but in no instance was anything beyond the presence of the troops necessary to restore order.

On the 13th of July the authorities of the Rock Island road reported that rioters were tearing up the track of that road at Enid and Pond Creek, in Oklahoma, and at Round Pond, in the Indian Territory; the mails obstructed, and interstate commerce interrupted. A bridge was blown up at Round Pond, trains derailed at several points, and a general cessation of all traffic ensued. The United States marshal, when called upon to arrest the leaders, reported himself powerless and without means to suppress the disorders. At the same time the acting governor of the Territory telegraphed for assistance, as follows:

Rioting in Oklahoma, July 13–20, 1894.

GUTHRIE, OKLA., *July 13, 1894.*

HON. HOKE SMITH,
Secretary of Interior, Washington, D. C.

SIR: In counties L and O, in this Territory, great violence toward the property of the Rock Island Railway Company has been, and is being, done. Mails are interrupted, interstate commerce stopped, and the track and bridges of the company torn up and wrecked; two bridges and a portion of the track having been destroyed within the past twenty-four hours. The civil authorities are unable to preserve order and protect property; the United States marshal is also unable to afford relief. I have no militia, and desire the assistance of the United States military to preserve order and protect property. I think one small troop, divided at Round Pond and Enid, will be sufficient.

THOS. J. LOWE,
Secretary, and Acting Governor.

We concur in the above.

E. D. NIX,
United States Marshal.
C. R. BROOKE,
United States Attorney.

Troops were accordingly sent to Enid on the 14th, and Round Pond, where the disorders continued for some days. All trains were completely blockaded from the 13th to the 20th; bridges were burned at eight different points, and much property destroyed. On the 23d two more companies were sent from Fort Supply to Round Pond, where a large number of arrests were made. These disorders were not altogether associated with the labor strikes, but were largely the result of growing dissatisfaction with the railroad companies on account of their failing to locate stations at every point desired by the settlers.

The railroad strike first reached California through the suspension of traffic on the Southern Pacific. On the 1st of July Major-General Ruger, then commanding the Department of California, was instructed to send a sufficient military force from San Francisco to Los Angeles "to enforce the mandates and warrants of the United States courts, and to prevent any obstruction of the United States mails." The First Infantry—eight companies—was sent in response to these instructions, and remained at that point for some two weeks, but beyond the moral effect of their presence no occasion arose for their active service. There was little delay in the sending out of trains along this section, and not much interruption to travel. The center of disturbance in this State was at Sacramento. On the 4th of July a force of National Guard, numbering about 1,000, in an attempt to clear the station of the Southern Pacific, was met by so defiant an attitude upon the part of the mob that the soldiers refused to obey orders to "charge," and as the United States marshal refused to give orders to fire the troops withdrew, leaving the station and vicinity in the hands of the mob. As a consequence, the Central Pacific and the northern section of the Southern Pacific between Sacramento and Oakland was practically in the hands of the strikers for something over a week. On the 10th a force of 18 officers and 345 men from the Presidio and Alcatraz, 2 officers and 50 men from Benicia, and 6 officers and 120 marines from Mare Island—total, 542 officers and men—left San Francisco by boat for Sacramento, arriving early the next morning and taking possession of the railroad depots and property without opposition. An attempt to start the trains resulted in the derailment of the leading section and the wounding of two of the strikers. A force of 350 sailors was sent to Oakland on the 14th, where some disturbance resulted from an attempt to send trains eastward. By the 16th all trains were running on time, but under escort of Regular troops or National Guard, and the block was broken by the 21st; but it was not until the middle of August that regular travel was resumed, so that the troops could be entirely withdrawn.

According to the testimony before the commission appointed by the President to inquire into the causes, etc., of this strike, the loss to the railroads in property destroyed, hire of deputy marshals, and other incidental expenses was at least $685,308. The loss of earnings of the roads is etimated at $4,672,916. The loss to the 3,100 Pullman employees in wages was at least $350,000; the loss in wages to the nearly 100,000 employees upon the 24 railroads centering at Chicago, at least $1,389,143. Besides these amounts, very great losses, widely distributed, were incidentally suffered throughout the country. The number of Federal troops brought to Chicago to protect the United States mail service and Federal buildings, and to sustain the execution of the orders of the United States courts, was 1,936; the number of State militia about 4,000; of extra deputy marshals, nearly 5,000; of extra deputy sher-

Riot at Sacramento, Cal., July 4, 1894.

Losses, etc., by the strike.

iffs, 250; to which should be added the police force of Chicago, 3,000, making a total force employed in the suppression of violence and the preservation of order of 14,186. The number of men who were shot or fatally wounded during the riots was 12; the number arrested by the police, 515; the number wounded, injured, or otherwise hurt, as nearly as can be ascertained, 875.[a]

It will be observed from the foregoing narrative of events that on the 10th of July the Government assumed the responsibility of arresting and holding in custody the leaders of the strike, and that from that date the disturbances ceased and the strike itself gradually declined. In his testimony before the United States strike commission, Mr. Eugene V. Debs, one of the prominent leaders of the strike, remarked (p. 143):

As soon as the employees found that we were arrested and taken from the scene of action they became demoralized, and that ended the strike. It was not the soldiers that ended the strike; it was not the old brotherhoods that ended the strike; it was simply the United States courts that ended the strike. Our men were in a position that never would have been shaken under any circumstances if we had been permitted to remain upon the field—remain among them. But once that we were taken from the scene of action and restrained from sending telegrams or issuing the orders necessary, or answering questions; when the minions of the corporations would be put to work at such a place, for instance, as Nickerson, Kans., where they would go and say that the men at Newton had gone back to work, and Nickerson would wire me to ask if that were true. No answer would come to the message, because I was under arrest, and we were all under arrest. The headquarters were demoralized and abandoned, and we could not answer any telegrams or questions that would come in. Our headquarters were temporarily demoralized and abandoned, and we could not answer any messages. The men went back to work, and the ranks were broken, and the strike was broken up by the Federal courts of the United States and not by the Army, and not by any other power, but simply and solely by the action of the United States courts in restraining us from discharging our duties as officers and representatives of the employees.

Debs and other officers of the American Railway Union were arrested, upon an indictment found by the grand jury, for contempt and violation of the injunction before issued by the circuit court of the United States for the northern district of Illinois. A hearing was had by the court, and on the 14th of December the defend-ants were found guilty of contempt and sentenced to imprisonment in the county jail for terms varying from three to six months. Having been committed to jail in pursuance of that order, they, on January 14, 1895, applied to the Supreme Court of the United States for a writ of error, and also one of habeas corpus. The former was denied; the latter was argued March 25–26, 1895, and on the 27th of May the court handed down its decision deny-

The case of In re Debs, Supreme Court, United States, 1895.

---

[a] Report on the Chicago strike of June–July, 1894, by the United States strike commission appointed by the President July 26, 1894, 736 pages. See also Annual Report Attorney-General, 1894.

ing the petition of a writ of habeas corpus.[a]   In the opinion of the Supreme Court the doctrine which had been laid down many years before in the Legal Tender cases (12 Wall., 457), Ex parte Siebold (100 U. S., 371, 395), and repeatedly reiterated, was again enunciated:

We hold it to be an incontrovertible principle that the Government of the United States may, by means of physical force, exercised through its official agents, execute on every foot of American soil the powers and functions that belong to it. This necessarily involves the power to command obedience to its laws, and hence the power to keep the peace to that extent. This power to enforce its laws and to execute its functions in all places does not derogate from the power of the State to execute its laws at the same time and in the same places. The one does not exclude the other, except where both can not be executed at the same time. In that case the words of the Constitution itself show which is to yield: "This Constitution, and all laws which shall be made in pursuance thereof, * * * shall be the supreme law of the land."

*   *   *   *   *   *   *

The entire strength of the nation may be used to enforce in any part of the land the full and free exercise of all national powers and the security of all rights intrusted by the Constitution to its care. The strong arm of the National Government may be put forth to brush away all obstructions to the freedom of interstate commerce or the transportation of the mails. If the emergency arises the Army of the nation, and all its militia, are at the service of the nation to compel obedience to its laws.

After a thorough review of the questions involved, the court thus concludes:

We have given to this case the most careful and anxious attention, for we realize that it touches closely questions of supreme importance to the people of this country. Summing up our conclusions, we hold that the Government of the United States is one having jurisdiction over every foot of soil within its territory and acting directly upon each citizen; that while it is a Government of enumerated powers, it has within the limits of those powers all the attributes of sovereignty; that to it is committed power over interstate commerce and the transmission of the mail; that the powers thus conferred upon the National Government are not dormant, but have been assumed and put into practical exercise by the legislation of Congress; that in the exercise of those powers it is competent for the Nation to remove all obstructions upon highways, natural or artificial, to the passage of interstate commerce or the carrying of the mail; that while it may be competent for the Government (through the executive branch and in the use of the entire executive power of the Nation) to forcibly remove all such obstructions, it is equally within its competency to appeal to the civil courts for an inquiry and determination as to the existence and character of any alleged obstructions, and if such are found to exist or threaten to occur, to invoke the powers of those courts to remove or restrain such obstructions; that the jurisdiction of courts to interfere in such matters by injunction is one recognized from ancient times and by indubitable authority; that such jurisdiction is not ousted by the fact that the obstructions are accompanied by or consist of acts in themselves violations of the criminal law; that the proceeding by injunction is of a civil character and may be enforced by proceedings in contempt; that such proceedings are not in execution of the criminal laws of the land; that the penalty for a violation of injunction is no substitute for and no defense to a prosecution for any criminal offenses committed in the

---

[a] In re Debs, Petitioner, 158 U. S. Reports (October term, 1894), 564.

course of such violation; that the complaint filed in this case clearly showed an existing obstruction of artificial highways for the passage of interstate commerce and transmission of the mail—an obstruction not only temporarily existing, but threatening to continue; that under such complaint the circuit court had power to issue its process of injunction; that it having been issued and served on these defendants, the circuit court had authority to inquire whether its orders had been disobeyed, and when it found that they had been, then to proceed under section 725, Revised Statutes, which grants power "to punish, by fine or imprisonment, * * * disobedience, * * * by any party * * * or other person, to any lawful writ, process, order, rule, decree, or command," and enter the order of punishment complained of; and finally that the circuit court having full jurisdiction in the premises, its finding of the fact of disobedience is not open to review on habeas corpus in this or any other court. (Ex parte Watkins, 3 Pet., 193; Ex parte Yarbrough, 110 U. S., 651; Ex parte Terry, 128 U. S., 289, 305; In re Swan, 150 U. S., 637; United States *v.* Pridgeon, 153 U. S., 48.)

XII. FROM THE RULING IN THE DEBS CASE TO THE END OF THE FIFTY-SEVENTH CONGRESS.

THE WAR WITH SPAIN, 1898—THE PHILIPPINE INSURRECTION, 1899-1901—THE CŒUR D'ALENE TROUBLES, 1899—THE REORGANIZATION OF THE ARMY, 1901—CONCLUSIONS.

It has doubtless been observed in the progress of this work that there has been an endeavor to show at the same time the various changes in the condition of the Army. The reasons for this are obvious. In the first place, it is to be remembered that the policy of our Government has invariably been to maintain an army in time of peace at the smallest possible strength consonant with the public benefit and interest, and yet to give it such organization as would enable it to expand in time of war; secondly, to regard the militia as a posse comitatus, to be "called out" and armed and equipped whenever the Regular Army is inadequate "to suppress insurrection, repel invasion, and to execute the laws of the Union." We have thus seen a paper-organized militia giving way to the "volunteer," and the latter to an organized militia under the name of the National Guard. The volunteer had demonstrated his effectiveness for work, and had carried the nation safely through a civil war of a magnitude such as has no parallel in history, and had merged in the body of the people, leaving scarcely any evidence that through four years 4,000,000 men, or more, had been withdrawn from peaceful avocations, and had devoted their lives, their fortunes, and their arduous labors to the pursuit of bitterly-contested war. To the volunteer succeeded the National Guard, which, patterning from the Regular Army, had slowly but steadily developed through the process of showy parades in harlequin uniforms, to solid bodies of picked men plainly and suitably clad, armed with rifles of latest pattern which they knew how to use, instructed in modern methods of skirmishing and effective fighting, and handled and fed by a trained staff. It is true that few of the men included in the National Guard of the States served more than the two or three years of enlistment; that many officers were appointed through political favor, or were elected by the men on account of their congenial natures rather than because of their fitness, and that many resigned through caprice or discontent. Those very facts inured to the greater benefit of the military system, on the principle that 1,000,000 men taught in the

240

elementary principles of the soldier are ten times more valuable than 100,000 who know it all. This apparent paradox, which to the military mind is the purest reason, was plainly demonstrated in the spring of 1898, and thus through experience afforded an opportunity for an advancement of the military system of the United States to a status and effectibility commensurate with the importance of the nation.

The joint resolution, approved April 20, 1898, demanding that Spain relinquish its authority and government in the island of Cuba and withdraw its land and naval forces from Cuba and Cuban. waters, authorized the President to use the land and naval forces of the United States to carry the resolve into effect. Congress followed this pregnant step by the passage of an act, approved April 22, 1898, providing for the temporary increase of the military establishment of the United States.

By this law the organized and active land forces were declared to consist of the Regular Army and of the militia of the several States when called into service, constituting two branches designated, respectively, as the Regular Army and the Volunteer Army of the United States. Section 6 provided that—

The war with Spain, 1898.

when the members of any company, troop, battery, battalion, or regiment of the organized militia of any State shall enlist in the Volunteer Army in a body, as such company, troop, battery, battalion, or regiment, the regimental company, troop, battery, and battalion officers in service with the militia organization thus enlisting may be appointed by the governors of the States and Territories, and shall when so appointed be officers of corresponding grades in the same organization when it shall have been received into the service of the United States as a part of the Volunteer Army.

The same section further provided that the President may authorize—

the Secretary of War to organize companies, troops, battalions, or regiments, possessing special qualifications, from the nation at large, not to exceed three thousand men, under such rules and regulations, including the appointment of the officers thereof, as may be prescribed by the Secretary of War.

Section 7 authorized the recruitment to their maximum strength of all the accepted organizations in the volunteer force, and provided for the organization of regular and volunteer troops into divisions of three brigades, each brigade to be composed of three or more regiments, and authorized the President, whenever three or more divisions are present in the same army, to organize them into army corps, each corps to consist of not more than three divisions. By section 13 not more than one officer of the Regular Army could hold a commission in any one of the regiments of the Volunteer Army at the same time.

Finally, by the act approved May 11, 1898, Congress authorized, in addition to the volunteer forces provided by the act of April 22, the organization of a volunteer brigade of engineers from the nation at large, to consist of not more than three regiments, and not more than

3,500 men, possessing the special qualifications for engineering troops; the officers of this brigade to be appointed by the Secretary of War. The same act authorized also the organization of an additional volunteer force, not exceeding 10,000 men, possessing immunity from disease incident to tropical climates, the officers of this force to be appointed by the President, by and with the advice of the Senate. Under the authority conferred upon him by the joint resolution of April 20 and the act of April 22, 1898, the President issued a proclamation, dated April 23, 1898, calling for volunteers to the number of 125,000 men, to be apportioned, as far as practicable, among the several States, Territories, and the District of Columbia, according to population, to serve for two years unless sooner discharged. The apportionment under this call aggregated 5 regiments and 17 troops of cavalry, 16 batteries of light artillery, 1 regiment and 7 batteries of heavy artillery, and 119 regiments and 10 battalions of infantry. May 25, 1898, the President issued a proclamation calling for an additional force of 75,000 men. For controlling military reasons it was determined to utilize so much of this additional force as was necessary to bring up the several State organizations in service to the full legal strength, the remainder to be apportioned among the several States and Territories according to their respective quotas as nearly as possible. The apportionment under this second call comprised 16 batteries of light artillery; 3 battalions of heavy artillery; and 22 regiments, 10 battalions, and 46 companies of infantry. The aggregate strength of the Regular and Volunteer armies for each of the months of May, June, July, and August was as follows:

	May.	June.	July.	August.
Officers..........	8,415	9,367	10,960	11,108
Enlisted men	160,514	202,868	257,392	263,609
Total..........	168,929	212,235	268,352	274,717

The suspension of hostilities, resulting from the short but brilliant operations of the army against Santiago, Cuba, leading to its capture and of that of the Spanish forces defending the city; the surrender of Spanish troops in Porto Rico, no less than the successful operation of our troops in the Philippines, led to the determination to muster out 100,000 men, nearly one-half of the entire volunteer force, and the first order looking to that end was issued on the 18th of August. [a]

The muster out of the volunteer regiments, except those in the Philippines, was commenced September 5, 1898, and was completed June 8, 1899. The withdrawal of the volunteer troops from the Philippines was commenced June 14, 1899, and all had been mustered out November 23, 1899, as likewise the men of the Regular Army who enlisted for the war with Spain.

[a] Report of the Adjutant-General of the Army for 1898.

The expectation of the War Department as to the preparedness of the National Guard as a line of first defense, an expectation which was based upon repeated reports from the State authorities, was not altogether realized.

The usual maximum per company of the organized State militia did not exceed 60, and many were not maintained at that number. Of the number actually borne upon company rolls a portion declined to volunteer upon reasonable grounds. About 25 per cent were rejected on physical examination prior to muster, and an additional number were rejected on physical reexamination after muster, a systematic inquiry having been made with a view to the elimination of all men unfitted for military service, so that about 30 of the original company is a fair estimate of the number of men previously trained, armed, and equipped in each company finally received into the United States service. The minimum number per company required for muster in was 77, and hence in many instances about 47 recruits, mostly untrained and without uniform or equipment, were hastily obtained and physically examined without opportunity to inquire into their moral or mental fitness, and a number were found on the expiration of muster-out furlough to be actual residents of neighboring or distant States. Deficiencies in numbers from these causes became immediately apparent, and the necessity of providing in almost every particular for the recruits necessary to expand State companies to the State maximum and thence to the minimum required for muster into the United States service at once developed deficiencies in clothing, arms, and equipment. Consolidation of military organizations urged by the War Department to meet this situation, presenting fewer regiments containing a greater number of trained men, fairly clothed, armed, and equipped was not accomplished. There were obtained for State organizations, mustered in under the first call, about 40,000 recruits to approximate to the maximum authorized by law— 106 per infantry company. States presented for muster into the United States service regimental and battalion, staff, and noncommissioned staff officers unknown to any law or regulation of the Army, viz: Regimental paymasters, regimental inspectors of rifle practice, regimental commissaries and ordnance officers, regimental signal officers, battalion adjutants and quartermasters, assistant surgeons (with the rank of captain); regimental and battalion commissary, quartermaster, and ordnance sergeants, and battalion sergeant-majors, presenting, on mobilization, a heterogeneous army, unsatisfactory not only from a military and economical view, but because of dissatisfaction created on account of officers performing precisely similar duties under different rank and emoluments. [a]

The necessity for an improvement in the method of expanding the Regular Army in the event of unexpected necessity, and which, perhaps, would have otherwise been delayed for many years, became apparent in the exigencies growing out of the situation in the Philippine Islands. At the end of 1898 the Eighth Army Corps, under the command of Maj. Gen. E. S. Otis—

held possession of the city of Manila under the provisions of the protocol of August 12, 1898, which required the United States to occupy and hold that city pending the conclusion of the treaty of peace, and which imposed upon the troops in possession at once the obligation to protect life and property within the city and to refrain from infringing upon Spanish territory outside of the city limits. In the performance of this duty many annoyances were experienced from the army of the Tagalogs who were in insurrection

The Philippine insurrection, 1899–1902.

---

[a] Report of the Adjutant-General of the Army for 1899.

against the Government of Spain, and who had been collected about the city after its capture by the American forces had become inevitable, under the promise of their leaders that they should share in the plunder of the inhabitants. General Otis was ordered to avoid any conflict with them, and, strictly complying with these orders, he made every effort to secure a peaceable understanding.

The peaceable attitude of the American forces was unfortunately misconstrued as indicating weakness and fear of a conflict. On the night of the 4th of February, 1899, our forces were attacked by the Tagalogs, who attempted to capture the city. They were promptly repulsed in a series of active engagements which extended through the night of the 4th, and the 5th, 6th, and 10th days of February. Our lines were extended and established at a considerable distance from the city in every direction. On the 22d of February a concerted rising of the Tagalogs in the city of Manila, of whom there are about 200,000, was attempted under instructions to massacre all the Americans and Europeans in the city. This attempt was promptly suppressed and the city was placed under strict control. The troops composing the Eighth Army Corps under General Otis's command at that time were of regulars 171 officers and 5,201 enlisted men, and of volunteers 667 officers and 14,831 enlisted men, making an aggregate of 838 officers and 20,032 enlisted men. All of the volunteers and 1,650 of the regulars were, or were about to become, entitled to their discharge, and their right was perfected by the exchange of ratifications of the treaty on the 11th of April. The total force which Major-General Otis was thus entitled to command for any considerable period consisted of only 171 officers and 3,551 enlisted men. The numbers of the Eighth Army Corps above stated give the entire numerical strength of all troops present in the islands, including those at Cavite and Iloilo, the sick and wounded, those serving in the civil departments and in the staff organizations, and, deducting these, the effective men of the line, officers and soldiers, were about 14,000. Of these 3,000 constituted a provost guard necessary to preserve order within Manila and prevent the known intention of the secret hostile organizations in that city to burn and sack the city when our troops were engaged on the lines of defense. Including, therefore, all the troops who were entitled to be discharged there were not more than 11,000 officers and men available to engage the insurgent army which was two or three times that number, well armed and equipped, and included many of the native troops formerly comprised in the Spanish army, and to occupy and hold positions in a comparatively unknown country, densely populated by inhabitants speaking, in the main, an unknown language. The months of the most intense heat, followed by the very severe rainy season of that climate, were immediately approaching, and for any effective occupation of the country it was necessary to await both the close of the rainy season and the supply of new troops to take the place of those about to be discharged. Practically all the volunteers who were then in the Philippines consented to forego the just expectation of an immediate return to their homes, and to remain in the field until their places could be supplied by new troops. They voluntarily subjected themselves to the dangers and casualties of numerous engagements and to the very great hardships of the climate. They exhibited fortitude and courage, and are entitled to high commendation for their patriotic spirit and soldierly conduct. The operations of the period extending from February to the 31st day of August, the date of the annual report of General Otis as commander of the Department of the Pacific, were marked by a steady maintenance and strengthening of the position occupied by our forces, a gradual extension of our lines, a restoration of security and confidence in the city of Manila, numerous sharp engagements in the field marked by unbroken success, and many instances of very gratifying conduct on the part of both officers and men. It is probable that at any time a column of troops could have been sent anywhere on the island of Luzon as against any armed resistance which the insurgents could have offered after the demoralization in their ranks, resulting from the severe defeats inflicted upon them in February; but there were not the troops necessary to garrison the towns or to maintain any far-extended lines of communication. No attempt was accordingly made to occupy the country, except in the vicinity of Manila and at such points as were important for the protection of our lines. Such movements as passed beyond this territory were designed primarily to break up threatening concentrations of insurgent troops and prevent undue annoyance to the positions which we occupied. *a*

To take the place of the volunteers, who under the law were required to be returned to the United States and mustered out, the President, under the provisions of the act of March 2, 1899, authorized the organization of ten regiments of volunteers, to be designated as the Twenty-sixth, Twenty-seventh, Twenty-eighth, Twenty-ninth, Thirtieth, Thirty-first, Thirty-second, Thirty-third, Thirty-fourth, and Thirty-fifth regiments of infantry, U. S. Volunteers; on July 18, 1899, of two regiments of volunteers, to be known as the Thirty-sixth and Thirty-seventh regiments of infantry, U. S. Volunteers, to be recruited and organized in the Philippine Islands; on August 10, 1899, of a regiment of cavalry to be known as the Eleventh Regiment of Cavalry, U. S. Volunteers; on August 17, 1899, of ten additional regiments of volunteer infantry to be known as the Thirty-eighth, Thirty-ninth, Fortieth, Forty-first, Forty-second, Forty-third, Forty-fourth, Forty-fifth, Forty-sixth, and Forty-seventh regiments of infantry, U. S. Volunteers; and on September 2, 1899, of two additional regiments to be designated as the Forty-eighth and Forty-ninth regiments of infantry, U. S. Volunteers. Of the two latter regiments, the enlisted men and company officers (captains and lieutenants) to be colored; the field officers to be appointed from the commissioned officers of the Regular Army. The captains and lieutenants were selected with much care from among the noncommissioned officers of the colored regiments of the Regular Army, those having distinguished themselves in battle in the Santiago campaign being given preference. After this class had been given recognition, men having had service in the Spanish-American war were considered, and an equal number from each organization of colored volunteers serving in the Spanish-American war was selected. It is believed that the best-equipped men of our colored citizens were commissioned in these regiments, many of them having given evidence of fitness by long service in the Regular Army and excellent conduct in battle. *b*

As has been stated, this volunteer force, which was raised under the provisions of the act of March 2, 1899, by the terms of that act was to continue in service not later than July 1, 1901. It was accordingly brought back from the Philippines, where it was substantially all stationed, between the 1st of January and the 30th of June, 1901, to San Francisco, where it was mustered out.

"It is very gratifying to note," says the Adjutant-General in his Annual Report for 1901, "from the reports made that the discipline of the volunteers while in camp was so uniformly good as to call for little criticism, fully justifying in that respect the wisdom of the method adopted of organizing them and of selecting the senior officers from the regular establishment. These officers were in every instance selected for purely military reasons. The line officers were selected on their efficiency records as volunteer officers. All in all, the Government has never had more satisfactory troops than these

---

a Report of the Secretary of War for 1899.
b Report of the Adjutant-General of the Army for 1899.

volunteers, and these troops are entitled to the gratitude of the people and the Government."[a]

In view of the provisions of the act of March 2, 1899, requiring the muster out of the United States Volunteers not later than July 1, 1901, and of the utter inadequacy of the Regular Army after that date to meet existing conditions, Congress, by the act of February 2, 1901, authorized its increase, on the basis of a three-battalion organization, to 15 regiments of cavalry, 1 corps of artillery, and 30 regiments of infantry, together with a suitable increase in the several staff departments. The artillery corps (substituted for the existing regimental organizations of the artillery arm of the Army) to comprise two branches—the coast artillery and the field artillery; the chief of that corps, selected from the colonels of artillery, to serve on the staff of the Lieutenant-General Commanding. The coast artillery to consist of 126 companies and the field artillery of 30 batteries, the aggregate number of enlisted men not to exceed 18,920, exclusive of electrician sergeants, and the increase provided for the artillery to be made as follows: Not less than 20 per cent before July 1, 1901, and not less than 20 per cent in each succeeding year until the entire number shall have been attained. Section 30 of the act above quoted authorizes the President to maintain the enlisted force of the several organizations of the Army at their maximum strength during the present exigencies of the service, or until such time as Congress may otherwise direct.[b]

The disturbances in the Cœur d'Alene district of Shoshone County, Idaho, in April, 1899, growing out of troubles between the miners' unions and the mine owners, came into unusual public prominence through a Congressional investigation made the following year, and while not important in itself became so through charges against the conduct of the United States troops in arresting, at the instance of the governor of Idaho, and holding as prisoners, parties implicated in the disturbances. The mines of the Cœur d'Alene are in Shoshone County, Idaho, and lie near the northern end of the Pan Handle of the State. The principal towns of the county are Murray, Wallace, Burke, Gem, Mullan, Kellogg, and Wardner. They are principally miners' camps, and are strung along the base of the Cœur d'Alene and Bitter Root mountains, which bound the region on the north. In some of the towns there is only room for a single narrow street between the mountains and the deep canyon of the river. The Northern Pacific and Oregon Railway and Navigation Company's railroad furnishes the natural and easy ingress and egress from said district; the only other approach or escape is over rough and almost impassable mountain trails, which in winter are filled in places with snow to a depth of 20 or 25 feet. It is one of the richest

The Cœur d'Alene labor troubles, April–May, 1899.

---

[a] Annual reports of the War Department for 1901, vol. 1, part 2, p. 20.
[b] Annual Report of the Adjutant-General of the Army for 1901.

lead-mining regions in the world, the ore carrying considerable silver, and the annual output of ore amounting to over $5,000,000. By reason of the mountainous condition of the country, Shoshone County is practically cut off from the rest of the State. The population of the county of Shoshone is about 10,000, the greater portion of which is engaged in mining. Owing to differences between the miners and the owners, and the difficulties of easy communication, Shoshone County had been in a state of insurrection since 1892, and during that time the courts had not been in the free and unobstructed exercise of their functions and justice had not been administered.

On the 29th of April, 1899, and for some time prior thereto, the miners' unions at Mullan, Burke, Gem, and Wardner, constituting a large part of the mining community of the Cœur d'Alene, held secret and largely attended meetings at their halls and distributed firearms and ammunition. The Burke union, about 200 strong, seized a Northern Pacific train and proceeded to Gem, where from 150 to 200 members of the Gem union joined them, seized some 80 kegs of powder belonging to the Helena-Frisco Mining Company, then proceeded to Wallace, where they were joined by the Mullan union, about 200 strong, which had marched over from Mullan to Wallace in time to intercept said train, obtaining numerous firearms which had been concealed along the roadside, and then proceeded to Wardner, where they destroyed property aggregating $250,000 and murdered two men and wounded a third. This was accomplished with military precision, under direct command of leaders and without delay, from which fact and from the evidence adduced at one of the trials drawing thereout there seems little doubt that there existed at that time in the mining district of Cœur d'Alene a widespread, deep-seated, and thoroughly-organized conspiracy.[a]

Immediately on being advised of the above occurrences the governor of Idaho sent the President the following message:

BOISE, IDAHO, *April 29, 1899.*

The PRESIDENT, *Washington, D. C.:*

In pursuance to the statute in such case made and provided, I, Frank Steunenberg, governor of Idaho, the legislature not being in session and it not being possible to convene it, do hereby apply to the President of the United States to call forth the military forces of the United States to suppress insurrection in Shoshone County, State of Idaho. This action is sustained in the fact that all the available Idaho National Guard volunteered for service in the Philippines, and said county is in a state of insurrection. I am of the opinion that at least 500 troops in the aggregate will be necessary, but smaller detachments should be ordered in as rapidly as possible.

FRANK STEUNENBERG,
Governor.

---

[a] H. R. Report No. 1999, Fifty-sixth Congress, first session; Idaho State Tribune, Wallace, Idaho, May 3, 1899.

The President, on receipt of the telegram, directed the Secretary of War to aid the governor of Idaho as requested, and under date of April 30, 1899, the following telegrams were sent to the commanding general, Department of the Columbia, in whose geographical limits the State of Idaho is located, and to the governor of Idaho:

ADJUTANT-GENERAL'S OFFICE,
Washington, April 30, 1899.

COMMANDING GENERAL, DEPARTMENTS CALIFORNIA AND COLUMBIA,
San Francisco, Cal.:

General Merriam has been ordered to Idaho in connection with insurrection in that State reported by governor to be beyond power of State to control. General Merriam has been authorized to call to his assistance such troops as may be most convenient without regard to department lines. Acting Secretary of War directs you send commanding officers of posts under your command to hold their troops in readiness to respond promptly to his calls.

By command of Major-General Miles:

H. C. CORBIN,
Adjutant-General.

ADJUTANT-GENERAL'S OFFICE,
Washington, April 30, 1899.

The GOVERNOR OF IDAHO, *Boise, Idaho:*

In compliance with your telegram of April 29, concerning insurrection in Shoshone County of your State, the President has directed that request be complied with, and following instructions have been sent to General Merriam, at Denver, Colo.: "The governor of Idaho reports an insurrection, beyond the power of the State to control, existing in Shoshone County of that State. The Acting Secretary of War directs that you repair at once to the capital of that State, and after conference with the authorities thence you go to the seat of action, calling to your aid such troops as may be most convenient, regardless of department lines. Department commanders will be notified. You will take with you the necessary staff officers. The travel s necessary to the public service."

H. C. CORBIN,
Adjutant-General.

In accordance with this order, General Merriam proceeded to the State of Idaho, conferred with the governor, ordered the United States troops stationed at Boise, Walla Walla, Vancouver, Harrison, Assinniboine, Russell, and Douglas to go to Wardner, Shoshone County, Idaho, and went there at once himself. Upon his arrival at Wardner he stationed his troops to control outlets from the mining camps and scrutinized outward travel with a view to detaining rioters. On the 3d of May, 1899, the governor of Idaho declared the county of Shoshone in a state of insurrection and rebellion, and asked General Merriam to have all trains stopped and suspicious persons returned, as will be seen by the following proclamation and telegram:

STATE OF IDAHO, EXECUTIVE OFFICE.

Whereas, it appearing to my satisfaction that the execution of process is frustrated and defied in Shoshone County, State of Idaho, by bodies of men and others, and that combinations of armed men, to resist the execution of process and to commit deeds of violence, exist in said county of Shoshone; and

Whereas, the civil authorities of said county of Shoshone do not appear to be able to control such bodies of men or prevent the destruction of property and other acts of violence; and

Whereas, on Saturday, the 29th day of April, 1899, at or near the town of Wardner Junction, in said county of Shoshone, State of Idaho, an armed mob did then and there wantonly destroy property of great value, with attendant loss of life; and

Whereas, said destruction of property, with attendant loss of life by mob violence (as above set forth), is but one and a repetition of a series of similar outrages covering a period of six years or more just passed, the perpetrators of said outrages seeming to enjoy immunity from arrest and punishment through subserviency of peace officers of said county of Shoshone (or through fear on the part of said officers) to such bodies of lawless and armed men; and

Whereas, I have reason to believe that similar outrages may occur at any time, and believing the civil authorities of said county of Shoshone are entirely unable to preserve order and protect property:

Now, therefore, I, Frank Steunenberg, governor of the State of Idaho, by virtue of authority in me vested, do hereby proclaim and declare the said county of Shoshone, in the State of Idaho, to be in a state of insurrection and rebellion. In testimony whereof, I have hereunto set my hand and caused to be affixed the great seal of the State. Done at the city of Boise, the capital of the State of Idaho, this 3d day of May, in the year of our Lord 1899, and of the Independence of the United States the one hundred and twenty-third.

[SEAL.] FRANK STEUNENBERG.

By the governor:
  M. PATRIE, *Secretary of State.*

BOISE, IDAHO, *May 3.*
General MERRIAM, *Tekoa:*
  My representative informs me that rioters are fleeing toward Spokane. Have all trains stopped and suspicious persons returned. Martial law declared.

FRANK STEUNENBERG.

On receipt of this information General Merriam informed the officers commanding at Wardner and Mullan that martial law had been declared in Shoshone County, and to arrest all persons attempting to leave the mining region of Cœur d'Alene unless fully satisfied that they were not implicated in the riots. On his arrival at Wardner he found that the two avenues of escape, via Mullan and Wardner, although occupied by troops, were not to be relied upon solely, and that escaping criminals were passing over the divide into Montana through the snow on foot, and that some had already arrived at Missoula and others at Thompsons Falls, on the Northern Pacific Railroad. Correspondence by wire was immediately opened by the representative of the governor of Idaho with the governor of Montana, looking to the arrest of fugitives in Montana, which resulted in assurances that civil officers of the latter State would assist in arresting and restoring these fugitives to the State of Idaho.

In the narration of earlier disturbances in which United States troops were called into service to assist State authorities, and as has been stated in the introductory chapter of this work, it will be remembered that the procedure following a proper and formal application to the President and a decision upon his part that the case is one in which the Government of the United States is bound to interfere, and obedient to section 5300, Revised Statutes, a proclamation was issued by the President reciting the situation and the law and commanding the insurgents to disperse and retire peaceably to their respective abodes within a specified time. Following this rule a proclamation was duly prepared in the office of the Adjutant-General of the Army, but before promulgating it General Merriam was called upon by telegraph, for the information of the President, for his opinion "If the situation is such as to require issuance of proclamation as required by section 5300, Revised Statutes." To this General Merriam replied on May 4 that "there is now no sign of organized resistance," but that indications are that most of the leaders of the mob have escaped, going east or west into Montana or Washington; that others are hidden in the mountains, and that troops are in position to do all that is possible. The governor of Idaho had duly proclaimed martial law and the circumstances did not require any such step on the part of the President.[a] It is to be remarked in this connection that at the time these troubles occurred Governor Steunenberg was sick and in the hospital, although not incapacitated from exercising his functions as chief executive, but in order to inform himself of the situation he dispatched Mr. Bartlett Sinclair, then auditor of the State, to the scene of trouble, and on the 1st of May Mr. Sinclair had telegraphed the governor as follows:

WARDNER, *May 1, 1899.*

FRANK STEUNENBERG, *Governor:*

Have thoroughly investigated advisability of declaring martial law, and fully nine-tenths, if not more, of citizens favor it. I recommend that course for the entire county. The present county administration is a perfect farce. There is only one organized town in the county. All other settlements are directly under county mal-administration. Successful prosecution of the rioters is impossible without presence of the troops. People are afraid to testify without Federal or State protection. Masked men are prowling about town to-night and the people are frightened.

BARTLETT SINCLAIR.

The situation, therefore, was apparently not such as required the issuance of the proclamation provided for in section 5300 of the Revised Statutes.

On the 5th, General Merriam telegraphed that 350 arrests had been made so far; that the prisoners were guarded by troops, and that the State officers were investigating the situation. The arrests of men suspected of complicity in the crimes of April 29, which began at once on the arrival of the troops, were continued daily in the different mining camps by deputies under escorts of troops. As they were brought in to Wardner they were placed in a large building two stories high, which had been constructed and used as a warehouse for

---

[a] H. R. Report No. 1999, Fifty-sixth Congress, first session, p. 11.

storage of hay and grain and other articles by a merchant. It was a good building for the purpose in every way, except that it had no provision for fires and was of course without furniture, so that camp fires outside were resorted to and the prisoners were compelled to sleep on the floors, but had an abundant supply of hay to lie upon. The prisoners were also fed at the expense of the State by an experienced caterer, who had managed a large miners' boarding house and had both the necessary means and experience for that purpose. After about May 5 the number of prisoners exceeded the capacity of the building, and it became necessary to hold perhaps 200 of them quartered in box cars, side tracked near Wardner station. Although abundance of hay was furnished here also, it is probable the men so confined were less comfortable than those in the warehouse, yet they were not obliged to sleep on the ground, as did the troops who were guarding them. Meanwhile the State authorities had begun the construction of a new prison, and were pushing forward the work with energy among many difficulties. However, General Merriam became dissatisfied with the apparently slow progress being made for the comfort of the prisoners, and on May 11 sent the following telegram to Governor Steunenberg:

WARDNER, *May 11, 1899.*

Governor STEUNENBERG, *Boise, Idaho:*

I am still holding nearly 500 prisoners in a barn and box cars. All are very uncomfortable and with unsanitary conditions which will soon become intolerable. Something must be done to hurry preliminary examination and release of those not prima facie guilty. It is impracticable to make this large number of prisoners reasonably comfortable here without considerable time and expense. Can you not personally inspect the situation at once and bring help?

MERRIAM,
Brigadier-General.[a]

In response to this telegram Governor Steunenberg proceeded at once to Wardner, where he arrived on the 12th, and from that moment assumed charge of the situation.

During the progress of making arrests at the instance of the State authorities General Merriam was informed by Mr. Sinclair that he had served notice upon all the mine owners of the district, by which, during the continuance of martial law, they were forbidden to employ miners unless they were able to present permits from the State authorities and presented to him a draft of a proclamation to that end, at the same time requesting General Merriam to join in said proclamation. General Merriam authorized his name to be printed at the bottom of the poster under the words "Examined and approved," on condition that a certain amendment by which an innocent member of an innocent union might receive the State permit and retain his employment was inserted, and such posters were printed and sent out.

---

[a] Report of General Merriam, dated July 31, 1899 (pamphlet).

It was not intended that the troops should assume any part whatever in carrying into effect these or any other rules affecting laborers or labor in the State of Idaho, nor did they do so in the remotest degree. There were no disturbances whatever after the arrival of the troops. The total number of men arrested and held in military custody exceeded 700, but many of those were almost immediately released on investigation, so that the number remaining in custody long enough to make a statistical record was 528.   Of the number arrested 330 were citizens of the United States and 396 foreign born, of which latter number only one-half, or 198, had taken out citizenship papers.

The coroner's jury began its examination into the circumstances of the murder of the two men on April 29, on the 3d of May, and continued its sessions for several weeks, examining hundreds of witnesses. A special term of the court was called for the purpose of bringing to light those who were engaged in the riot.   The county commissioners and sheriff were impeached and removed from office by decree of the court for misconduct in office, and particularly in encouraging and conniving at the crime of April 29.   A grand jury was afterwards called and a number of parties were indicted for murder, among others Paul Corcoran, one of the prominent officials of the union.   A great many of the prominent officials of the union immediately fled and were not intercepted.   Corcoran was brought to trial, and the trial resulted in a conviction of murder in the second degree, and he was sentenced to a term in the State penitentiary.   The troops were withdrawn from the custody of the prisoners on October 20, but remained in camp, holding themselves in readiness to meet any emergency that might arise.

On the 8th day of December, 1899, Mr. Lentz (Ohio) introduced House Resolution No. 31, to provide a committee to investigate the conduct of the United States Army and its officers in Idaho, which, as amended, was adopted January 8, 1900.   This committee held frequent sessions, examining a multitude of witnesses, including all parties concerned, representatives from the labor unions, the officials of the State of Idaho, General Merriam and his officers, and on June 5, 1900, presented its report, to the following effect:

First. The governor of Idaho, in his efforts to establish order and enforce the laws of the State, is to be commended for his courage and fearlessness.   The blind hatred excited by the mob, the consequent disturbance of public business, and the reign of lawlessness is in a fair way to be adjusted.   The citizens of Idaho are to be congratulated on the removal of a dangerous cancer that had long threatened the peace and order of the State.   Better ideas prevail as to the rights and duties of men in relation to the preservation of society, and this improved condition of affairs is in a great measure due to the conduct of the governor of that State.

Second. The conduct of the military in the trying hours from May 2 to the present amid the disturbing elements of the Cœur d'Alenes, when fierce passion flamed unchecked, when no hand was raised to stay the dynamiter and the murderer, where the mob had been supreme, is a matter of earnest congratulation to the country—

and recommended the adoption of the following resolution:

Resolved, That the charges set forth in House resolution No. 31 have not been sustained.

A minority report was also submitted, recommending the adoption of the following resolution:

Resolved by the House of Representatives, That the conduct of the President and of the military forces of the United States in Shoshone County, Idaho, has been reprehensible, violative of the liberty of the citizen, and totally unwarranted by the laws and Constitution of the United States.

Congress, however, adjourned June 7, 1900, without taking action, and the subject was not renewed during the following session, and the Fifty-sixth Congress adjourned without action. [a]

The situation with regard to the military system of the United States at the end of 1901 was concisely expressed in the report of the Secretary of War of November 27.   He said:

The act of February 2, 1901, entitled "An act to increase the efficiency of the permanent military establishment of the United States," provided for an increase of line organizations from 25 regiments of infantry to 30, from 10 regiments of cavalry to 15, from 7 regiments of artillery, including 16 field batteries, to a corps of artillery, practically equivalent to 13 regiments under the old organization, and including 30 field batteries, and from 1 battalion of engineers to 3.   Minimum and maximum numbers of enlisted men for the different organizations were established by the same statute, so that the total number of enlisted men might be varied by the President, according to the exigencies of the time, from a minimum of 59,131 to a maximum of 100,000, without any change of commissioned officers or in the number of organizations.   The improvement of conditions in the Philippines during the spring and summer of this year made it unnecessary to provide the maximum number allowed by the law, and on the 8th of May an order was made fixing the enlisted strength of the several organizations in such a manner as to establish the aggregate enlisted strength of the Army, including staff departments but exclusive of hospital corps men, at 77,287, composed as follows:

The reorganized Army, 1901.

Cavalry		15,840
Artillery:		
Coast	13,734	
Field	4,800	
Noncommissioned staff and band	328	
		18,862
Infantry		38,520
Engineer battalions and band		1,282
Enlisted men, staff departments, etc		2,783
Total Army		77,287

[a] H. Res. 31, Dec. 8, 1899, by Hon. J. J. Lentz; H. Rept. 24 and 1999 (H. Rept. 1999, majority and minority, submitted June 5, 1900, and ordered printed, p. 7389; see 7453, 7209); S. Res. 18, Dec. 11, 1899, by Senator Pettigrew (307519 A. G. O.); S. Docs. 24, 25 ("The Crime of the Century"), and 142, also 42; S. Res. 111; S. J. Res. 110; S. Con. Res. 71; H. J. Res. 214; H. Con. Res. 52; Cong. Record, pp. 187, 188, 234, 320, 696, 1181, 6511 (7527 to 7556, speech of Mr. Lentz).

The new organizations authorized were recruited upon the basis thus prescribed, leaving the organizations in the Philippines and Cuba, which had been temporarily increased to greater numbers, to be reduced to that basis by the ordinary expiration of enlistments and casualties. The regular establishment now consists, according to the latest reports which have been received, of 3,253 officers and 76,084 enlisted men. There are also 4,336 men of the hospital corps, 172 volunteer surgeons in the Philippines appointed under section 18 of the act of February 2, 1901, 4,973 native scouts under the command of 98 officers in the Philippines, and 25 officers and 815 men of the Porto Rico Provisional Regiment.[a]

The present provisions of law relating to the militia, and to the raising of volunteer forces, are quite imperfect and unsatisfactory. The militia law stands to-day practically as it was enacted in 1792, and is practically obsolete. It is very desirable that Congress should now exercise the power conferred upon it by the Constitution to provide for organizing, arming, and disciplining the militia. The organization and armament of the National Guards of the several States, which are treated as militia in the appropriations made by Congress, should be made the same as those provided by Congress for the regular and volunteer forces. The relations of the National Guard organizations to the national forces, and the obligations and duties of those organizations in time of war, should be clearly defined, so that the confusion and distress regarding their action which accompanied the outbreak of the war with Spain may not again occur. The reliance of the country for the large forces necessary in modern warfare must necessarily be chiefly upon volunteers. The method and procedure of raising volunteer forces should be prescribed in advance, so that instead of waiting to devise plans for a volunteer army until the excitement and haste of impending war makes perfection of design difficult and satisfactory execution impossible, Congress will have but to direct the execution of a well-understood plan by officers, each one of whom has long been familiar with the part he is to play. It is desirable that any plans adopted should provide for utilizing, in the earlier volunteer organizations called out, the training of those citizens who shall have served already in the Regular and Volunteer forces. If the earlier volunteer organizations can be constituted of these trained men, much valuable time and expense can be saved, and many dangers may be averted during the period while the ordinary volunteers are receiving the necessary training. Provision should also be made for the selection in advance of the officers of any volunteer force which may be raised. Careful selection is impossible at the outbreak of a war. It is entirely practicable in time of peace. I recommend that the President be authorized to convene boards of officers (including the general service and staff college board) for the examination of officers of the National Guard, and other citizens who may apply to be examined, as to their qualifications to hold volunteer commissions; that the persons passing such examinations shall receive certificates, stating the office for which they are found to be qualified, and upon the calling out of a volunteer force shall be entitled to receive commissions for such offices. I recommend that the War Department be authorized to arm the National Guard with the present service small arms, used by the Regular Army, Navy, and Marine Corps; that the National Guard of the several States be treated as a first reserve, to be called into the service of the United States to execute the laws of the Union, suppress insurrections, and repel invasions, the term of service under any call to be limited to nine months; that the President be authorized, on the request of the governor of any State, to detail officers of the Regular Army for instruction, staff, and inspection duties with the National Guard of such State; that the War Department be authorized to furnish transportation, rations, and tentage to officers and men of National Guard organizations, who shall take part with the forces of the Regular Army in annual encampment and maneuvers at national

[a] Annual Report of the Secretary of War for 1901.

military camps; that the Department be authorized to allow travel pay, commutation of rations and quarters, or commutation of quarters, to officers of the National Guard attending and regularly taking part in the courses of instruction at the general service and staff college at Fort Leavenworth. Both of these provisions should be within reasonable limits, proportional to the numbers of National Guard organizations in the several States. I recommend that the President be now empowered to organize the volunteer forces whenever called out, in the manner provided for by the act of March 2, 1899, for the organization of the volunteer force which has recently returned from the Philippines, with such modifications as shall be necessary to give effect to the views above expressed.[a]

The result of this recommendation was the act of January 21, 1903, entitled "An act to promote the efficiency of the militia, and for other purposes," and is given in full in Document No. 191. Briefly, sections 1625 to 1660, both inclusive, of the Revised Statutes—which are the acts of May 8, 1792, February 28, 1795, and March 19, 1836, all of which have been heretofore cited—are repealed and a more modern system devised which, although in its present shape far from satisfactory to the War Department, is regarded as at least a beginning of what it is hoped may result in bringing the organized militia more closely in touch with the Army.

The law provides that in order to participate in the annual apportionment of the annual appropriations of $1,000,000 "the organization, armament, and discipline of the organ-

Conclusions.   ized militia" must conform to that of the Regular

Army, except that the President may prescribe a minimum strength of companies, and five years are allowed for the transformation; that the organized militia is to be immediately armed with the United States standard service magazine arms and equipments; shall receive the "same pay, subsistence, and transportation or clothing allowances as officers and men of corresponding grades of the regular arm" when engaged in actual field or camp service for instruction or in combined maneuvers; officers of the militia may attend military schools and colleges, and while in attendance on such course of study shall receive travel allowance and quarters, or commutation of quarters, and of subsistence at $1 per day; that officers of the Army may be assigned to duty with the States and Territories; that ammunition for instruction in firing and target practice shall be furnished by the United States. It is further provided that for the purpose of securing a list of persons specially qualified to hold commissions in any future volunteer forces, men who have served in the Regular or Volunteer Army or organized militias, or taken a regular course of instruction at a military school or college, may appear before boards of officers to be convened from time to time at Army posts for examination and, if found qualified, their names shall be inscribed in a register at the War Department.

---

[a] Annual Report of the Secretary of War for 1901.

It will be deduced from the foregoing pages that inasmuch as the States are prohibited from maintaining a standing army in time of peace,[a] or from engaging in war, the United States is under constitutional obligation to guarantee them a republican form of government; to come to the aid of the States, or any one of them, and to protect them—

1. Against *invasion;* from—
   (a) Any foreign nation, or
   (b) Any Indian tribe; and
2. Against *domestic violence;* which may be caused—
   (a) By an insurrection against the State government,
   (b) By an insurrection against the United States Government, or
   (c) By unlawful obstructions, hindrances, combinations, and assemblages, or rebellion against the authority of the United States Government, or against the execution of its laws.

It will furthermore be observed that the agencies by which this aid is to be rendered and the protection thus guaranteed extended are—

1. The land and naval forces of the United States;
2. The militia of the State in which the disturbances exist;[b]
3. The militia of the State or States most convenient to the scene of disturbance; and
4. The militia of any other State or States.

In the same manner it will be seen that the procedure necessary to secure such Federal aid and protection, to set in motion these agencies, and to carry out the constitutional and statutory guaranties are—

---

[a] While a State has no right to establish and maintain a permanent military government, it is not to be inferred that it has no power over the militia resident within its borders. Unquestionably a State may use its military power to put down an armed insurrection too strong to be controlled by the civil authority. The power is essential to the existence of every government, essential to the preservation of order and free institutions, and is as necessary to the States of this Union as to any other government. (Luther *v.* Borden, 7 Howard 1.)

[b] Mr. Attorney-General Cushing (8 Opin., 12), in a consideration of the circumstances in which the President may employ the military and naval force to suppress insurrection in a State, remarks that the statute does not *by expression* empower the President to call forth the militia of the State in which the insurrection exists, but only upon the application of such State to call forth the militia of *some other* State or States. It presumes that when occasion arises the militia of the particular State will be brought into action by its own executive and legislative authority. But this is to assume a harmony of purpose or of action between the State and Federal authorities that does not always exist. Illustrations of this are many, beginning with the nullification insurrection of 1832 and ending with the railroad riots of 1894, and the case of *In re Debs,* in which the Supreme Court laid down the doctrine that when the powers of the State and those of the United States from any reason can not be executed at the same time, the powers of the latter are paramount. (158 U. S. Reports, 564.)

1. A proper and formal application to the President of the United States by—

   (*a*) The legislature of the State in which the insurrection or disturbances exist, or

   (*b*) By the executive of such State, in cases where the legislature is not in session, or can not reasonably be convened in time to meet the emergency.

2. A decision upon the part of the President that the case is one in which the Government of the United States is bound to interfere.

3. A proclamation of the President reciting the situation and the law provided in such cases, and commanding the insurgents to disperse and retire peaceably to their respective abodes within a specified time.

4. A formal call of the President upon the executive of the State wherein the disturbance exists, or a requisition upon the executive of neighboring or other States for such number of their militia as he (the President) may judge sufficient to suppress such insurrection or disturbance, or orders to the Secretary of War, the commanding general of the Army, or of a geographical divison or department of the Army, for such number of regular troops as he may deem necessary for the purpose.

5. Proper and formal instructions from the President to the commanding officer of the troops for his guidance in responding ιo the call of the State authorities, and for his conduct during the period he is engaged in such service.

It has been shown that in the development of the incidents leading up to the furnishing of Federal troops for the suppression of domestic disturbances; in the demonstration of the various and varied situations that were likely to arise, and have naturally arisen, during the progress of the one hundred years and more since the foundation of the Government, and in the lessons drawn from the experiences of more recent years under changed social conditions, many important and interesting questions have arisen that have called for the exercise of the widest and wisest discretion. "It shall be lawful," say the statutes, for the President to employ the land and naval forces; to call out the militia; to suppress such insurrections and remove such obstructions and hindrances to the execution of the laws; but nowhere is it made imperative that he shall do so. The President is the sole judge of the exigency.[a] To his judgment is left the deter-

---

[a] It is the function of the President of the United States, indubitably, to decide in his discretion what facts existing constitute the case of insurrection contemplated by the statutes and by the Constitution. (Martin *v.* Mott, 12 Wheaton, 29, 31; Luther *v.* Borden, 7 Howard, 1; Attorney-General Cushing, 8 Opin., 8; Black, 9 Opin., 922; Williams, 14 Opin., 344.)

mination of every possible doubt that may arise. He may furnish prompt and sufficient assistance upon the first sign of disorder; he may await the slow movement of every piece of the legal machinery necessary to put the troops in motion, or he may refuse to render any aid whatever. He is to judge whether a legislature or a governor has not overestimated the danger; whether the State has or has not exhausted its own resources; whether the opposition to the State government is one that justifies the term "insurrection." There may be two contesting executives of a State, or two disputing legislatures, and the President must determine which is the legal one before he can perform the duty imposed upon him by the law. An insurrection may exist within a State—palpable and indisputable according to the opinion of the ordinary observer—and the executive, who may be a party to the insurrection or in sympathy with it, may refuse to make the constitutional demand upon the Federal Government; or a legislature, in the face of self-evident facts, may declare that no insurrection exists, or that the State is fully able to suppress it without Federal aid.[a]

Nor are these the only questions that have grown out of domestic insurrections, such as are contemplated by the Constitution. The President being the sole judge of what steps are necessary to suppress such insurrection, and having called for militia, he may muster them into the service of the United States, and thus be in a position

---

[a] *Insurrection* (*sedition, rebellion, revolt, mutiny, riot*).—The first five conterminous words are distinguished from the last, in that they express action directed against government or authority, while riot has only this implication incidentally. They express actual and open resistance to authority; except sedition, which may be either secret or open, and often is only of a nature to lead to overt acts. An *insurrection* goes beyond *sedition* in that it is an actual uprising against the government, in discontent, in resistance to a law, or the like. *Rebellion* goes beyond *insurrection* in aim, being an attempt actually to overthrow the government, while an insurrection seeks only some change of a minor importance, and is generally on a larger scale than an insurrection. A *revolt* has generally the same aim as a rebellion, but is on a smaller scale. A revolt may be against military government, but is generally, like insurrection, sedition, and rebellion, against civil government. A *mutiny* is organized resistance to law in the army or navy, or perhaps a similar act by an individual. All these words have figurative uses. When literally used, only *insurrection* and revolt may be employed in a good sense. The success of a rebellion often dignifies it with the name of revolution, but insurrection, though it may be the beginning of what may subsequently develop into revolution, is not to be confounded with the larger word. A riot is generally a blind and misguided outburst of popular fury, with violence to property and persons, and may develop into insurrection. (Century Dictionary.) Insurrection is rebellion in its initial stage. (Standard Dictionary.)

Insurrection is the rising of people in arm against their government, or a portion of it; or against one or more of its laws, or against an officer or officers of the government. It may be confined to mere armed resistence, or it may have greater ends in view. (Glenn. International Law, St. Paul, 1895, p. 362.)

Insurrection against a government may or may not culminate in an organized rebellion, but a civil war always begins by insurrection against the lawful authority of the government. (Grier, J., in the Prize cases, 2 Black, 666.)

to arm and equip and supply them with food, clothing, and everything necessary to enable them to perform the duty he may require of them; or by retaining them as militia he may require the State to arm, equip, and supply them. It is a recognized principle of a republican form of government that the civil authority must be everywhere supreme; that the Federal troops, like all other citizens, must be always subject and subordinate to the civil powers. We have seen that every President has yielded to that doctrine during the past century so that in no single instance when a State has called for Federal assistance have other instructions been given to the troops than to report to and hold themselves at all times subject to the orders of the civil authorities of the State. At the same time it has been contended by most eminent authorities, and perhaps with reason, that the act of a State in calling for Federal aid is a confession of failure upon its part and an acknowledgment of its inability to preserve order within its own dominion or to enforce its own laws, and that, as a consequence, the power that is called in under such circumstances is the one that should exercise control. Is it expedient and proper that the President should transfer the Federal troops to the command of State officials who have already failed to preserve order or to suppress insurrection? If so, when would the time arrive when this State control should cease and the President resume control? And of this, who is to be the judge? And if these questions present themselves as between the Federal Government and that of a State in insurrection, what complications are likely to grow out of a situation where the militia of other States are called in.

We have seen that since the adoption of the Constitution there have been fourteen well-defined instances of domestic violence against the established laws of State or Federal Government sufficient to have warranted the President in proclaiming a state of insurrection. Many other occasions have arisen where Federal aid has been solicited, and in most cases has been furnished, but were not regarded as of sufficient importance to warrant the application of all the rules laid down by the statutes. This has been rather a narrative statement of these several insurrections, and of the events leading up to them, than an attempt to discuss the various questions that grew out of them. The latter have been so fully covered by writers on military law, by committees of Congress, and by the courts (to which authorities reference has been made in every instance) that their repetition in this connection is needless.

It is not to be understood that every occasion of domestic insurrection is herein reported, nor indeed every occasion in which the Federal troops were applied for or furnished. Whatever difficulty has been experienced in the handling of the voluminous mass of documentary material that has been consulted has been rather in the direction of selecting, without needless repetition, those events that are of importance because of some principle involved, some particular phase of the subject, some complication or involution calling for particular treatment, and hence becoming for the time being, if not permanently, a precedent for future emergencies. At the same time, and in order that the continuity of historical record need not be broken, it has been thought best to omit no conspicuous insurrectionary occurrence for the sole reason that it presents phases of precisely the same or similar character as others that had been already noticed. The result is a continuous and reasonably complete narrative of the domestic insurrections, riots, revolts, and miscellaneous disturbances that have entered into the history of the United States since its beginning, and of the measures that have been taken by the Executive, by Congress, and by the courts to meet, to suppress, to punish them, or to prevent their recurrence.

Aside from this, the record possesses a contemporary interest that is not wholly historical. When it is considered that there has been scarcely a year since the beginning of the Government that the Army has not been called upon to quell disturbances too great for the State authorities to handle; that since the reorganization of the militia on the national guard system, say during the past twenty-five years, the State troops, or some portion of them, have been called out more than five hundred times,[a] the extent to which the civil authorities are dependent upon the military arm as a police force is brought into startling prominence. It is a favorite argument of the opponents of a military system, since the beginning of history, that the existence of organized troops is, in itself, a temptation to use them. In the face of our compilation, one can not but wonder what would have been the course of our history without them.

---

[a] The number is rather under than over stated. General Cutting, M. C., in his remarks on the militia bill in the House of Representatives January 12, 1893, inserted a schedule made up from incomplete reports of adjutants-general of States, in which the number of such calls for the twenty-five years ending with 1892 is something over 400. And more recently Major Alexander, D. C. N. G., in the Journal of the United Service Institution for July, 1896 (vol. 19, p. 1), gives a list of about 400 calls for the ten years ending with 1896, which he has since increased (per a revised list in possession of the writer) to 425 specific calls during the period between January, 1886, and September, 1897.

APPENDIX.

XIII. DOCUMENTS.

NEGRO INSURRECTIONS.

(1.)

FORTRESS MONROE, *August 24, 1831.*

COLONEL: 1 send, inclosed, a copy of a communication which I received, by express, from the mayor of Norfolk at 3 a. m. this morning, and I have to report, for the information of the general in chief, that, from the serious nature of the circumstances stated and the pressing solicitation of the mayor, I have felt it my duty to afford the aid required; accordingly, I have detached three companies, under the command of Lieutenant-Colonel Worth, for the service required.

The detachment, with four days' provision, 1 field piece, 100 stands of spare arms with ammunition, etc., were embarked at 5 a. m., this morning, with orders to proceed to Suffolk, for the purpose of suppressing the disturbances in this district.

Colonel Worth has orders to consult with the civil authorities and to be governed in his movements (with a view to the object of the expedition) according to circumstances and his best judgment.

I have the honor to be, with the greatest respect, your obedient servant,

JAS. HOUSE,
Colonel First Artillery.

Col. R. JONES,
Adjutant-General.

(2.)

NORFOLK, *August 23, 1831.*

SIR: Information has been received by express from Suffolk, confirmed by other intelligence, that an insurrection of slaves commenced in the lower part of the county of Southampton on Sunday night; that about 50 persons were murdered; that some skirmishes have taken place between the militia and the insurgents, but without any decisive effect. It is believed to be of the utmost moment to crush this movement instantly to prevent the mischief of its extension. The imminent and pressing necessity of the occasion seems to justify on our part all formal scruples in applying to you for aid, and we trust that the same considerations will induce you to afford it promptly without regard to the informality of the measure. A steamboat is sent down, on board of which is Captain Capron, who will deliver you this letter. Our purpose is to obtain from the United States ships in Hampton Roads and Fortress Monroe a force from 150 to 200 men, to be conveyed immediately to Suffolk by the steamboat, with a supply of ammunition, and, if convenient, provisions for four or five days. The movement of the troops there will be directed to the point of danger according to the discretion of the officer in command.

We rely with confidence on your cheerful cooperation in the execution of this measure.

I have the honor to be your obedient servant,

JNO. E. HOLT,
Mayor.

P. S.—Sufficient time has not been allowed to address a separate letter to each of the commanding officers.

(3.)

FORTRESS MONROE, *August 30, 1831.*

COLONEL: I beg leave to report that, representations having been made to me of the exposed and defenseless situation of the village of Hampton and of the alarm of the inhabitants in consequence of the insurrectionary movements of the blacks in the neighboring counties, I have caused to be delivered, on the requisition of Colonel Jones, of this place, commanding the One hundred and fifteenth Regiment of Virginia Militia, 26 muskets, with the accouterments, and 300 rounds of ball cartridges, which are to be returned when the alarm shall have subsided.

Colonel Worth, with his detachments, are at Smithfield on their return and will be here this morning.

Respectfully, your obedient servant,

JAS. HOUSE,
Colonel First Artillery.

Col. R. JONES,
Adjutant-General.

(4.)

ADJUTANT-GENERAL'S OFFICE,
Washington, August 26, 1831.

Col. JAMES HOUSE,
First Artillery, Commanding Fortress Monroe, Va.

SIR: Your communication of the 24th instant, reporting the insurrection of the blacks in Southampton County and the succor furnished from Fortress Monroe, in compliance with the call made on you by the mayor of the borough of Norfolk, has been received.

I have it in command to express to you the entire satisfaction of the President and Secretary of War at the promptitude with which you detached three companies of artillery, under command of Brevet Lieutenant-Colonel Worth, at the request of the civil authority, on this lamentable and unforeseen occasion.

I am, sir, with great respect, your obedient servant,

R. JONES,
Adjutant-General.

(5.)

ADJUTANT-GENERAL'S OFFICE,
Washington, September 6, 1831.

Col. JAMES HOUSE,
First Regiment of Artillery, Commanding Fortress Monroe, Va.

SIR: I am instructed by the Secretary of War to direct that you will detach from the garrison of Fortress Monroe without delay one company of artillery, with orders to proceed to Newbern, N. C., by the most convenient and expeditious route.

The captain of the company will be instructed to furnish any aid towards the maintenance of the public peace in that quarter that may be required by the civil authorities at Newbern, for which purpose he will be ordered to take position and temporarily encamp within the town or its immediate vicinity until further orders.

The company will take with it one field piece, equipped for service.

I am, sir, very respectfully, your obedient servant,

R. JONES,
Adjutant-General.

(6.)

HEADQUARTERS FIRST REGIMENT ARTILLERY,
Fortress Monroe, September 9, 1831.

SIR: You will proceed with the company under your command to Newbern, N. C., and on your arrival you will confer with the civil authorities, on whose requisition you will afford any aid towards the maintenance of the public peace, for which purpose you will take position and temporarily encamp in the town or its immediate vicinity until further orders.

You will report your arrival to the headquarters of the regiment and keep me informed of any further movements or circumstances interesting to your command.

Wishing you a pleasant tour of duty, I remain, with great respect,

Your obedient servant,

JAMES HOUSE,
Colonel First Artillery.

Capt. F. WHITING,
First Regiment Artillery.

(7.)

NEWBERN, N. C., *September 26, 1831.*

SIR: The petition from this town, which resulted in the detachment of my company on its present service, was predicated upon the late servile insurrection in Virginia. Whatever degree of alarm may have been excited by that event, and by the many idle reports of more recent similar disturbances in this State, I am well assured that a large majority of, if not all, the principal citizens, including the civil authorities of Newbern, are now of the opinion that the presence of United States troops is no longer necessary for their protection against their slave population. The Hon. Mr. Gaston—certainly very high authority—has expressed these sentiments openly, in my hearing. Indeed some citizens, whose opinions are entitled to every respect, have from the first been opposed to the call upon Government for troops, either from doubts of the existence of any cause that would justify it, or from a belief that if the alleged danger actually existed, their own citizens were fully competent to guard against and that the presence of a regular force, even not exceeding one company, would have the effect of rendering the citizens less vigilant than they otherwise would, and at all times should, be.

There are many persons, to be sure, in this town (probably it would be the same in most other places), who are in favor of having the troops stationed among them permanently, and no doubt a petition, followed by an array of names at least numerically imposing, might at any moment be got up in support of their views. Some of this class, I fear a large proportion of it, are actuated in the adoption of such views by motives not altogether disinterested. But I speak advisedly when I say again that a large majority of, if not all, the principal citizens of Newbern are of the opinion that the presence of United States troops is no longer necessary as a protection against their slaves; and would not therefore be opposed to their departure hence within a few weeks, by which time it is believed that all the beneficial effects that could reasonably be expected from their appearance here will have been realized.

On this authority I now respectfully solicit an order to return with my company to Fortress Monroe, in the course of the ensuing month, or before it will be necessary to go upon a winter establishment, provided the civil authorities of Newbern shall concur in the measure.

It is my own settled conviction that a detention of my company here beyond the period above proposed would be more than useless, for the position it occupies within a populous town, is highly prejudicial to its discipline and moral efficiency, where no possible vigilance on the part of the officers can effectually prevent an intercourse with the rabble, which is always most debasing to the character of the soldier. A just professional pride therefore impels me to urge a compliance with my request for a removal.

I am, sir, very respectfully, your obedient servant,

F. WHITING,
Captain Commanding.

Col. R. JONES,
Adjutant-General, Washington, D. C.

THE DORR REBELLION.

(8.)

PROVIDENCE, *April 4, 1842.*

The PRESIDENT OF THE UNITED STATES.

SIR: The State of Rhode Island is threatened with domestic violence. Apprehending that the legislature can not be convened in sufficient season to apply to the Government of the United States for effectual protection in this case, I hereby apply to you, as the executive of the State of Rhode Island, for the protection which is required by the Constitution of the United States. To communicate more fully with you on this subject, I have appointed John Whipple, John Brown Francis, and Elisha R. Potter, esqs., three of our most distinguished citizens, to proceed to Washington and to make known to you in behalf of this State the circumstances which call for the interposition of the Government of the United States for our protection.

I am, sir, very respectfully, your obedient servant,

SAM W. KING,
Governor of Rhode Island.

(9.)

PROVIDENCE, *April 4, 1842.*

The PRESIDENT OF THE UNITED STATES.

SIR: For nearly a year past the State of Rhode Island has been agitated by revolutionary movements, and is now threatened with domestic violence.

The report of a joint committee of both branches of the legislature of this State, with an act and resolutions accompanying the same, herewith communicated, were passed unanimously by the senate and by a vote of 60 to 6 in the house of representatives. The legislature adjourned to the first Tuesday of May next.

It has become my duty by one of these resolutions to adopt such measures as in my opinion may be necessary in the recess of the legislature to execute the laws and preserve the State from domestic violence.

The provisions of the said act "in relation to offenses against the sovereign power of this State" have created much excitement among that portion of the people who have unequivocally declared their intention to set up another government in this State and to put down the existing government, and they threaten, individually and collectively, to resist the execution of this act. The numbers of this party are sufficiently formidable to threaten seriously our peace, and in some portions of the State and in this city particularly, may constitute a majority of the physical force, though they are a minority of the people of the State.

Under the dangers which now threaten us I have appointed John Whipple, John Brown Francis, and Elisha R. Potter, esqs., three of our most distinguished citizens, to proceed to Washington and consult with you in behalf of this State, with a view that such precautionary measures may be taken by the Government of the United States as may afford us that protection which the Constitution of the United States requires. There is but little doubt that a proclamation from the President of the United States and the presence here of a military officer to act under the authority of the United States, would destroy the delusion which is now so prevalent and convince the deluded that in a contest with the government of this State they would be involved in a contest with the Government of the United States, which could only eventuate in their destruction.

As no State can keep troops in time of peace without the consent of Congress, there is the more necessity that we should be protected by those who have the means of protection. We shall do all we can for ourselves. The Government of the United States has the power to prevent as well as to defend us from violence. The protection provided by the Constitution of the United States will not be effectual unless such precautionary measures may be taken as are necessary to prevent lawless men from breaking out into violence as well as to protect the State from further violence after it has broken out. Preventive measures are the most prudent and safe, and also the most merciful.

The protective power would be lamentably deficient if "the beginning of strife," which "is like the letting out of waters," can not be prevented and no protection can be afforded the State until to many it would be too late.

The above-named gentlemen are fully authorized to act in behalf of the State of Rhode Island in this emergency, and carry with them such documents and proof as will, no doubt, satisfy you that the interposition of the authority of the Government of the United States will be salutary and effectual.

I am, sir, very respectfully, your obedient servant,

SAM. W. KING.

(10.)

WASHINGTON, *April 11, 1842.*

His Excellency the GOVERNOR OF RHODE ISLAND.

SIR: Your letter dated the 4th instant was handed me on Friday by Mr. Whipple, who, in company with Mr. Francis and Mr. Potter, called upon me on Saturday and placed me, both verbally and in writing, in possession of the prominent facts which have led to the present unhappy condition of things in Rhode Island—a state of things which every lover of peace and good order must deplore. I shall not adventure the expression of opinion upon those questions of domestic policy which seem to have given rise to the unfortunate controversies between a portion of the citizens and the existing government of the State. They are questions of municipal regulation, the adjustment of which belongs exclusively to the people of Rhode Island, and with which this Government can have nothing to do. For the regulation of my conduct in any interposition which I may be called upon to make between the government of a State and any portion of its citizens who may assail it with domestic violence, or may be in actual insurrection against it, I can only look to the Constitution and laws of the United States, which plainly declare the obligations of the executive department and leave it no alternative as to the course it shall pursue.

By the fourth section of the fourth article of the Constitution of the United States it is provided that "the United States shall guarantee to every State in this Union a republican form of government, and shall protect each of them against invasion, and, on application of the legislature or executive (when the legislature can not be convened), against domestic violence." And by the act of Congress approved on the 28th February, 1795, it is declared "that in case of an insurrection in any State against the government thereof it shall be lawful for the President of the United States, upon application of the legislature of such State or by the executive (when the legislature can not be convened), to call forth such numbers of the militia of any other State or States as may be applied for, as he may judge sufficient to suppress such insurrection." By the third section of the same act it is provided "that whenever it may be necessary, in the judgment of the President, to use the military force hereby directed to be called forth, the President shall forthwith, by proclamation, command such insurgents to disperse and retire peaceably to their respective abodes within a reasonable time." By the act of March 3, 1807, it is provided "that in all cases of insurrection or obstruction to the laws, either of the United States or of any individual State or Territory where it is lawful for the President of the United States to call forth the militia for the purpose of suppressing such insurrection or of causing the laws to be duly executed, it shall be lawful for him to employ for the same purposes such part of the land or naval force of the United States as shall be judged necessary, having first observed all the prerequisites of the law in that respect."

This is the first occasion, so far as the government of a State and its people are concerned, on which it has become necessary to consider of the propriety of exercising those high and most important of constitutional and legal functions.

By a careful consideration of the above recited acts of Congress your excellency will not fail to see that no power is vested in the Executive of the United States to anticipate insurrectionary movements against the government of Rhode Island so as to sanction the interposition of the military authority, but that there must be an actual insurrection, manifested by lawless assemblages of the people or otherwise, to whom a proclamation may be addressed and who may be required to betake themselves to their respective abodes. I have, however, to assure your excellency that should the time arrive—and my fervent prayer is that it may never come—when an insurrection shall exist against the government of Rhode Island, and a requisition shall be made upon the Executive of the United States to furnish that protection which is guaranteed to each State by the Constitution and laws, I shall not be found to shrink from the performance of a duty which, while it would be the most painful, is at the same time the most imperative. I have also to say that in such a contingency the Executive could not look into real or supposed defects of the existing government in order to ascertain whether some other plan of government proposed for adoption was better suited to the wants and more in accordance with the wishes of any portion of her citizens. To throw the Executive power of this Government into any such controversy would be to make the President the armed arbitrator between the people of the different States and their constituted authorities, and might lead to a usurped power, dangerous alike to the stability of the State governments and the liberties of the people. It will be my duty, on the contrary, to respect the requisitions of that government which has been recognized as the existing government of the State through all time past until I shall be advised in regular manner that it has been altered and abolished and another substituted in its place by legal and peaceable proceedings adopted and pursued by the authorities and people of the State. Nor can I readily bring myself to believe that any such contingency will arise as shall render the interference of this Government at all necessary. The people of the State of Rhode Island have been too long distinguished for their love of order and of regular government to rush into revolution in order to obtain a redress of grievances, real or supposed, which a government under which their fathers lived in peace would not in due season redress. No portion of her people will be willing to drench her fair fields with the blood of their own brethren in order to obtain a redress of grievances which their constituted authorities can not for any length of time resist if properly appealed to by the popular voice. None of them will be willing to set an example, in the bosom of this Union, of such frightful disorder, such needless convulsions of society, such danger to life, liberty, and property, and likely to bring so much discredit on the character of popular governments. My reliance on the virtue, intelligence, and patriotism of her citizens is great and abiding, and I will not doubt but that a spirit of conciliation will prevail over rash councils, that all actual grievances will be promptly redressed by the existing government, and that another bright example will be added to the many already prevailing among the North American Republics of change without revolution and a redress of grievances without force or violence.

I tender to your excellency assurances of my high respect and consideration.

JOHN TYLER.

(11.)

State of Rhode Island and Providence Plantations, in general assembly, May session, 1842.

Whereas, a portion of the people of this State, for the purpose of subverting the laws and existing government thereof, have framed a pretended constitution, and for the same unlawful purposes have met in lawless assemblages and elected officers for the future government of this State; and

Whereas, the persons so elected in violation of law, but in conformity to the said pretended constitution, have, on the 3d day of May instant, organized themselves into executive and legislative departments of government, and under oath assumed the duties and exercise of said powers; and

Whereas, in order to prevent the due execution of the laws a strong military force was called out and did array themselves to protect the said unlawful organization of government and to set at defiance the due enforcement of law: Therefore,

Resolved by the general assembly, That there now exists in this State an insurrection against the laws and constituted authorities thereof, and that, in pursuance of the Constitution and laws of the United States, a requisition be, and hereby is, made by this legislature upon the President of the United States forthwith to interpose the authority and power of the United States to suppress such insurrectionary and lawless assemblages, to support the existing government and laws, and protect the State from domestic violence.

Resolved, That his excellency the governor be requested immediately to transmit a copy of these resolutions to the President of the United States.

True copy.

Witness:
HENRY BOWEN,
Secretary of State.

(12.)

WASHINGTON, *May 7, 1842.*

The GOVERNOR OF THE STATE OF RHODE ISLAND.

SIR: Your letter of the 4th instant, transmitting resolutions of the legislature of Rhode Island, informing me that there existed in that State " certain lawless assemblages of a portion of the people " " for the purpose of subverting the laws and overthrowing the existing government," and calling upon the Executive " forthwith to interpose the authority and power of the United States to suppress such insurrectionary and lawless assemblages and to support the existing government and laws and protect the State from domestic violence," was handed me on yesterday by Messrs. Randolph and Potter.

I have the honor to inform your excellency in reply that my opinions as to the duties of this Government to protect the State of Rhode Island against domestic violence remain unchanged; yet from information received by the Executive since your dispatches came to hand I am led to believe that the lawless assemblages to which reference is made have already dispersed, and that the danger of domestic violence is hourly diminishing, if it has not wholly disappeared. I have with difficulty brought myself at any time to believe that violence would be resorted to or an exigency arise which the unaided power of the State could not meet, especially as I have from the first felt persuaded that your excellency and others associated with yourself in the administration of the government would exhibit a temper of conciliation as well as of energy and decision. To the insurgents themselves it ought to be obvious, when the excitement of the moment shall have passed away, that changes achieved by regular and, if necessary, repeated appeals to the constituted authorities, in a country so much under the influence of public opinion, and by recourse to argument and remonstrance, are more likely to insure lasting blessings than those accomplished by violence and bloodshed on one day, and liable to overthrow by similar agents on another.

I freely confess that I should experience great reluctance in employing the military power of this Government against any portion of the people; but, however painful the duty, I have to assure your excellency that if resistance be made to the execution of the laws of Rhode Island by such force as the civil power shall be unable to overcome, it will be the duty of this Government to enforce the constitutional guaranty—a guaranty given and adopted mutually by all the original States, of which number Rhode Island was one, and which in the same way has been given and adopted by each of the States since admitted into the Union; and if an exigency of lawless violence shall actually arise the Executive Government of the United States, on the application of your excellency under the authority of the resolutions of the legislature already transmitted, will stand ready to succor the authorities of the State in their efforts to maintain a due respect for the laws. I sincerely hope, however, that no such exigency may occur, and that every citizen of Rhode Island will manifest his love of peace and good order by submitting to the laws and seeking a redress of grievances by other means than intestine commotions.

I tender to your excellency assurances of my distinguished consideration.

JOHN TYLER.

(13.)

STATE OF RHODE ISLAND AND PROVIDENCE PLANTATIONS.

A PROCLAMATION BY THOMAS W. DORR, GOVERNOR AND COMMANDER IN CHIEF OF THE SAME.

FELLOW-CITIZENS: Shortly after the adjournment of the general assembly and the completion of indispensable executive business, I was induced by the request of the most active friends of our cause to undertake the duty (which had been previously suggested) of representing in person the interests of the people of Rhode Island in other States and at the seat of the General Government. By virtue of a resolution of the general assembly, I appointed Messrs. Pearce and Anthony commissioners for the same purpose.

Of the proposed action of the Executive in the affairs of our State you have been already apprised. In case of the failure of the civil posse (which expression was intended by the President, as I have been informed, to embrace the military power) to execute any of the laws of the charter assembly, including their law of pains and penalties and of treason, as it has been for the first time defined, the President intimates an intention of resorting to the forces of the United States to check the movements of the people of this State in support of their republican constitution recently adopted.

From a decision which conflicts with the right of sovereignty inherent in the people of this State, and with the principles which lie at the foundation of a democratic republic, an appeal has been taken to the people of our country. They understand our cause; they sympathize in the injuries which have been inflicted upon us; they disapprove the course which the National Executive has adopted toward this State, and they assure us of their disposition and intention to interpose a barrier between the supporters of the people's constitution and the hired soldiery of the United States. The democracy of the country are slow to move in any matter which involves an issue so momentous as that which is presented by the controversy in Rhode Island, but when they have once put themselves in motion they are not to be easily diverted from their purposes. They believe that the people of Rhode Island are in the right; that they are contending for equal justice in their political system; that they have properly adopted a constitution of government for themselves, as they were entitled to do, and they can not and will not remain indifferent to any act, from whatever motive it may proceed, which they deem to be an invasion of the sacred right of self-government, of which the people of the respective States can not be divested.

As your representative, I have been everywhere received with the utmost kindness and cordiality. To the people of the city of New York, who have extended to us the hand of a generous fraternity, it is impossible to overrate our obligation at this most important crisis.

It has become my duty to say that so soon as a soldier of the United States shall be set in motion, by whatever direction, to act against the people of this State in aid of the charter government, I shall call for that aid to oppose all such force, which, I am fully authorized to say, will be immediately and most cheerfully tendered to the service of the people of Rhode Island from the city of New York and from other places. The contest will then become national, and our State the battle ground of American freedom.

As a Rhode Island man, I regret that the constitutional question in this State can not be adjusted among our own citizens, but as the minority have asked that the sword of the national Executive may be thrown into the scale against the people, it is imperative upon them to make the same appeal to their brethren of the States—an appeal which they are well assured will not be made in vain. They who have been the first to ask assistance from abroad can have no reason to complain of any consequences which may ensue.

No further arrests under the law of pains and penalties, which was repealed by the general assembly of the people at their May session, will be permitted. I hereby direct the military, under their respective officers, promptly to prevent the same and to release all who may be arrested under said law.

As requested by the general assembly, I enjoin upon the militia forthwith to elect their company officers, and I call upon volunteers to organize themselves without delay. The military are directed to hold themselves in readiness for immediate service.

Given under my hand and the seal of the State, at the city of Providence, this 6th day of May, A. D. 1842.

[L. S.]   THOMAS W. DORR,
Governor and Commander in Chief of the State of
Rhode Island and Providence Plantations.

By the governor's command:
    WILLIAM H. SMITH,
       Secretary of State.

(14.)

PROVIDENCE, R. I., *May 25, 1842.*

The PRESIDENT OF THE UNITED STATES.

SIR: Since my last communication the surface of things in this city and State has been more quiet. The complete dispersing of the insurgents and flight of their leader on Wednesday last (18th instant) seems to have broken their strength and prevented them from making head openly in any quarter.

But another crisis now appears to be approaching. By the private advices received by myself and the council from our messengers in the neighboring States we learn that Dorr and his agents are enlisting men and collecting arms for the purpose of again attempting to subvert by open war the government of this State. Those who have assisted him at home in his extreme measures are again holding secret councils and making preparations to rally on his return. Companies of men pledged to support him have met and drilled in the north part of this State during the present week.

From the forces which he can collect among our own citizens we have nothing to fear. Our own military strength has once scattered them and could as easily do so a second time, but, if the bands which are now organizing in Massachusetts, Connecticut, and New York should make the incursion which they threaten, with Dorr at their head, we have reason to apprehend a civil war of the most destructive and vindictive character. Our own forces might be sufficient to repel them, but, having little discipline and no officer of military experience to lead them, they could not do it without the loss of many valuable lives.

For the evidence that such forces are organizing in other States, I refer Your Excellency to a letter from Governor Seward, of New York, and to a statement made by one of our messengers to the council, which will be handed you. Other messengers confirm to the fullest extent the same intelligence.

In this posture of affairs I deem it my duty to call upon Your Excellency for the support guaranteed by the Constitution and laws of the United States to this government. I would submit to Your Excellency whether a movement of a sufficient body of troops to this quarter, to be stationed at Fort Adams, and to be subject to the requisitions of the executive of this State whenever, in his opinion, the exigency should arise to require their assistance, would not be the best measure to insure peace and respect for the laws and to deter invasions.

You will see by the statement of the secret agent of the Government that the time set for this incursion is very near. The mustering of the insurgents and their movement upon the city will probably be with the greatest expedition when once commenced—in a time too short for a messenger to reach Washington and return with aid. I therefore make this application before any movement of magnitude on their part, in order that we may be prepared at the briefest notice to quell domestic insurrection and repel invasion.

SAM. W. KING,
Governor of Rhode Island.

(15.)

WASHINGTON CITY, *May 28, 1842.*

His Excellency Governor KING.

SIR: I have received your excellency's communication of the 25th instant, informing me of efforts making by Mr. Dorr and others to embody a force in the contiguous States for the invasion of the State of Rhode Island, and calling upon the Executive of the United States for military aid.

In answer I have to inform your excellency that means have been taken to ascertain the extent of the danger of any armed invasion by the citizens of other States of the State of Rhode Island, either to put down her government or to disturb her peace. The apparent improbability of a violation so flagrant and unprecedented of all our laws and institutions makes me, I confess, slow to believe that any serious attempts will be made to execute the designs which some evil-minded persons may have formed.

But should the necessity of the case require the interposition of the authority of the United States it will be rendered in the manner prescribed by the laws.

In the meantime I indulge a confident expectation, founded upon the recent manifestations of public opinion in your State in favor of law and order, that your own resources and means will be abundantly adequate to preserve the public peace, and that the difficulties which have arisen will be soon amicably and permanently adjusted by the exercise of a spirit of liberality and forbearance.

JOHN TYLER.

[Indorsement.]

The Secretary of War will issue a private order to Colonel Bankhead, commanding at Newport, to employ, if necessary, a private and confidential person or persons to go into all such places and among all such persons as he may have reason to believe to be likely to give any information touching Rhode Island affairs, and to report with the greatest dispatch, if necessary, to the President. He will also address a letter to General Wool, conveying to him the fears entertained of a hostile invasion contemplated to place Dorr in the chair of state of Rhode Island by persons in the States of Connecticut and New York, and also to General Eustis, at Boston, of a similar character, with instructions to adopt such inquiries (to be secretly made) as they may deem necessary, and to report with the greatest dispatch all information which from time to time they may acquire. (Indorsed:) "President's instructions, May 28, 1842."

(16.)

WAR DEPARTMENT, *May 28, 1842.*

Colonel BANKHEAD,

Newport, R. I.

SIR: The governor of Rhode Island has represented to the President that preparations are making by Mr. Dorr and some of his adherents to recruit men in the neighboring States for the purpose of supporting his usurpation of the powers of government, and that he has provided arms and camp equipage for a large number of men. It is very important that we should have accurate information on this subject, and particularly in relation to the movements made in other States. I have therefore to desire you to employ proper persons to go to the places where it may be supposed such preparations are making to possess themselves fully of all that is doing and in contemplation, and report frequently to you. It is said that Mr. Dorr's principal headquarters are at the town of Thompson, in the State of Connecticut. It may be well for you personally to communicate with Governor King and ascertain from him the points and places at which any preparations for embodying men are supposed to be making, and to direct your inquiries accordingly.

It is important that you should select persons on whose integrity and accuracy the fullest reliance can be placed. They should not be partisans on either side, although to effect the object it will, of course, be necessary that some of them should obtain (if they do not already possess) the confidence of the friends of Mr. Dorr. You will please communicate directly to me all the information you obtain and your own views of it.

It is scarcely necessary to say that this communication is of the most private and confidential character, and it is not to be made known to anyone.

Respectfully, your obedient servant,

J. C. SPENCER.

(17.)

WAR DEPARTMENT, *May 29, 1842.*

Brigadier-General EUSTIS,
        Boston.

SIR: The governor of Rhode Island has represented to the President that preparations are making in other States (particularly in Massachusetts) for an armed invasion of that State to support the usurpation of Mr. Dorr and his friends and foment
domestic insurrection. It is very important that we should have accurate information on this subject, and I have to desire you to take all necessary means to acquire
it, and communicate directly to me as speedily and frequently as possible. It is said
that 1,000 stand of arms have been procured in Boston, some pieces of artillery, and
a large quantity of camp equipage for the use of the insurgents. Your attention to
this is particularly desired to ascertain its truth or falsehood. It is also stated that
there are 200 men enrolled and embodied in a town upon the borders of Rhode
Island, the name of which has escaped me. Please inquire into this. If it becomes
necessary to employ confidential persons to discover what is doing, you will do so,
being careful to select those only that are entirely trustworthy; and it will be desirable to avoid heated partisans on either side. Their inquiries should be conducted
quietly and privately.

I desire you to communicate fully and freely what you may learn and your views
concerning it for the information of the President and the Department.

It is scarcely necessary to say that this communication is strictly private and confidential.

Respectfully, your obedient servant,   J. C. SPENCER.

———

(18.)

EXECUTIVE DEPARTMENT,
        Providence, June 23, 1842.

His Excellency JOHN TYLER,
        President of the United States.

SIR: After my last communication the excitement and military operations of the
insurgents against the government of this State appeared to subside, and I indulged
in hopes that no open violence would be attempted, but that they were disposed to
await the action of the general assembly, now in session at Newport. I regret that
I am obliged to inform Your Excellency that within a few days past appearances
have become more alarming. Several iron cannon have been stolen from citizens of
Providence, and during the night of the 19th a powder house, owned by a merchant
of Providence, was broken open and about 1,200 pounds of powder stolen therefrom.
Yesterday the military operations of the insurgents became more decided in their
character. At Woonsocket and Chepachet there were gatherings of men in military
array, pretending to act under the authority of Thomas W. Dorr. They established
a kind of martial law in those villages, stopped peaceable citizens in the highways,
and at Chepachet four citizens of Providence were seized by an armed force, pinioned
and compelled to march about 10 miles under a guard of about forty men to Woonsocket, where they were cruelly treated under pretense of being spies. The insurgents are provided with cannon, tents, ammunition, and stores.

It is ascertained that Thomas W. Dorr has returned from the city of New York to
the State of Connecticut, and I have reason to believe he will be at Chepachet this
day, where he will concentrate what forces he has already under arms with such
others as he can collect. Those already assembled are composed of citizens of other
States as well as of our own, and are variously estimated at 500 to 1,000 men.

I have this morning had an interview with Colonel Bankhead, who will communicate to the War Department such facts as have come to his knowledge. I would further state to Your Excellency that in those villages and their vicinity the civil authority is disregarded and paralyzed.

Under these circumstances I respectfully submit to Your Excellency that the crisis has arrived when the aid demanded by the legislature of the State from the Federal Government is imperatively required to furnish that protection to our citizens from domestic violence which is guaranteed by the Constitution and laws of the United States.

I confidently trust that Your Excellency will adopt such measures as will afford us prompt and efficient relief.

I remain, with great consideration, your obedient servant,

SAM. W. KING.

———

(19.)

WASHINGTON, *June 25, 1842.*

Governor KING.

SIR: Your letter of the 23d instant was this day received by the hands of Governor Sprague, together with the documents accompanying the same. Your excellency has unintentionally overlooked the fact that the legislature of Rhode Island is now in session. The act of Congress gives to the Executive of the United States no power to summon to the aid of the State the military force of the United States unless an application shall be made by the legislature, if in session; and that the State executive can not make such application except when the legislature can not be convened. (See act of Congress, February 28, 1795.)

I presume that your excellency has been led into the error of making this application (the legislature of the State being in session at the date of your dispatch) from a misapprehension of the true import of my letter of 7th May last. I lose no time in correcting such misapprehension if it exist.

Should the legislature of Rhode Island deem it proper to make a similar application to that addressed to me by your excellency, their communication shall receive all the attention which will be justly due to the high source from which such application shall emanate.

I renew to your excellency assurances of high consideration.

J. TYLER.

———

(20.)

PROVIDENCE, R. I., *June 27, 1842.*

SIR: As there was no mail yesterday from this, I could make no report to the major-general commanding of the military movements in this quarter up to that time. Since my last letter to you most of the volunteers and other military companies called out by the governor have assembled here, to the amount of about 2,000 men. The force of the insurgents under the immediate direction of Mr. Dorr, and concentrated at Chepachet, is estimated at from 800 to 1,000 men armed with muskets, about 1,500 without arms, and ten or twelve cannon mounted.

It seems to be impossible to avoid a conflict between the contending parties without the interposition of a strong Regular force.

The State force here can defend this city, and it might successfully attack the insurgent force at Chepachet; but there would be danger in leaving the city without adequate means of protection to it, as there is doubtless a large number within the city, with concealed arms, ready to commence hostilities.

The position taken by Dorr's troops at Chepachet is naturally strong, and has been much strengthened by intrenchments, etc. It would, therefore, be highly imprudent to make the attack, even if no secret foes were left behind within the city, without a positive certainty of success; and with the aid of a few disciplined troops a defeat there would be ruinous and irreparable.

A force of 300 Regular troops would insure success, and probably without bloodshed.

I am, sir, very respectfully, your obedient servant,

JAS. BANKHEAD,
Colonel, Second Regiment Artillery.

The SECRETARY OF WAR,
Washington, D. C.

(21.)

WASHINGTON, *June 27, 1842.*

The PRESIDENT OF THE UNITED STATES.

SIR: The intelligence from Rhode Island since the call was made on you by the Senators of that State is of a character still more serious and urgent than that then communicated to you by Mr. Sprague, who was charged with communications to Your Excellency from Governor King. We are informed that a requisition was made upon the Government of the United States by the governor of Rhode Island, pursuant to resolutions passed by the general assembly of that State when in session in May last, calling for a proclamation against those engaged in an armed rebellion against the government of Rhode Island and for military aid in suppressing the same; that Your Excellency replied to Governor King that in the opinion of the Executive the force arrayed against the government of the State was not then such as to warrant immediate action on his part, but that Your Excellency in your reply proceeded to say: "If an exigency of lawless violence shall actually arise, the Executive Government of the United States, on the application of your excellency under the authority of the resolutions of the legislature already submitted, will stand ready to succor the authorities of the State in their efforts to maintain a due respect for the laws." Whereby it was understood that in the event of the assembling of such an armed force as would require the interference contemplated by the Constitution and laws of the United States, the Executive of the United States, upon being duly notified of the fact by the governor of the State, would act upon the requisition already made by the legislature without further action on the part of that body.

We understand that upon this notice being given through the communications handed you by Mr. Sprague on Saturday, containing proof of the existence and array of a large body of armed men within the State of Rhode Island, who had already committed acts of lawless violence, both by depredating largely upon property in various parts of the State and by capturing and confining citizens, as well as owning and manifesting a determination to attack the constituted authorities, you considered that it was desirable that this communication should have been accompanied with a further resolution of the general assembly authorizing the governor to act in this instance, from the fact that the assembly was then in session by adjournment.

It is the purpose of this communication respectfully to state that we conceive the existing circumstances call for the immediate action of the Executive upon the information and papers now in its possession.

The meeting of the legislature during the last week was by adjournment. It is in law regarded as the May session of the general assembly, and can be regarded in no other light than if it had been a continuous session of that body held from day to day by usual adjournments. Had this last been the case, it can not be conceived that new action on its part would have been required to give notice of any movements of hostile forces engaged in the same enterprise which was made known to the Executive by its resolutions of May last.

Our intelligence authorizes us to believe that a multitude of lawless and violent men, not citizens of Rhode Island, but inhabitants of other States, wickedly induced by pay and by hopes of spoil, and perhaps instigated also by motives arising from exasperation on the part of their instigators and of themselves at the course heretofore indicated in this matter by the Executive Government of the Union, have congregated themselves and are daily increasing their numbers within the borders of our State, organized, armed, and arrayed in open war upon the State authorities, and ready to be led, and avowedly about to be led, to the attack of the principal city of the State as part of the same original plan to overthrow the government, and that in the prosecution of this plan our citizens have reason to apprehend the most desperate and reckless assaults of ruffianly violence upon their property, their habitations, and their lives.

We beg leave to refer you, in addition, to a letter which we understand was received yesterday by General Scott from Colonel Bankhead, detailing some information in his possession.

We therefore respectfully request an immediate compliance on the part of the Executive with the requisition communicated in the papers from Governor King as the most effectual, and, in our opinion, the only measure that can now prevent the effusion of blood and the calamities of intestine violence, if each has not already occurred.

We are, with the highest respect, Your Excellency's obedient servants,

JAMES F. SIMMONS,
WM. SPRAGUE,
JOSEPH L. TILLINGHAST.

(22.)

WASHINGTON, *June 29, 1842.*

The SECRETARY OF WAR.

SIR: From the official communication of Colonel Bankhead to you, this day laid before me, it is evident that the difficulties in Rhode Island have arrived at a crisis which may require a prompt interposition of the Executive of the United States to prevent the effusion of blood. From the correspondence already had with the governor of Rhode Island, I have reason to expect that a requisition will be immediately made by the government of that State for the assistance guaranteed by the Constitution to protect its citizens from domestic violence. With a view to ascertain the true condition of things and to render the assistance of this Government (if any shall be required) as prompt as may be, you are instructed to proceed to Rhode Island, and, in the event of a requisition being made upon the President in conformity with the laws of the United States, you will cause the proclamation herewith delivered to be published. And should circumstances, in your opinion, render it necessary, you will also call upon the governors of Massachusetts and Connecticut, or either of them, for such number and description of the militia of their respective States as may be sufficient to terminate at once the insurrection in Rhode Island. And in the meantime the troops in the vicinity of Providence may with propriety be placed in such positions as will enable them to defend that city from assault.

JOHN TYLER.

[Inclosure.]

By the President of the United States of America.

A PROCLAMATION.

Whereas, the legislature of the State of Rhode Island has applied to the President of the United States setting forth the existence of a dangerous insurrection in that State, composed partly of deluded citizens of the State, but chiefly of intruders of dangerous and abandoned character coming from other States, and requiring the immediate interposition of the constitutional power vested in him to be exercised in such cases, I do issue this my proclamation, according to law, hereby commanding all insurgents, and all persons connected with said insurrection to disperse and retire peaceably to their respective abodes within twenty-four hours from the time when this proclamation shall be made public in Rhode Island.

In testimony whereof, I have caused the seal of the United States to be hereunto affixed, and signed the same with my hand.

Done at the city of Washington, this —— day of ——, A. D. 1842, and of the Independence of the United States the sixty-sixth.

[L. S.]   JOHN TYLER.

By the President:
    DANL. WEBSTER,
        Secretary of State.

(23.)

[Proclamation of Governor King, temporarily suspending martial law in Rhode Island, dated August 8, 1842.]

By His Excellency Samuel Ward King, Governor, Captain-General, Commander-in-Chief of the State of Rhode Island and Providence Plantations.

A PROCLAMATION.

Whereas, the general assembly of the State of Rhode Island and Providence Plantations did, on the 25th day of June last, pass the following act, viz:

"AN ACT establishing martial law in this State.

"*Be it enacted by the general assembly as follows:*

"SECTION 1. The State of Rhode Island and Providence Plantations is hereby placed under martial law; and the same is declared to be in full force until otherwise ordered by the general assembly, or suspended by proclamation of his excellency the governor of the State."

I do, therefore, pursuant to the authority aforesaid and by the advice of the council, hereby suspend the operation of said act from the date hereof until the 1st day of September next, and the same is suspended accordingly.

In testimony whereof, I have caused the seal of said State to be affixed to these presents, and have signed the same with my hand. Given at the city of Providence, on the 8th day of August in the year of our Lord eighteen hundred and forty-two, and of the Independence of the United States of America the sixty-seventh.

[L. S.]   SAMUEL WARD KING.

By his excellency's command:
    HENRY BOWEN,
        Secretary of State.

(24.)

[Proclamation of Governor King, indefinitely suspending martial law in Rhode Island, dated August 30, 1842.]

By His Excellency Samuel Ward King, Governor, Captain - General, and Commander-in-Chief of the State of Rhode Island and Providence Plantations.

A PROCLAMATION.

"Whereas, the general assembly of said State, on the 25th day of June last, passed the act following, viz:

"AN ACT establishing martial law in this State.

"*Be it enacted by the general assembly as follows:*
"Section 1. The State of Rhode Island and Providence Plantations is hereby placed under martial law; and the same is declared to be in full force until otherwise ordered by the general assembly, or suspended by proclamation of his excellency the governor of the State."

And whereas, on the 8th day of August instant, I issued a proclamation suspending the operation of said act until the 1st day of September then next; I do now, therefore, pursuant to the authority in said act to me given, and by advice of the council, hereby further suspend the operation of said act on and after the said 1st day of September, indefinitely.

Given under my hand and seal of said State, at the city of Providence, this 30th day of August, in the year of our Lord eighteen hundred and forty-two, and of the Independence of the United States of America the sixty-seventh.

[L. S.]   Samuel Ward King.

True copy.
Witness:
　Henry Bowen,
　　　Secretary.

DISTURBANCES IN KANSAS.

(25.)

[By telegraph.]

Westport, Mo., *December 1, 1855.*

I desire authority to call on the United States forces at Leavenworth to preserve the peace of this Territory, to protect the sheriff of Douglas County, and enable him to execute the legal process in his hands. If the laws are not executed, civil war is inevitable. An armed force of 1,000 men, with all the implements of war, it is said, are at Lawrence. They have rescued a prisoner from the sheriff, burnt houses, and threatened the lives of citizens. Immediate assistance is desired. This is the only means to save bloodshed.

Particulars by mail.   Wilson Shannon.

His Excellency Franklin Pierce.

(Received, Washington, December 3, 1855, 10 o'clock 5 minutes a. m.)

(26.)

DECEMBER 3, 1855.

Your dispatch is received.   All the power vested in the Executive will be exerted to preserve order and enforce the laws.   On the receipt of your letter the preliminary measures necessary to be taken before calling out troops will be promptly executed, and you will then be fully advised.

FRANKLIN PIERCE.

WILSON SHANNON,
    Governor of the Territory of Kansas.

(27.)

LAWRENCE, KANS. TER., *January 21, 1856.*

SIR: We have authentic information that an overwhelming force of the citizens of Missouri are organizing upon our border, amply supplied with artillery, for the avowed purpose of invading this Territory, demolishing our towns, and butchering our unoffending free State citizens.   We respectfully demand, on behalf of the citizens of Kansas, that the commandants of the United States troops in this vicinity be immediately instructed to interfere to prevent such an inhuman outrage.

Respectfully,

J. H. LANE,
    Chairman Executive Committee, Kansas Territory.
C. ROBINSON,
    Chairman Committee of Safety.

Attest:
    J. H. GOODIN,
        Secretary Executive Committee, Kansas Territory.
    GEO. W. DEITZLER,
        Secretary Committee of Safety.
FRANKLIN PIERCE,
    President United States.

(28.)

LAWRENCE CITY, *January 23, 1856.*

SIR: We notified you that an overwhelming force, supplied with artillery, was organizing upon our border for the avowed purpose of invading Kansas, demolishing the towns, and butchering the unoffending free State citizens—they constituting nineteen-twentieths of the entire population.   In addition to the relief respectfully demanded in that notice, we earnestly request you to issue your proclamation immediately, forbidding the invasion.   We trust there may be no delay in taking so important a step to prevent an outrage which, if carried out as planned, will stand forth without a parallel in the world's history.

Yours, respectfully,   J. H. LANE,
    Chairman Executive Committee, Kansas Territory.
C. ROBINSON,
    Chairman Committee of Safety.

PRESIDENT OF THE UNITED STATES.

(29.)

By the President of the United States of America.

A PROCLAMATION.

Whereas, indications exist that public tranquillity and the supremacy of law in the Territory of Kansas are endangered by the reprehensible acts or purposes of persons, both within and without the same, who propose to direct and control its political organization by force; it appearing that combinations have been formed therein to resist the execution of the Territorial laws, and thus in effect subvert by violence all present constitutional and legal authority; it also appearing that persons residing without the Territory, but near its borders, contemplate armed intervention in the affairs thereof; it also appearing that other persons, inhabitants of remote States, are collecting money, engaging men, and providing arms for the same purpose; and it further appearing that combinations within the Territory are endeavoring, by the agency of emissaries and otherwise, to induce individual States of the Union to intervene in the affairs thereof, in violation of the Constitution of the United States;

And whereas, all such plans for the determination of the future institutions of the Territory, if carried into action from within the same, will constitute the fact of insurrection, and if from without, that of invasive aggression, and will in either case justify and require the forcible interposition of the whole power of the General Government, as well to maintain the laws of the Territory as those of the Union:

Now, therefore, I, Franklin Pierce, President of the United States, do issue this my proclamation to command all persons engaged in unlawful combinations against the constituted authority of the Territory of Kansas, or of the United States, to disperse and retire peaceably to their respective abodes; and to warn all such persons that any attempted insurrection in said Territory, or aggressive intrusion into the same, will be resisted not only by the employment of the local militia, but also by that of any available forces of the United States, to the end of assuring immunity from violence and full protection to the persons, property, and civil rights of all peaceable and law-abiding inhabitants of the Territory.

If, in any part of the Union, the fury of faction or fanaticism, inflamed into disregard of the great principles of popular sovereignty, which, under the Constitution, are fundamental in the whole structure of our institutions, is to bring on the country the dire calamity of an arbitrament of arms in that Territory, it shall be between lawless violence on the one side and conservative force on the other, wielded by legal authority of the General Government.

I call on the citizens, both of adjoining and of distant States, to abstain from unauthorized intermeddling in the local concerns of the Territory, admonishing them that its organic law is to be executed with impartial justice, that all individual acts of illegal interference will incur condign punishment, and that any endeavor to intervene by organized force will be firmly withstood.

I invoke all good citizens to promote order by rendering obedience to the law; to seek remedy for temporary evils by peaceful means; to discountenance and repulse the counsels and the instigations of agitators and of disorganizers; and to testify their attachment to their country, their pride in its greatness, their appreciation of the blessings they enjoy, and their determination that republican institutions shall not fail in their hands, by cooperating to uphold the majesty of the laws and to vindicate the sanctity of the Constitution.

In testimony whereof, I have hereunto set my hand and caused the seal of the United States to be affixed to these presents.

Done at the city of Washington, the 11th day of February, in the year of our Lord eighteen hundred and fifty-six, and of the Independence of the United States the eightieth.

[L. S.]   FRANKLIN PIERCE.

By the President:
    W. L. MARCY,
       Secretary of State.

(30.)

WAR DEPARTMENT,
Washington, February 15, 1856.

SIR: The President has, by proclamation, warned all persons combined for insurrection or invasive aggression against the organized government of the Territory of Kansas, or associated to resist the due execution of the laws therein, to abstain from such revolutionary and lawless proceedings, and has commanded them to disperse and retire peaceably to their respective abodes, on pain of being resisted by his whole constitutional power. If, therefore, the governor of the Territory, finding the ordinary course of judicial proceedings and the powers vested in United States marshals inadequate for the suppression of insurrectionary combinations or armed resistance to the execution of the law, should make requisition upon you to furnish a military force to aid him in the performance of that official duty, you are hereby directed to employ for that purpose such part of your command as may in your judgment consistently be detached from their ordinary duty.

In executing this delicate function of the military power of the United States, you will exercise much caution, to avoid, if possible, collision with even insurgent citizens, and will endeavor to suppress resistance to the laws and constituted authorities by that moral force which, happily, in our country, is ordinarily sufficient to secure respect to the laws of the land and the regularly constituted authorities of the Government. You will use a sound discretion as to the moment at which the further employment of the military force may be discontinued, and avail yourself of the first opportunity to return with your command to the more grateful and prouder service of the soldier, that of the common defense.

For your guidance in the premises you are referred to the acts of 28th of February, 1795, and 3d of March, 1807 (see Military Laws, pp. 301 and 123), and to the proclamation of the President, a copy of which is herewith transmitted.

Should you need further or more specific instructions, or should, in the progress of events, doubts arise in your mind as to the course which it may be proper for you to pursue, you will communicate directly with this Department, stating the points upon which you wish to be informed.

Very respectfully, your obedient servant,

JEFFERSON DAVIS,
Secretary of War.

Col. EDWIN V. SUMNER and
Lieut. Col. P. ST. GEORGE COOKE.

(31.)

DEPARTMENT OF STATE,
Washington, February 16, 1856.

SIR: I herewith inclose to you a copy of a proclamation by the President, dated the 11th instant, duly authenticated, and also a copy of orders issued from the Department of War to Colonel Sumner and Brevet Colonel Cooke, of the United States Army.

The President is unwilling to believe that, in executing your duties as governor of the Territory of Kansas, there will be any occasion to call in the aid of the United

States troops for that purpose, and it is enjoined upon you to do all that possibly can be done before resorting to that measure; yet if it becomes indispensably necessary to do so in order to execute the laws and preserve the peace, you are hereby authorized by the President to make requisitions upon the officers commanding the United States military forces at Fort Leavenworth and Fort Riley for such assistance as may be needed for the above specified purpose.

While confiding in the respect of our citizens for the laws, and the efficiency of the ordinary means provided for protecting their rights and property, he deems it, however, not improper, considering the peculiar situation of affairs in the Territory of Kansas, that you should be authorized to have the power herein conferred, with a view to meet any extraordinary emergency that may arise, trusting that it will not be used until you shall find a resort to it unavoidable in order to insure the due execution of the laws and to preserve the public peace.

Before any actual interposition of the military force on any occasion, you will cause the proclamation of the President, with which you are herewith furnished, to be publicly read.

I am, sir, very respectfully, your obedient servant,

W. L. MARCY.

Hon. WILSON SHANNON,
    Governor of the Territory of Kansas.

(32.)

DEPARTMENT OF STATE,
Washington, September 2, 1856.

SIR: Reliable information having reached the President that armed and organized bodies of men, avowedly in rebellion against the Territorial government, have concentrated in such numbers as to require additional military forces for their dispersion, you will have the militia of the Territory completely enrolled and organized, to the end that they may on short notice be brought into the service of the United States. Upon requisition of the commander of the military department in which Kansas is embraced you will furnish by companies, or regiments, or brigades, or divisions, such number and composition of troops as from time to time you may find in his report to you to be necessary for the suppression of all combinations to resist the laws of the United States too powerful to be suppressed by the civil authority, and for the maintenance of public order and civil government.

I am, sir, your obedient servant,

W. L. MARCY.

His Excellency JOHN W. GEARY,
    Governor of the Territory of Kansas, Lecompton.

(33.)

[By telegraph.]

DEPARTMENT OF STATE,
Washington, September 27, 1856.

Your dispatch, 16th instant, received. Your course is fully approved. To the troops in service military law can properly be applied, but you have not power to proclaim martial law. You must get along without doing so.

W. L. MARCY.

JOHN W. GEARY,
    Governor of Kansas Territory, Lecompton, Kans. Ter.

(34.)

PROCLAMATION.

Whereas, a large number of volunteer militia have been called into the service of the Territory of Kansas, by authority of the late acting governor, for the maintenance of order, many of whom have been taken from their occupations or business and deprived of their ordinary means of support and of their domestic enjoyments; and

Whereas, the employment of the militia is not authorized by my instructions from the General Government, except upon requisition of the commander of the military department in·which Kansas is embraced; and

Whereas, an authorized regular force has been placed at my disposal sufficient to insure the execution of the laws that may be obstructed by combinations too powerful to be suppressed by the ordinary course of judicial proceedings: Now,

Therefore, I, John W. Geary, governor of the Territory of Kansas, do issue this my proclamation, declaring that the services of such volunteer militia are no longer required, and hereby order that they be immediately discharged. The secretary and the adjutant-general of the Territory will muster out of service each command at its place of rendezvous.

And I command all bodies of men, combined, armed, and equipped with munitions of war, without authority of the Government, instantly to disband or quit the Territory, as they will answer the country at their peril.

In testimony whereof, I have hereunto set my hand and affixed the seal of the Territory of Kansas. Done at Lecompton, this 11th day of September, in the year of our Lord eighteen hundred and fifty-six.

[SEAL.]
                                          JOHN W. GEARY,
                                            Governor of Kansas.

By the Governor:
DANIEL WOODSON, Secretary.

———

(35.)

PROCLAMATION.

Whereas, it is the true policy of every State or Territory to be prepared for any emergency that may arise from internal dissension or foreign invasion:

Therefore, I, John W. Geary, governor of the Territory of Kansas, do issue this my proclamation, ordering all free male citizens qualified to bear arms, between the ages of 18 and 45 years, to enroll themselves in accordance with the act to organize the militia of the Territory, that they may be completely organized by companies, regiments, brigades, or divisions, and hold themselves in readiness to be mustered, by my order, into the service of the United States, upon the requisition of the commander of the military department in which Kansas is embraced, for the suppression of all combinations to resist the laws, and for the maintenance of public order and civil government.

In testimony whereof, I have hereunto set my hand and the seal of the Territory of Kansas. Done at Lecompton, this 11th day of September, in the year of our Lord eighteen hundred and fifty-six.

[SEAL.]
                                          JOHN W. GEARY,
                                            Governor of Kansas.

By the Governor:
DANIEL WOODSON,
          Secretary.

(36.)

EXECUTIVE DEPARTMENT,
Lecompton, Kans. Ter., September 12, 1856.

DEAR SIR: You will proceed without a moment's delay to disarm and disband the present organized militia of the Territory, in accordance with the instructions of the President and the proclamations which I have issued, copies of which you will find inclosed.

You will also take care to have the arms belonging to the Territory deposited in a place of safety and under proper accountability.

Yours, etc.,

JOHN W. GEARY,
Governor of Kansas Territory.

By the Governor:
DANIEL WOODSON,
Secretary.

Adjt. Gen. H. J. STRICKLER.

(37.)

EXECUTIVE DEPARTMENT,
Lecompton, Kans. Ter., September 13, 1856—1.30 a. m.

DEAR SIR: The accompanying dispatch just received from Lawrence gives sufficient reason to believe that trouble of a serious character is likely to take place there. Mr. Adams, the writer of the dispatch, is the special agent whom I sent down last evening to ascertain the state of affairs.

I think that you had better send immediately to Lawrence a force sufficient to prevent bloodshed, as it is my orders from the President to use every possible means to prevent collisions between belligerent forces. If desirable, I will accompany the troops myself, and should be glad to have you go along.

Truly yours, etc.,

JOHN W. GEARY,
Governor of Kansas Territory.

Col. P. St. GEORGE COOKE.

(38.)

LAWRENCE, *September 14, 1856—12 o'clock.*

SIR: I went, as directed, to the camp of the militia and found at the town of Franklin, 3 miles from this place, encamped 300 men, with four pieces of artillery. One mile to the right, on the Wakarusa, I found a very large encampment of 300 tents and wagons. They claim to have 2,500 men, and from the appearance of the camp I have no doubt they have that number.

General Reid is in command. I saw and was introduced to General Atchison, Colonel Titus, Sheriff Jones, General Richardson, etc. The proclamations were distributed.

Secretary Woodson and General Strickler had not, up to the time I left, delivered their orders, but were about doing so as soon as they could get the officers together. The outposts of both parties were fighting about an hour before sunset; one man killed of the militia, and one house burned at Franklin. There were but few people at Lawrence, most of them having gone to their homes after your visit here.

I reported these facts to the officers in command here, and your prompt action has undoubtedly been the means of saving the loss of blood and valuable property.

Secretary Woodson thought you had better come with the militia on to the camp as soon as you can. I think a prompt visit would have a good effect. I will see you as you come this way and communicate with you more fully.

Very respectfully, your obedient servant,

THEODORE ADAMS.

His Excellency GOVERNOR GEARY,
Kansas Territory.

(39.)

DEAR SIR: Proceed at all speed with your command to Lawrence and prevent a collision, if possible, and leave a portion of your troops there for that purpose.

Yours, etc.,

JNO. W. GEARY,
Governor of Kansas Territory.

Col. P. ST. G. COOKE.

———

(40.)

[Dated Washington, September 9, 1856.]

ST. LOUIS, *September 10, 1856.*

I presume the orders sent by Colonel Emory on the 3d instant have already reached you. If the militia which those orders made subject to the requisition of General Smith are not sufficient for the emergency, notify me by telegraph. The insurrectionary invasions of the Territory by way of Nebraska, and the subsequent hostile attacks on the post-office at Franklin and on the dwellings of Titus and of Clark, seem to have stimulated to unlawful acts of the same character on the borders of Missouri. The President expects you to maintain the public peace and bring to punishment all acts of violence and disorder by whomsoever perpetrated and on whatever pretext, and he relies on your energy and discretion and the approved capacity, decision, and coolness of character of General Smith to prevent or suppress all attempts to kindle civil war in the Territory of Kansas. A communication on the same subject has this day been telegraphed to General Smith by the Secretary of War, with positive directions that no parties or bodies of armed men shall be allowed to carry on military operations in the Territory, save such persons as are enrolled by him into the service of the United States.

W. L. MARCY,
Secretary of State.

To JOHN W. GEARY.

———

(41.)

HEADQUARTERS DEPARTMENT OF THE WEST,
Fort Leavenworth, September 17, 1856.

SIR: By virtue of the authority given me by the President of the United States, a copy of which is in your possession, I have the honor to make a requisition on you for two companies of militia (infantry), for the service of the United States.

Each company to consist of 1 captain, 1 first lieutenant, 1 second lieutenant, 4 sergeants, 4 corporals, 2 musicians, and 74 privates.

The companies when ready will be mustered into the service of the United States by an officer who will be detailed for that purpose by Lieutenant-Colonel Cooke, from his command.

With the highest respect, your obedient servant,

PERSIFOR F. SMITH,
Brevet Major-General, Commanding Department.

His Excellency J. W. GEARY,
Governor of Kansas Territory.

(42.)

EXECUTIVE DEPARTMENT,
Lecompton, Kans. Ter., September 30, 1856.

SIR: Peace now reigns in Kansas. Confidence is gradually being restored. Citizens are returning to their claims. Men are resuming their ordinary pursuits, and a general gladness pervades the entire community.

When I arrived here everything was at the lowest point of depression. Opposing parties saw no hope of peace save in mutual extermination, and they were taking the most effectual means to produce that terrible result.

I will shortly issue a proclamation announcing the fact that tranquillity prevails, and inviting the return of all citizens who have been ejected from the Territory either by fraud or force.

In a day or two I will transmit you a full account of my proceedings.

Your obedient servant,

JOHN W. GEARY,
Governor of Kansas Territory.

Hon. WM. L. MARCY,
Secretary of State.

(43.)

DEPARTMENT OF STATE,
Washington, September 23, 1856.

SIR: Your letter of the 9th instant, from Fort Leavenworth, has been received and laid before the President. He is much gratified with your assurance that you shall be able ere long to restore peace and quiet to the Territory of Kansas. Such aid as he can give toward accomplishing this most desirable result will be promptly afforded.

In General Smith's dispatch to the Secretary of War, of the same date with that of your letter, he expresses a decided opinion that the military force which he now has under his command, together with that which can be organized in the Territory, will be sufficient for all the purposes for which such a force is needed, and that he shall have no occasion to use the authority given to him to call for any additional force from the States of Kentucky and Illinois.

The President indulges the hope that, by the judicious measures which he does not doubt will be adopted by you, and the concerted action between yourself and General Smith, outrages will cease, order be restored, and the civil authority reestablished and found competent to preserve peace and afford complete protection to the settlers, both in their persons and property. Those who have committed crimes within the Territory should not be permitted to escape punishment, and there can be no ground for any discrimination between offenders acting individually and those acting as members of organized or associated bands. Your prompt and vigorous attention will be directed toward those who meditate further mischief and are disposed to obstruct your efforts to restore the supremacy of the civil authority.

The President relies upon your energy and discretion to overcome the difficulties which surround you, and to restore tranquillity to Kansas. The exigencies of affairs, as they shall be presented to you on the spot, will indicate the course of proceeding in particular cases calculated to lead to such results better than any definite instructions emanating from this Department.

The President directs you to keep the Government here constantly advised of the state of things in Kansas, and the measures you may take in carrying out the general instructions you have received.

I am, etc., W. L. MARCY.

His Excellency JOHN W. GEARY,
Governor of Kansas Territory, Lecompton.

(44.)

EXECUTIVE DEPARTMENT,
Lecompton, Kans. Ter., November 11, 1856.

SIR: Peace prevails throughout the Territory at this time, and, as the season of the year is now so far advanced into autumn as to make it extremely uncomfortable for the encampment of troops and the picketing of horses, I have the honor to inform you that I can at present dispense with all the troops which you have been pleased to place at my disposal for maintaining the peace of the Territory, with the exception of a squadron of dragoons and one company of United States infantry to be left at Lecompton subject to my orders.

I can not forbear on this occasion to thank you most cordially for the very efficient aid you have rendered me during the late disturbances, and for the truly magnanimous conduct of all the officers and soldiers placed by you at my disposal, the services of whom, I trust, will never again be required under similar circumstances.

With high respect, your friend and obedient servant,

JNO. W. GEARY,
Governor of Kansas Territory.

Maj. Gen. P. F. SMITH,
Commanding Department of the West.

(45.)

ORDERS, No. 14.]   HEADQUARTERS DEPARTMENT OF THE WEST,
Fort Leavenworth, Kans. Ter., November 12, 1856.

The governor of Kansas has announced to the general commanding the department that peace prevails throughout the Territory at the present time, and that the services of the troops for the maintenance of order can in a measure be dispensed with.   In consideration, therefore, of this announcement, and in view also of the approach of winter, the several commands now in the field will return to their respective permanent stations at once, but by easy marches, with the exception of two companies of the First Regiment of Cavalry and one company of the Sixth Regiment of Infantry, to be designated by the senior field officer of each corps, under instructions of Lieut. Col. P. St. George Cooke, Second Dragoons, commanding the troops in the field, and to be by him reported to Governor Geary.   Each company will constitute a distinct and separate command, to be held subject to such orders or requisitions as they may from time to time receive from the executive of the Territory.

By order of Brevet Major-General Smith:

GEO. DEAS,
Assistant Adjutant-General.

(46.)

LEAVENWORTH, *July 14, 1857.*

SIR: I have received authentic intelligence that a dangerous rebellion has occurred in the city of Lawrence, in this Territory, involving an open defiance of the laws and the establishment of an insurgent government in that city.

This movement, if not speedily arrested, I am also assured, will be extended throughout the Territory, and must result in a renewal of civil war.

It becomes, then, my painful duty, under my instructions from the President of the United States, to request you to furnish a regiment of dragoons, to proceed at once to the immediate vicinage of Lawrence, to act as a posse comitatus in aid of the civil authorities in the due execution of the laws and for the preservation of the public peace. The service of the troops for this purpose will be discontinued so soon as the public exigency will permit.

Respectfully yours,

R. J. WALKER,
Governor of Kansas Territory.

Brevet Brig. Gen. W. S. HARNEY,
Commanding Troops in Kansas, etc.

(47.)

HEADQUARTERS TROOPS SERVING IN KANSAS,
Fort Leavenworth, July 15, 1857.

GOVERNOR: I have the honor to acknowledge the receipt of your communication of yesterday's date, requesting a regiment of dragoons to proceed at once to the immediate vicinage of the city of Lawrence, in this Territory, to act as a posse comitatus in aid of the civil authorities in the due execution of the laws, and for the preservation of the public peace.

In answer I desire to inform you that I have directed Lieutenant-Colonel Cook, of the Second Dragoons, to proceed with seven companies of his regiment, all the disposable force of that arm, to the vicinity of the city of Lawrence, and report his force to yourself, as a posse comitatus to execute such orders as you may deem proper to give him in that capacity.

I am, governor, very respectfully, your obedient servant,

WM. S. HARNEY,
Colonel Second Dragoons, Brevet Brigadier-General Commanding.

His Excellency ROBT. J. WALKER,
Governor of Kansas Territory, Leavenworth, Kans. Ter.

(48.)

DEPARTMENT OF STATE,
Washington, July 25, 1857.

SIR: Your letter of the 15th instant and the accompanying papers have been received and submitted to the President.

I am instructed by him to inform you that he indulges the hope that by the prudence and firmness of your measures, supported by the patriotism and intelligence of the people of Kansas, peace and order will be firmly established in that Territory, without the necessity of resorting to the employment of force.

The President has learned with surprise, as well as regret, that the design has been avowed by some of the citizens of Kansas to adopt measures which, if carried into full effect, must inevitably lead to a collision between the lawful authorities of the Territory and the persons thus placing themselves in opposition to the law. Should such a contingency unfortunately arise, the President will employ all the necessary power confided to him by the Constitution and the laws to put an end to this illegal state of things.

The pretension of a portion of the people of Lawrence to establish a municipal government for that place and to clothe it with legal authority to act is so destitute of all just foundation in itself, and in any view so unnecessary in a Territory with a government established by Congress in full operation, that the President can not believe this illegal project will be carried into execution; and he trusts that, independently of other considerations, the able and patriotic appeal made by you to the people of Kansas in your recent proclamation will stop all further progress in this dangerous career.

The President approves the precautionary measures you have adopted in calling into the vicinity of Lawrence a military force to act as a posse comitatus to aid in the enforcement of the laws should it be necessary.

He confidently relies upon your discretion, as well as your firmness, and feels assured that this force will be actually employed in those cases only where there is a resistance to the law which can not be overcome by the proper civil officers with the ordinary means at their command. There must be not a mere declaration of intention to do acts contrary to law, but there must be an act of resistance before the military force can properly intervene.

When a civil officer has reason to believe that process placed in his hands will be resisted by force, he has the right to call for the aid of such portions of the posse comitatus as he may think necessary. And at this point may rightfully commence the action of the military force. It may be called upon as a part of the posse comitatus to aid such officer in the execution of his duty, and while so acting the troops act under his authority; and as the head of the executive department of the Territorial government it is your duty to provide the necessary instructions in these cases; and to render them the more effectual the troops of the United States have been directed to act as a posse comitatus when you shall require their services for that purpose.

In conclusion, I repeat that the authority of the law must be maintained under any circumstances that may happen.

I am, sir, etc.,

LEWIS CASS.

ROBERT J. WALKER, Esq.,
Governor of the Territory of Kansas, Lecompton.

THE SAN FRANCISCO VIGILANCE COMMITTEE.

(49.)

BY AUTHORITY—PROCLAMATION.

EXECUTIVE DEPARTMENT,
Sacramento City, Cal., June 3, 1856.

Whereas, satisfactory information has been received by me that combinations to resist the execution of legal process by force exist in the county of San Francisco, in this State, and that an unlawful organization, styling themselves the "Vigilance Committee," have resisted by force the execution of criminal process, and that the power of said county has been exerted and has not been sufficient to enable the sheriff of said county to execute such process: Now, therefore, I, J. Neely Johnson, governor of the State of California, by virtue of the power vested in me by the constitution and laws thereof, do hereby declare said county of San Francisco in a state of insurrection; and I hereby order and direct all of the volunteer companies within the county of San Francisco, also all persons subject to military duty within said county, to report themselves for duty immediately to Maj. Gen. William T. Sherman, commanding second division California militia, to serve in the performance of military duty under the command of said Sherman until disbanded from service by his orders. Also, that all volunteer military companies now organized, or which may be organized within the third, fourth, and fifth military divisions of this State; also all persons subject to military duty in said military divisions do hold themselves in readiness to respond to and obey the orders of the governor of this State, or said Sherman, for the performance of military duty in such manner and at such time and place as may be directed by the governor of the State. I furthermore order and direct that all associations, combinations, or organizations, whatsover, existing in said county of San Francisco, or elsewhere in this State, in opposition to or in violation of the laws thereof, more particularly the association known as the "Vigilance Committee" of San Francisco, do disband, and each and every individual thereof yield obedience to the constitution and laws of this State, the writs and process of the courts, and all legal orders of the officers of this State and the county of San Francisco.

J. NEELY JOHNSON.

(50.)

EXECUTIVE DEPARTMENT,
Sacramento City, Cal., November 3, 1856.

Whereas, on the 2d day of June, 1856, satisfactory information having been received by me that combinations for the purpose of resisting the execution of legal process by force existed in the county of San Francisco, in this State, and that an unlawful organization styling themselves the Vigilance Committee had resisted by force the execution of criminal process, and the power of said county had been exhausted, and was not sufficient to enable the sheriff of said county to execute said process, I did, in performance of my duty and the exercise of the power and authority vested in me by the constitution and laws, as the governor of the State of California, on the aforesaid day, issue a proclamation declaring the said county of San Francisco in a state of insurrection; and whereas, I have this day received satisfactory information that the causes which required the issuance of the same no longer exist, I do therefore revoke and withdraw the said proclamation.

J. NEELY JOHNSON.

(51.)

INSURRECTION IN A STATE.

CONSIDERATION OF THE CIRCUMSTANCES IN WHICH THE PRESIDENT MAY EMPLOY THE MILITARY AND NAVAL FORCE OF THE UNION TO SUPPRESS INSURRECTION IN ONE OF THE STATES.

ATTORNEY-GENERAL'S OFFICE, July 19, 1856.

SIR: I have the honor to lay before you herewith conclusions of law on the questions presented by the application of the governor of the State of California, concerning which you have required my official opinion.

It appears by the representation of the governor and by other documents communicated on the subject that, on the 26th day of May last, there was formed, in the city of San Francisco, a voluntary association, composed of persons whose names are not disclosed, styling themselves a "vigilance committee," who proceeded to organize a numerous military force of all arms, to establish a strongly fortified post in the heart of the city, and by these means to overawe and supersede the city and county officers, and to usurp the local authority of the State.

It further appears that the professed inducement of this combination and organization was the commission, in the city of San Francisco, of an act of individual homicide; that the so-called committee overpowered the sheriff, abstracted from the prison force the alleged murderer, and also another person under commitment on the charge of murder, and took the lives of said persons by hanging them publicly, without law, in front of the headquarters of the association in San Francisco.

It further appears that the committee thereafter continued to assume and exercise a summary police jurisdiction in the city and county of San Francisco, making domiciliary visits, arresting by force numerous individuals, subjecting the same to imprisonment or deportation without law, and, at the date of the governor's representation, the 19th of June last, still holding the military possession of the city, with daily augmentation of armed force, and with no definite indication of any purpose to desist from the usurped exercise of the public authority of the State.

It further appears that most of the organized companies of militia in the city of San Francisco uphold the proceedings of the committee and yield obedience to its orders in preference to, and in open disregard of, those of the constituted military authorities of the State.

It does not appear distinctly how far this outward submission of the inhabitants of San Francisco to the assumed authority of the committee is attributable to approbation of its acts, and how far to want of preparation and means to withstand it; nor is that material to the question of law involved, since whatever may be the local opinion regarding the committee, its organization and its acts do not the less constitute a lawless usurpatiou of the powers of the State.

Thus it appears that, independently of the specific acts of violation of law perpetrated by the committee, there is peculiar aggravation of illegality in its organization and action, by reason of the secrecy of its direction, its demonstrative ostentation of military force, the excessive disproportion of the means which it employs to its professed ends, and the duration of its violent power. If circumstances are supposable in which the exertion of illegal force for a moment may be justified, or at least extenuated, none are possible which suffice to warrant the permanent substitution of such force in the place of constitutional government.

It also requires to be stated that, while the so-called vigilance committee is acting in usurpation of public right and assuming to punish, at its mere discretion, alleged malefactors without lawful authority and in contempt of the established forms of justice, while its illegal power is rendered still more objectionable by reason of its anonymous secret and irresponsible constitution, and while the good which it may have done or which it professes to aim to do in the punishment of a few alleged criminal or disorderly persons is altogether incommensurate with the extraordinary means adopted for its accomplishment, and while these considerations tend to subject the committee to suspicion of unavowed ulterior purposes, still there is no evidence in the documents referred or in other authentic information that, in what has thus occurred at San Francisco, there has been committed or threatened any act of resistance or obstruction to the Constitution, laws, or official authority of the United States.

But the incidents in question exhibited a case of such persistent disturbance of public tranquillity as to have constrained the interposition of the governor of the State, who, on the 8th of June, issued his official proclamation, setting forth the existence of the unlawful combination, calling on its members to disband, and summoning to arms the militia of the State for the purpose of restoring public order and of enforcing obedience to law in the city and county of San Francisco.

Upon these facts the governor of the State now represents to you that insurrection exists therein and prefers the following requests:

1. That you will transmit orders to the officer of the United States commanding the Pacific division to issue to the State, on the requisition of the governor, such arms and ammunition as may be needed for the object of suppressing the said insurrection.

2. That you will transmit orders to the said commanding officer to render such assistance in arms and ammunition at any future time as may be required by the governor for the purpose of enforcing obedience to the constitution and laws of the State.

Such, specifically, is the tenor of this application, and the question is of your constitutional and legal power in the premises.

With reference to such a case of insurrection in a State against the government thereof the Constitution declares that Congress shall have power "to provide for calling forth the militia to execute the laws of the Union, suppress insurrections, and repel invasions." The present is one of the forms of the second of the three specified emergencies, namely, insurrection against, not the Government of the United States, but that of a State.

I do not perceive in the Constitution any other provision of specific pertinency; but something will be said in the sequel regarding the relations of Congress and of the President, in such a case, to the military and naval force of the United States.

As to the clause of the Constitution which makes it the duty of the President "to take care that the laws be faithfully executed," that, it is apprehended, refers primarily to the laws of the United States, and to those of a State or Territory only in the contingency when the case of insurrection therein is presented according to the Constitution and to acts of Congress.

The Congress of the United States has executed that clause of the Constitution which empowers it "to provide for calling forth the militia to execute the laws of the Union, suppress insurrections, and repel invasions," and also its general power in the same relation over the Federal, military, and naval forces by the enactment of two subsisting laws, the material parts of which are as follows:

The act of February 28, 1795, entitled an act to provide for calling forth the militia for the purposes, and in the words of the Constitution, enacts that "in case of an insurrection in any State against the government thereof, it shall be lawful for the President of the United States, on application of the legislature of such State, or of the executive, when the legislature can not be convened, to call forth such number of the militia of any other State or States as may be applied for, as he may judge sufficient to suppress such insurrection."

And it further enacts, "that whenever it may be necessary, in the judgment of the President, to use the military force hereby directed to be called forth, the President shall forthwith, by proclamation, command such insurgents to disperse and retire peaceably to their respective abodes within a limited time." (1 Stat. L., p. 424.)

The act of March 3, 1807, entitled an act authorizing the employment of the land and naval forces of the United States in case of insurrections, provides: "That in all cases of insurrection, or obstruction to the laws, either of the United States or any individual State or Territory, where it is lawful for the President of the United States to call forth the militia for the purpose of suppressing such insurgents, or of causing the laws to be duly executed, it shall be lawful for him to employ, for the same purposes, such part of the land or naval force of the United States as shall be judged necessary, having first observed all the prerequisites of the law in that respect." (11 Stat. L., p. 443.)

These are the only subsisting provisions of statute material to the subject-matter of inquiry.

It is observable that the statute does not, by expression, empower the President to call forth the militia of the State in which the insurrection exists, but only upon the application of such State to call forth the militia of some other State or States. It presumes, of course, that when occasion arises the militia of the particular State will be brought into action by its own executive and legislative authority. (Luther v. Borden, 7 Howard, pp. 1–45.)

It is likewise observable that, in so far as the statute goes to determine the point, the President is only to be moved to action by the "legislature" of the State in which the insurrection exists, or of the executive of such State when the legislature can not be convened.

Now, the call here made on the President in the name of the State of California is not according to the conditions of the statute, for it is made by the governor of the State, not by its legislature, and made by him without any allegation that the legislature could not be convened.

That he had lawful power to convene the legislature can not be doubted, for it is expressly conferred by the constitution of the State. (Art. V, sec. 9.)

Moreover, the governor of the State does not request the President to call forth the militia of some other State or States in aid of his authority, nor does he in terms request you to employ for that purpose the land and naval force of the United States.

On the other hand, there is no room for question here as to legitimacy of government between two contending parties in the same State or Territory. If there were, it would be for you to determine that question, in the first instance, as the Supreme Court have decided in the case of the political controversy which some years ago agitated the State of Rhode Island. (Luther v. Borden, ubi supra, p. 43.)   But in the present case there is no pretext or claim whatever that the vigilance committee is the government of the State, which beyond all peradventure has its lawful representation in the person of the governor.

And it is the function of the President of the United States, indubitably, to decide, in his discretion, what facts existing constitute the case of insurrection contemplated by the statutes and by the Constitution. (Martin v. Mott, 12 Wheaton, 29, 31; Luther v. Borden, ubi supra, p. 45.)

In a word, the present case seems to be wholly exempt from difficulties of a political nature, and the only questions involved are of the duty and power of the President, in view of the peculiarities before mentioned in the tenor of the application made by the governor of California.

Can the President call forth the militia of one State for the purpose of suppressing insurrection in another, or employ the land and naval forces of the United States for the same purpose, when he has sufficient knowledge of the fact of insurrection, but no request for his interposition has been made in due conformity with the conditions of the statute?

And supposing the emergency of insurrection to occur and to be duly brought to his knowledge, can he furnish to the public authorities of the State in which the insurrection exists arms and munitions of war, distinct from and not in the hands of officers and troops of the United States?

I feel reluctant to go beyond the actual case in the undertaking to pronounce rules of law applicable to the gravest and the most critical of all the emergencies possible to occur in the relations between the United States and the respective States of the Union. I am not willing to say that circumstances may not arise in which the President might furnish arms without furnishing men at the same time, under the authority of the act of 1807, and on the principle that as the whole includes all its parts, so the furnishing of arms alone may be comprehended in the power to employ all the land and naval "force" of the United States. I am not less unwilling to assume to foresee or conceive all the possible contingencies of such a public question, and to presume, by conjectural supposition in anticipation of fact, to exhaust the legal conditions of the power of the General Government in the premises.

This, however, it seems safe to say—that the application of this high power of the President to cases of doubtful legal condition ought to be reserved for circumstances of the most exigent emergency, such as, for instance, a case of indisputable *bellum flagrans* in a given State, and in which all the constitutional powers of the State shall have been exerted in vain to prevent or suppress domestic war, and in which, also, imminent or extreme public disaster can be averted only by such interposition of the Federal Government.

I do not perceive such circumstances of superlative exigency in the present case.

There is obstruction of law in California, but not actual shock of arms between the insurgents and the State.

Besides, the whole constitutional power of the State in the case has not yet been exerted; for, in the space of time which the illegal incidents had already occupied— of one whole month—it does not appear that the governor took any steps to convene the legislature of the State, although that remedy might have been adopted, and have had its effectual application to the evil, long before any such remedy could be derived from the President of the United States.

The legal considerations herein submitted apply more particularly to the first of the two requests made by the governor, namely, that for the supply of arms and munitions of war to the State in the specific present emergency. The same objections, with others of a more serious nature, which it is unnecessary to discuss in detail, apply to the second request—that of orders for the supply of arms and ammunition "at any future time," on the call of the governor. It is obvious that the President of the United States must himself determine the conditions of actual or apprehended insurrection in a State, demanding and justifying the interposition of the military force of the United States.

In regard to the supply of arms to the State, it is taken for granted by me that in the ordinary course of its administrative action the War Department had delivered to the State the distributive quantity of arms to which it was entitled under standing provisions of acts of Congress.

In conclusion, then, permit me to observe that, without presuming to say that there may not be in the present case some act of moral authority competent for you in your discretion to perform, still, in my opinion, the circumstances do not afford sufficient legal justification for acceding to the actual requests of the governor of the State of California.

I am, with the highest consideration,

C. CUSHING.

The PRESIDENT.

THE MORMON REBELLION.

(53.)

PROCLAMATION BY THE GOVERNOR.

CITIZENS OF UTAH: We are invaded by a hostile force, who are evidently assailing us to accomplish our overthrow and destruction.

For the last twenty-five years we have trusted officials of the Government, from constables and justices to judges, governors, and Presidents, only to be scorned, held in derision, insulted, and betrayed. Our houses have been plundered and then burned, our fields laid waste, our principal men butchered while under the pledged faith of the Government for their safety, and our families driven from their homes to find that shelter in the barren wilderness, and that protection among hostile savages which were denied them in the boasted abodes of Christianity and civilization.

The Constitution of our common country guarantees unto us all that we do now or have ever claimed. If the constitutional rights which pertain unto us as American citizens were extended to Utah according to the spirit and meaning thereof, and fairly and impartially administered, it is all that we could ask—all that we have ever asked.

Our opponents have availed themselves of prejudice existing against us, because of our religious faith, to send out a formidable host to accomplish our destruction. We have had no privilege or opportunity of defending ourselves from the false, foul, and unjust aspersions against us before the nation. The Government has not condescended to cause an investigating committee, or other person, to be sent to inquire into and ascertain the truth, as is customary in such cases. We know those aspersions to be false, but that avails us nothing. We are condemned unheard, and forced to an issue with an armed mercenary mob, which has been sent against us at the instigation of anonymous letter writers ashamed to father the base, slanderous falsehoods which they have given to the public, of corrupt officials who have brought false accusations against us to screen themselves in their own infamy, and of hireling priests and howling editors who prostitute the truth for filthy lucre's sake.

The issue which has thus been forced upon us compels us to resort to the great first law of self-preservation, and stand in our own defense, a right guaranteed to us by the genius of the institutions of our country, and upon which the Government is based. Our duty to ourselves, to our families, requires us not to tamely submit to be driven and slain without an attempt to preserve ourselves. Our duty to our country, our holy religion, our God, to freedom and liberty, requires that we should not quietly stand still and see those fetters forging around us which are calculated to enslave and bring us in subjection to an unlawful military despotism, such as can only emanate in a country of constitutional law from usurpation, tyranny, and oppression.

Therefore, I, Brigham Young, governor and superintendent of Indian affairs for the Territory of Utah, in the name of the people of the United States in the Territory of Utah forbid:

First. All armed forces of every description from coming into this Territory under any pretense whatever.

Second. That all the forces in said Territory hold themselves in readiness to march at a moment's notice to repel any and all such invasion.

Third. Martial law is hereby declared to exist in this Territory from and after the publication of this proclamation, and no person shall be allowed to pass or repass into or through or from this Territory without a permit from the proper officer.

Given under my hand and seal, at Great Salt Lake City, Territory of Utah, this 15th day of September, A. D. 1857, and of the Independence of the United States of America the eighty-second.

BRIGHAM YOUNG.

(54.)

GREEN RIVER COUNTY, NEAR FORT BRIDGER,
Utah Territory, November 21, 1857.

To the people of Utah Territory:

On the 11th of July, 1857, the President appointed me to preside over the executive department of this Territory. I arrived at this point on the 19th of this month and shall probably be detained some time, in consequence of the loss of animals during the recent snowstorm. I will proceed at this point to make the preliminary arrangements for the temporary organization of the Territorial government.

Many treasonable acts of violence having been committed by lawless individuals, supposed to have been countenanced by the late executive, such persons are in a state of rebellion. Proceedings will be instituted against them in a court organized by Chief Justice Eckels, held in this county, which will supersede the necessity of appointing a military commission for the trial of such offenders. It is my duty to enforce unconditional obedience to the Constitution, to the organic laws of this Territory, and to all the other laws of Congress applicable to you. To enable me to effect this object, I will, in the event of resistance, rely, first upon a posse comitatus of the well-disposed portion of the inhabitants of this Territory, and will only resort to a military posse in case of necessity. I trust that this necessity will not occur.

I come upon you with no prejudices or enmities, and by the exertion of a just and firm administration I hope to command your confidence. Freedom of conscience and the use of your own peculiar mode of serving God are sacred rights guaranteed by the Constitution, with which it is not the province of the Government or the disposition of its representatives in this Territory to interfere.

In virtue of my authority as commander in chief of the militia of this Territory, I hereby command all armed bodies of individuals, by whomsoever organized, to disband and return to their respective homes. The penalty of disobedience to this command will subject the offenders to the punishment due to traitors.

A. CUMMING,
Governor of Utah Territory.

(55.)

To the people of Utah:

The commissioners of the United States, deputed by the President to urge upon the people of this Territory the necessity of obedience to the Constitution and laws, as enjoined by his proclamation, have this day informed me that there will be no obstruction to the administration and execution of the laws of the Federal Government, nor any opposition on the part of the people of this Territory to the military force of the Government in the execution of their orders. I therefore feel it incumbent on me, and have great satisfaction in doing so, to assure those citizens of the Territory who, I learn, apprehend from the army ill treatment, that no person whatever will be in anywise interfered with or molested in his person or rights, or in the peaceful pursuit of his avocations; and, should protection be needed, that they will find the army (always faithful to the obligations of duty) as ready now to assist and protect them as it was to oppose them while it was believed they were resisting the laws of their Government.

A. S. JOHNSTON,
Colonel Second Cavalry and Brevet Brigadier-General, Commanding.

HEADQUARTERS DEPARTMENT OF UTAH,
Camp on Bear River, June 14, 1858.

(56.)

PROCLAMATION OF GOVERNOR CUMMING.

To the inhabitants of Utah and others whom it may concern:

Whereas, James Buchanan, President of the United States, at the city of Washington, the 6th day of April, 1858, did, by his proclamation, offer to the inhabitants of Utah who submit to the laws a free and full pardon for all treasons and seditions heretofore committed; and

Whereas, the proffered pardon was accepted, with the prescribed terms of the proclamation, by the citizens of Utah:

Now, therefore, I, Alfred Cumming, governor of Utah Territory, in the name of James Buchanan, President of the United States, do proclaim that all persons who submit themselves to the laws and to the authority of the Federal Government are by him freely and fully pardoned for all treasons and seditions heretofore committed. All criminal offenses associated with or growing out of the overt acts of sedition and treason are merged in them, and are embraced in the "free and full pardon" of the President. And I exhort all persons to persevere in a faithful submission to the laws and patriotic devotion to the Constitution and government of our common country.

Peace is restored to our Territory.

All civil officers, both Federal and Territorial, will resume the performance of the duties of their respective offices without delay, and be diligent and faithful in the execution of the laws. All citizens of the United States in this Territory will aid and assist the officers in the performance of their duties.

Fellow-citizens, I offer you my congratulations for the peaceful and honorable adjustment of recent difficulties.

Those citizens who have left their homes I invite to return as soon as they can do so with propriety and convenience.

To all I announce my determination to enforce obedience to the laws, both Federal and Territorial.

Trespasses upon property, whether real or personal, must be scrupulously avoided.

Gaming and other vices are punished by Territorial statutes with peculiar severity, and I commend the perusal of these statutes to those persons who may not have had an opportunity of doing so previously.

In testimony whereof, I have hereunto set my hand and caused the official seal of the Territory to be affixed at Great Salt Lake City, in the Territory of Utah, this 14th day of June, one thousand eight hundred and fifty-eight, and of the Independence of the United States the eighty-second.

[SEAL.]   A. CUMMING.

By the governor:

JOHN HARTNETT,
        Secretary.

THE AFFAIR AT HARPERS FERRY, VA.

(57.)

[By telegraph.]

BALTIMORE, *October 17, 1859.*

CALDWELL, *Chief Operator:*

Hear by train that negroes have taken possession of United States arsenal in Harpers Ferry; fired into express train. Town in great excitement; both our wires cut. Negroes are led by about two fifty (250) white men. They gave Conductor Phelps notice would allow no more trains to pass.

JONES, *Operator.*

(57a.)

[By telegraph.]

CAMDEN STATION, *Baltimore, October 17, 1859.*

Hon. J. B. FLOYD,
        Secretary of War:

Telegraph advices present a serious affair at Harpers Ferry, where United States armory and our bridges are in full possession of large bands of armed men said to be abolitionists, but thought to be armory men. The guns from armory have been taken for offensive use and the leaders notified our men that no trains shall pass the armory and bridge. Our officers were fired upon and a laborer nearly killed. The wires being cut, we got our advices from next station, but they are entirely reliable, although it may be exaggerated in some degree. Can you authorize the Government officers and military from Washington to go on our train at three twenty this afternoon to the scene or send us full authority for volunteers from Baltimore to act? We will take them up on afternoon express if necessary. Please advise us immediately what the Government will do. Our operations on road being in meantime suspended.

JOHN W. GARRETT,
President, Baltimore and Ohio Railroad.

(57b.)

RICHMOND, VA., *October 24, 1859.*

His Excellency JAMES BUCHANAN,
President of the United States.

SIR: I have lately returned from Harpers Ferry, to which place I was suddenly called on the 17th instant by causes the most disturbing and destructive to the peace of this State.

A regularly organized band of lawless invaders, with the purpose of emancipating slaves in Maryland and Virginia by force and arms at the expense of the lives and property of our people, seized the United States arsenal, with its arms, munition, and treasure, and made that arsenal a positive danger instead of being a protection to the surrounding country and its peaceful inhabitants. They seized upon the Baltimore and Ohio Railroad, one of the great national thoroughfares, and arrested the superintendents and cars with their passengers, and shot one of the company's servants; they cut the telegraph wires and prevented the transmission of intelligence on the highway; they shot down several of the most worthy and respectable of the citizens of the town, and shot and wounded dangerously several citizens of the adjoining neighborhood in Virginia who went to the lawful defense of the arsenal and the town of Harpers Ferry. Particulars of these high crimes and felonies are or will be duly reported to you by the proper officers of the United States. And I obey my duty to the Commonwealth, whose people I am bound to protect by a due execution of the laws, to inform you that after due personal examination of the causes of these outrages, and of the opportunities for their commission, I am convinced that they could not have been perpetrated as they were, by less than 20 men, if a proper police and guard, under a military officer, had been duly organized and kept in force at the arsenal of Harpers Ferry. There was no watch worth naming kept at the arsenal, and no military or civil guard whatever. Finding, on Thursday morning last, that the United States marines under Colonel Lee had been ordered away from Harpers Ferry, and that there was no guard left there, I organized a corps of volunteers to watch and guard the confines of Virginia contiguous to and around the arsenal and grounds attached thereto ceded to the United States, and incidentally to afford protection to the same, as well as to the people and territory of Virginia, until the Executive of the United States shall order such police and guard as it may deem necessary and proper for such a place.

I have the honor to be, most respectfully, yours,

HENRY A. WISE.

POLITICAL DISTURBANCES IN LOUISIANA.

(58.)

NEW ORLEANS, *August 1. 1866.*

U. S. GRANT, *General:*

You are doubtless aware of the serious riot which occurred in this city on the 30th. A political body, styling itself the convention of 1864, met on the 30th for, as it is alleged, the purpose of remodeling the present constitution of the State. The leaders were political agitators and revolutionary men, and the action of the convention was liable to produce breaches of the public peace. I had made up my mind to arrest the head men if the proceedings of the convention were calculated to disturb the tranquillity of the department, but I had no cause for action until they committed the overt act. In the meantime official duty called me to Texas, and the mayor of the city, during my absence, suppressed the convention by the use of the police force, and, in so doing, attacked the members of the convention and a party of 200 negroes with firearms, clubs, and knives in a manner so unnecessary and atrocious as to compel me to say that it was murder. About 40 whites and blacks were thus killed and about 160 wounded. Everything is now quiet, but I deem it best to maintain a military supremacy in the city for a few days until the affair is fully investigated. I believe the sentiment of the general community is great regret at this unnecessary cruelty, and that the police could have made any arrest they saw fit without sacrificing lives.

P. H. SHERIDAN,
Major-General, Commanding.

———

(59.)

EXECUTIVE MANSION,
Washington, D. C., August 4, 1866.

Major-General SHERIDAN,
　　Commanding, etc., New Orleans, La.:

We have been advised here that, prior to the assembling of the illegal and extinct convention elected in 1864, inflammatory and insurrectionary speeches were made to a mob, composed of white and colored persons, urging them to arm and equip themselves for the purpose of protecting and sustaining the convention in its illegal and unauthorized proceedings, intended and calculated to upturn and supersede the existing State government of Louisiana, which had been recognized by the Government of the United States. Further, did the mob assemble, and was it armed for the purpose of sustaining the convention in its usurpation and revolutionary proceedings? Have any arms been taken from persons since the 30th ultimo, who were supposed or known to be connected with this mob? Have not various individuals been assaulted and shot by persons connected with this mob without good cause and in violation with the public peace and good order? Was not the assembling of this convention and the gathering of the mob for its defense and protection the main cause of the riotous and unlawful proceedings of the civil authorities of New Orleans? Have steps been taken by the civil authorities to arrest and try any and all those who were engaged in this riot, and those who have committed offenses in violation of law? Can ample justice be meted by the civil authorities to all offenders against the law? Will General Sheridan please furnish me a brief reply to the above inquiries, with such other information as he may be in possession of?

Please answer by telegraph at your earliest convenience.

ANDREW JOHNSON,
President of the United States.

(60.)

NEW ORLEANS, LA., *August 6, 1866—12 m.*

His Excellency ANDREW JOHNSON,
President United States:

I have the honor to make the following reply to your dispatch of August 4: A very large number of colored people marched in procession on Friday night, July 27, and were addressed from the steps of the city hall by Dr. Dostie, ex-Governor Hahn, and others. The speech of Dostie was intemperate in language and sentiment. The speeches of the others, so far as I can learn, were characterized by moderation. I have not given you the words of Dostie's speech, as the version published was denied, but from what I have learned of the man I believe they were intemperate.

The convention assembled at 12 m. on the 30th, the timid members absenting themselves, because the tone of the general public was ominous of trouble. I think there were but about 26 members present. In the front of the Mechanics' Institute, where the meeting was held, there were assembled some colored men, women, and children, perhaps 18 or 20, and in the institute a number of colored men, probably 150. Among those outside and inside there might have been a pistol in the possession of every tenth man.

About 1 p. m. a procession of, say, from 60 to 130 colored men marched up Burgundy street and across Canal street toward the convention, carrying the American flag.

These men had about one pistol to every 10 men, and canes and clubs in addition. While crossing Canal street a row occurred. There were many spectators in the streets, and their manner and tone toward the procession unfriendly. A shot was fired, by whom I am not able to state, but believe it to have been a policeman or some colored man in the procession. This led to other shots and a rush after the procession. On arrival at the front of the institute there was some throwing of brickbats by both sides. The police, who had been held well in hand, were vigorously marched to the scene of disorder. The procession entered the institute with the flag, about six or eight remaining outside. A row occurred between a policeman and one of those colored men, and a shot was again fired by one of the parties, which led to an indiscriminate fire on the building through the windows by the policemen. This had been going on for a short time when a white flag was displayed from the windows of the institute, whereupon the firing ceased and the police rushed into the building.

From the testimony of wounded men and others who were inside the building, the policemen opened an indiscriminate fire upon the audience until they had emptied their revolvers, when they retired, and those inside barricaded the doors. The door was broken in and the firing again commenced, when many of the colored and white people either escaped through the door or were passed out by the policemen inside, but as they came out the policemen, who formed the circle nearest the building, fired upon them, and they were again fired upon by the citizens that formed the outer circle. Many of those wounded and taken prisoners and others who were prisoners and not wounded were fired upon by their captors and by citizens. The wounded were stabbed while lying on the ground, and their heads beaten with brickbats in the yard of the building, whither some of the colored men had escaped and partially secreted themselves. They were fired upon and killed or wounded by policemen. Some were killed and wounded several squares from the scene. Members of the convention were wounded by the policemen while in their hands as prisoners—some of them mortally.

The immediate cause of this terrible affair was the assemblage of this convention; the remote cause was the bitter and antagonistic feeling which has been growing in this community since the advent of the present mayor, who, in the organization of his police force, selected many desperate men, and some of them known murderers.

People of clear views were overawed by want of confidence in the mayor and fear of the thugs, many of which he had selected for his police force. I have frequently been spoken to by prominent citizens on this subject, and have heard them express fear and want of confidence in Mayor Monroe. Ever since the intimation of this last convention movement I most condemn the course of several of the city papers for supporting by their articles the bitter feeling of bad men. As to the merciless manner in which the convention was broken up, I feel obliged to confess strong repugnance.

It is useless to attempt to disguise the hostility that exists on the part of a great many here toward Northern men, and this unfortunate affair has so precipitated matters that there is now a test of what shall be the status of Northern men. Whether they can live here without being in constant dread or not; whether they can be protected in life and property and have justice in the courts. If this matter is permitted to pass over without a thorough and determined prosecution of those engaged in it we may look out for frequent scenes of the same kind, not only here, but in other places. No steps have as yet been taken by the civil authorities to arrest citizens who were engaged in this massacre or policemen who perpetrated such cruelties. The members of the convention have been indicted by the grand jury and many of them arrested and held to bail. As to whether the civil authorities can mete out ample justice to the guilty parties on both sides, I must say that it is my opinion unequivocally that they can not. Judge Abell, whose course I have closely watched for nearly a year, I now consider one of the most dangerous men that we have here to the peace and quiet of the city. The leading men of the convention—King, Cutler, Hahn, and others—have been political agitators and are bad men. I regret to say that the course of Governor Wells has been vacillating, and that during the late trouble he has shown very little of the man.

P. H. Sheridan,
Major-General, Commanding.

War Department,
Washington City, August 7, 1866.

Maj. Gen. P. H. Sheridan,
  Commanding, etc., New Orleans, La.:

The President directs me to acknowledge your telegram of the 6th in answer to his inquiries of the 4th instant. On the 3d instant instructions were sent you by General Grant, in conformity with the President's directions, authorizing you to "continue to enforce martial law so far as might be necessary to preserve the public peace, and ordering you not to allow any of the civil authorities to act as you deem such action dangerous to the public safety, and also that no time be lost in investigating the causes that led to the riot and the facts which occurred." By these instructions the President designed to invest in you, as the chief military commander, full authority for the maintenance of the public peace and safety, as he does not see that anything more is needed pending the investigation with which you are intrusted. But if, in your judgment, your powers are inadequate to preserve the peace until the facts connected with the riot are ascertained, you will please report to this Department for the information of the President.

Edwin M. Stanton,
Secretary of War.

(62.)

HEADQUARTERS DEPARTMENT OF LOUISIANA,
CIRCULAR No. 2.] *New Orleans, La., September 1, 1868.*

In order that the official relations between the commanders of military posts and detachments, and the sheriffs of the various parishes and counties of the States comprising this Department, may be fully understood by all concerned, the following instructions are communicated for the government of such commanders:

The sheriff, being a State officer, usually appointed for a particular county or parish, is restricted in the execution of his duties to the territorial limits of such county or parish. His right to require the assistance of the posse comitatus is supreme within such limits. He is therefore authorized, in cases of unlawful resistance to his authority clearly shown to exist, to require the assistance of any troops serving within his district. In such cases the military commander will be required to render the assistance called for; provided that, in the exercise of a sound discretion, he is satisfied that the necessity for such service exists. But should he not be thoroughly satisfied of this, he will decline to act until he can make a report to, and receive special instructions from, these headquarters, in each case.

The official relations of military commanders and United States marshals are to be defined as follows: The marshal, being a United States officer, is acting under the same authority as that which governs the military commander himself; and his district being ordinarily restricted to the limits of the State, his authority to call for the assistance of troops in cases arising out of a resistance to the laws of the United States, is coextensive with the limits of such State. He will, therefore, have a right to call upon any military commander, within his district, for such assistance as the nature of the case may require; but the military commander will, as before indicated, exercise a sound discretion in deciding upon the necessity for the use of his troops.

In no case is it deemed proper to consider a mere riotous demonstration as a case of calling for the interposition of the military forces, which should not be displayed until it shall be absolutely necessary for them to act.

By command of Bvt. Maj. Gen. R. C. Buchanan:

THOS. H. NEILL,
Major, Twentieth Infantry; Brevet Brigadier-General, U. S. A.,
Acting Assistant Adjutant-General.

Official:

NATHANIEL BURBANK,
Second Lieutenant, Thirty-seventh Infantry;
Bvt. First Lieut., U. S. A., Acting Assistant Adjutant-General.

(63.)

GENERAL ORDERS, HEADQUARTERS, DEPARTMENT OF LOUISIANA,
No. 3. *New Orleans, La., August 18, 1868.*

In order to carry out the instructions from the Secretary of War relative to the assistance to be afforded by the troops on duty in this Department to the civil authorities in case of domestic disturbances or insurrections arising therein, officers commanding districts, detachments, and posts will be governed by the following directions:

Every officer will keep himself well informed of the condition of affairs in his vicinity. Should a necessity arise which, in his opinion, would render the services of troops requisite he will immediately communicate by telegraph with these headquarters, stating the essential facts in the case and asking for the necessary instructions for his government.

Under no circumstances will any interference of the military with the civil authorities be permitted; nor will the services of the troops be made use of unless upon special instructions, previously communicated, in each case, from these headquarters.
By command of Bvt. Maj. Gen. R. C. Buchanan:

THOS. H. NEILL,
Major, Twentieth Infantry; Brevet Brigadier-General, U. S. A.,
Acting Assistant Adjutant-General.

Official:

NATHANIEL BURBANK,
Second Lieutenant, Thirty-seventh Infantry;
Bvt. First Lieut., U. S. A., Acting Assistant Adjutant-General.

(64.)

[Telegram.]

NEW ORLEANS, *December 9, 1872.*
President GRANT:

Having taken the oath of office and being in the possession of the gubernatorial office, it devolves upon me to urge the necessity of a favorable consideration of the request of the general assembly as conveyed in the concurrent resolution of this day telegraphed to you requesting the protection of the United States Government. Be pleased to send the necessary orders to General Emory. This seems to me a necessary measure of precaution, although all is quiet here.

P. B. S. PINCHBACK,
Lieutenant-Governor, Acting Governor of Louisiana.

(65.)

[Telegram.]

NEW ORLEANS, *December 9, 1872.*

We have the honor to transmit to Your Excellency the following concurrent resolutions of both houses of the general assembly, and to request an early reply:

Whereas, the general assembly is now convened in compliance with the call of the governor, and certain evil-disposed persons are reported to be forming combinations to disturb the public peace, defy the lawful authority, and the State is threatened with violence: Therefore,

Be it resolved by the senate and house of representatives of the State of Louisiana in general assembly convened, That the President of the United States be requested to afford the protection guaranteed each State by the Constitution of the United States when threatened with domestic violence, and that the presiding officers of the general assembly transmit this resolution immediately, by telegraph or otherwise, to the President of the United States.

Adopted in general assembly convened this 9th day of December, A. D. 1872.

P. B. S. PINCHBACK,
Lieutenant-Governor and President of the Senate.
CHAS. W. LOWELL,
Speaker of the House of Representatives.

The PRESIDENT OF THE UNITED STATES.

(66.)

[Telegram.]

NEW ORLEANS, *December 11, 1872.*

The PRESIDENT OF THE UNITED STATES:

Under an order from the judge of the United States district court, investing James Longstreet, Jacob Hawkins, and others, with the powers and duties of returning officers under State election law, and charging them with the duty of completing the legal returns and declaring the result in accordance therewith, those persons have promulgated results based upon no returns whatever and no evidence except ex parte statements. They have constructed a pretended general assembly, composed mainly of candidates defeated at the election, and those candidates protected by United States military forces have taken possession of the statehouse and have organized a pretended legislature, which to-day has passed pretended articles of impeachment against the governor; in pursuance of which the person claiming to be a lieutenant-governor, but whose term had expired, proclaimed himself acting governor, broke into the executive office under the protection of United States soldiers and took possession of the archives. In the meantime the general assembly has met in the city hall and organized for business with 60 members in the house and 21 in the senate, being more than a quorum of both bodies. I ask and believe that no violent action be taken and no force used by the Government, at least until the supreme court shall have passed final judgment on the case. A full statement of the facts will be laid before you and the Congress in a few days.

H. C. WARMOTH,
Governor of Louisiana.

(67.)

DEPARTMENT OF JUSTICE, *December 11, 1872.*

P. B. S. PINCHBACK,
Acting Governor of Louisiana:

Requisition of legislature transmitted by you is received. Whenever it becomes necessary, in the judgment of the President, the State will be protected from domestic violence.

GEO. H. WILLIAMS,
Attorney-General.

(68.)

[Telegram.]

NEW ORLEANS, *12th, 1872.*

President U. S. GRANT:

In view of the fact that H. C. Warmoth, assuming to act as governor after having been impeached and suspended from his office of governor in strict compliance with the court and laws of this State, has issued a proclamation declaring himself as still governor of the State, and has assumed to convene an illegal body of men styling themselves a legislature, thus endangering the public peace and tranquillity, and threatening domestic violence, I respectfully request that the commanding officer of this department be instructed, in compliance with the requisition of the legislature, to aid and assist me in maintaining the public peace and protection and sustaining the legal State government.

P. B. S. PINCHBACK,
Acting Governor of Louisiana.

(69.)

DEPARTMENT OF JUSTICE, *December 12, 1872.*

Acting Governor PINCHBACK,

  New Orleans, La.:

Let it be understood that you are recognized by the President as the lawful executive of Louisiana, ana the body assembled at Mechanics' Institute as the lawful legislature of the State, and it is suggested that you make proclamation to that effect, and also that all necessary assistance will be given to you and the legislature herein recog.iized to protect the State from disorder and violence.

GEO. H. WILLIAMS,

Attorney-General.

(70.)

[Telegram.]

NEW ORLEANS, [*December*] *12th, 1872.*

His Excellency U. S. GRANT,

  President United States:

Claiming to be governor-elect of this State, I beg you, in the name of all justice, to suspend recognition of either of the dual governments now in operation here until there can be laid before you all facts and both sides touching the legitimacy of either government. The people denying the legitimacy of Pinchback government and its legislature simply ask to be heard, through committee of many of our best citizens on eve of departure for Washington, before you recognize the one or the other of said governments. I do not believe we will be condemned before we are fully heard.

JNO. MCENERY.

(71.)

[Telegram.]

NEW ORLEANS, *December 14, 1872.*

President U. S. GRANT,

  Washington, D. C.:

Louisiana Field Artillery, 4 Napoleon guns, 2 companies infantry, armed with Winchester rifles, numbering 500 men, nearly all the militia force acting under the command of H. C. Warmoth, stationed in the State armory, with arms loaded, are in open mutiny and disobedience of the civil and military authorities of the State government. They have been repeatedly commanded to lay down their arms. A large armed police force, under the command of Gen. A. S. Badger, of the State militia, has been ordered to take the position. General Badger reports the position too strong for his force. They offer to surrender to any United States military force. I have sent a copy of the dispatch from the Attorney-General, dated the 12th instant, to the commanding general of this department, calling upon him for a military force for the purpose of suppressing this mutiny. He has refused to comply with my demand, and alleges a want of proper authority in the premises. I would respectfully request, in compliance with the requisition of the legislature, that you place a military force at my disposal in order to enable me to suppress this armed revolt and execute the laws.

P. B. S. PINCHBACK,

Lieutenant-Governor, Acting Governor Louisiana.

(72.)

[Telegram.]

NEW ORLEANS, *December 13, 1872.*

ADJUTANT-GENERAL, U. S. ARMY,
        Washington:

There is imminent danger of immediate conflict between two armed bodies of men of some considerable numbers—one body of State militia, representing Governor Warmoth, holding an arsenal; the other an armed body of police, representing Governor Pinchback. I have been appealed to to interfere. Shall I do so; and if I interfere, to which party shall the arsenal be delivered? The parties are face to face with arms in their hands. I beg an immediate answer. I sent an officer to try what can be done by persuasion to suspend the conflict until an answer can be received. There will be no resistance to the Federal forces.

W. H. EMORY,
Colonel, Commanding.

(73.)

[Telegram.]

WASHINGTON, *December 14, 1872.*

Gen. W. H. EMORY, U. S. Army,
        Commanding, New Orleans, La.:

You may use all necessary force to preserve the peace, and will recognize the authority of Governor Pinchback.

By order of the President:

E. D. TOWNSEND,
Adjutant-General.

(74.)

[Telegram.]

NEW ORLEANS, *December 14, 1872.*

The ADJUTANT-GENERAL, U. S. ARMY:

On the receipt of your telegram last night an officer was sent to the contesting parties to ask the evacuation of the arsenal and the dispersion of the armed forces. The demand was promptly complied with and the arsenal turned over to the State authorities this morning. Everything now is quiet.

W. H. EMORY,
Colonel Commanding, Brevet Major-General.

(75.)

[Telegram.]

NEW ORLEANS, *January 3, 1873.*

To President GRANT:

Several persons who claim to have been elected to the legislature, in conjunction with H. C. Warmoth, the impeached and suspended executive, and John McEnery, late Democratic candidate for governor, propose to meet in this city on next Monday and organize a so-called general assembly in conflict with the legislature now in session at the statehouse, and to inaugurate said McEnery as governor. To prevent a subversion of the present State government and to suppress riot, it may be necessary for me, as executive, to use police or other forces to prevent this revolutionary movement, and, in my judgment, under present orders, as contained in the telegrams to General Emory from the President, he would be authorized to furnish troops to sustain the State government. I have just ascertained that General Emory construes the orders already given to have been intended only for the particular occasion upon which they were issued, and unless further instructions are given he will decline responding to my demands for troops and will interfere only in case of actual riot. I respectfully request that the order be repeated or extended so as to fully cover the case, if maintenance of State government and good order require me to make the demand on him.

P. B. S. PINCHBACK,
Acting Governor of Louisiana.

(76.)

[Telegram.]

HEADQUARTERS ARMY OF THE UNITED STATES,
Washington, D. C., January 4, 1873.

Col. W. H. EMORY,
  Commanding Department, New Orleans, La.:
  Your dispatch, through General McDowell, has been laid before the War Department and the President, and you are hereby authorized to use your troops to preserve peace, should a contingency arise which, in your judgment, calls for it.

By command of General Sherman:

WM. D. WHIPPLE,
Assistant Adjutant-General.

(77.)

[Telegram.—Private.]

JANUARY 4, 1873.

S. B. PACKARD,
  United States Marshal, New Orleans, La.:
  I think there ought to be no forcible interference with any proceedings to inaugurate McEnery, if they are not accompanied by violence and there is no attempt to take control of the State government.

GEO. H. WILLIAMS,
Attorney-General.

(78.)

[Telegram. Dated New Orleans, January 5, 1872; received at northeast corner Fourteenth street and Pennsylvania avenue 8.15 p. m.]

Hon. GEORGE H. WILLIAMS,
  Attorney-General United States, Washington:
  Members of legislature returned, as elected by the State board, recognized by Governor Warmoth before the assemblage of the body at Mechanic's Institute, are compelled to meet to-morrow, under our constitution, in order to preserve their status. Their assemblage will be peaceable, without arms, and with no purpose of aggression, but simply to organize.

The organization presided over by Pinchback has threatened violent interference, from which serious trouble may arise. That organization derives its authority from the attitude of the Federal Executive and will be controlled by the President.

We trust that he will discountenance interference with this assemblage, which has a lawful object and is rendered necessary by the situation. Please see the President immediately.

F. N. OGDEN,
Attorney-General, Louisiana.

(79.)

EXECUTIVE MANSION,
Washington, D. C., January 5, 1873.

GENERAL: The President directs that General Emory be telegraphed immediately that he inform Governor Pinchback that the troops will not be furnished to disperse any body of men claiming to be a legislature, or otherwise assembling peaceably and not obstructing the administration of the recognized government of the State.

Very respectfully,

WM. W. BELKNAP,
Secretary of War.

Gen. W. T. SHERMAN,
Commanding the Army, etc.

(80.)

[Telegram.]

WESTERN UNION TELEGRAPH COMPANY,
New Orleans, —— 11, 1873.
(Received at Washington January 11—10.15.)

Col. W. D. WHIPPLE,
Assistant Adjutant-General:

As Mr. Kellogg has been declared by Governor Pinchback and the legislature which he recognizes as the governor-elect of Louisiana, I presume it is intended by my instructions that I shall also recognize him, and shall accordingly do so unless otherwise instructed. Addressed letters to the General Commanding Army on 8th and 9th instant, but they may not reach in time for action. The situation is becoming more complicated, and, in my opinion, the use of the troops simply to keep the peace can not lead to a satisfactory or permanent solution of the difficulties here.

W. H. EMORY,
Colonel, Commanding.

[Document No. 81. Not found.]

POLITICAL DISTURBANCES IN ARKANSAS.

(82.)

[Telegram.]

DEPARTMENT OF JUSTICE,
Washington, April 16, 1874.

ISAAC C. MILLS, Esq.,
United States Marshal, Little Rock, Ark.:

Take notice of existing troubles and notify the officer commanding United States troops if collision is imminent. He is expected to prevent bloodshed.

GEORGE H. WILLIAMS,
Attorney-General.

(83.)

EXECUTIVE MANSION,
Washington, D. C., April 16, 1874.

SIR: The President directs me to request that you will please instruct the commanding officer at Little Rock, Ark., to take no part in the political controversy in that State, unless it should be necessary to prevent bloodshed or collision of armed bodies.

I am, sir, your obedient servant,

O. E. BABCOCK,
Secretary.

The SECRETARY OF WAR.

(84.)

[Telegram.]

LITTLE ROCK, ARK., *April 17, 1874.*

Attorney-General WILLIAMS,
Washington, D. C.:

In your dispatch to Governor Brooks I infer that you intend to be understood as saying that the President can not recognize him as governor until his right has been fully and finally recognized by the courts. I understand from your dispatch to Governor Baxter that the President can not recognize him as governor until his right has been settled by the supreme court. The supreme court will not be in session until June. Now, what are we to do in the meantime? Governor Baxter has issued a proclamation putting this county under martial law, and armed men, pretending to act under his orders, are patrolling the streets, stopping peaceable and unarmed citizens, and setting the authority of the city officers at defiance and arresting the police. Not only this, private property is being forcibly seized and appropriated in a like manner. The construction placed on your dispatch by Governor Baxter is that it is a license to make an attack on the Brooks faction, with an assurance that in so doing the Federal Government will not interfere. You will readily see that the city is sure to become a scene of bloodshed, and over a strife they are not responsible for and which they have not the power to settle under the case of facts stated and placed, when an appeal to either one of the persons claiming to be governor lays the city authorities liable to the charge of being the partisans of the one appealed to. I desire to ask you if the Federal Government is powerless to protect the lives and property of 20,000 inhabitants who are situated as we are. If you will instruct the officers in command of the arsenal to aid the city police in making the arrest of men who are openly violating the law and setting the same at defiance, I could preserve the peace of the city without being compelled to take sides with either of the contending factions. This question of one who is the rightful governor can only be settled by the courts, a thing that may not be done for the next twelve months, and I now implore you, in the name of peace, to aid me all in your power until the other question is settled.

FRED K. KRAMER,
Mayor, City of Little Rock, Ark.

(85.)

[Telegram.]

DEPARTMENT OF JUSTICE,
Washington, April 17, 1874.

S. R. HARRINGTON, Esq.,
United States Attorney, Little Rock, Ark.:

Colonel Rose must execute the orders of the War Department to prevent bloodshed and the collision of armed bodies according to his own judgment.

GEORGE H. WILLIAMS,
Attorney-General.

(86.)

EXECUTIVE MANSION,
Washington, D. C., April 18, 1874.

Captain ROSE,
Commanding United States Troops, Little Rock, Ark.:

I have a dispatch from the acting president of the Western Union Telegraph Company, saying that "Baxter's officers now inspect all messages at Little Rock before transmission, and will allow no messengers to pass out with any message for the Brooks party, whether from the United States officials, or otherwise. Under these circumstances it will be seen that this company is unable at present to maintain the sanctity of telegraphic correspondence."

While the Government takes no part in the unhappy state of affairs existing in Arkansas at this time, you will see that all official dispatches of the Government, whether from the military or civil departments, are transmitted without molestation by either of the contestants for the gubernatorial chair. Report to the Secretary of War the situation of affairs.

U. S. GRANT.

———

(87.)

EXECUTIVE OFFICE,
Little Rock, Ark., April 20, 1874.

SIR: I hereby inform you that one Elisha Baxter, a private citizen, pretending to be governor of Arkansas, without warrant or authority of law, assumed to declare martial law in the capital county of the State, and to appoint a pretended military governor of the city of Little Rock, the seat of government.

That he has called out armed bodies of men for the avowed purpose of attacking and capturing the capitol of the State, by military force, and forcibly installing himself as governor of such State.

That large bodies of armed men have assembled and are continually assembling under said Baxter's proclamation of martial law, and are in close proximity to the statehouse; and have this day actually advanced on the statehouse, and confronted a body of Federal troops stationed in front of the statehouse under orders from their commanding officer acting under your commands to preserve the peace; and were only prevented from making the attack by the presence of Federal troops.

That those armed bodies have seized and appropriated private property, and are hourly seizing and appropriating private property, without compensation; have conscripted and are continually conscripting private citizens, and compelling them to aid and abet them in their insurrectionary purposes; and have seized and are daily seizing railroads in the State, and appropriating them to the same illegal and insurrectionary purposes.

That those armed bodies at this moment are assembled within a few hundred yards of the statehouse, and have threatened an immediate attack upon it.

That the legislature of the State adjourned sine die in April last; has not since been convened; is not now in session; and can not be convened in time to prevent the threatened attack.

That domestic violence now actually exists in this State, and at the seat of government, which the civil and military authorities under my control are powerless to prevent or suppress. Therefore, I, Joseph Brooks, governor of the State of Arkansas, in pursuance of the Constitution and laws of the United States, hereby make application to Your Excellency to protect the State capitol and the State of Arkansas against domestic violence and insurrection.

In testimony whereof, I have hereunto set my hand and caused the great seal of the State to be affixed, at Little Rock, this 20th day of April, A. D. 1874.

[SEAL.]

JOSEPH BROOKS,
Governor.

By the Governor:
EDWARD CURREY,
Secretary of State ad interim.

His Excellency U. S. GRANT,
President United States.

(88.)

[Telegram.]

WASHINGTON, D. C., *April 23, 1874.*

Captain ROSE, U. S. Army,
Little Rock, Ark.:

You may retire to the arsenal with your command as soon as danger to life is no longer threatened, and leave the question to be settled by the contestants, by the courts, or other peaceable methods.

W. W. BELKNAP,
Secretary of War.

(89.)

[Telegram.]

LITTLE ROCK, ARK., *May 9, 1874.*

Hon. GEORGE H. WILLIAMS,
Attorney-General United States.

SIR: Yours of this date, submitting a proposition for the settlement of the troubles in Arkansas, is received and fully considered. A similar proposition in all respects, except so far as relates to the joint call of the legislature, was submitted by me some two weeks since and rejected by Brooks. I can not consent to anything that will in whole or part recognize Brooks as governor. I am governor or I am not governor. The legislature has been called together for the 11th of this month. The members are rapidly assembling, with nearly a quorum present now, with the belief that they will receive the protection of the General Government in their meeting and deliberations. I could not lawfully disperse them if I would; nor have I any means of compelling a legislature that might be convened under the proposed joint call to conform to the terms proposed. The legislature might as well meet now and act under my call, because it might not return two weeks hence, and in the meantime we are in confusion, with no recognized governor and the State in war. To dispose of all these matters I have called the legislature for the 11th instant, under the conviction it would assemble and be protected by the General Government. I now renew my appeal to the President to protect the legislature now called. If the legislature meets now the question may be submitted to it fairly and I will abide its decision fully. I am therefore constrained to decline the terms proposed.

ELISHA BAXTER,
Governor of Arkansas.

(90.)

[Telegram.]

BARING CROSS, ARK., *May 10, 1874.*

Attorney-General WILLIAMS, *Washington:*

Your dispatch submitting proposition to submit question of who was duly elected governor, and to refrain from all warlike demonstrations until the question is finally decided by the legislature or the National Government, as proposed in your dispatch, is accepted. My claims to the governorship of Arkansas have already been adjudged in the circuit court and the right to exercise the office declared by the supreme court in a proceeding where the main question at issue was, Who is the governor of Arkansas? Notwithstanding this, I feel so confident of my election and the justness of my cause that I am willing to submit the question to any other tribunals you have named, and peacefully abide the determination, at all times asserting that the only tribunal that can or has the right to construe the constitution is the supreme court of the State, which, in its late decision in the case of Brooks against Page, determined that the circuit court had both the power and jurisdiction to adjudicate my right to the office.

JOSEPH BROOKS,
Governor of Arkansas.

(91.)

[Telegram.]

LITTLE ROCK, ARK., *May 10, 1874.*

The PRESIDENT OF THE UNITED STATES:

We, the undersigned, members of the legislature of this State, have come here to meet, under the call of Governor Baxter, on to-morrow, and we wish to meet and settle the troubles now existing here, as the country requires it, and we respectfully ask protection of the General Government while we meet and deliberate. We hold the matter should not be postponed, and all that we can do to have a fair and honorable adjustment shall be done, and unless we are protected there may be bloodshed here in a very short time, and the consequence no one can tell. We are well satisfied there will be a quorum of the legislature present to-morrow under the call of Governor Baxter, and we are satisfied a quorum would be here now were it not for the unwarranted seizure and suppression of the trains on the Little Rock and Fort Smith Railroad, necessarily delaying the members of the legislature from the northwestern portions of the State.

B. F. ASKEN.
(And 28 others.)

(92.)

[Telegram.]

LITTLE ROCK, ARK., *May 10, 1874.*

Hon. W. W. WILSHIRE, J. M. JOHNSON, or Governor P. LOWE,
Washington, D. C.:

The Little Rock, Fort Smith and Memphis Railroad, all in the interest of Brooks, have ceased running, the tracks being torn up to prevent the arrival of members of the legislature. The salvation of the people is in the convening of the legislature. Forty members are here and the balance will come to make a quorum if they have to fight over every inch of ground until they reach the capital. Seventy-five thousand legal voters of Arkansas are unit in this cause until an investigation is had by the legislature into the office of governor, the only legal tribunal under our constitution having jurisdiction. We will stand by Elisha Baxter, as we will obey no other.

B. F. ASKEN,

B. B. BEAVERS,

R. W. McCHESNEY,

(and 37 other members of general assembly present to-night).

(93.)

[Telegram.]

WASHINGTON, *May 11, 1874.*

Hon. JOSEPH BROOKS,
    Little Rock, Ark.:

I have suggested to Mr. Baxter that the members of the general assembly now in Little Rock adjourn for a reasonable time, say ten days, to give you opportunity to call in those members who may not respond to his call, so that there may be a full legislature. The United States will give all necessary protection to the legislature in meeting and transacting its business as usual at the statehouse, and prevent as far as practicable all violence and disturbance of the public peace. I urgently request that the military of both parties be at once disbanded, which is the first step toward a peaceable settlement.

U. S. GRANT.

(94.)

[Telegram.]

WASHINGTON, *May 11, 1874.*

Hon. ELISHA BAXTER,
    Little Rock, Ark.:

I recommend that the members of the general assembly now at Little Rock adjourn for a reasonable time, say for ten days, to enable Brooks to call into the body his supposed adherents, so that there may be a full legislature. Any hasty action by a part of the assembly will not be satisfactory to the people. Brooks's friends here agree that if this course is pursued no opposition will be made to the meeting of the assembly in the statehouse as usual, and that he will at once dismiss his forces if you will do the same. I urgently request that all armed forces on both sides be disbanded, so that the general assembly may act free from any military pressure or influence. The United States will give all necessary protection to the legislature, and prevent as far as practicable all violence and disturbance of the public peace. Answer.

U. S. GRANT.

(95.)

[Telegram. Dated Little Rock, Ark., May 11, 1874, 3 a. m.   Received at ——, 2.45 a. m.]

U. S. GRANT, *President:*

On the 9th of May the Attorney-General submitted to me a proposition that he said had your approval. On the 10th I accepted the same out of deference to your wishes, feeling that in doing so I was humiliating myself and the courts of the State. This I did solely in the interest of peace, supposing that Baxter would be required to assent to your proposed plan of settlement. In accordance with the proposition of the Attorney-General I issued a proclamation convening the legislature on the fourth Monday of the present month. To my surprise Baxter has declined to submit the question of his election to the legislature. In conversation with members thereof he boldly proclaims that he does not and will not permit an investigation of his right to the office. Yet you ask me to recognize a call of the legislature at the instance of one who declares the question at issue, and for which you insist on its being assembled, shall not be settled by the tribunal you desire convened. In the attempted organization made to-day, which failed, although persons were sworn in as members from districts in which no vacancies had been declared. Both houses of the legislature now have a quorum in existence. This quorum should pass upon the election return and qualifications of the newly elected members instead of the newly elected members themselves. This action I can not and will not willingly submit to. Section 1, article IV, of the Constitution of the United States declares that full faith and credit shall be given to the judicial proceedings of every State; and if in the face of the decision of the supreme and circuit courts of the States deciding that I am and recognizing me as the legal governor you can recognize Baxter as governor, it is your duty to respond to his application for Federal help. If you can not, it is your duty to assist me to suppress the present domestic violence. To disband my troops at this time under no other assurance than is contained in your telegram of to-day would result not only in the assassination of the judges of the supreme court, but of many of my friends and especially the colored men, who have been guilty of no crime save fidelity to law and order. I shall hold my troops together for the purpose of protecting the citizens of the State who believe the expression of the will of the people at the ballot box should be enforced, and for the protection of those who stand by the Constitution, laws, and the adjudications of the courts of the country. Federal bayonets can put Baxter's legislature in the statehouse, but I am ignorant of the clause of the Constitution under which the President has this power; nothing else will, and when there I doubt if you can compel them to determine who is governor. It is time this agony, doubt, and uncertainty was over; the interests of humanity demand it shall be settled, and if you have the power under the Constitution and laws of the United States to settle the question of who is governor of Arkansas adverse to the decision of the courts of the State, settle it, and settle it at once. I shall not resist what you may order United States troops to do, but shall with all the power at my command repel any and all attempts by Baxter's forces to take possession of the statehouse. I am confident that a legal quorum of the legislature will not respond to Baxter's call, and I shall not assent nor be a party to convening the legislature under any other agreement than that submitted by yourself through the Attorney-General on the 9th instant.

JOSEPH BROOKS,
Governor of Arkansas.

———

(96.)

[Telegram.]

MARIANNA, ARK., April 21, 1874.
(Received at War Department 11.20.)

President GRANT, Washington, D. C.:

For the sake of law and order, take some steps to suppress the riot in Arkansas. Every good citizen will abide your command. Speak and we'll obey. The general impression is that you will not interfere; thus they keep up the fight. Will you save us? We are in a pitiable condition. For God's sake help us! Our whole salvation depends upon our crops. If this matter continues much longer we are ruined.

There is not a man in Arkansas but what will obey your orders, if you will only demand. President Grant, you can stop this muddle if you will, and if you do not you are responsible for our ruin. Know from whence this comes. We do not care—and I speak the sentiments of the people of Arkansas without egotism—who is governor; all we want is peace. The people will obey. Answer.

W. H. FORBISH,
Sheriff, Lee County, Ark.

(97.)

By the President of the United States of America.

A PROCLAMATION.

Whereas, certain turbulent and disorderly persons, pretending that Elisha Baxter, the present executive of Arkansas, was not elected, have combined together with force and arms to resist his authority as such executive, and other authorities of said State; and whereas, said Elisha Baxter has been declared duly elected by the general assembly of said State, as provided in the constitution thereof, and has for a long period been exercising the functions of said office, into which he was inducted according to the constitution and laws of said State, and ought by its citizens to be considered the lawful executive thereof; and whereas, it is provided in the Constitution of the United States that the United States shall protect every State in the Union, on application of the legislature, or of the executive when the legislature can not be convened, against domestic violence; and whereas, said Elisha Baxter, under section 4 of Article IV of the Constitution of the United States and the laws passed in pursuance thereof, has heretofore made application to me to protect said State and the citizens thereof against domestic violence; and whereas, the general assembly of said State was convened in extra session at the capital thereof on the 11th instant, pursuant to a call made by said Elisha Baxter, and both houses thereof have passed a joint resolution also applying to me to protect the State against domestic violence; and whereas, it is provided in the laws of the United States that in all cases of insurrection in any State, or of obstruction to the laws thereof, it shall be lawful for the President of the United States, on application of the legislature of such State, or of the executive when the legislature can not be convened, to employ such part of the land and naval forces as shall be judged necessary for the purpose of suppressing such insurrection, or causing the laws to be duly executed; and whereas, it is required that whenever it may be necessary, in the judgment of the President, to use the military force for the purpose aforesaid, he shall forthwith by proclamation command such insurgents to disperse and retire peaceably to their respective homes within a limited time:

Now, therefore, I, Ulysses S. Grant, President of the United States, do hereby make proclamation and command all turbulent and disorderly persons to disperse and retire peaceably to their respective abodes within ten days from this date, and hereafter to submit themselves to the lawful authority of said executive and the other constituted authorities of said State; and I invoke the aid and cooperation of all good citizens thereof to uphold law and preserve public peace.

In witness whereof, I have hereunto set my hand and caused the seal of the United States to be affixed.

Done at the city of Washington, this 15th day of May in the year of our Lord eighteen hundred and seventy-four, and of the Independence of the United States the ninety-eighth.

U. S. GRANT.

By the President:
    HAMILTON FISH,
        Secretary of State.

LABOR DISTURBANCES, 1877.

(98.)

WHEELING, W. VA., *July 18, 1877.*

His Excellency R. B. HAYES,
President of the United States:

Owing to unlawful combinations and domestic violence now existing at Martinsburg and other points along the line of the Baltimore and Ohio Railroad it is impossible with any force at my command to execute the laws of the State, I therefore call upon your Excellency for the assistance of the United States military to protect the law-abiding people of the State against domestic violence and to maintain the supremacy of the law. The legislature is not now in session and could not be assembled in time to take any action in the emergency. A force of from two to three hundred should be sent without delay to Martinsburg, where my aid, Colonel Delaplaine, will meet and confer with the officer in charge.

HENRY M. MATHEWS,
Governor of West Virginia.

(99.)

WHEELING, W. VA., *July 18, 1877.*

Hon. GEO. W. McCRARY,
Secretary of War:

The only organized force in the State consists of four companies. Two of them are at Martinsburg and in sympathy with rioters, who are believed to be 800 strong. Another company is 38 miles from railroad; only one company of 40 men efficient. No organized militia in the State. Will send Colonel Delaplaine to see the President if desired. He is at Martinsburg. I have been reluctant to call on the President, but deemed it necessary to prevent bloodshed.

HENRY M. MATHEWS.

(100.)

WHEELING, W. VA., *July 18, 1877.*

Hon. GEO. W. McCRARY,
Secretary of War:

The legislature of 1875 prohibited the enrollment of the militia of this State. There is now but one volunteer company which is valuable in this emergency. I have no doubt that within ten days I could organize within the State a force sufficient to suppress any riot, but in the meantime much property will be destroyed, and what is more important, valuable lives lost. I regret the necessity, but have not hesitated to assume the responsibility of applying to the President for assistance.

HENRY M. MATHEWS.

(101.)

[Telegram.]

WAR DEPARTMENT,
Washington, D. C., July 18, 1877.

Governor HENRY M. MATHEWS,
Wheeling, W. Va..

Your dispatch to the President asking for troops is received. The President is averse to intervention unless it is clearly shown that the State is unable to suppress the insurrection. Please furnish a full statement of facts. What force can the State raise? How strong are the insurgents?

GEORGE W. McCRARY,
Secretary of War.

(102.)

[Telegram.]

WAR DEPARTMENT, ADJUTANT-GENERAL'S OFFICE,
Washington, July 18, 1877.

The COMMANDING OFFICER, TROOPS AT WASHINGTON ARSENAL:

The Secretary of War directs that you proceed with the companies of your command, every available man, as infantry, and with the least practicable delay, to Martinsburg, W. Va., there to report and confer with Colonel Delaplaine, aid to the governor of the State.

The companies from Fort McHenry have also been ordered, and you will, on their arrival, assume command of all. Your services will be in connection with the existing riots on the Baltimore and Ohio Railroad.

You will confer with the authorities of the Baltimore and Ohio Railroad at the depot in this city, where it is understood the company will have transportation ready to move at a moment's notice.

THOMAS M. VINCENT,
Assistant Adjutant-General.

(103.)

[Telegram.]

ADJUTANT-GENERAL'S OFFICE,
Washington, July 18, 1877.

The COMMANDING OFFICER,
Fort McHenry, Md.:

The Secretary of War directs that you send the companies of your command, every available man, as infantry, and with the least practicable delay, to Martinsburg, W. Va., there to report and confer with Colonel Delaplaine, aid to the governor of the State.

Their services will be in connection with the existing riots on the Baltimore and Ohio Railroad.

Confer with the Baltimore and Ohio Railroad authorities, who. it is believed, will have transportation ready to move at a moment's notice.

Acknowledge receipt.

THOMAS M. VINCENT,
Assistant Adjutant-General.

(104.)

WAR DEPARTMENT, *Washington, July 18, 1877.*

GENERAL: Please direct the officer in command of troops to be sent to Martinsburg to await the President's proclamation commanding the insurgents to disperse and retire peaceably to places of abode. The proclamation will issue at once—probably this evening or early in the morning—and will be published at the scene of the disturbance doubtless by the time our forces arrive there, but if not they will delay until its publication.

Respectfully,

GEO. W. McCRARY,
Secretary of War.

Gen. THOS. M. VINCENT,
Assistant Adjutant-General, U. S. Army.

(105.)

HEADQUARTERS U. S. TROOPS,
Martinsburg, W. Va., July 20, 1877.

Due notification having been given by the proclamation of the President of the United States to those concerned, the undersigned warns all persons engaged in the interruption of travel on the Baltimore and Ohio Railroad that the United States troops must not be impeded, and whoever undertake it do so at their own peril.

WM. H. FRENCH,
Bvt. Maj. Gen., U. S. Army, Colonel Fourth Artillery, Commanding.

(106.)

[Telegram by A. & P. Co.]

MARTINSBURG, W. VA., *July 19, 1877.*
(Received at War Department July 19, 1877.)

Colonel VINCENT,
   Adjutant-General, Washington:

Proclamation printed; now being circulated. After 12 o'clock, if the insurgents have not dispersed, the troops under my command will proceed to enforce the orders of the President. At present everything seems quiet and I doubt whether anything more than a demonstration will be required. Whatever action I may determine upon, will be after consultation with and full concurrence of Colonel Delaplaine, aid to the governor.

FRENCH,
Colonel, Commanding.

(107.)

BALTIMORE, CAMDEN STATION, *July 20, 1877.*

His Excellency R. B. HAYES.

SIR: An assemblage of rioters, to be dispersed by any force at my command, has taken possession of the Baltimore and Ohio Railroad depot here. Set fire the same and have driven off the firemen who attempted to extinguish the same, and it is impossible with force at my command to disperse the rioters. Under circumstances, as governor of the State of Maryland, I call upon you as President of the United States to furnish the force necessary to protect the State against domestic violence. The legislature of the State not in session and can not be convened in time to meet the emergency.

JOHN LEE CARROLL,
Governor of Maryland.

(108.)

[Duplicate of Document 107.]

(109.)

Soldiers' Home, *Washington, July 21, 1877.*

Governor John Lee Carroll,
  Baltimore, Md.:

The President directs me to say that he will aid you to the extent of his power. Available troops will be sent, but a call upon neighboring States will probably be necessary. Communicate with me here and I will advise you more definitely in a short time.

Geo. W. McCrary,
Secretary of War.

(110.)

[Telegram.]

Soldiers' Home, *July 21—1.55 a. m.*

General Vincent,
  Assistant Adjutant-General, Washington:

You will order any troops now at Fort McHenry to respond to call of governor of Maryland to aid in suppressing riot in Baltimore. Also order any artillery at Fort McHenry, to be used for same purpose, under the governor's orders. Also direct General French to use, in his discretion, for same purpose, any troops under his command not needed in West Virginia.

The President directs that all possible aid be extended the State authorities, and you may use discretion in ordering any force in reach to be sent to the governor.

Geo. W. McCrary,
Secretary of War.

(111.)

[Telegram.]

Soldiers' Home, *July 21—2.40 a. m.*

General Vincent: Without waiting further orders consider yourself authorized to send any troops in reach to aid the State authorities of Maryland in suppressing riot.

Geo. W. McCrary,
Secretary of War.

(112.)

[Telegram.]

July 21—2.36 a. m.

Hon. Secretary of War,
  Soldiers' Home:

Can the marines at the Marine Barracks in this city be ordered?

Vincent,
Assistant Adjutant-General.

(113.)

[Telegram.]

SOLDIERS' HOME, *July 21, 1877—2.44 a. m.*

General VINCENT: The President wishes all available forces sent, if necessary. If marines are needed have Secretary of Navy order them.

GEO. W. McCRARY,
Secretary of War.

_____

(114.)

[Telegram by A. & P. Co., 1.30 p. m.]

HEADQUARTERS OF THE ARMY,
ADJUTANT-GENERAL'S OFFICE,
Washington, July 21, 1877.

General FRENCH,
Commanding, Martinsburg, W. Va.:

Secretary of War directs that you send such portions of your command as you can spare to Cumberland, there to report to Colonel Douglass, of Governor Carroll's staff, to act under orders of governor. Acknowledge receipt and report action, keeping governor of West Virginia advised.

VINCENT,
Assistant Adjutant-General.

_____

(115.)

[Telegram.]

WAR DEPARTMENT, *July 21, 1877 — a. m.*

General BARRY,
Commanding Fort McHenry, Baltimore:

Secretary of War directs that you report to the governor of Maryland with your guns and all available men to aid in quelling riot.

You will act under the governor's orders.

Acknowledge receipt.

VINCENT,
Assistant Adjutant-General.

_____

(116.)

[Telegram.]

CAMDEN STATION, *July 21, 1877.*

Hon. GEO. W. McCRARY:

Order has been restored for the present and I hope we may be able to restrain violence with our military and the police. There is increased lawlessness at Cumberland, and as I will not be able to send a force from here I may be obliged to ask the Government for aid. I will communicate again in the morning. Please convey my thanks to the President for promptly responding to my request.

JOHN LEE CARROLL.

(117.)

[Telegram.]

WAR DEPARTMENT,
ADJUTANT-GENERAL'S OFFICE,
Washington, July 22, 1877—2.50 p. m.

General HANCOCK, U. S. Army,
Barnum's Hotel, Baltimore:

Your dispatch of 12.11 p. m. received. Colonel French, now at Martinsburg, has been instructed to act under your orders. The President thinks he had better be directed to change his headquarters to Cumberland.

Two officers and 50 men have been ordered from Columbus, Ohio, to Allegheny Arsenal, and 2 officers and 50 men from St. Louis Depot to Indianapolis Arsenal. These and all United States troops in the disturbed districts are under your orders. The President leaves it to your discretion whether to transfer any from Martinsburg to Cumberland.

E. D. TOWNSEND,
Adjutant-General.

(118.)

[Telegram.]

WAR DEPARTMENT,
Washington, D. C., July 22, 1877.

General HANCOCK,
Barnum's Hotel, Baltimore:

The President directs that you go to Philadelphia as soon as you can leave Baltimore, taking the battalion of marines with you, and take steps to protect United States property there against mob violence. If you think proper, send the marines in advance of you. After your arrival, telegraph if you need more troops from here. There are 160 army and about 100 marines, but they ought not to be moved if it can be avoided. Some time to-morrow morning there will be about 400 more sailors and marines here. You can halt the troops from the New England forts at Philadelphia, if you think best. The governor of Pennsylvania has not yet made a formal call for troops, but the President wishes to prepare in season for emergencies. The state of things is exceedingly threatening at Philadelphia. You had better see Mr. Scott. Your dispatch about company at Pittsburg just received. If not wanted there, it might be ordered to Indianapolis, at your discretion. The Secretary does not think it advisable to move troops from Detroit, etc.

Please acknowledge receipt.

E. D. TOWNSEND,
Adjutant-General.

(119.)

[Telegram.]

PHILADELPHIA, *July 22, 1877.*

Hon. GEO. W. McCRARY,
Secretary War:

We have been advised to-night from reliable authority of a most serious state of affairs at Buffalo, as between the rioters who are obstructing the Lake Shore road and the Erie Railway and the State and city authorities at that point, which shows a complete state of anarchy; everything being in the hands of the mob; every power of the General Government should be used at once, and there is no doubt that any call you may make for additional troops from the States will arouse the people and be responded to most enthusiastically, and it will be the means of saving the country from further violence to persons and property.

Please acknowledge receipt of message.

W. T. Stokeley,
Mayor, City of Philadelphia

(120.)

[Telegram.]

Sunday Evening, *July 22, 1877*

The Mayor of the City of Philadelphia:

Troops will be immediately placed in Philadelphia under command of General Hancock to meet any emergency, and the President will exert every constitutional power to restore order and protect property.

Geo. W. McCrary,
Secretary of War.

(Sent 11.35 p. m.)

(121.)

[Telegram.]

War Department,
Adjutant-General's Office,
Washington, July 23, 1877.

Major-General Hancock, *Philadelphia:*

The Secretary of War directs me to say the President desires you to understand that you have full authority to move any troops within your division as you may think necessary during these disturbances, only informing this office. All information which may aid you concerning any point within your division will be sent from here, and the President relies on your discretion to do all that is possible within the law to preserve peace.

E. D. Townsend,
Adjutant-General

(122.)

[Telegram.]

Philadelphia, Pa., *July 24, 1877.*
(Received at War Department July 24, 1877.)

Adjutant-General of the Army,
Washington, D. C.:

The Federal troops in Maryland as they reached there were, by direction of the President, ordered to be reported to the governor of the State. No instructions concerning that matter have been received regarding the United States troops arriving in Pennsylvania for like purposes. As the governor is, before long, expected to arrive here, it might be well that I should know by the time of his arrival whether the same course is to be pursued here as in Maryland.

W. S. Hancock,
Major-General, Commanding.

S. Doc. 209——21

(123.)

[Telegram.]

PHILADELPHIA, *July 24, 1877—2.36 p. m.*

Hon. GEO. W. MCCRARY,

 Secretary of War, Washington, D. C.:

I send herewith copies of dispatches received by me this afternoon from commanders of State troops within 20 miles of Philadelphia. My replies are also communicated. These dispatches show on the part of the governor, if truly represented, and of those commanders, a certain misapprehension as to the attitude of the United States troops, especially my own, as commander, but which exhibits an excellent intention and spirit on the part of all concerned, and to which I respectfully invite your attention in connection with the future consideration of the important subject now before us. My dispatches from the War Department plainly indicate to me the attitude of the Government at the present date, and my duties are clearly understood; on the first representation by the State authorities in Maryland and West Virginia of their inability to preserve order, and when the troops were first ordered they were directed to be reported to the governors of the States in which they were placed, subject to the civil authorities thereof. The governor of this State has been far away and is not now probably within its limits, and it may be understood that he is not fully advised of the situation here. These show an uncertainty, however, of the course to be pursued under present circumstances. I am convinced that, in the interest of our institutions, the State authorities should be first required to develop the fact so as to be patent to the world whether they can preserve order within the limits of their States or not, under such circumstances as are now existing, and especially in such a great State as Pennsylvania, and that this question should first be determined before any further action should be taken by the General Government. The legal minds of this country have proclaimed that the civil authorities are supreme under the Constitution and they could not be so unless the Federal troops are always subject to the civil authorities in the same way as other people. I have yielded to that doctrine, although I have been always of the impression that under our system of government, Federal and State, each claiming certain sovereign functions, that by a logical sequence there is a point when if civil authority of the State should prove powerless, it should, for the time being, cease to reign, and the Federal authority assume control.

My impression is that when the State governments declare their inability to suppress domestic insurrection through the ordinary channels and call upon the President of the United States to intervene to their assistance, he should not do it through the civil powers of the States which have already failed, but that it should be done by the intervention of Federal authority by military force and by the President exercising the control. Should the President transfer his troops to the control of the governors of the States who have already acknowledged their inability to preserve order under such circumstances, when would the time arrive when the control of the State authorities should cease and the President assume control through his own officials?

My impression is that when the governor of a State has declared his inability to suppress an insurrection and has called upon the President of the United States under the Constitution to do so, that from that time commences a state not of peace but of war, and that although civil local authority still exists, yet the only outcome is to resort to force through the Federal military authorities, and that can only be through a subordination of the State authorities for the time being and until lawful order is restored; otherwise there can be no complete exercise of power in a military way within the limits of the State by the Federal officers. I only present these views for your personal consideration, and I do not desire them to be urged in connection with the present condition of affairs. It may be unnecessary, but you are at liberty to use them if you deem it best.

W. S. HANCOCK,
Major-General, Commanding.

READING, PA.

Maj. Gen. W. S. HANCOCK,
St. George's Hotel, Philadelphia:
Have just received orders from Governor Hartranft to report to you with Sixteenth Regiment Infantry, National Guard, and two staff officers will leave here this evening with Sixteenth Regiment. Please advise.

W. J. BOLTON.

PHILADELPHIA, *July 24—6.25 p. m.*

Maj. Gen. W. J. BOLTON, *Reading, Pa.:*
Your dispatch received. I have heard nothing of Governor Hartranft on the subject of your reporting to me. My dispatch to you of last night indicates my position in the State at this time. My impression is that the governor supposed that I was in command here. I would advise you to consult with him further before morning. I think he only intended that you should hold yourself in readiness subject to my orders, supposing that I had authority over the State troops. The governor will soon be here, when the matter will be determined, and I advise you to communicate with him further before morning.

HANCOCK,
Major-General.

MALVERN, PA., *July 24.*

Major-General HANCOCK
St. George's Hotel, Philadelphia:
The following order was received at these headquarters:
"To Gen. J. R. Dobson, Tenth Division, National Guard, of Pennsylvania. Report with your command to General Hancock, Philadelphia. J. F. Hartranft."
Pennsylvania Railroad Company have made arrangements for our transportation.

J. R. DOBSON,
Major-General.

PHILADELPHIA.

Gen. J. R. DOBSON, *Malvern, Pa.:*
Your dispatch received. I have heard nothing from Governor Hartranft on the subject of your reporting to me. The order was doubtless given under a misapprehension on the part of the governor as to extent of the authority being exercised by me here. I would advise you to consult with him further before moving your troops.

W. S. HANCOCK,
Major-General, Commanding.

(124.)

[Duplicate of Document 122.]

(125.)

[Telegram.]

WAR DEPARTMENT,
ADJUTANT-GENERAL'S OFFICE,
Washington, July 24, 1877—7.50 p. m.

General HANCOCK,
St. George's Hotel, Philadelphia:

In reply to your inquiry, received 4 p. m., Federal troops in Pennsylvania, the Secretary of War says, are to act under the orders of the governor, as in Maryland and West Virginia.

E. D. TOWNSEND,
Adjutant-General.

(126.)

[Telegram.]

PHILADELPHIA, PA., *July 24, 1877.*

Gen. E. D. TOWNSEND,
Adjutant-General, U. S. Army, Washington, D. C.:

Your dispatch giving decision of Secretary of War that Federal troops in Pennsylvania are to act under orders of the governor is received.

W. S. HANCOCK,
Major-General, Commanding.

(127.)

[Telegram.]

WAR DEPARTMENT,
Washington City, July 25, 1877.

Gen. W. S. HANCOCK,
St. George's Hotel, Philadelphia:

Your telegram of yesterday has been duly considered. It is for the General Government to determine whether it will direct you and the troops under your command to act under the direction of the State which calls for the aid of the United States.

Under existing circumstances the President thinks you should take command of all troops engaged in suppressing domestic violence within the State of Pennsylvania, including both the United States forces and the forces furnished by the State.

GEO. W. MCCRARY,
Secretary of War.

(128.)

[Telegram.]

ST. GEORGE'S HOTEL,
Philadelphia, July 25, 1877.

ADJUTANT-GENERAL OF THE ARMY,
Washington, D. C.:

Reports received from all points to-day within reach of my troops indicate that matters are very quiet. It may be the lull before the storm elsewhere, or that the backbone of the disorders within these limits is broken. I am informed that Governor Hartranft will reach here about 4 p. m. to-day, and I will then report the troops in this State to him in the same manner they were tendered to the governor of Maryland and West Virginia.

HANCOCK,
Major-General.

(129.)

[Telegram.]

PHILADELPHIA, *July 26, 1877—1.30 p. m.*

Hon. SECRETARY OF WAR,
        Washington, D. C.:

I have just given the following instructions to Maj. John Hamilton, First U. S. Artillery, at West Philadelphia depot: You will be placed in command of a detachment of about five hundred men, to go on a special train over the Pennsylvania Railroad from here to Pittsburg, for the purpose of assisting the State authorities in opening the road to traffic and in protection of property. Your troops have been reported to the governor of the State for service in connection with the restoration of order and the preservation of the peace in this State. The same instructions will govern as were given you on the occasion of your taking your command to Reading. A division of State troops, in different bodies, will follow your command closely at certain intervals, and the governor informs Major-General Hancock that he will accompany the command. The hour of starting will be intimated to you; it will probably be about 2 p. m. to-day, if the troops ordered from Washington and Baltimore shall have arrived. The train for your command is now in waiting for you at West Philadelphia depot. The general in command of these State troops is Major-General Beaver, who is known to General Hancock to be a thoroughly reliable soldier and equal to the occasion. You will take ten days' rations and 200 rounds of ammunition per man, and what reserve ammunition Colonel Brannan can give you.

HANCOCK,
Major-General.

————

(130.)

PHILADELPHIA, *July 26, 1877.*

R. B. HAYES,
        President, Washington, D. C.:

I invite your attention to the following telegram, just received. The committee of safety represents the business and capital of the city, and is practically in control there at present:

"Pittsburg, July 26, 1877. To Governor Hartranft, Philadelphia: The unanimous judgment of the committee of safety is, that the peril in which our city stands demands that the President be strenuously urged to place here immediately a prominent army officer of nerve and judgment to take charge of the entire situation in this city and county; and the committee ask your immediate attention in this matter. Wm. G. Johnston, Chairman."

The programme arranged by General Hancock, General Schofield, and myself will be promptly and vigorously carried out.

J. F. HARTRANFT,
Governor of Pennsylvania.

————

(131.)

[Telegram.]

PHILADELPHIA, PA.,
St. George's Hotel, July 26, 1877.

Hon. GEORGE W. McCRARY,
        Washington, D. C.:

Your dispatch of this date received. In view of the action already taken—the United States troops having been placed under the control of the governor, after the proclamations of the President and Governor Hartranft—being ready and willing to proceed in the direction of maintaining the supremacy of the law, and with the promise of success with the Federal assistance, I think he should be permitted to develop that fact, and that the determination of the question you submit to me should now be deferred at least until there has been an absolute failure to accomplish successful results under that system.

HANCOCK,
Major-General, Commanding.

(132.)

[Telegram by Western Union line.]

PHILADELPHIA, *July 27, 1877.*
(Received Washington, 8.55 p. m.)

Hon. GEO. W. McCRARY,
    Secretary of War, Washington, D. C.:

If the great paternal prestige heretofore recognized by all citizens of the Federal Government with the people, the measures that have already been taken with the Federal force at their disposal, together with the change of sentiment among the substantial law-abiding and interested people to preserve order, have had a sufficient influence upon the insurrectionary element, the present troubles will, I think, soon be concluded. Otherwise, I believe the great railroad and other corporations will make such terms with their employees as to restore order promptly. In either case the truce will be a hollow one. The corporations will gain time, believing that time will strengthen the Federal authority before other outbreaks can recur, and believing that if once the Federal authorities are prepared, by legislation or otherwise, to enter into such matters in the future in a powerful way that order will certainly then be maintained, and their points will have been substantially gained, or the opposition elements, feeling themselves unprepared to contest this question further at this moment, in view of their lack of preparation to meet even the present action of the Federal power, will endeavor to gain by time the sympathies of large masses of the people, backed by the prestige of certain successes in the past, and not an entire defeat for the present, and will be confident that by the votes attainable by that sympathy they will be enabled to so influence legislation, State and National, in the direction of their interests, as to finally accomplish their purposes. It will soon be determined whether the State authorities have sufficient strength to preserve order, and I think that fact will be known in this State when Governor Hartranft, with the troops at his disposal, reaches Pittsburg.

Without further legislation I presume the next probable action on the part of the Federal Government, when the States acknowledge themselves powerless, will be to order troops of the militia from other States, and not now in insurrection, for service in insurrectionary States, to subdue the turbulent spirit therein. That would seem to be, considering its past action, the next opportunity for the Federal Government to assume direct control through its own officials if the law was believed to admit of such a course.

Must there not be some process by which the troops of a State in insurrection should be made to bear their just proportion of the burden of service toward the restoration of order therein, when troops of other States are called from their homes for such duty in that State? There can not be two heads for military operations. Under these circumstances it must be that the governor of the State would exercise control of not only the forces of that State but of those called into it from other States, or the Federal military officials, of suitable rank, should command the whole force therein under Federal authority. I think that question can readily be determined at the proper time and by an examination of the law.

But whether all of these troops should be mustered into service of the United States or not, or whether they shall all serve as militia, acting under their own officers in conjunction with Federal troops and under Federal authority, is a matter of law; also in the latter case the United States would have to feed, clothe, and supply them.

I still believe it is necessary that the States should, after an effort, first establish and declare the fact whether they have sufficient vitality to meet such issues before action should be taken by the Federal authority, other than that which has already been taken.

There has been no previous opportunity under our present constitution, within my recollection, of sufficient magnitude to demand a proper investigation of the delicate question arising between Federal and State jurisdiction.

In such connection and as these occasions will probably be repeated, it may now be wisdom to seize the opportunity to declare, in anticipation of the future, what the law is in reference to the great questions which I have discussed in this and a previous dispatch as to the relative attitude of these powers. I present these views in continuation of the subject, as discussed in a former telegram to you, and I only send them now to show you how I look at these matters in the light of existing events.

You are at liberty to make such private or official use of them as you may deem best. It may be stated that it was not intended by the leaders that this outbreak should occur until the month of October, but certain events precipitated matters and the leaders were made to follow.

W. S. HANCOCK,
Major-General.

(133.)

[Telegram.]

INDIANAPOLIS, IND., *July 25, 1877.*

The PRESIDENT OF THE UNITED STATES,
Washington, D. C.:

The situation here is most critical and dangerous. The State authorities are doing nothing and the mob is the only supreme authority in the State at present. They commit no other violence but to interrupt railroads; but they keep together, stop all business, and by suspension of business large numbers of men will soon be out of employment, upon the streets, and swelling the mob there. No organization here able to resist or subdue them, and there is so much sympathy with the strike and so much distrust of the local authorities that I regard it impossible to get up any efficient organization of citizens. The town is full of idle mechanics and laborers. There may be an outbreak at any moment and the consequences will be most disastrous. Can not you order Gen. Jeff. C. Davis here to take command? He is a citizen of the State and has great influence with the State authorities.

W. Q. GRESHAM.

(134.)

INDIANAPOLIS, IND., *July 26.*

The PRESIDENT OF THE UNITED STATES,
Washington, D. C.:

In view of the threatened domestic violence growing out of the railroad strike, I request that authority be at once given to the commandant of the arsenal to render me all the aid possible in preserving the public peace.

JAMES D. WILLIAMS,
Governor of Indiana.

(135.)

WAR DEPARTMENT,
Washington City, July 27, 1877.

Governor JAMES D. WILLIAMS,
Indianapolis, Ind.:

I am directed by the President to say that in the absence of a call upon him under the Constitution and laws for military aid in suppressing domestic violence, the Federal troops at Indianapolis can only be used in protecting property of the United States and enforcing process of Federal courts.

GEO. W. McCRARY,
Secretary of War.

(136.)

[Telegram.]

WAR DEPARTMENT,
Washington, D. C., July 28, 1877.

Gen. W. S. HANCOCK,
St. George's Hotel, Philadelphia:

Dispatches have been received from United States judges and marshals in Indiana asking that troops be furnished to aid the marshal in enforcing process of United States courts. They have been referred to you. The President thinks the troops may, upon the application of the marshal, be employed for this purpose, and I suggest that you so inform the officers in command at Indianapolis and other points where disturbances exist or may occur. Before resorting to other means of compelling obedience, the officer in command of troops should in the name of the United States command the insurgents to disperse and desist from resisting the process of the United States.

GEO. W. McCRARY,
Secretary of War.

(137.)

WAR DEPARTMENT, *July 30, 1877*—6.05 p. m.

Major-General HANCOCK,
St. George's Hotel, Philadelphia:

The Secretary of War has decided that troops can not be furnished the governor of Indiana except on call made in due form upon the President of the United States.

E. D. TOWNSEND,
Adjutant-General.

(138.)

[Telegram.]

PHILADELPHIA, *August 2, 1877*—1.45 p. m.

ADJUTANT-GENERAL OF THE ARMY,
Washington, D. C.:

The following copies of dispatches are furnished for the information of the War Department:

TOLEDO DEPOT, *August 2, 1877*—11.15 a. m.

Major-General HANCOCK, U. S. Army,
Philadelphia, Pa.:

The authorities here request that I stay until evening and render assistance. Shall I proceed to Fort Wayne at once, or remain here for to-day?

OTIS, *Commanding.*

PHILADELPHIA, *August 2, 1877*—12 m.
Lieutenant-Colonel OTIS,
    Toledo, Ohio:
If there is is no riot at Toledo, nor one imminent, go on to Fort Wayne, where you will find orders to proceed to Pittsburg. If there is a riot at Toledo and you are legally summoned as part of a posse comitatus you will have to obey until order is restored. You must judge, but take no part there unless the civil authorities summon you in a legal way in case of disorder. The governor of Ohio has not asked for Federal troops and may not require them. Answer.
    By command of Major-General Hancock:

MITCHELL,
Acting Assistant Adjutant-General.
HANCOCK,
Major-General.

[Document 139 not found.]

(140.)

[Telegram.]

SPRINGFIELD, ILL., *July 24, 1877.*
(Received, Washington, D. C., 8.40 p. m.)
Hon. GEO. W. McCRARY,
    Secretary of War, Washington, D. C.:
Will there be any United States troops in Chicago to-morrow, or soon? Please answer.

S. M. CULLOM,
Governor.

(141.)

[Telegram.]

WAR DEPARTMENT, ADJUTANT-GENERAL'S OFFICE,
Washington, July 24, 1877—9.55 p. m.
GOVERNOR OF ILLINOIS,
    Springfield:
Telegram to Secretary of War received. Six companies Twenty-second Infantry are en route to Chicago. Part will arrive to-morrow or Thursday morning, remainder twenty-four hours later.
    Mayor of Chicago has expressed opinion that presence of troops there will only aggravate existing troubles, but thinks that as the companies of Twenty-second are en route, and that being known, will not matter.

E. D. TOWNSEND,
Adjutant-General.

(142.)

[Telegram.]

SPRINGFIELD, ILL., *July 25, 1877.*
Hon. GEO. W. McCRARY,
    Secretary of War, Washington:
The mayor of Chicago is appealing to me for all the troops that can possibly be sent in at once.

S. M. CULLOM,
Governor.

(143.)

SPRINGFIELD, ILL., *July 25, 1877.*

His Excellency R. B. HAYES, .
   President United States, Washington, D. C.:
   Lawlessness exists in this State to such an extent that I am unable with forces at
my command to quell the same and protect the law-abiding citizens in their rights.
I therefore call upon you for assistance by furnishing military aid without delay.
Can the six companies at Rock Island be forwarded to Chicago at once? Domestic
violence exists in the State.

S. M. CULLOM,
Governor.

(144.)

WAR DEPARTMENT,
Washington, D. C., July 26, 1877.

Col. R. C. DRUM,
   Asssistant Adjutant-General, Chicago, Ill.:
   The President directs that you use the United States troops in case of emergency
in suppressing riot at Chicago, under orders of governor of the State. The orders
you have given for movement of troops are approved. I have ordered Major Flagler
to send you the Gatlings and ammunition. Inform Governor Cullom of this in reply
to his request for them. Acknowledge receipt.

E. D. TOWNSEND,
Adjutant-General.

(145.)

[Telegram.]

HEADQUARTERS MILITARY DIVISION OF THE MISSOURI,
Chicago, Ill., July 26, 1877.

Gen. E. D. TOWNSEND,
   Washington, D. C.:
   Your dispatch received. Agreeably to instructions contained in your dispatch
received last night, I informed the governor of Illinois that the President had
directed me to use the United States troops, in case of emergency, in suppressing riot
in Chicago, under his, the governor's orders. In response the governor asked me to
report to the mayor of Chicago and act in concert with him in putting down mobs
and riots and in keeping the peace and protecting the property of the people.
   Immediately on receipt of this, at the urgent solicitation of the mayor, I ordered
the two companies of the Twenty-second Infantry—then the only national troops in
the city—to report to the mayor, and they were at once placed on duty. At 2 o'clock
p. m. to-day the other four companies of the Twenty-second and six companies of
the Ninth Infantry arrived and were at once placed at the disposal of the mayor. I
have not learned and do not believe that any of the companies of national troops
have been engaged in actual conflict with the mob, but think that thus far they have
been engaged in protecting property. At this hour, 5 o'clock, the troops are in the
quarters provided for them by the Government.

R. C. DRUM,
Assistant Adjutant-General.

(146.)

[Telegram.]

WAR DEPARTMENT,
Washington, D. C., July 27, 1877.

Col. R. C. DRUM,
Chicago, Ill:
  The President directs that the troops under your command are to be used in protecting the property of the United States and in enforcing the process of the courts of the United States. Should a pressing emergency again arise for their use otherwise, you will telegraph for further orders unless circumstances make it impossible. You will make such display of your force for moral effect as you may deem expedient, and will advise me as to situation.

GEO. W. McCRARY,
Secretary of War.

———

(147.)

[Telegram.]

WAR DEPARTMENT,
ADJUTANT-GENERAL'S OFFICE,
Washington, July 30, 1877—8.55 p. m.

Lieut. Gen. P. H. SHERIDAN,
Chicago, Ill.:
  GENERAL: In reply to yours of 4.35 of this date, the President has hoped that a necessity would not arise for him to issue a proclamation to put the troops under the governor. Unless the governor urged this and you deem it necessary, the troops as at present can only be used to protect public property, assist in executing United States civil process, or to display such strength as to serve the moral purpose of keeping the peace.
  Very respectfully, your obedient servant,

E. D. TOWNSEND,
Adjutant-General.

———

(148.)

[Telegram.]

JULY 22, 1877.

Hon. G. W. McCRARY,
Secretary of War, Soldiers' Home:
  We are notified that a general strike will take place to-morrow on the Union Pacific. The wages paid our employees are liberal, far better than on Eastern roads. As the Government has a large interest in the Union Pacific, we think it proper to lay this matter before yourself and the President, and will be happy to adopt any suggestions you may make. What military protection can the Government afford our property against a lawless mob, which, judging from actions at Pittsburg and elsewhere, is likely to follow the strike? Please answer.

SIDNEY DILLON,
President, Union Pacific Railroad.

(149.)

[Telegram.]

HEADQUARTERS DEPARTMENT OF THE PLATTE,
ASSISTANT ADJUTANT-GENERAL'S OFFICE,
Omaha, Nebr., July 24, 1877.

The ADJUTANT-GENERAL, U. S. ARMY,
Washington, D. C.:

In the absence of the department commander, and in view of the condition of affairs along the lines of railroads between this place and Washington, by which communication, both by mail and telegraph, may be interrupted at any moment, I feel it my duty to report, for the information of the honorable Secretary of War, the condition of affairs in this vicinity, and to ask that his instructions may be furnished without delay, relative to the use of the troops, should the emergency occur requiring their use, and I be unable at the-time to communicate with the Headquarters of the Army. As yet there has been no strike among the railroad employees here, owing to the judicious manner in which they have been treated, but disaffection is rife among them, and with the bad element always existing in a frontier town, they are at any moment liable to be incited to strike by designing persons. If a strike occurs at either Omaha or Council Bluffs it will be attended with much destruction of property, including, perhaps, the bridge connecting the two places, and with serious loss of life.

As you are no doubt aware, there is no organized militia in either Nebraska or Wyoming, and if troops should be required, calls will no doubt be made by both governors upon the President for the use of the United States troops. To prevent the sacrifice of life as well as the destruction of property by timely action, if required, I would respectfully ask that such instructions may be given as to the use of the troops in this vicinity as will meet any emergency that may arise. From present indications it seems more than probable that communication will be interrupted, and to this I ask special attention.

I am, very respectfully, your obedient servant,

R. WILLIAMS,
Assistant Adjutant-General.

(150.)

[Telegram.]

WAR DEPARTMENT,
ADJUTANT-GENERAL'S OFFICE,
Washington, July 24, 1877—7.25 p. m.

Asst. Adjt. Gen. R. WILLIAMS,
Omaha, Nebr.:

Yours of this date asking instructions in certain events is received. Troops may be used to protect the property of the United States, and by their presence to promote peace and order. They can not, until a call is made by the State upon the United States and responded to, take part in suppressing insurrection against State law.

E. D. TOWNSEND,
Adjutant-General.

(151.)

WAR DEPARTMENT,
ADJUTANT-GENERAL'S OFFICE,
July 22, 1877.

Maj. JAS. MCMILLAN,
Second Artillery, Commanding Washington Arsenal, District of Columbia.

SIR: The President of the United States places under your command the entire force, consisting of detachments of the Army, Navy, and Marine Corps, to be assembled at Washington Arsenal, and charges you to confer with the civil government and chief of police of the District of Columbia and to take effective measures to prevent any riotous disturbance or unlawful violence within its limits.

I am, sir, very respectfully, your obedient servant,

E. D. TOWNSEND,
Adjutant-General.

(152.)

[Telegram.]

LEAVENWORTH, *July 23, 1877.*

ADJUTANT-GENERAL, U. S. ARMY,
Washington, D. C.:

Your dispatch received. Six companies of Twenty-third Infantry leave for St. Louis in three hours. No violence there yet; the difficulty is in East St. Louis, which is in Illinois. I have ordered Col. Jeff. C. Davis, a prompt and reliable officer, who is commanding the troops going down, to place men on arrival in the old arsenal, present recruiting depot, and to assume command at the post; this is the best place for them until they are to be used, as this recruiting depot is under the control of the Adjutant-General. I ask that my order to Colonel Davis be approved by the Secretary of War. I would wish to know whether these and other troops I can send forthwith are to act under my authority or whether I and they shall only act under the directions and authority of the State civil authorities of Missouri and Illinois, and whether for simple protection of persons and property or to break up blockade of trains. I will, if necessary, go down myself to-morrow, but should like answer to these questions before I leave.

JNO. POPE,
Brevet Major-General, Commanding.

(153.)

[Telegram.]

WAR DEPARTMENT,
Washington, July 24, 1877.

Gen. JOHN POPE,
Fort Leavenworth, Kans.:

Yours of 23d submitted to the Secretary; following his reply: Your order to Colonel Davis approved. The troops go to St. Louis to protect the property of the United States and by their presence promote peace and order. They can not, until a call is made by State upon the United States and responded to, take part in suppressing insurrection against State law. Let Colonel Davis report situation upon his arrival and keep the Department advised through you.

E. D. TOWNSEND,
Adjutant-General.

(154.)

DETROIT, MICH., *July 24, 1877.*

Hon. SECRETARY OF WAR,
        Washington, D. C.:

I am directed by the governor of this State to respectfully request, in view of the very unsettled and threatening condition of affairs in this immediate neighborhood, that the United States troops at Fort Wayne, near this city, may be made subject to his orders, in case of an emergency arising when their services would be absolutely necessary in maintaining peace and enforcing obedience to the laws.

J. M. ROBERTSON,
Adjutant-General, Michigan.

(155.)

WAR DEPARTMENT,
ADJUTANT-GENERAL'S OFFICE,
Washington, July 25, 1877.

GOVERNOR OF MICHIGAN,
        Detroit:

Your telegram to the Secretary of War, by your adjutant-general, received.

The troops of the United States are to protect public property and by presence promote peace and order.

They cannot, until call is made by State upon United States and responded to, take part in suppressing insurrection against State law.

E. D. TOWNSEND,
Adjutant-General.

(156.)

[Telegram.]

MILWAUKEE, WIS., *July 25, 1877.*

The PRESIDENT OF THE UNITED STATES:

There is danger that the labor insurrection may extend to this city. The State has little or no militia that can be relied upon. There are at the Soldiers' Home three hundred (300) old soldiers subject to the rules and articles of war who can be usefully organized and armed for effective guard duty in case of emergency. Can these men be used as a part of the national force or as a part of the State militia?

HARRISON LUDINGTON,
Governor of Wisconsin.

(157.)

WAR DEPARTMENT,
Washington City, August 2, 1877.

Governor HARRISON LUDINGTON,
        Madison, Wis.

SIR: Your dispatch relative to the employment of soldiers in the Soldiers' Home at Milwaukee to aid in suppressing riot was received and duly considered by the President, but before any action was had on the subject the danger apprehended seemed to have passed away. This, and the pressure of public business in this Department, must explain the delay in answering.

I have the honor to be, yours, very respectfully,

GEO. W. McCRARY,
Secretary of War.

(158.)

[Telegram.]

COSMOPOLITAN HOTEL,
San Francisco, July 25, 1877.

R. B. HAYES,
Washington, D. C.:

A riot is apprehended in this city, in which case more force will be required than the local police and State militia can supply. I respectfully request that you direct the United States vessels at Mare Island to take position in the harbor in front of the city and place the forces there, or subject to my call, to be used in quelling a disturbance in case of necessity. Will you also direct the proper officer to issue on my order such arms and ammunition as the emergency may require.

WILLIAM IRVIN,
Governor of State of California.

(159.)

[Telegram.]

WAR DEPARTMENT,
Washington, D. C., July 25, 1877.

His Excellency the GOVERNOR OF CALIFORNIA,
Sacramento, Cal.:

In reply to your request for arms the Secretary of War suggests you call on General McDowell, who has full discretion.

E. D. TOWNSEND,
Adjutant-General.

(160.)

WAR DEPARTMENT,
QUARTERMASTER-GENERAL'S OFFICE,
Washington, D. C., July 24, 1877.

The ADJUTANT-GENERAL, U. S. ARMY.

GENERAL: I hastily replied in pencil to a note from you early this morning in regard to requests for blankets, etc., upon the War Department for use of State militia engaged in putting down the riots attending the present strike of railroad hands.

I notice that one request for blankets is for a regiment of Ohio militia stationed at Columbus. Another is for Major-General Brinton's command of Pennsylvania militia, on duty in Pennsylvania.

There is no law or regulation providing for issue of military stores of the United States to troops not mustered into the service of the United States.

But the President is to see that the laws are faithfully executed, and he is to give the aid of the United States troops, or to call out the militia of any State in which is an insurrection beyond control of State authorities, and, if necessary, he can call on adjoining States for their militia.

In the present case he has issued proclamations to disperse riots in West Virginia, Maryland, and Pennsylvania, but not in Ohio.

It appears to me that the President is the sole judge of what steps he shall take to put down insurrection and domestic violence. That he, if the United States troops alone are not immediately available in sufficient numbers, may make use of the State militia to any extent. He need not muster them into the United States service, when it would become necessary to supply them outright with all that was necessary to efficiency in performing the duties imposed upon them. He may merely aid them to the extent necessary and proper. He is to use such other means as he finds necessary. (Rev. Stat., 5300.)

If they have not sufficient arms he can issue those of the United States. If not sufficient food, he can supply them from the stores or credit of the United States. If not clothing and equipage enough, he may order the Quartermaster's Department to supply such articles as are deficient and necessary from the stores provided for the defense of the United States by the Regular Army.

In fact, the whole matter is within his discretion, and while the property purchased with appropriations specially made by Congress to clothe and equip the Army should not be squandered or loaned or issued to irregular troops not engaged in actual campaign against a public, domestic, or foreign enemy, he may use this, the people's property, to protect the people whenever he deems necessary.

All such issues should be made known to Congress at the next session.

To apply these principles to the requests under consideration:

The proclamation of the President sanctions the action of the governor of Pennsylvania in calling out State troops, and under the call of the governor the United States troops themselves have in small numbers been sent into the field.

The State troops suffering for want of blankets may properly be furnished with such as are absolutely necessary from the stores of the War Department, and when Congress provides, as it will provide, to pay the State the expenses of putting down these riots, swollen to the extent of insurrection, these issues should be charged in the account with the State.

If the governor of Ohio has sent a regiment to protect the arsenal or other military establishment at Columbus denuded of troops by their removal to Pennsylvania or Maryland, then I think, at request of the governor, this regiment may be supplied with blankets in absence of any call for aid from the governor and proclamation from the President. But if the governor has not called upon the President for aid of troops but only in a time of insurrection for the issue of certain military stores, then this, it seems to me. is a call for aid under the Constitution, and I do not see that the President's discretion or his action is limited. He can grant the aid asked if he thinks it necessary, whether it be in the form of United States troops or of arms or of any other military stores which he has available.

All is for the protection of life and property, and all is at his command.

Very respectfully, your obedient servant,

M. C. MEIGS,
Quartermaster-General, U. S. Army.

LAWLESSNESS IN NEW MEXICO.

(161.)

[Telegram.]

HEADQUARTERS DEPARTMENT OF THE MISSOURI,
Fort Leavenworth, Kans., February 25, 1878.

ADJUTANT-GENERAL, U. S. ARMY,
Washington, D. C.:

Commanding officer, district of New Mexico, telegraphs that governor of Territory has applied to him officially for assistance of United States troops to enforce the laws in Lincoln County.

Have replied that troops can only be furnished for purpose indicated on the orders of the President, based on application made to him by the governor.

JOHN POPE,
Brevet Major-General, Commanding.

Official copy. Original sent by telegraph.

JNO. POPE,
Brevet Major-General, U. S. Army, Commanding.

(162.)

[Telegram.]

SANTA FE, N. MEX., *March 4, 1878.*

The PRESIDENT OF UNITED STATES,
    Washington, D. C.:

"Fort Stanton, N. Mex., February 28, 1878. Thomas B. Catron, esq., United States Attorney, Santa Fe, N. Mex. Dear Sir: A. A. McSween, Weideman, and others, have collected a well-armed mob of about 50 men, and are still getting more to join them. They defy the law. They threaten the lives and property of our best citizens. The good and law-abiding citizens, although far in majority, are not able to compete with them for want of arms. I can not serve any legal document or carry out the law if I am not assisted by the military. Please see his excellency the governor and ask him to obtain an order from General Hatch to the post commander of Fort Stanton to protect me in the discharge of my official duties. I am, sir, very respectfully, your obedient servant, Wm. Brady, sheriff Lincoln County."

"United States Attorney's Office, Santa Fe, N. Mex., March 3, 1878. Respectfully referred to His Excellency Governor Axtell. T. B. Catron, United States attorney." "I know the sheriff and believe his dispatch to be true. One man, an Englishman by the name of Truesdell, has been killed. I start in the morning for the scene of action. It will take me four days to go there. I hope orders may be given to General Hatch to render me such assistance as will enable me to keep the peace and protect life and property. S. B. Axtell, Governor of New Mexico."

Respectfully referred to General Sherman for proper orders. The military can be ordered to support the civil Territorial authorities in maintaining order and enforcing legal process.

GEO. W. McCRARY,
Secretary of War.

MARCH 5, 1878.

(163.)

[Telegram.]

HEADQUARTERS ARMY OF THE UNITED STATES,
    Washington, D. C., March 5, 1878.

Gen. P. H. SHERIDAN,
    Commanding Division, Chicago, Ill.:

The governor of New Mexico, Axtell, telegraphs the President that certain men at and near Fort Stanton have collected a well-armed mob of about 50 men who defy the law, threaten the lives of the best citizens, and resist the authority of the sheriff, Brady. The Secretary of War decides that the military authorities of the United States must support the civil Territorial authorities in maintaining order and in enforcing legal process. Please so order by telegraph, and if there be not sufficient force at Fort Stanton cause it to be reenforced so that prompt and decisive action may be taken.

W. T. SHERMAN,
General.

Copy to Secretary of War.

S. Doc. 209——22

(164.)

BUREAU OF MILITARY JUSTICE, WAR DEPARTMENT,
June 8, 1878.

Hon. GEO. W. McCRARY,
Secretary of War.

SIR: In response to your within indorsement of the 3d instant, requiring my opinion upon the question whether there has been any violation of law in the use of United States troops in Lincoln County, N. Mex., as set forth in the reports, herewith returned, of Lieut. Col. N. A. M. Dudley, Ninth Cavalry, commanding at Fort Stanton, N. Mex., of May 4 and 11 last, I have the honor to submit as follows:

In a report to the Secretary of War of March 1 last, in regard to the use of troops in Texas, I had the honor to express an opinion to the following effect:

"That a sheriff or other State official has no such authority as that possessed by a United States marshal to call upon United States troops as such to serve upon a posse, and that United States troops, on the other hand, while required to comply with the call of a marshal to assist him to execute the laws of the United States, can not legally serve on the posse comitatus of a sheriff or other State official. The Army is an instrument to assist the Executive of the United States to enforce the laws of the United States, and can not be employed to aid in executing the laws of a State or process of a State court except in the special case when ordered by the President to render such service under and by virtue of section 4, Article IV of the Constitution."

In my judgment the law as thus stated applies equally to the use of troops in a Territory as in a State.

In a Territory the sheriff is a local officer whose duty it is to execute process issued under the local law, i. e., the laws enacted by the Territorial legislature for purposes of internal government. He is vested with no authority to execute process in the name of the United States, the only officer whom I can find to be so authorized being the marshal of the United States for the Territory. Section 11 of the act of September 9, 1850, to establish the Territorial government of New Mexico (and see Rev. Stat., sec. 1876), provides for the appointment by the President of a marshal, who is required to "execute all process issuing from" the district courts of the Territory, "when exercising their jurisdiction as circuit and district courts of the United States;" that is to say (to cite from sec. 10 of the same act, establishing these courts), jurisdiction "in cases arising under the Constitution and laws of the United States."

As to the governor, while it appears that he made an application to the President for military aid, this application, which was of an informal character, was not accompanied by any statement that the legislature could not be convened—the contingency contemplated by the Constitution upon which only the application of a governor may be acceded to—nor does it elsewhere appear that such contingency existed. But even if it did the application would not have been within the constitutional provision, since the same provides for the protection from "domestic violence" only of "States in the Union," not Territories.

I may add that I do not find anything in the provisions in regard to the office and powers of the governor contained in the act of 1850 above cited (or the Revised Statutes) from which any general authority to require from the President a military force to assist in executing the local law can in my judgment be implied. He is indeed appointed by the President, and by section 3 of the act indicated (and see Rev. Stat., sec. 1841) is vested with "the executive power and authority in and over said Territory," but this is shown by the other provision of the section and of the act to mean power to execute the laws passed by the legislature created by the same act, his authority being thus local, not Federal.

"The theory," says Chief Justice Chase in Clinton *v.* Englebrecht (13 Wallace,

441), "upon which the various governments for portions of the territory of the United States have been organized has ever been that of leaving to the inhabitants all the powers of self-government consistent with the supremacy and supervision of national authority."

I can but arrive, therefore, at the conclusion that the furnishing of troops to aid the Territorial sheriff to serve warrants, guard prisoners, etc., in this case was without authority of law, as was also the furnishing of the same for any purpose at the demand of the district judge.

It would seem, indeed, that the governor of a Territory was in a position properly to be authorized, with even more reason than the governor of a State, to call upon the President for assistance such as was asked for in this instance. But, as it is observed by Attorney-General Cushing (VII Opin., 574), "it is remarkable how silent the Constitution is on the subject of a Territory, so called—that is, an organized government within the Union, but not of it." And in view of this silence and of the fact that Congress in the exercise of the " supremacy and supervision " referred to by the Chief Justice and vested in it by paragraph 2, section 3, Article IV of the Constitution has omitted to make any enactment authorizing the Executive to interpose for the enforcement of the local laws of a Territory, I can not believe that it would be safe to sanction the uses made of the United States troops, as stated in the report of Colonel Dudley, except in so far as they may have been employed at the call of the marshal or his deputy.

W. M. DUNN,

Judge-Advocate-General.

CHINESE OUTRAGES.

(165.)

[Telegram.]

WAR DEPARTMENT,

ADJUTANT-GENERAL'S OFFICE,

Washington, September 7, 1885.

Gen. JNO. M. SCHOFIELD,

Chicago, Ill.:

In reply to your dispatch of to-day I am instructed to say that by the third article of our treaty with China this Government has agreed to exert all its power to devise means to protect Chinese laborers from ill treatment at the hands of any other persons. In view of this treaty stipulation and of the representation of the governor of Wyoming that the civil powers of that Territory are unable to protect lives and property and preserve the peace in certain localities therein, the President directs that you send to the points where violence exists or is threatened a suitable military force. If necessity actually exists for the employment of this force in protecting life and property and aiding the civil authorities in preserving the peace and in the arrest of those committing offenses against the laws, you are authorized to use it for these purposes, but care should be taken that the military force is not needlessly employed.

The President desires that the commander of each detachment communicate directly with you and receive instructions directly from you, to make sure that the force is not unnecessarily used, and that you keep the Department frequently informed of the condition of affairs at each of the disturbed localities.

Please acknowledge receipt.

R. C. DRUM,

Adjutant-General.

(166.)

CHICAGO, ILL., *September 8, 1885.*

The GOVERNOR OF WYOMING TERRITORY,
          Rock Springs, Wyo.:

I am authorized by the President to use the United States troops, in case of actual necessity, to protect the lives and property of Chinese laborers in Wyoming and to aid the civil authorities in preserving the peace and arresting offenders against the law.

I have given the necessary orders for the action of the troops in any case of threatened attack which the civil authorities are not able to prevent.

Any further action which may be desired can be taken only upon express orders from me in each case, based upon an accurate report of the facts showing the necessity for such action. I have, therefore, to request that you will confer freely with the commanding officers of the several detachments of troops, inform them fully of the facts in each case, and show them the necessity for the action requested, so that they may report fully to me.

I hope that this authority from the President and the presence of troops ready to enforce it will suffice to prevent further violence in the Territory.

                                        J. M. SCHOFIELD,
                                        Major-General Commanding.

(167.)

[Telegram.]

EVANSTON, WYO., *September 9, 1885.*

R. C. DRUM,
          Adjutant-General, Washington, D. C.:

I have the honor to acknowledge receipt of your dispatch of yesterday; also one from Major-General Schofield. Please do me the favor to convey to the President my grateful thanks for prompt assistance rendered the Territory in protecting Chinese laborers. Chinamen who took refuge in Evanston when driven from Rock Springs are now aboard cars returning to Rock Springs under guard of civil authorities, followed by train transporting troops. In my judgment the presence of troops, with existing orders, will avert further violence and enable civil forces to overcome disorder.

                                        FRANCIS E. WARREN,
                                        Governor of Wyoming.

(168.)

[Telegram from Secretary of State to governor of Washington Territory.]

DEPARTMENT OF STATE,
          Washington, October 20, 1885.

The GOVERNOR OF WASHINGTON TERRITORY, *Olympia*:

Chinese minister represents the urgent necessity for measures of protection of Chinese at Seattle, and every power of law should be lent to secure them from assault.

                                        T. F. BAYARD.

(169.)

[Telegram from governor of Washington Territory to Secretary of State.]

OLYMPIA, WASH. TER., *October 21, 1885.*

T. F. BAYARD,

Secretary of State, Washington, D. C.:

My letter of October 12 to Secretary of Interior explains situation and organization at Seattle. Sheriff of county reports he is able to protect lives and property of all persons in county, and that in case disturbance nineteen-twentieths of the able-bodied men can be depended upon as a posse comitatus. I am taking every lawful precaution to preserve order, and will issue a proclamation, if deemed advisable, warning all persons against assaulting Chinese.

WATSON C. SQUIRE,
Governor.

(170.)

[Filed under November 4, 1885.]

PROCLAMATION BY THE GOVERNOR.

WASHINGTON TERRITORY,
EXECUTIVE OFFICE, OLYMPIA.

Whereas, it has recently appeared by published statements and various other evidences, commonly understood in certain counties bordering on Puget Sound, that certain persons have concerted together and determined to cause the removal of all Chinese residents from such counties in Washington Territory;

And whereas, all acts of violence and intimidation against Chinese residents are plainly against the laws of Washington Territory and the laws and treaty of the United States;

And whereas, it is represented by the sheriff of Pierce County and by the Chinese residents of the city of Tacoma, in said county, that said Chinese residents have been forcibly removed beyond the limits of said city;

And whereas, the mayor of the city of Seattle now represents the immediate danger of disturbances of the peace in that city on account of the present anti-Chinese agitation;

And whereas, the United States Government has, by the Secretary of the Department of State, instructed the executive of the Territory that every power of law should be lent to secure the Chinese from assault;

And whereas, the good name and prosperity of the Territory depend upon the preservation of peace and good order therein by the duly constituted civil authorities;

Now, therefore, I, Watson C. Squire, governor of the Territory of Washington, hereby warn all persons against participating in any riot or breach of the peace; and at this time I especially warn all persons against inciting others to riot or a breach of the peace, in that they will be held responsible for such acts under the penalties of the law.

And I call upon the sheriffs of the respective counties and other officers who are charged by law with the duty of keeping the peace therein, to secure all Chinese residents from assault, and I call upon all good citizens to assist them in so doing.

Fellow citizens, I appeal to you. Array yourselves on the side of the law! This is the time in the history of the Territory for an intelligent, law-abiding, and prosperous community, who love their country and their homes, who are blessed with boundless resources of forest, field, and mine, and who aspire to soon become a great self-governing State, to assert their power of self-control and self-preservation as against a spirit of lawlessness, which is destructive alike to immigration, to labor, and to capital.

If you do not protect yourselves you have only to look to the step beyond, which is simply the fate of Wyoming and the speedy interference of United States troops.

In testimony whereof, I have hereunto set my hand and caused the great seal of the Territory to be affixed at Olympia, this 4th day of November, A. D. 1885.

WATSON C. SQUIRE,
Governor.

By the governor:
    N. H. OWINGS,
        Secretary of Washington Territory.

(171.)

[Telegram.]

SEATTLE, WASH. TER., *February 8, 1886.*

Hon. WILLIAM M. EVARTS,
    Washington, D. C.:

This city is in armed insurrection. The governor, on my advice, has proclaimed martial law. Blood has been shed. The loyal citizens willing to stake their lives for law appear to be comparatively few. They can not stand the strain on them forever. The President has been telegraphed for troops. No word comes from him as yet. We had hoped United States troops would be here by nightfall. See him and hurry his order if possible.

ROGER S. GREENE.

(172.)

[Telegram.]

SEATTLE, WASH. TER., *February 9, 1886.*

Hon. GEORGE F. HOAR,
    United States Senate, Washington, D. C.:

The situation here is full of peril. There has been actual bloodshed, and the lawless and turbulent elements of the surrounding country are furious at the firm stand of the law-abiding people of this country and are moving in this direction. Great popular excitement here and throughout Puget Sound. Nothing short of prompt dispatch of troops can prevent fearful sacrifice of life and property. I greatly fear for the consequences of any delay. Wire communication with Seattle is liable to be cut any time. This is a national matter and United States troops should bear the brunt.

ROGER S. GREENE,
Chief Justice.

(173.)

PROCLAMATION.

To the people of Washington Territory:

Whereas, it is represented to me by the mayor of the city of Seattle as follows:

"Hon. W. C. Squire. Sir: The Chinese residents of this city of Seattle are being unlawfully removed from the city by a mob unlawfully gathered together; the authority of the city is not sufficient to keep the peace or preserve order; I appeal to you for aid and assistance. Henry L. Yesler, mayor."

Now, therefore, I, Watson C. Squire, governor of Washington Territory, do hereby publish this, my proclamation, warning all persons to desist from breach of the peace, and that peaceably disposed persons shall retire to their homes, except such persons as are disposed to assist the sheriff and the duly constituted civil authorities in maintaining law and order. And I request all persons who are disposed to assist in maintaining order to enroll themselves under the sheriff immediately for that purpose. Furthermore, I order the military companies of this city to immediately place themselves under arms, and that the commanding officers of such companies report forthwith to the sheriff of King County for the purpose of rendering him military assistance if need be in maintaining the law.

Done at Seattle, this 7th day of February, A. D. 1886.

WATSON C. SQUIRE,
Governor.

(174.)

PROCLAMATION OF MARTIAL LAW.

Whereas, heretofore, on the 7th day of February, in consequence of an inflamed condition of the public mind in the city of Seattle and grave disturbance of the public peace therein, I, Watson C. Squire, governor of the Territory of Washington, issued my proclamation warning all persons to desist from breaches of the peace and peaceably to return to their homes, except such as were disposed to assist the sheriff and the other duly constituted authorities in maintaining law and order, and requesting all persons who were disposed to assist in maintaining order to enroll themselves under the sheriff immediately for that purpose; and

Whereas, said proclamation has proven ineffectual to quiet the public mind and preserve the peace; and

Whereas, numerous breaches of the peace have occurred and more are threatened; and

Whereas, an insurrection exists in said city of Seattle by which the lives, liberties, and property of citizens of the Territory and sojourners within the Territory are endangered; and

Whereas, the civil authorities have proved powerless to suppress said insurrection or prevent such breaches of the peace; and

Whereas, the necessity for martial law within said city exists, and it is deemed proper that all needful measures should be taken for the protection of such citizens and sojourners and of all officers of the United States and of the Territory in the discharge of their public duties within said city:

Now, therefore, be it known that I, Watson C. Squire, as governor of said Territory, and commander in chief of the military forces thereof, do hereby assume military command of said city of Seattle, and do hereby order that no person exercise any office or authority in said city which may be inconsistent with the laws and Constitution of the United States or the laws of said Territory; and I do hereby suspend the writ of habeas corpus and declare martial law within said city.

Done at the city of Seattle, Territory of Washington, this 8th day of February, A. D. 1886.

Witness my hand and the seal of the Territory.

[SEAL.]

WATSON C. SQUIRE,
Governor.

(175.)

[Telegram.]

ADJUTANT-GENERAL'S OFFICE,
Washington, February 16, 1886.

Gen. JOHN GIBBON, *Seattle, Wash. Ter.:*

The remark in a telegram from the governor of Washington Territory to the Secretary of War that "arrests of leaders being made by General Gibbon" creates the impression that you have not clearly comprehended the purpose for which the troops were sent to Seattle. It was not intended that the troops should be used as a posse to do those things which the local magistracy are, so far as the authorities here are informed, capable of performing, but to preserve the peace, give security to life and property, and prevent obstruction to the enforcement of the laws. If the condition of affairs at Seattle or elsewhere in the Territory was such that the functions of the judiciary were virtually suspended by acts of violence and that the ordinary process could not issue, a report of the facts as they existed should have been made, when orders suitable to the condition of affairs would, if deemed necessary, have been issued.

Please inform the War Department fully of the present condition of affairs and how long the troops will probably·be required at Seattle.

R. C. DRUM,
Adjutant-General.

———

(176.)

[Telegram.]

SANTA FE, N. MEX., *January 14, 1886.*

The PRESIDENT, *Washington, D. C.:*

Please telegraph military commandant here to furnish troops on my request to suppress anti-Chinese riot when in his judgment necessary. Full advice by mail.

E. G. ROSS,
Governor.

———

(177.)

EXECUTIVE OFFICE, TERRITORY OF NEW MEXICO,
Santa Fe, N. Mex., January 14, 1886.

. on. GROVER CLEVELAND, *President.*

SIR: I have the honor to state that at two points in this Territory (Silver City and Raton) there is a high condition of public excitement against Chinese residents. At the latter place especially several hundred coal miners and others have united in a Knights of Labor organization, and there is imminent danger of violence. I have admonished the sheriffs to be vigilant, and am hopeful that they may be able to prevent an outbreak. It may become important that I should have authority to call on the troops to prevent bloodshed, and on the advice of Gen. L. P. Bradley, commanding here, have to-day telegraphed you for that authority. I shall of course not attempt the use of troops until every other resource for preserving the peace shall have failed.

Very respectfully, your obedient servant,

EDMUND G. ROSS,
Governor.

(178.)

WASHINGTON, D. C., *January 16, 1886.*

Hon. EDMUND G. ROSS,
  Governor, etc., Santa Fe, N. Mex.:

In reply to your telegram of the 14th, at the request of the President I would call your attention to sections 5297, 5298, 5299, 5300 of the Revised Statutes of the United States, which declare under what circumstances and in what manner troops are to be called out for the purpose of suppressing domestic violence. The President can not order out troops except in accordance with these provisions and section 4 of article IV of the Constitution of the United States.

WM. C. ENDICOTT,
  Secretary of War.

MINING RIOTS IN IDAHO.

(180.)

[Telegram.]

WAR DEPARTMENT,
  Washington, D. C., July 12, 1892.

Hon. NORMAN B. WILLEY,
  Governor of Idaho, Boise City, Idaho:

In response to your call and by order of the President orders have been telegraphed to Fort Sherman, Idaho, and Fort Missoula, Mont., to send troops to the scene of disturbance in northern Idaho to assist the civil authorities in preserving the peace and protecting life and property.

Please communicate directly to commanding officers of Fort Sherman and Fort Missoula all information necessary for their guidance; also communicate with Brigadier-General Ruger, San Francisco, Cal., who is in command of that department, and who will give all necessary orders for your support.

J. M. SCHOFIELD,
  Major-General Commanding and Acting Secretary of War.

(181.)

[Telegram.]

HEADQUARTERS OF THE ARMY,
  Washington, D. C. July 12, 1892.

The COMMANDING GENERAL, DEPARTMENT OF THE COLUMBIA,
  San Francisco, Cal.:

Please send immediately to the scene of disturbance in northern Idaho—Wardner is indicated as the center of the disturbance—all the infantry that can be spared from Fort Sherman. Send a discreet officer of rank in command, with orders to report to the governor of the State and to support the civil authorities in preserving peace and preventing the destruction of property and life. Three companies of infantry from Missoula will also be ordered to move by rail to the same point to assist the troops from Sherman if necessary, and with orders to report to the commanding officer of the latter force. If you find upon inquiry or experience additional troops are necessary, send them without delay from the nearest garrison or call upon me for additional troops from the Department of Dakota, if they are more convenient. Direct the commanding officer to give me full information by telegraph, as well as to communicate the same information to you. Report receipt and execution of this order.

By command of the President:

J. M. SCHOFIELD,
  Major-General Commanding and Acting Secretary of War.

(182.)

[Telegram.]

HEADQUARTERS OF THE ARMY,
Washington, D. C., July 12, 1892.

The COMMANDING GENERAL, DEPARTMENT OF DAKOTA,
St. Paul, Minn.:

Send three companies of infantry from Missoula by rail direct to the scene of disturbance in northern Idaho, with directions to report to the commanding officer of troops sent from Fort Sherman for like purpose, and with orders to assist the civil authorities in suppressing the existing disorder, preserving the peace, and protecting property and life. This by order of the President upon the call of the governor of Idaho. Report receipt and execution of this order. Direct the commanding officer to report to you frequently everything important, which you will transmit to me.

J. M. SCHOFIELD,
Major-General Commanding and Acting Secretary of War.

(183.)

[Telegram.]

BOISE CITY, IDAHO, *July 22, 1892.*

The SECRETARY OF WAR, *Washington, D. C.:*

Can I depend upon the continuance of the Federal troops now in the Cœur d'Alenes for a considerable period? The State troops were hastily assembled and can not remain longer away from business without very great difficulty. The presence of troops will be necessary for a considerable time. Nothing but their presence restrains the vicious and turbulent.

N. B. WILLEY,
Governor.

(184.)

[Telegram.]

WAR DEPARTMENT,
Washington, D. C., July 23, 1892.

Hon. N. B. WILLEY,
Governor of Idaho, Boise City, Idaho:

Replying to your message of the 22d, would say that the troops were placed at your disposal only temporarily and upon your statement that you were powerless to execute the laws and suppress disorder. The President does not desire that the troops shall remain under your orders longer than absolutely necessary to assist you to restore peace and order. He can not say how long they should remain, but hopes you can, through the militia and civil power, soon relieve the situation, so the troops can be withdrawn.

S. B. ELKINS,
Secretary of War.

RAILROAD STRIKE, 1894.

(185.)

[Telegram.]

INDIANAPOLIS, IND., *July 8, 1894.*

Hon. RICHARD OLNEY,
   Attorney-General, Washington, D. C.:
   Our information is that a mob is in possession of the city of Hammond, Ind., a suburb of Chicago. As rioters driven from Chicago are massing at this point, the lives of deputy marshals protecting the mail trains and serving process are in danger. All railroads from Chicago east pass through Lake County. Governor Matthews is in conference with us and will send available militia to Lake County. He asks the cooperation of Federal troops in protecting the mail trains and Federal officers. In that request we earnestly join, believing the necessity exists.

JOHN H. BAKER,
United States District Judge.
W. H. HAWKINS,
United States Marshal.
BURKE,
United States Attorney.

(186.)

[Telegram.]

DEPARTMENT OF JUSTICE,
Washington, D. C., July 8, 1894.

BURKE, *United States Attorney, Indianapolis, Ind.:*
   Have joint dispatch of yourself, judge, and marshal. Suggest to governor that use of Federal troops would be much more effective if he called upon the President for protection against domestic violence under Article IV, section 4, of the Constitution of the United States.

OLNEY,
Attorney-General.

(187.)

[Telegram.]

INDIANAPOLIS, IND., *July 8, 1894.*

Hon. GROVER CLEVELAND,
   President United States:
   Since Judge Baker and Marshal Hawkins wired Attorney-General situation at Hammond grows more alarming. Mail trains are held and all traffic stopped. The place in control of mob. Overrun by desperate characters from Chicago. Available State troops on way. Other points in State in threatening and dangerous condition. Will soon have entire force of State ordered out. It is absolutely necessary that at least three companies of United States troops be ordered to that point without delay. Will use every means at my command and cooperate with Government troops.

CLAUDE MATTHEWS,
Governor.

(188.)

[Telegram.]

WASHINGTON, D. C., *July 8, 1894.*

Hon. CLAUDE MATTHEWS,
        Governor, Indianapolis, Ind.:

Your telegram of this date, addressed to the President, has been referred to Major-General Miles, commanding Department of the Missouri, headquarters at Chicago, who has full authority to act in the premises. Please communicate with him at that place.

DANIEL S. LAMONT,
Secretary of War.

―――――

(189.)

[Telegram.]

HEADQUARTERS OF THE ARMY,
Washington, D. C., July 8, 1894.

Major-General MILES,
        Headquarters of the Army, Chicago, Ill.:

The President is informed by Governor Matthews, of Indiana, that the situation at Hammond, in that State, makes it absolutely necessary that at least three companies of Regular troops be ordered to that point at once. This being in the immediate vicinity of Chicago, your previous instructions are sufficient to authorize you to respond.

J. M. SCHOFIELD,
Major-General, Commanding.

―――――

(190.)

[Governor Altgeld's protest against the use of United States troops in Illinois.]

EXECUTIVE OFFICE,
State of Illinois, July 5 [1894].

Hon. GROVER CLEVELAND,
        President of the United States, Washington, D. C.

DEAR SIR: I am advised that you have ordered Federal troops to go into service in the State of Illinois. Surely the facts have not been correctly presented to you in this case, or you would not have taken this step, for it is entirely unnecessary, and, it seems to me, unjustifiable. Waiving all questions of courtesy, I will say that the State of Illinois is not only able to take care of itself, but it stands ready to-day to furnish the Federal Government any assistance it may need elsewhere.

Our military force is ample, and consists of as good soldiers as can be found in the country. They have been ordered out promptly whenever and wherever they were needed. We have stationed in Chicago alone three regiments of infantry, one battery, and one troop of cavalry, and no better soldiers can be found. They have been ready every moment to go, and have been and are now eager to go into service. But they have not been ordered out, because nobody in Cook County, whether official or private citizen, asked to have their assistance, or even intimated in any way that their assistance was desired or necessary.

So far as I have been advised the local officials have been able to handle the situation. But if any assistance were needed, the State stood ready to furnish one hundred men for every man required, and stood ready to do so at a moment's notice. Notwithstanding these facts, the Federal Government has been applied to by men who had political and selfish motives for wanting to ignore the State government. We have just gone through a long coal strike, more extensive here than in any other State, because our soft-coal field is larger than that of any other State; we have not had ten days of the railroad strike, and we have promptly furnished military aid wherever the local officials needed it.

In two instances the United States marshal for the southern district of Illinois applied for assistance to enable him to enforce the processes of the United States court, and troops were promptly furnished him and he was assisted in every way he desired. The law has been thoroughly executed, and every man guilty of violating it during the strike has been brought to justice. If the marshal for the northern district of Illinois or the authorities of Cook County needed military assistance, they had but to ask for it in order to get it from the State.

At present some of our railroads are paralyzed, not by reason of obstructions, but because they can not get men to operate their trains. For some reason they are anxious to keep this fact from the public, and for this purpose are making an outcry about obstructions in order to divert attention.

I will cite you two examples which illustrate the situation. Some days ago I was advised that the business of one of our railroads was obstructed at two railway centers—that there was a condition bordering on anarchy there, and I was asked to furnish protection so as to enable the employees of the road to operate the trains. Troops were promptly ordered to both points. Then it transpired that the company had not sufficient men on its line to operate one train. All the old hands were orderly but refused to go. The company had large shops in which worked a number of men who did not belong to the railway union, and who could run an engine. They were appealed to to run the train, but flatly refused. We were obliged to hunt up soldiers who could run an engine and operate a train.

Again, two days ago, appeals which were almost frantic came from officials of another road, stating that at an important point on their lines trains were forcibly obstructed, and that there was a reign of anarchy at that place, and that they asked for protection so that they could move their trains. Troops were put on the ground in a few hours' time, when the officer in command telegraphed me that there was no trouble and had been none at that point, but that the road seemed to have no men to run trains; and the sheriff telegraphed me that he did not need troops, but would himself move every train if the company would only furnish an engineer. The result was that the troops were there over twelve hours before a single train was moved, although there was no attempt at interference by anybody. It is true that in several instances a road made efforts to work a few green men, and a crowd standing around insulted them and tried to drive them off, and in a few instances they cut off Pullman sleepers from the train. But all these troubles were local in character and could easily be handled by the State authorities. Illinois has more railroad men than any State in the Union, but as a rule they are orderly and well behaved.

This is shown by the fact that so very little actual violence has been committed. Only a very small per cent of these men has been guilty of any infraction of the law. The newspaper accounts have in some cases been pure fabrications, and in others wild exaggeration.

I have gone thus into details to show that it is not soldiers that the railroads need so much as it is men to operate trains, and that the conditions do not exist here which bring the case within the Federal statute, a statute that was passed in 1861, and was in reality a war measure. This statute authorized the use of Federal troops in a State whenever it shall be impracticable to enforce the laws of the United States within such State by the ordinary judicial proceedings. Such a condition does not exist in Illinois. There have been a few local disturbances, but nothing that seriously interfered with the administration of justice, or that could not be easily controlled by the local or State authorities, for the Federal troops can do nothing that the State troops can not do.

I repeat that you have been imposed upon in this matter, but even if by a forced construction it were held that the conditions here came within the letter of the statute, then I submit that local self-government is a fundamental principle of our Constitution. Each community shall govern itself so long as it can and is ready and able to enforce the law, and it is in harmony with this fundamental principle that the statute authorizing the President to send troops into States must be construed. Especially is this so in matters relating to the exercise of the police power and the preservation of law and order.

To absolutely ignore a local government in matters of this kind, when the local government is ready to furnish any assistance needed, and is amply able to enforce the law, not only insults the people of the State by imputing to them an inability to govern themselves or unwillingness to enforce the law, but is in violation of a basic principle of our institutions. The question of Federal supremacy is in no way involved. No one disputes it for a moment, but, under our Constitution, Federal supremacy and local self-government must go hand in hand, and to ignore the latter is to do violence to the Constitution.

As governor of the State of Illinois, I protest against this, and ask the immediate withdrawal of the Federal troops from active duty in this State. Should the situation at any time get so serious that we can not control it with the State forces, we will promptly and freely ask for Federal assistance, but until such time I protest with all due deference against this uncalled-for reflection upon our people, and again ask the immediate withdrawal of these troops.

I have the honor to be, yours, respectfully,

JOHN P. ALTGELD,
Governor of Illinois.

(191.)

AN ACT To promote the efficiency of the militia, and for other purposes.

Be it enacted by the Senate and House of Representatives of the United States of America in Congress assembled, That the militia shall consist of every able-bodied male citizen of the respective States, Territories, and the District of Columbia, and every able-bodied male of foreign birth who has declared his intention to become a citizen, who is more than eighteen and less than forty-five years of age, and shall be divided into two classes—the organized militia, to be known as the National Guard of the State, Territory, or District of Columbia, or by such other designations as may be given them by the laws of the respective States or Territories, and the remainder to be known as the reserve militia.

SEC. 2. That the Vice-President of the United States, the officers, judicial and executive, of the Government of the United States, the members and officers of each House of Congress, persons in the military or naval service of the United States, all custom-house officers, with their clerks, postmasters, and persons employed by the United States in the transmission of the mail, ferrymen employed at any ferry on a post-road, artificers and workmen employed in the armories and arsenals of the United States, pilots, mariners actually employed in the sea service of any citizen or merchant within the United States, and all persons who are exempted by the laws of the respective States or Territories shall be exempted from militia duty, without regard to age: *Provided,* That nothing in this act shall be construed to require or compel any member of any well-recognized religious sect or organization at present organized and existing whose creed forbids its members to participate in war in any form, and whose religious convictions are against war or participation therein, in accordance with the creed of said religious organization, to serve in the militia or any other armed or volunteer force under the jurisdiction and authority of the United States.

SEC. 3. That the regularly enlisted, organized, and uniformed active militia in the several States and Territories and the District of Columbia who have heretofore participated or shall hereafter participate in the apportionment of the annual appropriation provided by section sixteen hundred and sixty-one of the Revised Statutes of the United States, as amended, whether known and designated as National Guard, militia, or otherwise, shall constitute the organized militia. The organization, armament, and discipline of the organized militia in the several States and Territories and in the District of Columbia shall be the same as that which is now or may hereafter be prescribed for the regular and volunteer armies of the United States, within five years from the date of the approval of this act: *Provided*, That the President of the United States, in time of peace, may by order fix the minimum number of enlisted men in each company, troop, battery, signal corps, engineer corps, and hospital corps: *And provided further*, That any corps of artillery, cavalry, and infantry existing in any of the States at the passage of the act of May eighth, seventeen hundred and ninety-two, which, by the laws, customs, or usages of the said States have been in continuous existence since the passage of said act under its provisions and under the provisions of section two hundred and thirty-two and sections sixteen hundred and twenty-five to sixteen hundred and sixty, both inclusive, of title sixteen of the Revised Statutes of the United States relating to the militia, shall be allowed to retain their accustomed privileges, subject, nevertheless, to all other duties required by law in like manner as the other militia.

SEC. 4. That whenever the United States is invaded, or in danger of invasion from any foreign nation, or of rebellion against the authority of the Government of the United States, or the President is unable, with the other forces at his command, to execute the laws of the Union in any part thereof, it shall be lawful for the President to call forth, for a period not exceeding nine months, such number of the militia of the State or of the States or Territories or of the District of Columbia as he may deem necessary to repel such invasion, suppress such rebellion, or to enable him to execute such laws, and to issue his orders for that purpose to such officers of the militia as he may think proper.

SEC. 5. That whenever the President calls forth the militia of any State or Territory or of the District of Columbia to be employed in the service of the United States, he may specify in his call the period for which such service is required, not exceeding nine months, and the militia so called shall continue to serve during the term so specified, unless sooner discharged by order of the President.

SEC. 6. That when the militia of more than one State is called into the actual service of the United States by the President he may, in his discretion, apportion them among such States or Territories or to the District of Columbia according to representative population.

SEC. 7. That every officer and enlisted man of the militia who shall be called forth in the manner hereinbefore prescribed and shall be found fit for military service shall be mustered or accepted into the United States service by a duly authorized mustering officer of the United States: *Provided, however*, That any officer or enlisted man of the militia who shall refuse or neglect to present himself to such mustering officer upon being called forth as herein prescribed shall be subject to trial by court-martial, and shall be punished as such court-martial may direct.

SEC. 8. That courts-martial for the trial of officers or men of the militia, when in the service of the United States, shall be composed of militia officers only.

SEC. 9. That the militia, when called into the actual service of the United States, shall be subject to the same rules and articles of war as the regular troops of the United States.

SEC. 10 That the militia, when called into the actual service of the United States, shall, during their time of service, be entitled to the same pay and allowances as are or may be provided by law for the Regular Army.

SEC. 11. That when the militia is called into the actual service of the United States, or any portion of the militia is accepted under the provisions of this act, their pay shall commence from the day of their appearing at the place of company rendezvous. But this provision shall not be construed to authorize any species of expenditure previous to arriving at such places of rendezvous which is not provided by existing laws to be paid after their arrival at such places of rendezvous.

SEC. 12. That there shall be appointed in each State, Territory, and District of Columbia, an adjutant-general, who shall perform such duties as may be prescribed by the laws of such State, Territory, and District, respectively, and make returns to the Secretary of War, at such times and in such form as he shall from time to time prescribe, of the strength of the organized militia, and also make such reports as may from time to time be required by the Secretary of War. That the Secretary of War shall, with his annual report of each year, transmit to Congress an abstract of the returns and reports of the adjutants-general of the States, Territories, and the District of Columbia, with such observations thereon as he may deem necessary for the information of Congress.

SEC. 13. That the Secretary of War is hereby authorized to issue, on the requisitions of the governors of the several States and Territories, or of the commanding general of the militia of the District of Columbia, such number of the United States standard service magazine arms, with bayonets, bayonet scabbards, gun slings, belts, and such other necessary accouterments and equipments as are required for the Army of the United States, for arming all of the organized militia in said States and Territories and District of Columbia, without charging the cost or value thereof, or any which have been issued since December first, nineteen hundred and one, or any expense connected therewith, against the allotment to said State, Territory, or District of Columbia, out of the annual appropriation provided by section sixteen hundred and sixty-one of the Revised Statutes, as amended, or requiring payment therefor, and to exchange, without receiving any money credit therefor, ammunition, or parts thereof, suitable to the new arms, round for round, for corresponding ammunition suitable to the old arms theretofore issued to said State, Territory, or District by the United States: *Provided*, That said rifles and carbines and other property shall be receipted for and shall remain the property of the United States and be annually accounted for by the governors of the States and Territories as now required by law, and that each State, Territory, and District shall, on receipt of the new arms, turn in to the Ordnance Department of the United States Army, without receiving any money credit therefor, and without expense for transportation, all United States rifles and carbines now in its possession.

To provide means to carry into effect the provisions of this section, the necessary money to recover the cost of exchanging or issuing the new arms, accouterments, equipments, and ammunition to be exchanged or issued hereunder is hereby appropriated out of any moneys in the Treasury not otherwise appropriated.

SEC. 14. That whenever it shall appear by the report of inspections, which it shall be the duty of the Secretary of War to cause to be made at least once in each year by officers detailed by him for that purpose, that the organized militia of a State or Territory or of the District of Columbia is sufficiently armed, uniformed, and equipped for active duty in the field, the Secretary of War is authorized, on the requisition of the governor of such State or Territory, to pay to the quartermaster-general thereof, or to such other officer of the militia of said State as the said governor may designate and appoint for the purpose, so much of its allotment out of the said annual appropriation under section sixteen hundred and sixty-one of the Revised Statutes as amended as shall be necessary for the payment, subsistence, and transportation of such portion of said organized militia as shall engage in actual field or camp service for instruction; and the officers and enlisted men of such militia while so engaged shall be entitled to the same pay, subsistence, and transportation or travel allowances as officers and enlisted men of corresponding grades of the Regular Army are or may hereafter be entitled by law, and the officer so designated and appointed shall be regarded as a disbursing officer of the United States, and shall render his accounts through the War Department to the proper accounting officers of the Treasury for settlement; and he shall be required to give good and sufficient bonds to the United States, in such sums as the Secretary of War may direct, faithfully to account for the safe-keeping and payment of the public moneys so intrusted to him for disbursement.

SEC. 15. That the Secretary of War is hereby authorized to provide for participation by any part of the organized militia of any State or Territory on the request of the governor thereof in the encampment, maneuvers, and field instruction of any part of the Regular Army at or near any military post or camp or lake or seacoast defenses of the United States. In such case the organized militia so participating shall receive the same pay, subsistence, and transportation as is provided by law for the officers and men of the Regular Army, to be paid out of the appropriation for the pay, subsistence, and transportation of the Army: *Provided*, That the command of such military post or camp and of the officers and troops of the United States there stationed shall remain with the regular commander of the post without regard to the rank of the commanding or other officers of the militia temporarily so encamped within its limits or in its vicinity.

SEC. 16. That whenever any officer of the organized militia shall, upon recommendation of the governor of any State, Territory, or general commanding the District of Columbia, and when authorized by the President, attend and pursue a regular course of study at any military school or college of the United States such officer shall receive from the annual appropriation for the support of the Army the same travel allowances and quarters, or commutation of quarters, to which an officer of the Regular Army would be entitled if attending such school or college under orders from proper military authority, and shall also receive commutation of subsistence at the rate of one dollar per day while in actual attendance upon the course of instruction.

SEC. 17. That the annual appropriation made by section sixteen hundred and sixty-one, Revised Statutes, as amended, shall be available for the purpose of providing for issue to the organized militia any stores and supplies or publications which are supplied to the Army by any department. Any State, Territory, or the District of Columbia may, with the approval of the Secretary of War, purchase for cash from the War Department, for the use of its militia, stores, supplies, material of war, or military publications, such as are furnished to the Army, in addition to those issued under the provisions of this act, at the price at which they are listed for issue to the Army, with the cost of transportation added, and funds received from such sales shall be credited to the appropriations to which they belong and shall not be covered into the Treasury, but shall be available until expended to replace therewith the supplies sold to the States and Territories and to the District of Columbia in the manner herein provided.

SEC. 18. That each State or Territory furnished with material of war under the provisions of this or former acts of Congress shall, during the year next preceding each annual allotment of funds, in accordance with section sixteen hundred and sixty-one of the Revised Statutes as amended, have required every company, troop, and battery in its organized militia not excused by the governor of such State or Territory to participate in practice marches or go into camp of instruction at least five consecutive days, and to assemble for drill and instruction at company, battalion, or regimental armories or rendezvous or for target practice not less than twenty-four times, and shall also have required during such year an inspection of each such company, troop, and battery to be made by an officer of such militia or an officer of the Regular Army.

S. Doc. 209——23

SEC. 19. That upon the application of the governor of any State or Territory furnished with material of war under the provisions of this act or former laws of Congress, the Secretary of War may detail one or more officers of the Army to attend any encampment of the organized militia, and to give such instruction and information to the officers and men assembled in such camp as may be requested by the governor. Such officer or officers shall immediately make a report of such encampment to the Secretary of War, who shall furnish a copy thereof to the governor of the State or Territory.

SEC. 20. That upon application of the governor of any State or Territory furnished with material of war under the provisions of this act or former laws of Congress, the Secretary of War may, in his discretion, detail one or more officers of the Army to report to the governor of such State or Territory for duty in connection with the organized militia. All such assignments may be revoked at the request of the governor of such State or Territory or at the pleasure of the Secretary of War.

SEC. 21. That the troops of the militia encamped at any military post or camp of the United States may be furnished such amounts of ammunition for instruction in firing and target practice as may be prescribed by the Secretary of War, and such instruction in firing shall be carried on under the direction of an officer selected for that purpose by the proper military commander.

SEC. 22. That when any officer, noncommissioned officer, or private of the militia is disabled by reason of wounds or disabilities received or incurred in the service of the United States he shall be entitled to all the benefits of the pension laws existing at the time of his service, and in case such officer, noncommissioned officer, or private dies in the service of the United States or in returning to his place of residence after being mustered out of such service, or at any time, in consequence of wounds or disabilities received in such service, his widow and children, if any, shall be entitled to all the benefits of such pension laws.

SEC. 23. That for the purpose of securing a list of persons specially qualified to hold commissions in any volunteer force which may hereafter be called for and organized under the authority of Congress, other than a force composed of organized militia, the Secretary of War is authorized from time to time to convene boards of officers at suitable and convenient army posts in different parts of the United States, who shall examine as to their qualifications for the command of troops or for the performance of staff duties all applicants who shall have served in the Regular Army of the United States, in any of the volunteer forces of the United States, or in the organized militia of any State or Territory or District of Columbia, or who, being a citizen of the United States, shall have attended or pursued a regular course of instruction in any military school or college of the United States Army, or shall have graduated from any educational institution to which an officer of the Army or Navy has been detailed as superintendent or professor pursuant to law after having creditably pursued the course of military instruction therein provided. Such examinations shall be under rules and regulations prescribed by the Secretary of War, and shall be especially directed to ascertain the practical capacity of the applicant. The record of previous service of the applicant shall be considered as a part of the examination. Upon the conclusion of each examination the board shall certify to the War Department its judgment as to the fitness of the applicant, stating the office, if any, which it deems him qualified to fill, and, upon approval by the President, the names of the persons certified to be qualified shall be inscribed in a register to be kept in the War Department for that purpose. The persons so certified and registered shall, subject to a physical examination at the time, constitute an eligible class for commissions pursuant to such certificates in any volunteer force hereafter called for and organized under the authority of Congress, other than a force composed of organized militia, and the President may authorize persons from this class to attend and pursue a regular course of study at any military school or college of the United States other than the

Military Academy at West Point and to receive from the annual appropriation for the support of the Army the same allowances and commutations as provided in this act for officers of the organized militia: *Provided*, That no person shall be entitled to receive a commission as a second lieutenant after he shall have passed the age of thirty; as first lieutenant after he shall have passsd the age of thirty-five; as captain after he shall have passed the age of forty; as major after he shall have passed the age of forty-five; as lieutenant-colonel after he shall have passed the age of fifty, or as colonel after he shall have passed the age of fifty-five: *And provided further*, That such appointments shall be distributed proportionately, as near as may be, among the various States contributing such volunteer force: *And provided*, That the appointments in this section provided for shall not be deemed to include appointments to any office in any company, troop, battery, battalion, or regiment of the organized militia which volunteers as a body or the officers of which are appointed by the governor of a State or Territory.

SEC. 24. That all the volunteer forces of the United States called for by authority of Congress shall, except as hereinbefore provided, be organized in the manner provided by the act entitled "An act to provide for temporarily increasing the military establishment of the United States in time of war, and for other purposes," approved April twenty-second, eighteen hundred and ninety-eight.

SEC. 25. That sections sixteen hundred and twenty-five to sixteen hundred and sixty, both included, of title sixteen of the Revised Statutes, and section two hundred and thirty-two thereof, relating to the militia, are hereby repealed.

SEC. 26. That this act shall take effect upon the date of its approval.

Approved, January 21, 1903.

INDEX.

357

Ku-Klux-Klan—Continued.
Operations of the organization, 1866-1872—Con.
Extract from report of General Thomas re, 117.
General Forrest's statements re, 116.
Governor calls out State troops, 117.
Martial law declared, 118.
Mentioned, 182.
Operations in different States, 119.
Operations in Tennessee, 117.
Outrages committed by, 119.
Position of Federal authorities, 117.
Proclamations against, 118.
State militia called out, 118.
Statement by General Gordon re, 119.
Strength of, 118.
Labor Strikes of 1877, 189-205, 315-336.
Causes, 189.
Commencement, 189.
Documents re, 315-336.
Other points affected by, 203.
Rendering of assistance to civil authorities of Toledo, Ohio, 328, 329.
Use of Federal troops, 189.
Lafayette County, Ark.
Martial law declared in, 125.
Lake Shore Railroad.
Strike ordered on, 228.
Lamar, L. Q. C., Secretary of the Interior.
Correspondence with Watson C. Squire, governor of Washington, 276.
Lamont, Daniel S., Secretary of War.
Instructions for use of troops at Denver, Colo., 226.
Instructions for troops to enforce mandates of U. S. court, 234.
Letters re Federal aid to—
Matthews, Claude, governor of Indiana, 348.
Thornton. W. T., governor of New Mexico, 234.
Lancaster County, S. C.
Martial law declared in, 122.
Lane, J. H., Chairman Executive Committee, Kansas Territory.
Demand for Federal aid, 278.
Laurens, S C.
Martial law declared in, 122.
Riot of October 20, 1870, at, 119.
Causes, 119.
Organization of colored militia, 119.
Law, Enforcement of.
Employment of troops in, 5-12.
Arrest of criminal refugees in Indian country, 6.
Discoverers of guano islands, protection of rights, 10.
Domestic violence, suppression of, 9.
Extradition, provision of Revised Statutes in re, 8.
Indian—
Hostilities, prevention or termination, 6.
Lands, trespassing on and prevention, 6.
Offenders, arrest of, how procured, 6.
Insurgents, authority of President to disperse, 5.
Insurrection, suppression, 9.

Law, Enforcement of—Continued.
Employment of troops in—Continued.
Mails—
Passage, obstructing or retarding, punishment, 9.
Robbing or interruption, prevention, 11.
Military force, detention of persons by, 6.
Military roads and postal routes, 10.
Militia, when may be called out by President, 9.
Mob violence, government of troops in action against, 12.
Neutrality, violation, punishment, 8.
Procedure in re foreign vessels, 8.
Officer of Army, when may use troops to preserve order, etc., 11.
Peonage, abolishment of, 6.
Posse comitatus, use of troops as, 11.
Public lands—
Occupation, laws relating to, 7.
Prevention of trespassing, 7.
Unlawful inclosures, removal or destruction, 7.
Validity of title, 7.
Punishment, to whom properly pertains, 12.
Quarantine laws, execution of, 8.
Trade and commerce, protection against restraints and monopolies, 9.
Vessels or cargo, detained, unlawful to take from customs officer, 10.
Warrants and other processes, appointments for service, 5.
Lawful Government.
How determined, 148, 150.
Lawrence, Kans.
Violence at, 80-85.
Lee, Henry, Governor of Virginia.
Commanding troops in whisky insurrection, 37.
Influence of presence, 41.
Instructions of President to, 39.
Lee, Richard Henry, Member Virginia Constitutional Convention.
Opposes adoption of Constitution, 21.
Lee, Robert E., Lieutenant-Colonel, U. S. A.
Commands troops at Harpers Ferry, 100, 101, 297.
Lehigh County, Pa.
Resistance to domiciliary visitation, 43.
Lennox, David, United States Marshal, District of Pennsylvania.
Whisky insurrection, 35, 36.
Seized by insurrectionists, 35.
Release and flight, 36.
Lentz, John J., Member of Congress.
Resolution to investigate conduct of Army in Idaho, 252, 253.
Lincoln, Abraham, President United States.
Conditions existing at first inauguration, 101.
First reconstruction proclamation, 107.
Mentioned, 112.
Message regarding secession of Southern States, 107.
Power invested in, for suppression of rebellion, 106.
Proclamation declaring insurrection in certain States, 103.
Restoration of rights to secessionists, 107.
War of the rebellion, 101-106.